Mamotte! Lollipop

Michiyo Kikuta

Translated and adapted by
Elina Ishikawa

Lettered by
North Market Street Graphics

Ballantine Books · New York

A Del Rey Manga/Kodansha Trade Paperback Original

Published in the United States by Del Rey Books, an imprint of The Random House Publishing Group, a division of Random House, Inc., New York.

DEL REY is a registered trademark and the Del Rey colophon is a trademark of Random House, Inc.

Publication rights arranged through Kodansha Ltd.

First published in Japan in 2005 by Kodansha Ltd., Tokyo

ISBN 978-0-345-49894-6

Printed in the United States of America

www.delreymanga.com

9 8 7 6 5 4 3 2 1

Translator/Adapter—Elina Ishikawa
Lettering—North Market Street Graphics

Contents

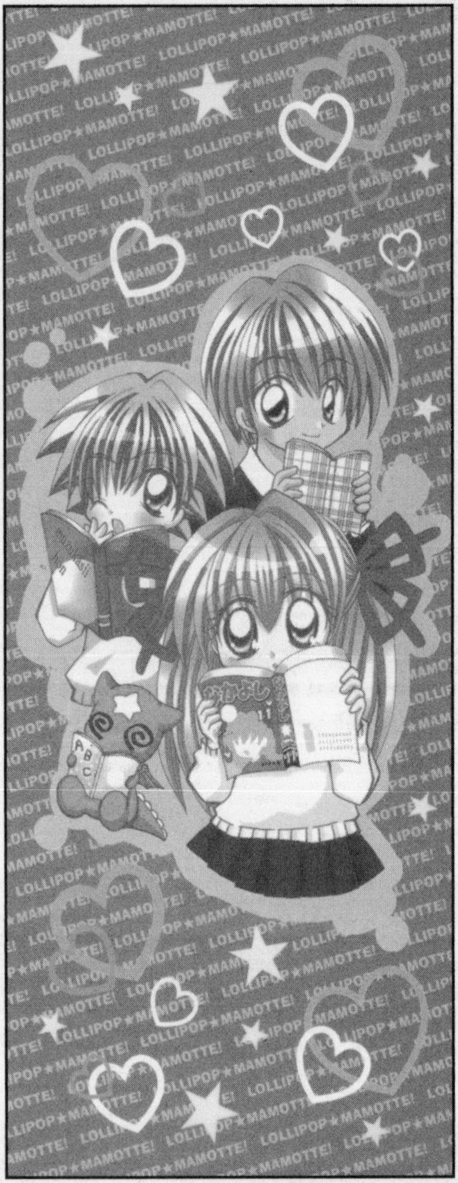
LOLLIPOP★MAMOTTE!

Honorifics Explained

Throughout the Del Rey Manga books, you will find Japanese honorifics left intact in the translations. For those not familiar with how the Japanese use honorifics and, more important, how they differ from American honorifics, we present this brief overview.

Politeness has always been a critical facet of Japanese culture. Ever since the feudal era, when Japan was a highly stratified society, use of honorifics—which can be defined as polite speech that indicates relationship or status—has played an essential role in the Japanese language. When addressing someone in Japanese, an honorific usually takes the form of a suffix attached to one's name (example: "Asuna-san"), is used as a title at the end of one's name, or appears in place of the name itself (example: "Negi-sensei," or simply "Sensei!").

Honorifics can be expressions of respect or endearment. In the context of manga and anime, honorifics give insight into the nature of the relationship between characters. Many English translations leave out these important honorifics and therefore distort the feel of the original Japanese. Because Japanese honorifics contain nuances that English honorifics lack, it is our policy at Del Rey not to translate them. Here, instead, is a guide to some of the honorifics you may encounter in Del Rey Manga.

-**san:**   *This is the most common honorific and is equivalent to Mr., Miss, Ms., or Mrs. It is the all-purpose honorific and can be used in any situation where politeness is required.*

-**sama:**   *This is one level higher than "-san" and is used to confer great respect.*

-**dono:**   *This comes from the word "tono," which means "lord." It is an even higher level than "-sama" and confers utmost respect.*

-kun: This suffix is used at the end of boys' names to express familiarity or endearment. It is also sometimes used by men among friends, or when addressing someone younger or of a lower station.

-chan: This is used to express endearment, mostly toward girls. It is also used for little boys, pets, and even among lovers. It gives a sense of childish cuteness.

Bozu: This is an informal way to refer to a boy, similar to the English terms "kid" and "squirt."

**Sempai/
Senpai:** This title suggests that the addressee is one's senior in a group or organization. It is most often used in a school setting, where underclassmen refer to their upperclassmen as "sempai." It can also be used in the workplace, such as when a newer employee addresses an employee who has seniority in the company.

Kohai: This is the opposite of "sempai" and is used toward underclassmen in school or newcomers in the workplace. It connotes that the addressee is of a lower station.

Sensei: Literally meaning "one who has come before," this title is used for teachers, doctors, or masters of any profession or art.

-[blank]: This is usually forgotten in these lists, but it is perhaps the most significant difference between Japanese and English. The lack of honorific means that the speaker has permission to address the person in a very intimate way. Usually, only family, spouses, or very close friends have this kind of permission. Known as yobisute, it can be gratifying when someone who has earned the intimacy starts to call one by one's name without an honorific. But when that intimacy hasn't been earned, it can be very insulting.

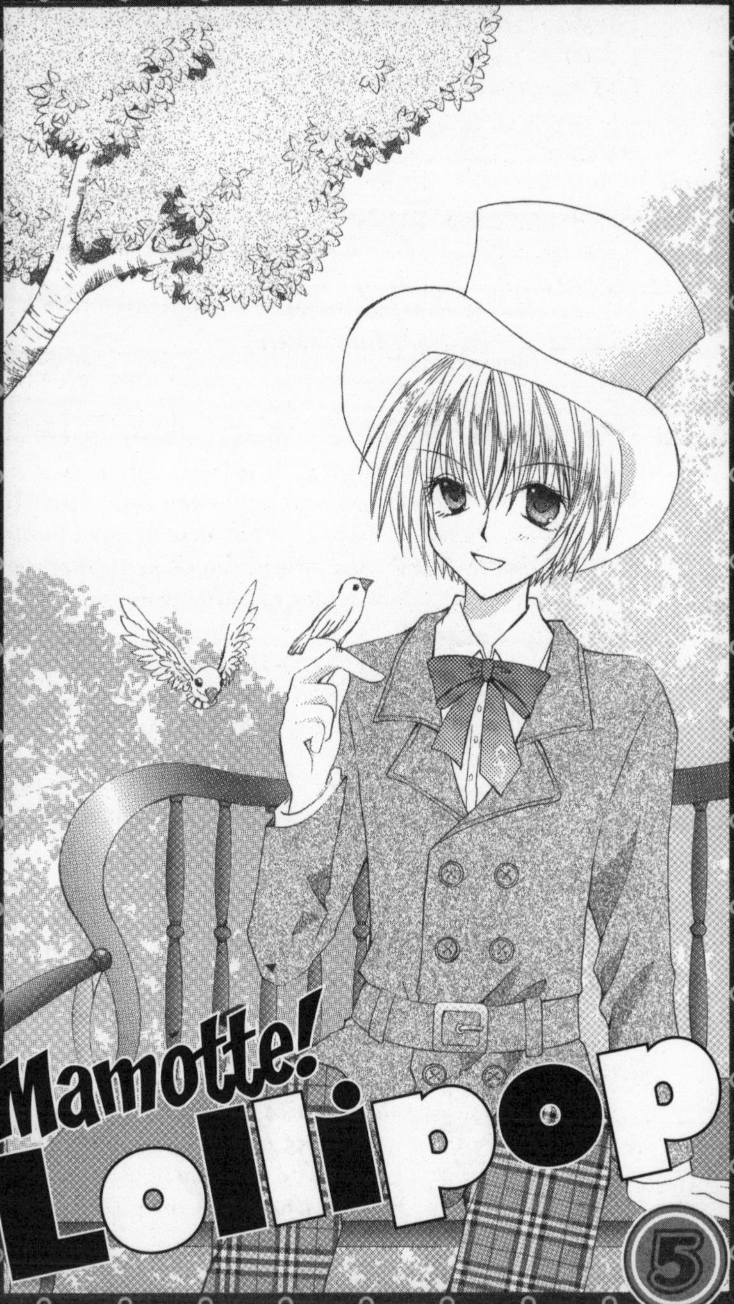
Mamotte!
Lollipop
5

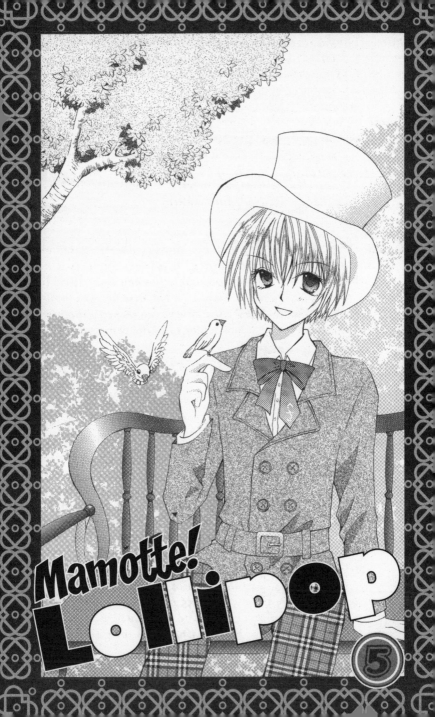

CONTENTS

MAMOTTE! LOLLIPOP

Let's go to the magical pop story!!

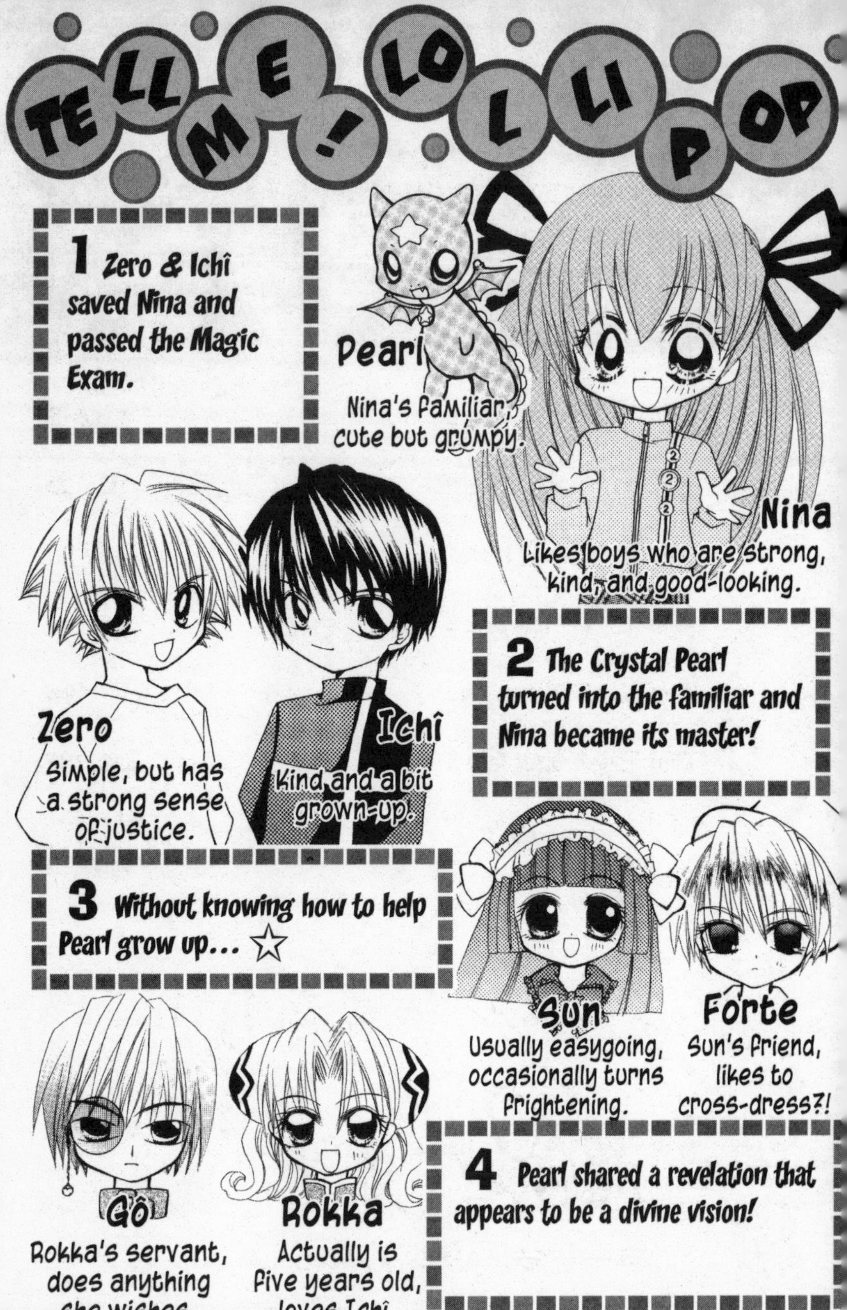
TELL ME! LOLLIPOP
1 Zero & Ichî saved Nina and passed the Magic Exam.
Pearl
Nina's familiar, cute but grumpy.
Nina
Likes boys who are strong, kind, and good-looking.
Zero
Simple, but has a strong sense of justice.
Ichî
Kind and a bit grown-up.
2 The Crystal Pearl turned into the familiar and Nina became its master!
3 Without knowing how to help Pearl grow up... ☆
Sun
Usually easygoing, occasionally turns frightening.
Forte
Sun's friend, likes to cross-dress?!
Gô
Rokka's servant, does anything she wishes.
Rokka
Actually is five years old, loves Ichî.
4 Pearl shared a revelation that appears to be a divine vision!

And now the exciting magical pop story begins.

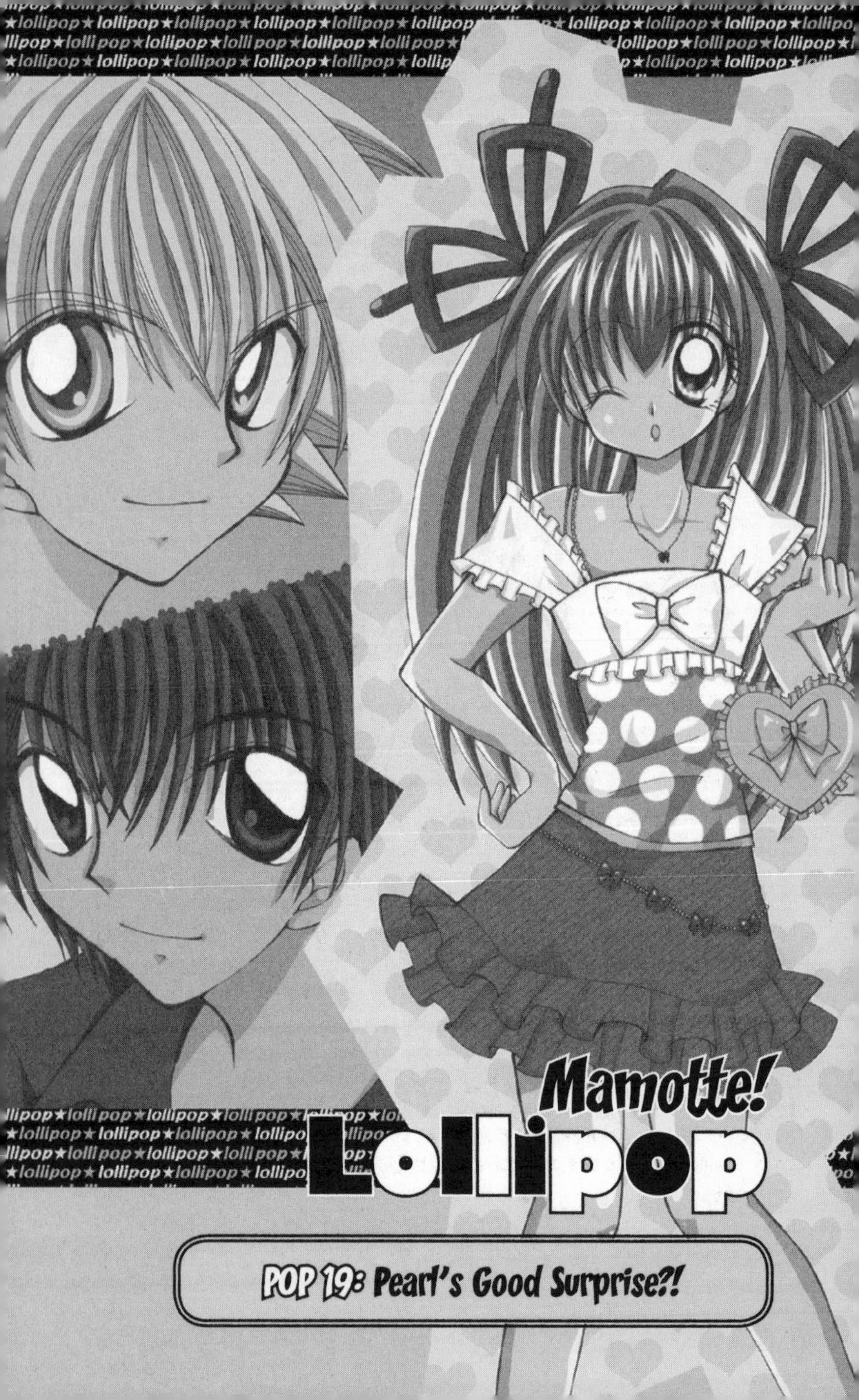
Mamotte!
Lollipop
POP 19: Pearl's Good Surprise?!

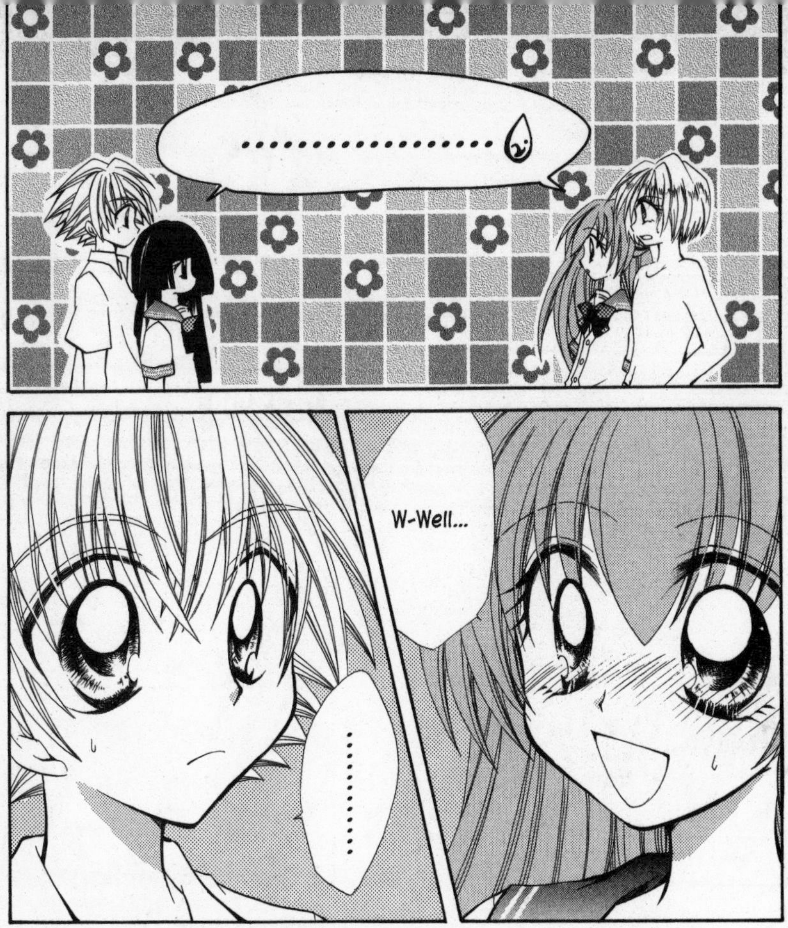
....
W-Well...
....

PoP 19 Pearl's Good Surprise?!

I like the outfit Nina is wearing on this splash page. I think it would be so cute to see something like this in a store window.

The story was funny, with all the jokes about Pearl (laugh). I was happy that I was able to bring out Eleven and Twelve, even though it was just for a little while. The guy next to the detective was popular at the office.

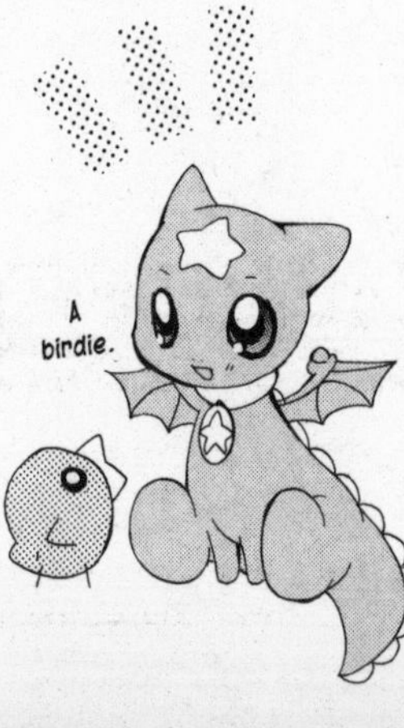
A birdie.

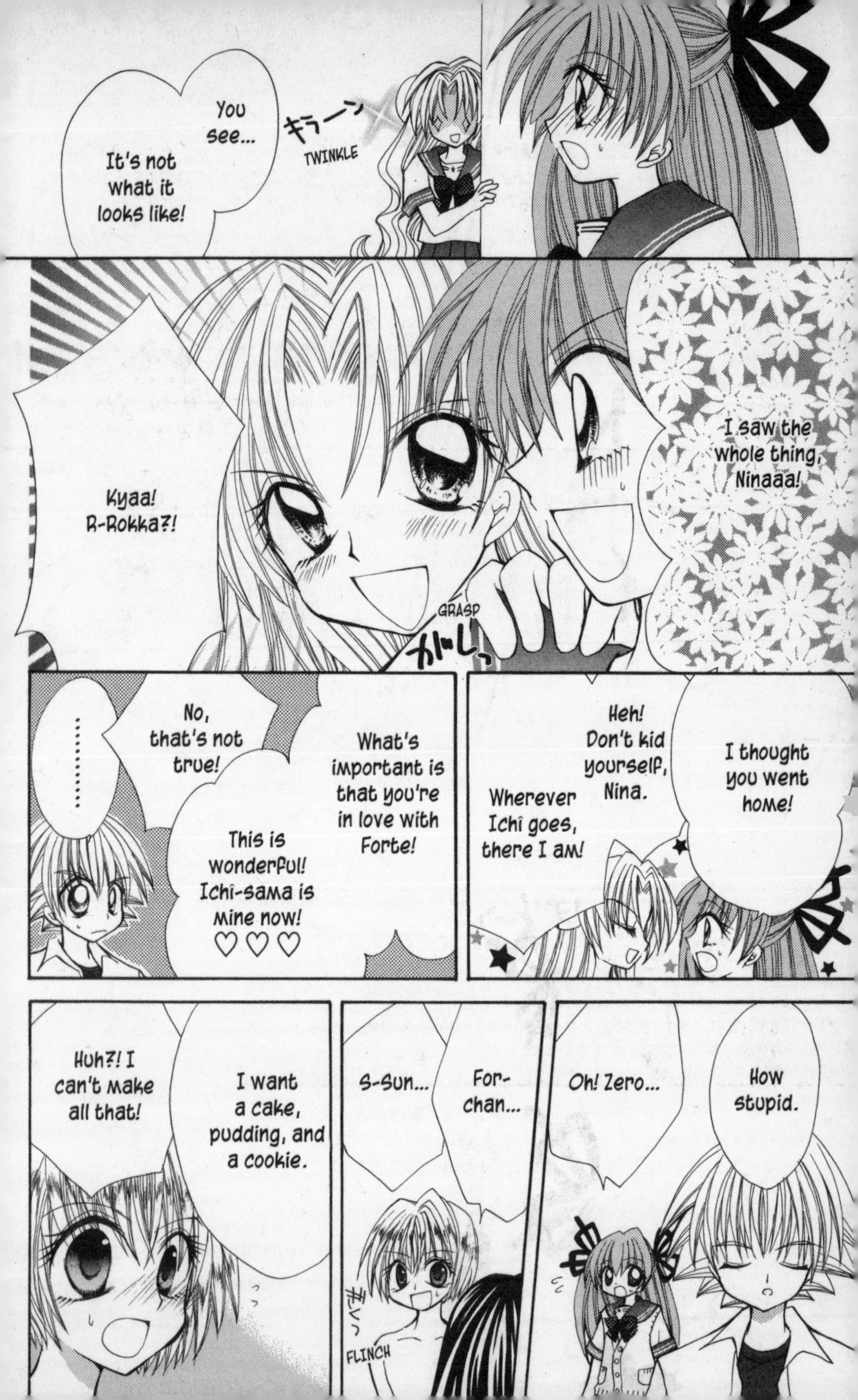

You see...
It's not what it looks like!
キラーン
TWINKLE
I saw the whole thing, Ninaaa!
Kyaa! R-Rokka?!
GRASP
がしっ
I thought you went home!
Heh! Don't kid yourself, Nina.
Wherever Ichî goes, there I am!
What's important is that you're in love with Forte!
No, that's not true!
This is wonderful! Ichî-sama is mine now! ♡ ♡ ♡
......
How stupid.
Oh! Zero...
For-chan...
S-Sun...
FLINCH
I want a cake, pudding, and a cookie.
Huh?! I can't make all that!

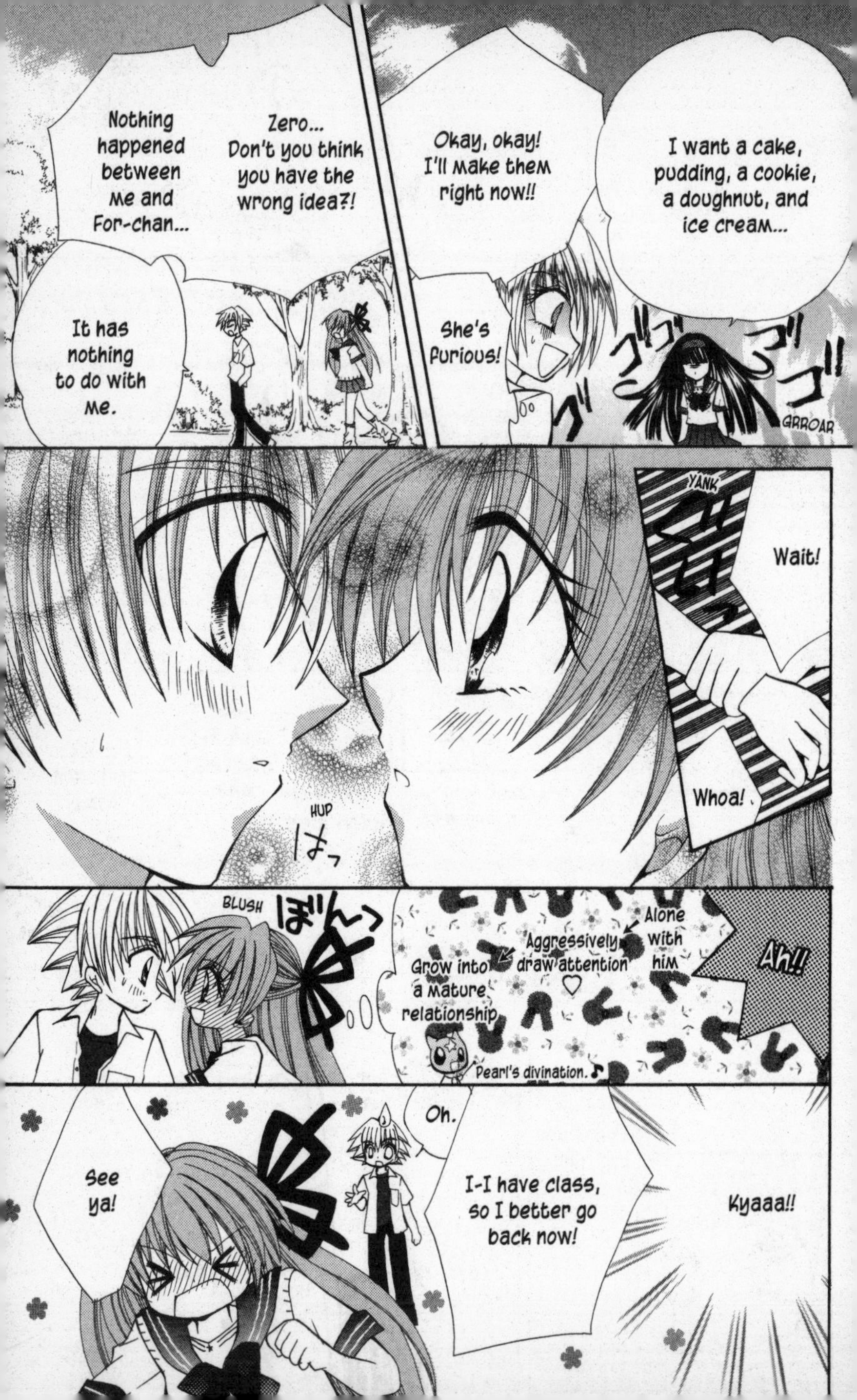
I want a cake, pudding, a cookie, a doughnut, and ice cream...
Okay, okay! I'll make them right now!!
GRROAR
She's furious!
Zero... Don't you think you have the wrong idea?!
Nothing happened between me and For-chan...
It has nothing to do with me.
YANK
Wait!
Whoa!
HUP
Ah!!
Alone with him
Aggressively draw attention ♡
Grow into a mature relationship
Pearl's divination.♪
BLUSH
Kyaaa!!
I-I have class, so I better go back now!
Oh.
See ya!

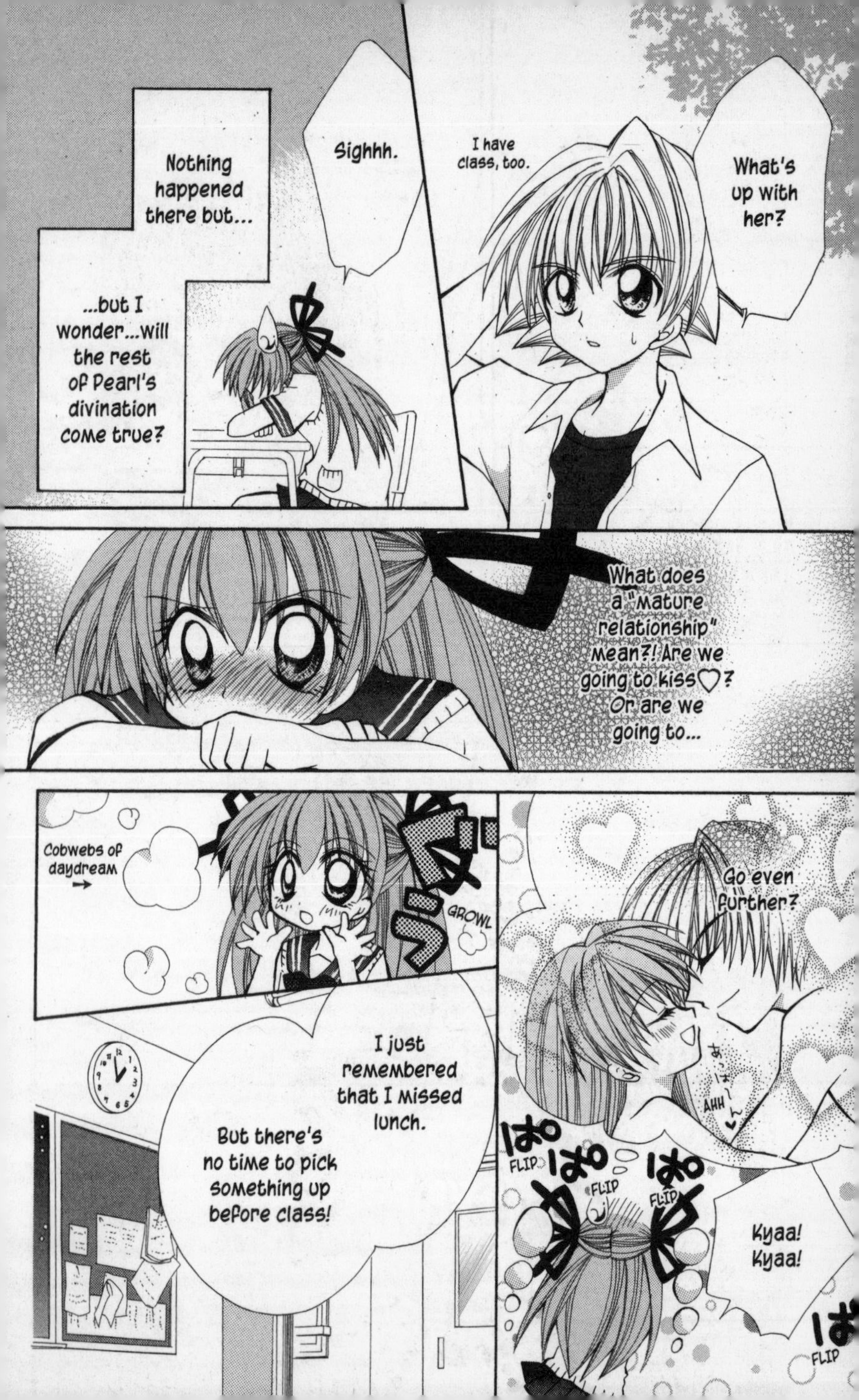

What's up with her?
I have class, too.
Sighhh.
Nothing happened there but...
...but I wonder...will the rest of Pearl's divination come true?
What does a "mature relationship" mean?! Are we going to kiss♡? Or are we going to...
Go even further?
AHH
FLIP
FLIP
FLIP
FLIP
Kyaa! Kyaa!
Cobwebs of daydream →
GROWL
I just remembered that I missed lunch.
But there's no time to pick something up before class!

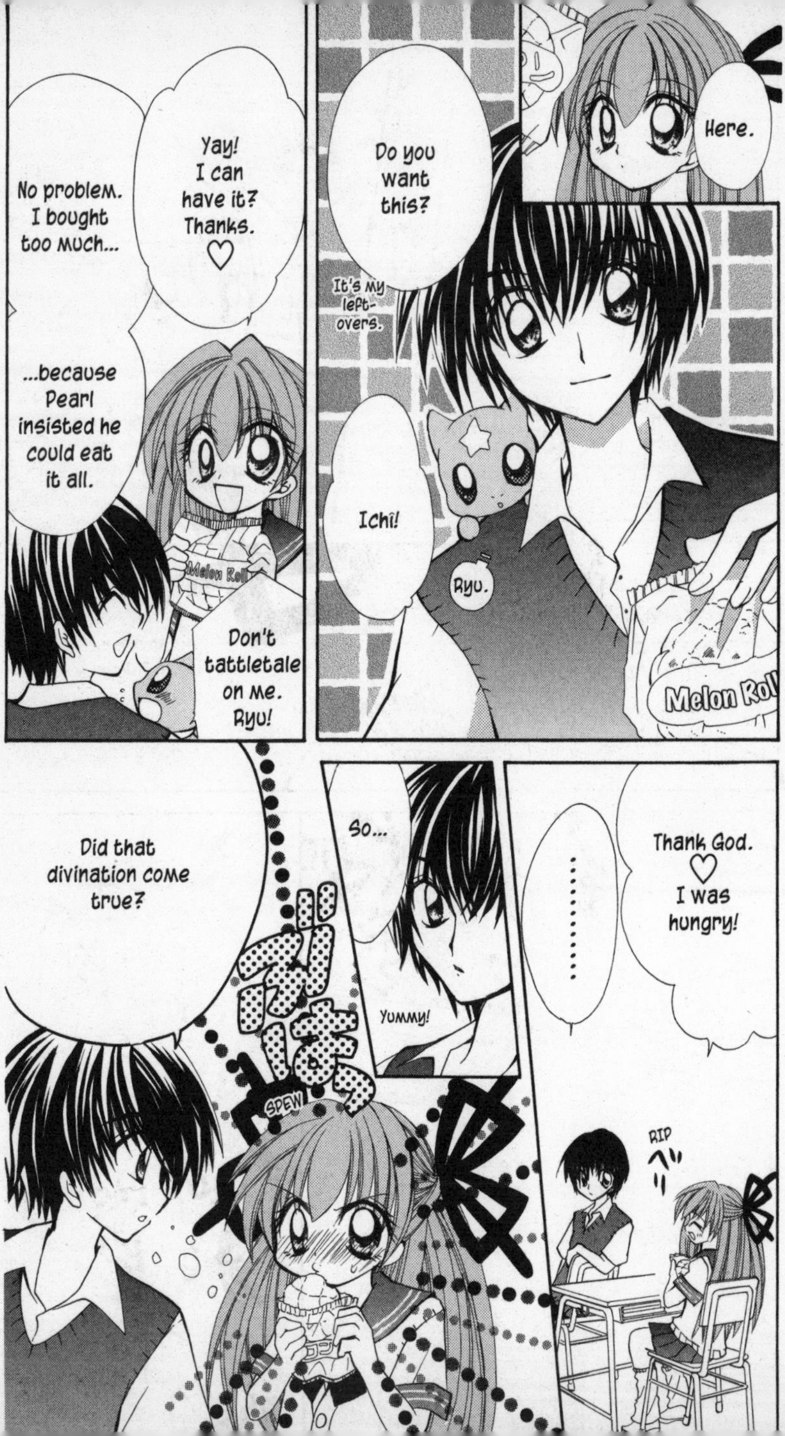
Here.
Do you want this?
It's my left-overs.
Ichi!
Ryu.
Melon Roll
Yay! I can have it? Thanks. ♡
No problem. I bought too much...
...because Pearl insisted he could eat it all.
Melon Roll
Don't tattletale on me. Ryu!
Thank God. ♡ I was hungry!
......
So...
Yummy!
Did that divination come true?
RIP
SPEW

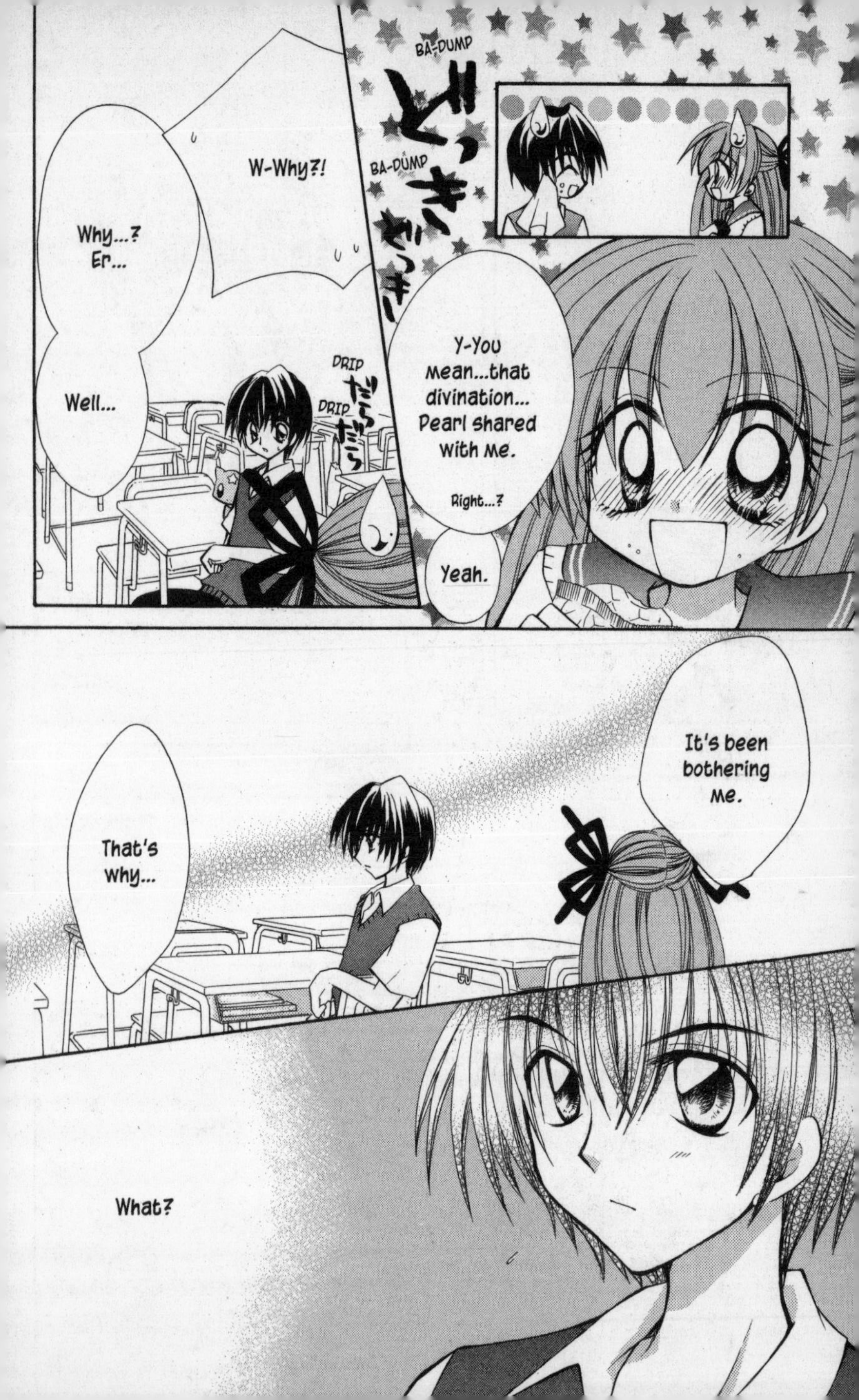
BA-DUMP
BA-DUMP
どっきどっき
Y-You mean...that divination... Pearl shared with me.
Right...?
Yeah.
W-Why?!
Why...? Er...
Well...
DRIP
DRIP
だらだら
It's been bothering me.
That's why...
What?

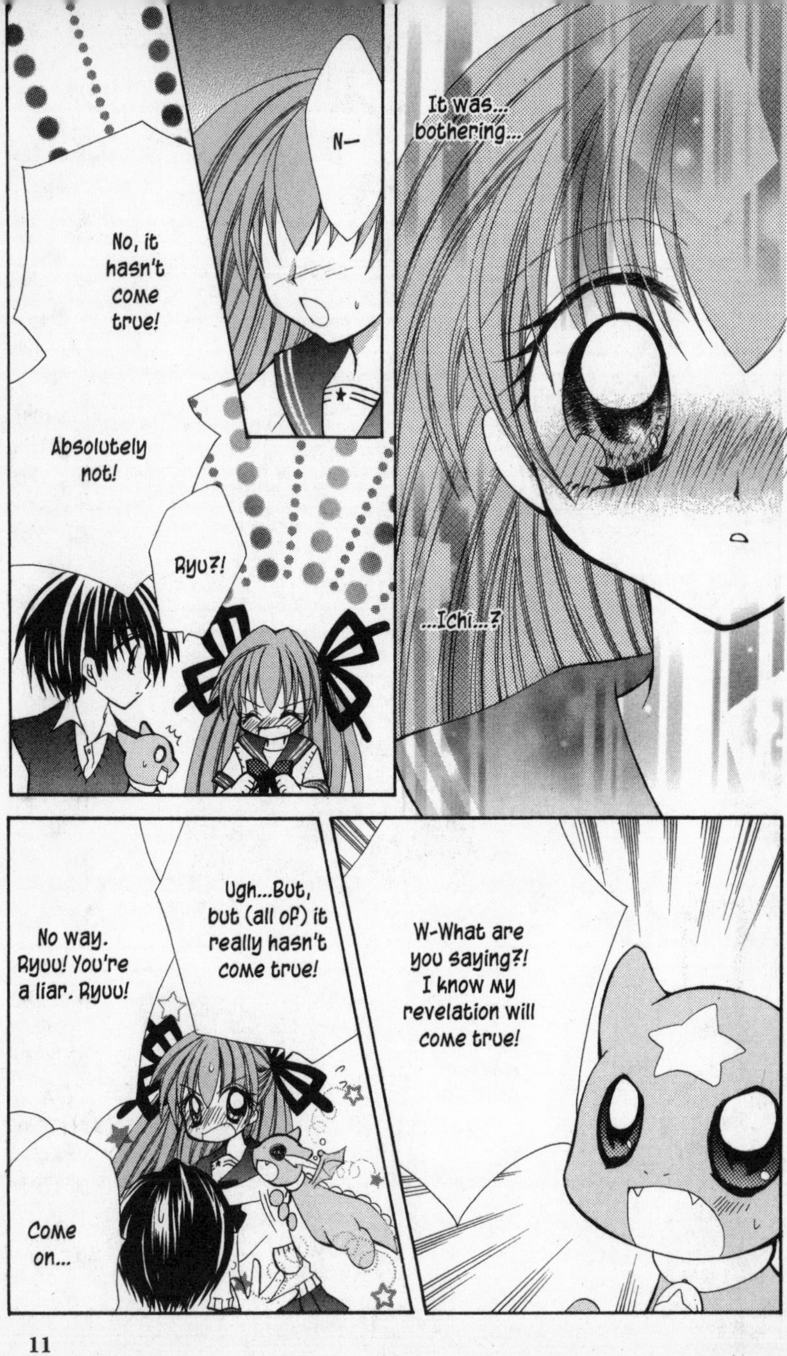
It was... bothering...
...Ichi...?
N—
No, it hasn't come true!
Absolutely not!
Ryu?!
W-What are you saying?! I know my revelation will come true!
Ugh...But, but (all of) it really hasn't come true!
No way. Ryuu! You're a liar. Ryuu!
Come on...

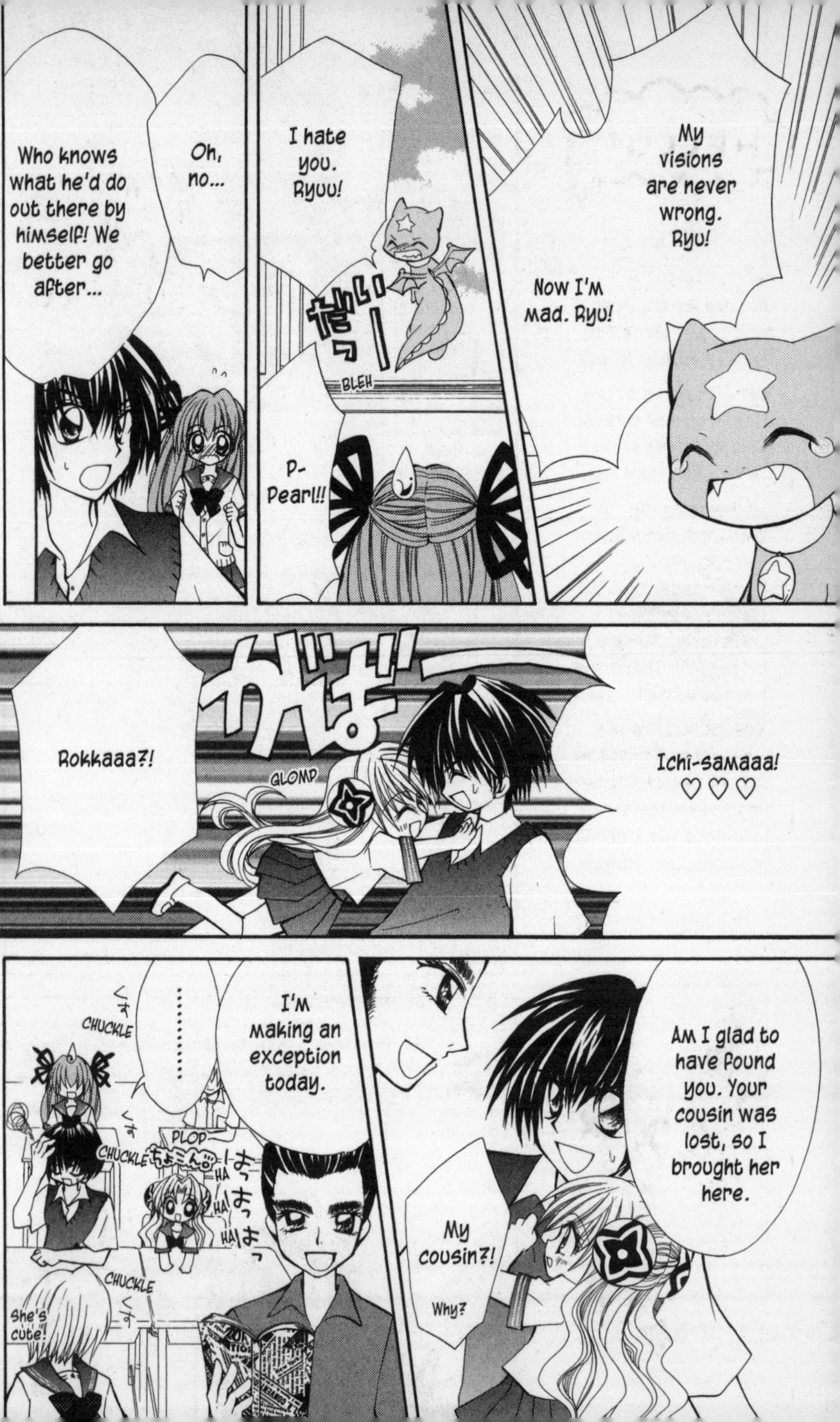
My visions are never wrong. Ryu!
Now I'm mad. Ryu!
I hate you. Ryuu!
だっ
BLEH
P-Pearl!!
Oh, no...
Who knows what he'd do out there by himself! We better go after...
Ichi-samaaa! ♡ ♡ ♡
がばー
GLOMP
Rokkaaa?!
Am I glad to have found you. Your cousin was lost, so I brought her here.
My cousin?!
Why?
I'm making an exception today.
......
くす
CHUCKLE
くす
CHUCKLE
PLOP
ちょこん
HA HA HA
くす
CHUCKLE
She's cute!

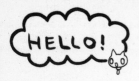

HELLO!

Hello to those I'm meeting for the first time and to those I'm not!! I'm Michiyo Kikuta.

We're finally up to the fifth volume of *Mamotte! Lollipop!* I can't believe we've gotten this far.

I'm inserting my comments, requested illustrations, four-frame manga, and Q&A again! I've included a bonus story, *Nanapachi*, and the Mini-Theatre is included as well.

Personally, I like the bonus story *Nanapachi* and the new characters, King and his comrades. I hope everyone will like this book, too. Enjoy.

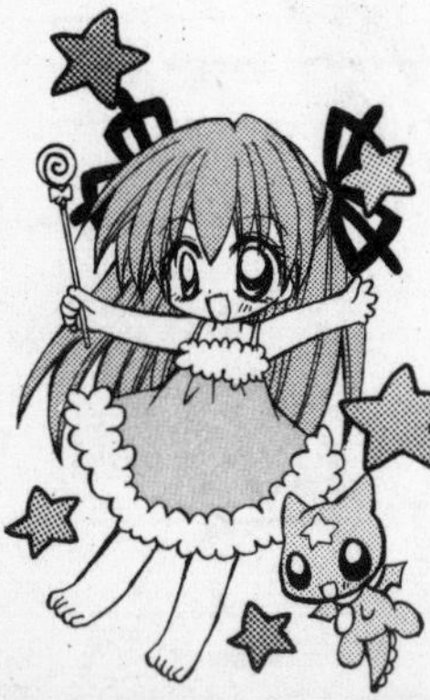

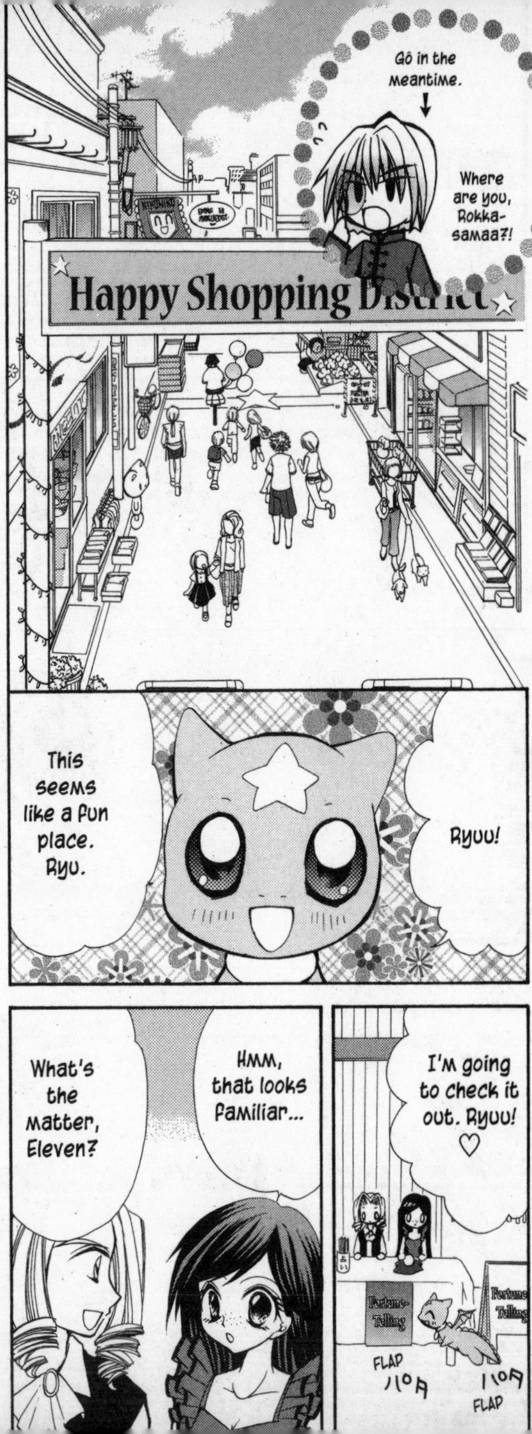
Happy Shopping District
Gô in the meantime.
Where are you, Rokka-samaa?!
Ryuu!
This seems like a fun place. Ryu.
I'm going to check it out. Ryuu! ♡
FLAP FLAP
Hmm, that looks familiar...
What's the matter, Eleven?

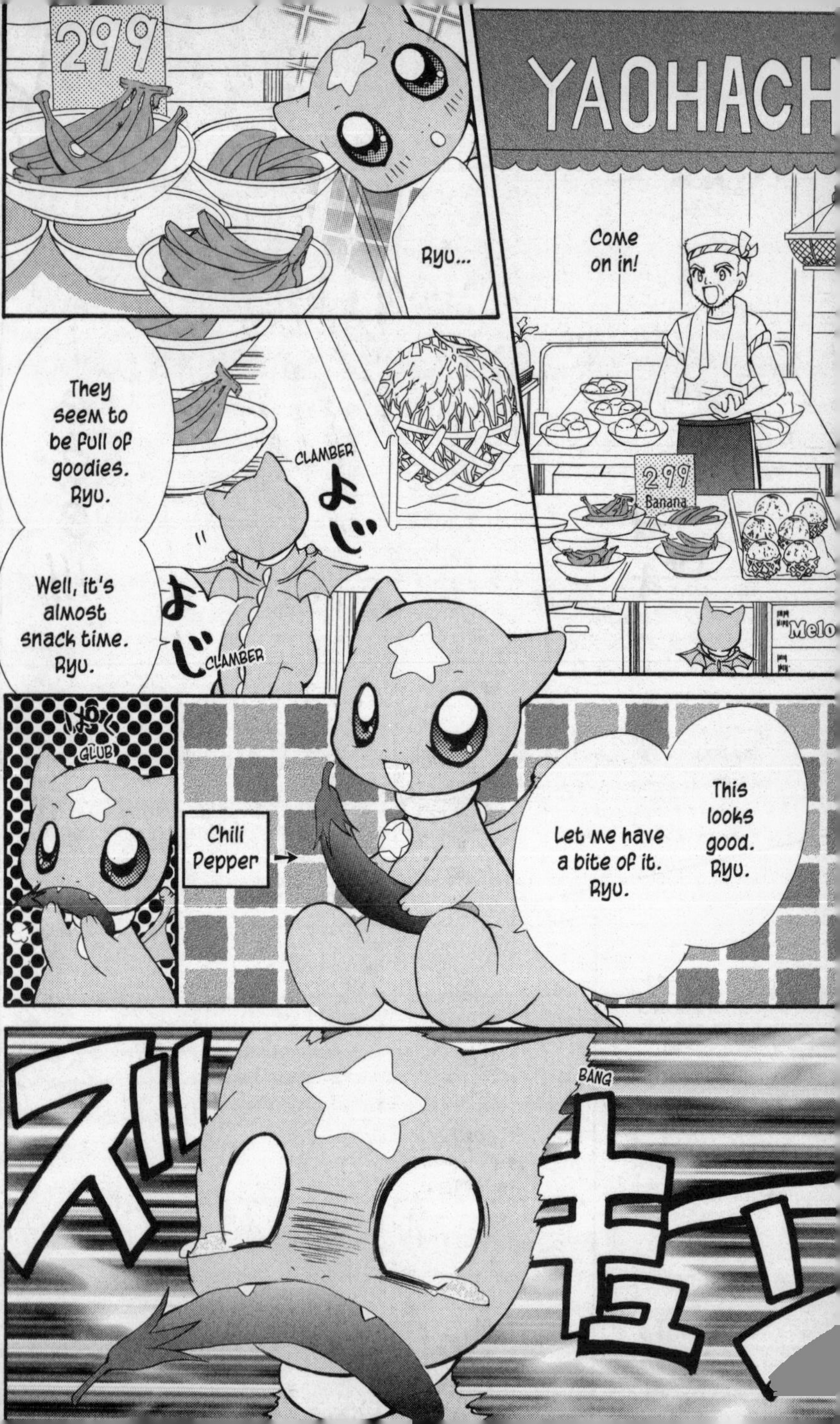
YAOHACH
Come on in!
299
Banana
Melo
299
Ryu...
They seem to be full of goodies. Ryu.
CLAMBER
よじ
Well, it's almost snack time. Ryu.
よじ
CLAMBER
This looks good. Ryu.
Let me have a bite of it. Ryu.
Chili Pepper
GLUB
BANG

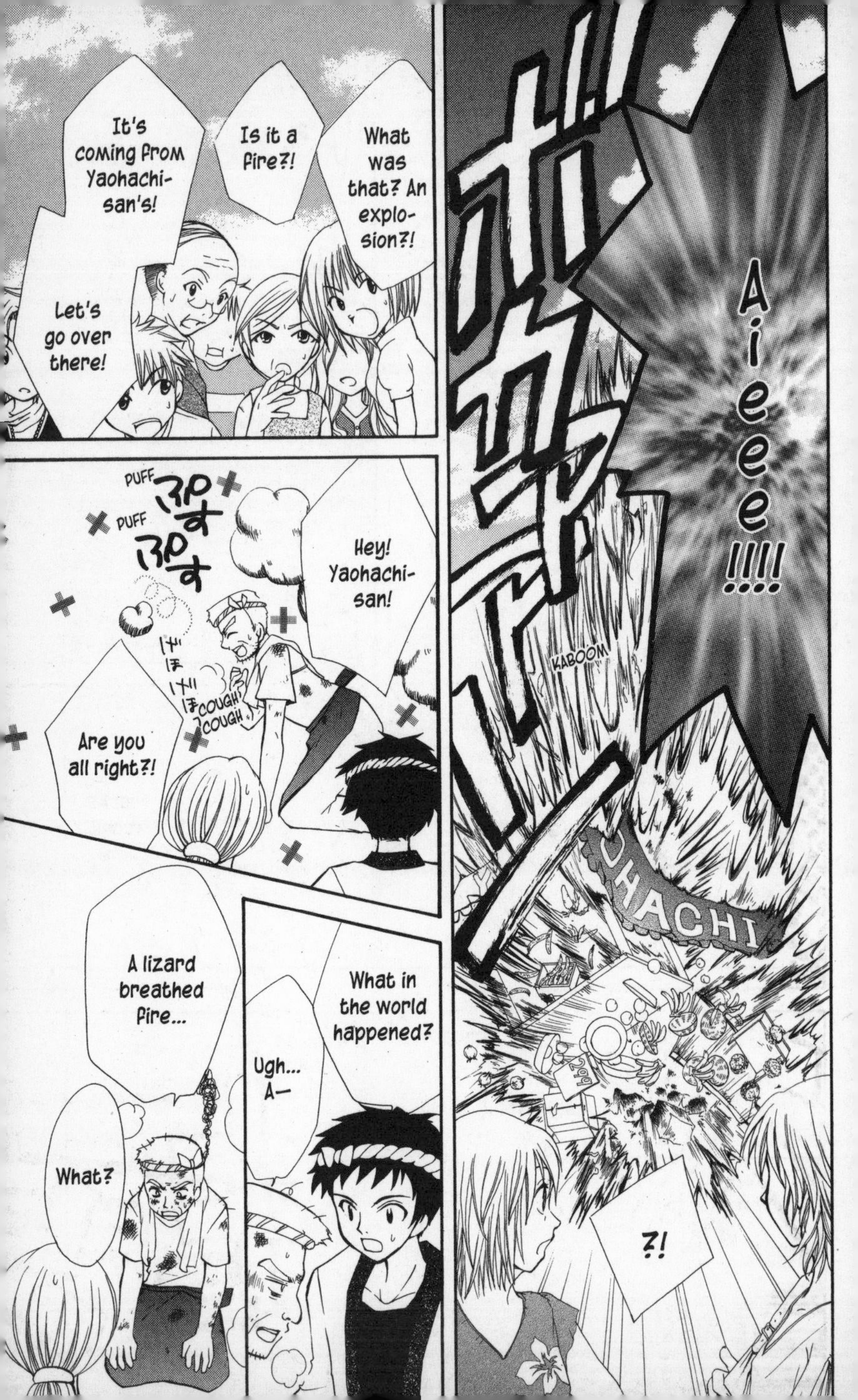

KABOOM
Aieeee!!!!
UHACHI
?!
What was that? An explosion?!
Is it a fire?!
It's coming from Yaohachi-san's!
Let's go over there!
ぷすぷす
PUFF PUFF
Hey! Yaohachi-san!
げほげほ
COUGH COUGH
Are you all right?!
What in the world happened?
Ugh... A—
A lizard breathed fire...
What?

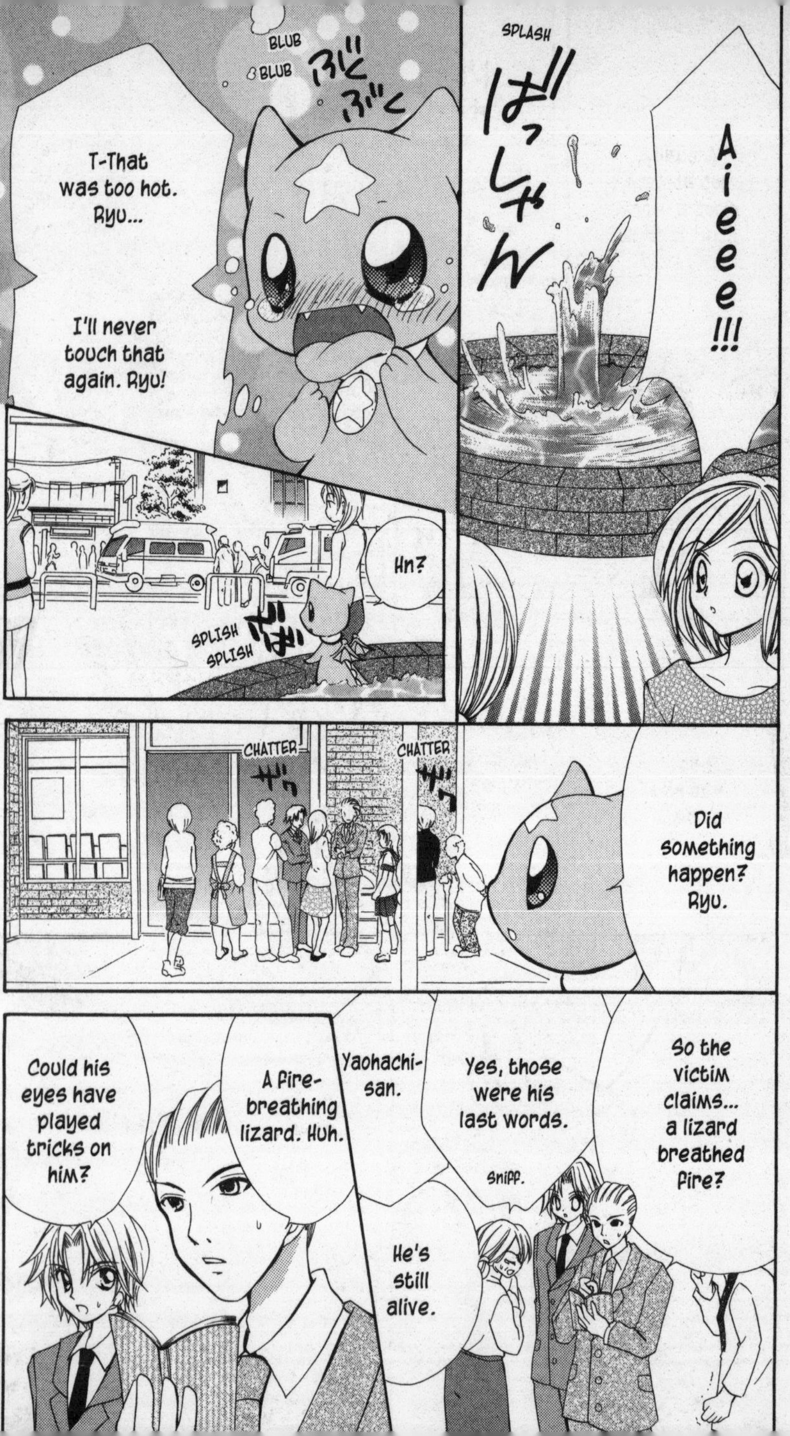
SPLASH
ばっしゃん
Aieeee!!!
BLUB
BLUB
ぶくぶく
T-That was too hot. Ryu...
I'll never touch that again. Ryu!
Hn?
SPLISH
SPLISH
Did something happen? Ryu.
CHATTER
ザワ
CHATTER
ザワ
So the victim claims... a lizard breathed fire?
Yes, those were his last words.
Sniff.
Yaohachi-san.
He's still alive.
A fire-breathing lizard. Huh.
Could his eyes have played tricks on him?

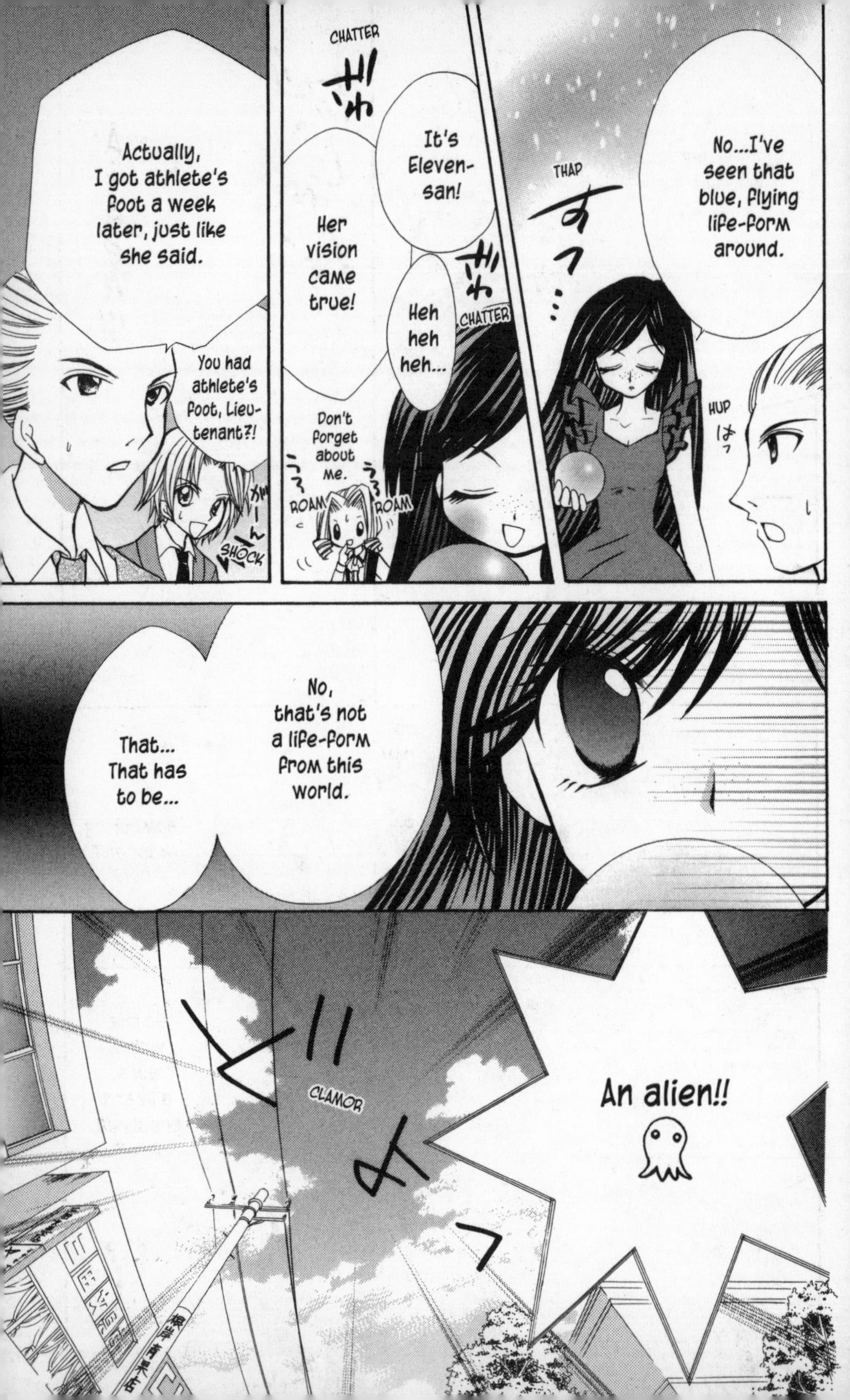
No...I've seen that blue, flying life-form around.
THAP
HUP
CHATTER
It's Eleven-san!
Her vision came true!
Heh heh heh...
CHATTER
Don't forget about me.
ROAM
ROAM
Actually, I got athlete's foot a week later, just like she said.
You had athlete's foot, Lieutenant?!
SHOCK
No, that's not a life-form from this world.
That... That has to be...
An alien!!
CLAMOR

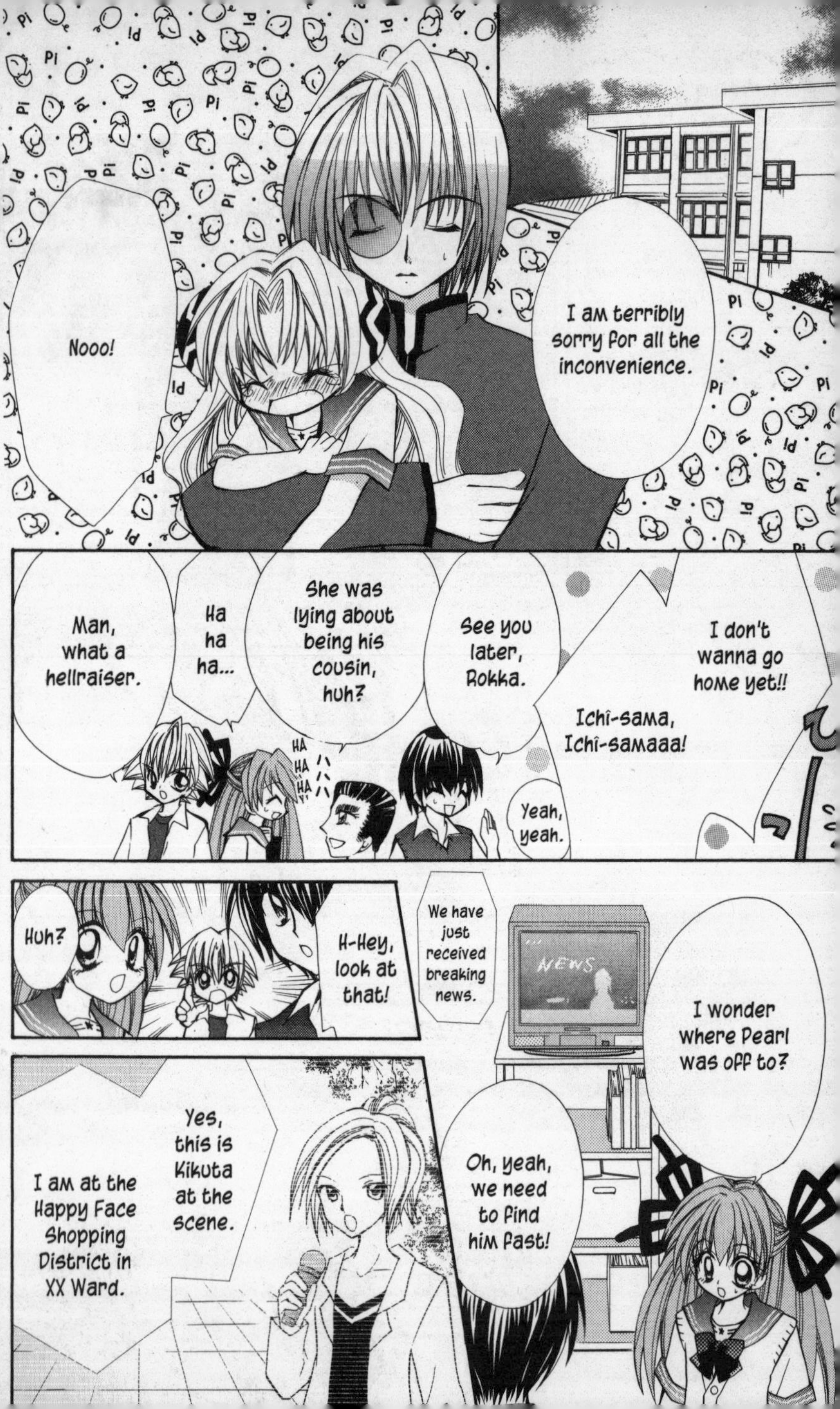
I am terribly sorry for all the inconvenience.
Nooo!
I don't wanna go home yet!!
Ichî-sama, Ichî-samaaa!
See you later, Rokka.
Yeah, yeah.
She was lying about being his cousin, huh?
HA HA HA
Ha ha ha...
Man, what a hellraiser.
I wonder where Pearl was off to?
Oh, yeah, we need to find him fast!
H-Hey, look at that!
Huh?
We have just received breaking news.
NEWS
Yes, this is Kikuta at the scene.
I am at the Happy Face Shopping District in XX Ward.

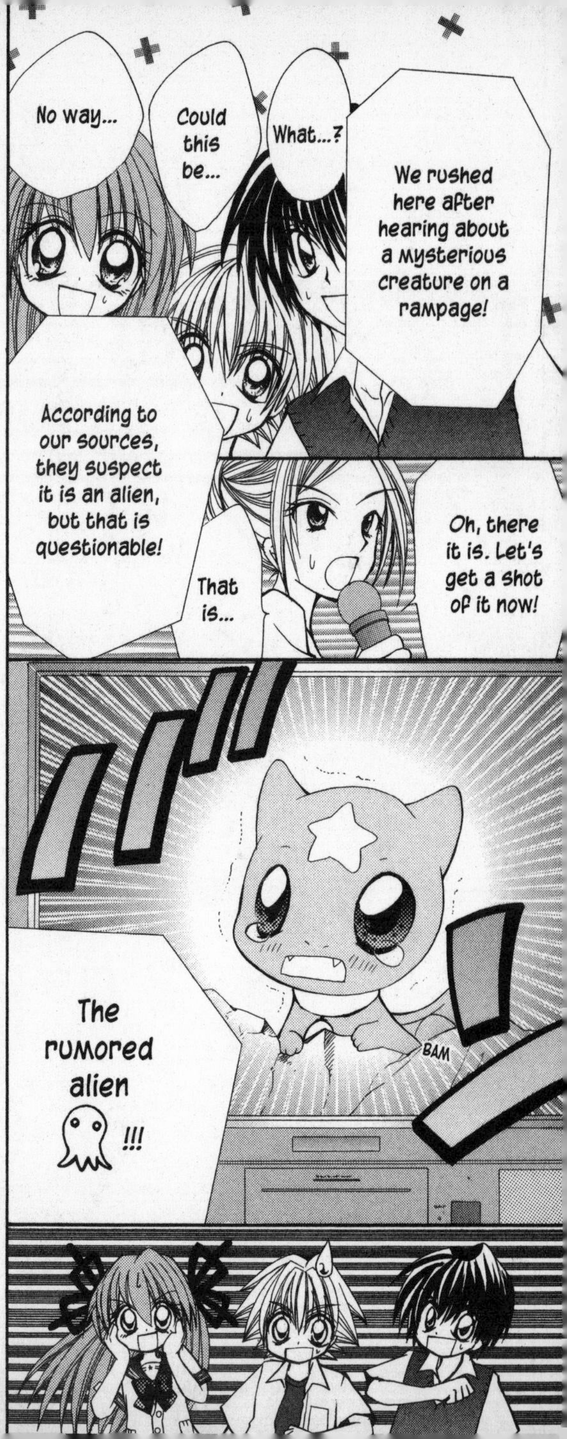

We rushed here after hearing about a mysterious creature on a rampage!
What...?
Could this be...
No way...
According to our sources, they suspect it is an alien, but that is questionable!
Oh, there it is. Let's get a shot of it now!
That is...
BAM
The rumored alien !!!

Lollipop in Other Countries Part One

It's a late announcement, but *Mamotte! Lollipop* is being published in Taiwan, Hong Kong, and South Korea. I don't understand these languages, but it's interesting to look at the alphabets! I'm thrilled that they offer their own original bonus items, too!! Even the character names look different in each country! I'll use this space to show them to you.

Continued on page 57!

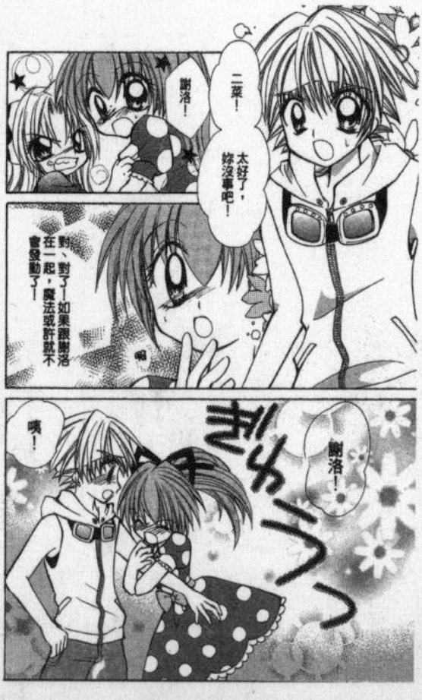

二葉！
太好了，妳沒事吧！
謝洛！
對、對了！如果跟謝洛在一起，魔法或許就不會發動了！
嗯
謝洛！
ぎゅうっ
咦！

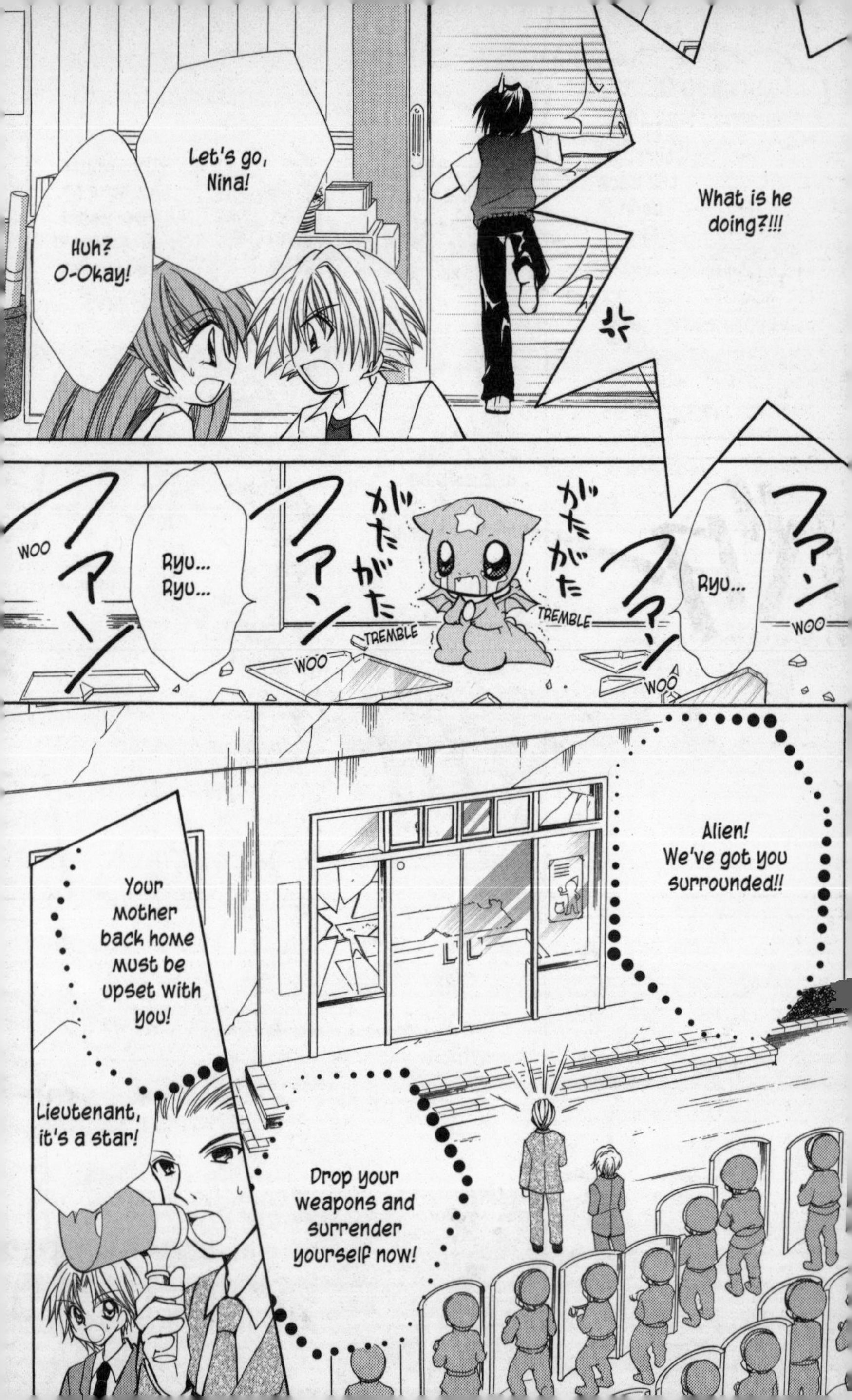
What is he doing?!!!
Let's go, Nina!
Huh? O-Okay!
ファン
WOO
Ryu...
ファン
WOO
がたがた
TREMBLE
がたがた
TREMBLE
ファン
WOO
Ryu... Ryu...
ファン
WOO
Alien! We've got you surrounded!!
Your mother back home must be upset with you!
Drop your weapons and surrender yourself now!
Lieutenant, it's a star!

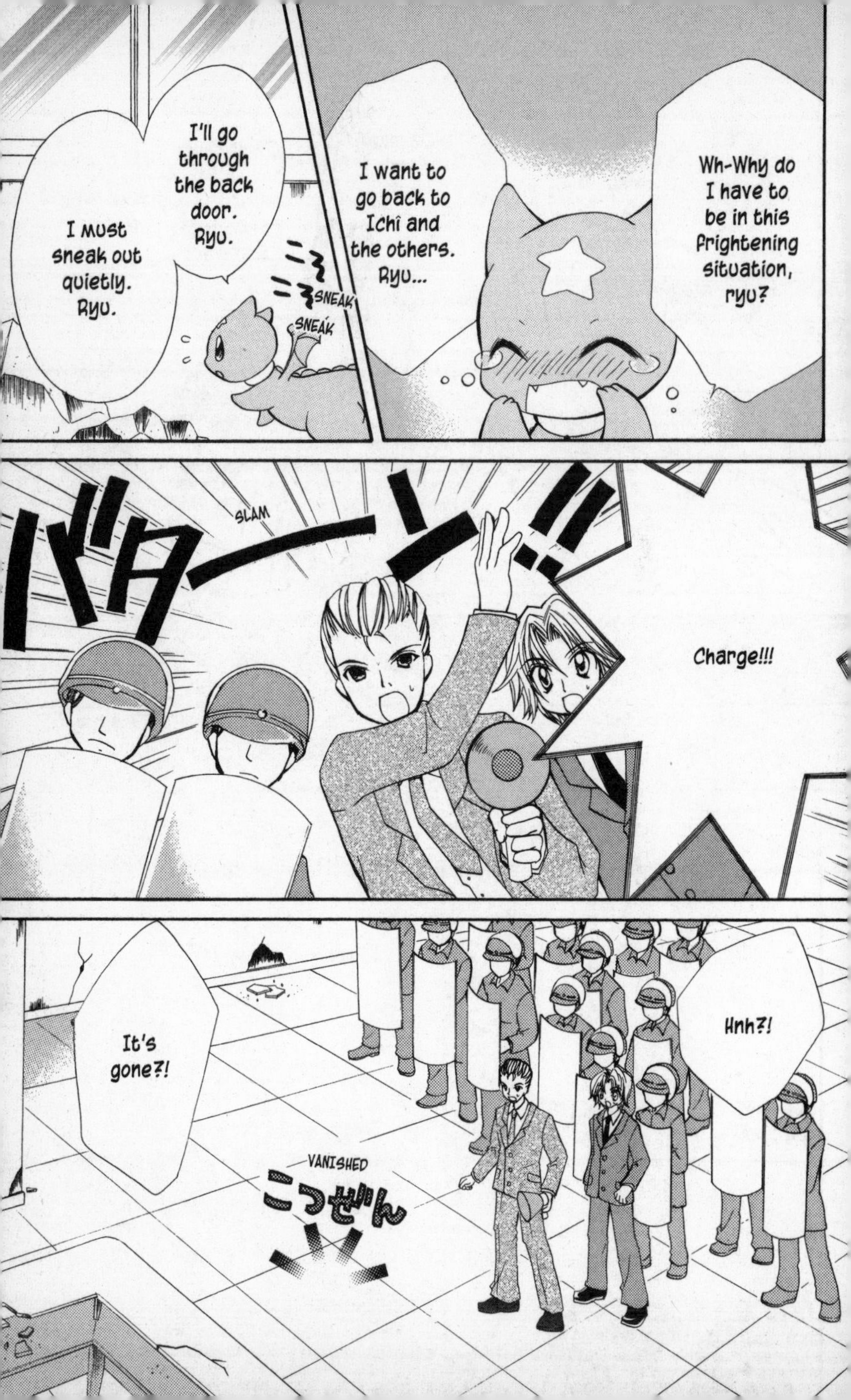
Wh-Why do I have to be in this frightening situation, ryu?
I want to go back to Ichi and the others. Ryu...
I'll go through the back door. Ryu.
I must sneak out quietly. Ryu.
こそ
こそ
SNEAK
SNEAK
Charge!!!
バターン!!
SLAM
Hnh?!
It's gone?!
こつぜん
VANISHED

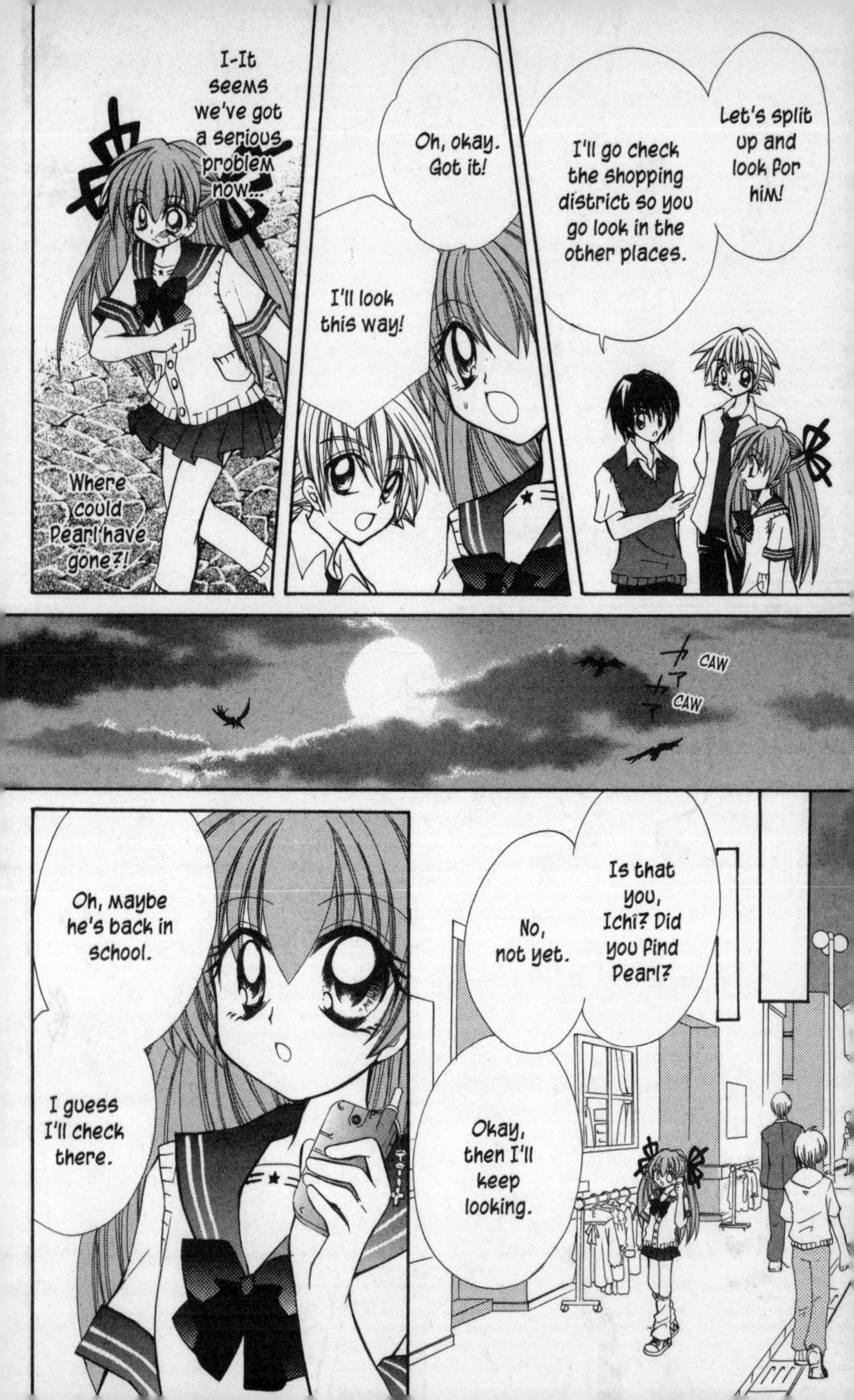

Let's split up and look for him!
I'll go check the shopping district so you go look in the other places.
Oh, okay. Got it!
I'll look this way!
I-It seems we've got a serious problem now...
Where could Pearl have gone?!
CAW
CAW
Is that you, Ichi? Did you find Pearl?
No, not yet.
Okay, then I'll keep looking.
Oh, maybe he's back in school.
I guess I'll check there.

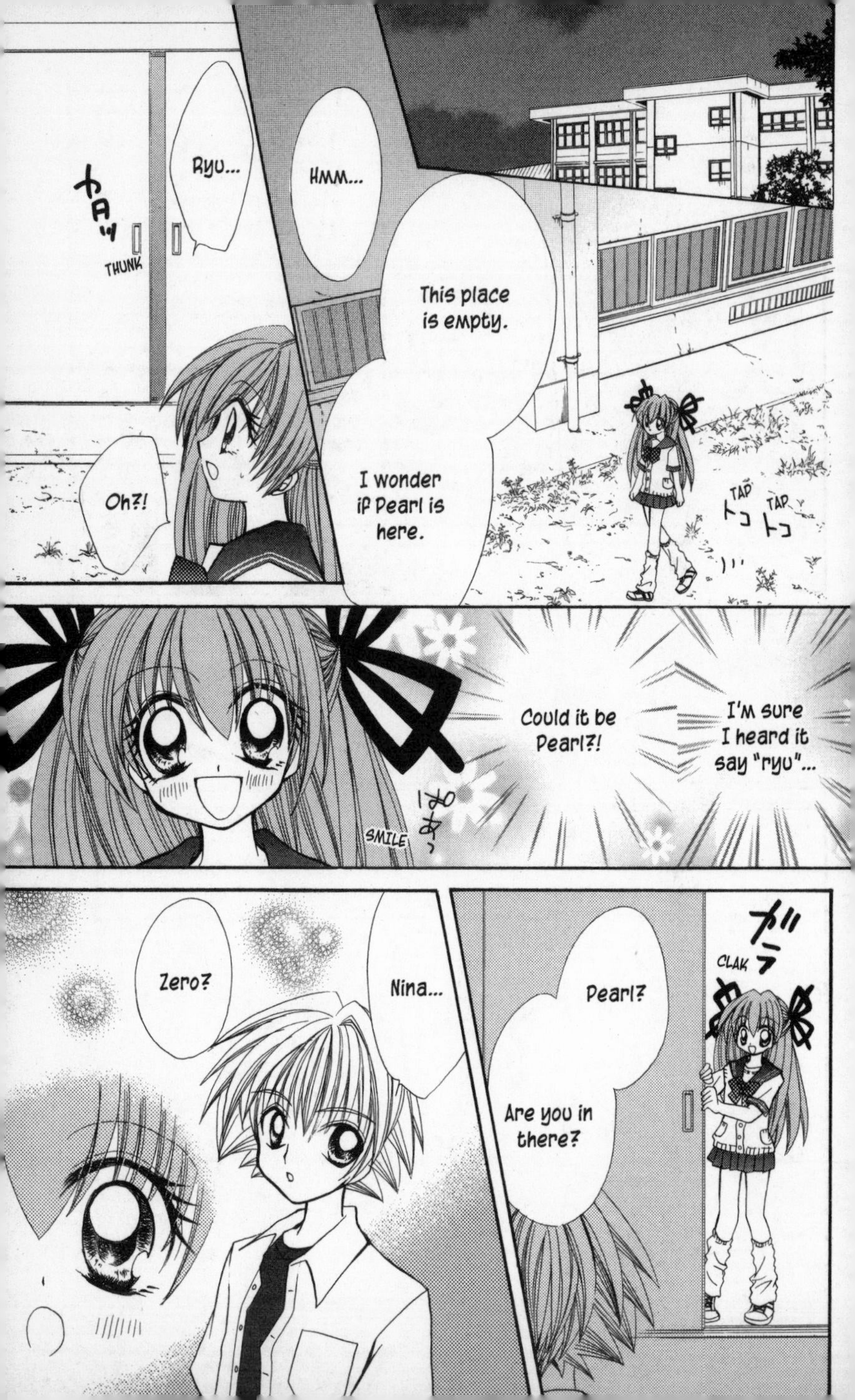
Hmm...
This place is empty.
I wonder if Pearl is here.
TAP
TAP
Ryu...
THUNK
Oh?!
I'm sure I heard it say "ryu"...
Could it be Pearl?!
SMILE
CLAK
Pearl?
Are you in there?
Nina...
Zero?

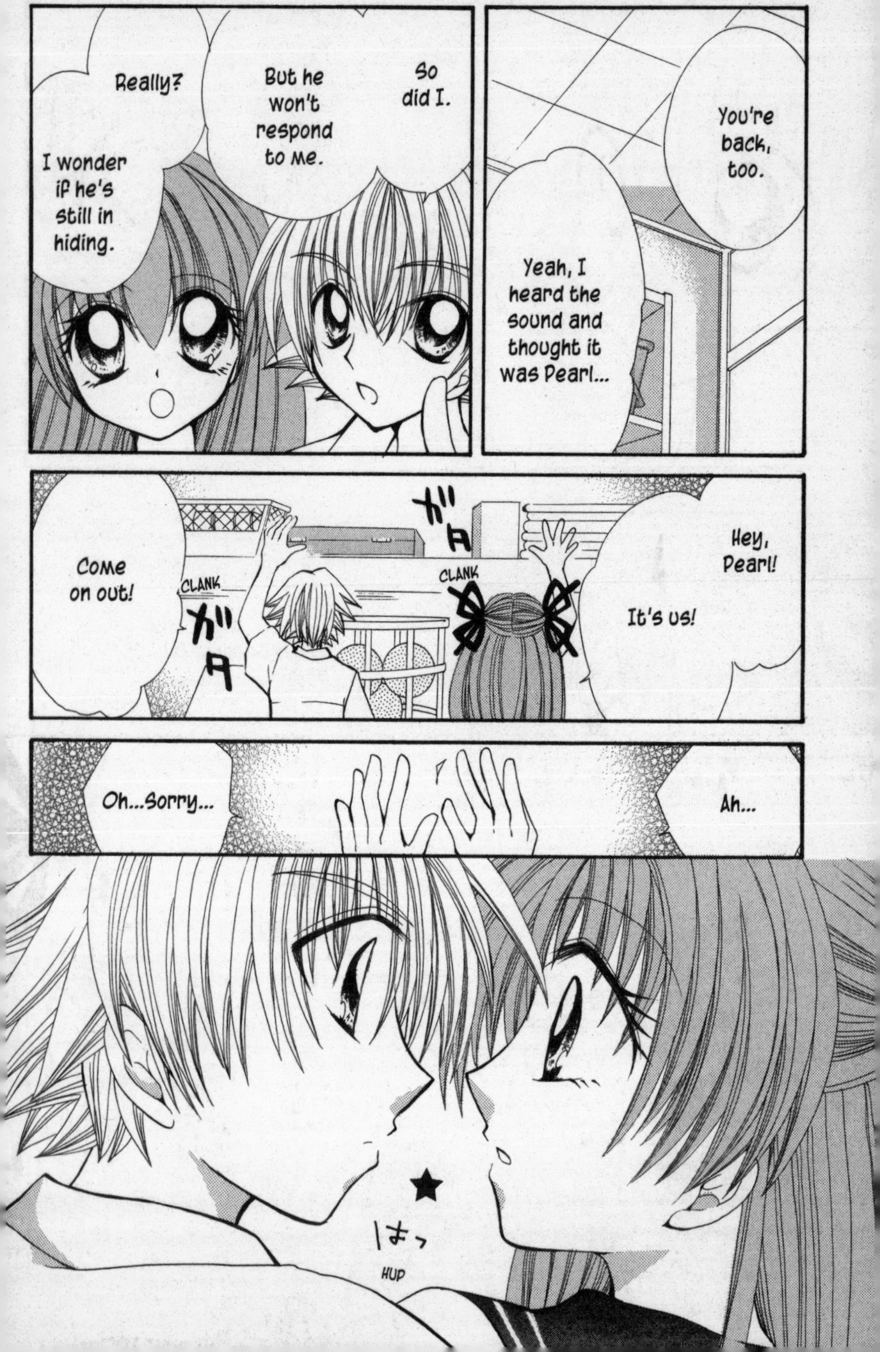
You're back, too.
Yeah, I heard the sound and thought it was Pearl...
So did I.
But he won't respond to me.
Really?
I wonder if he's still in hiding.
Hey, Pearl!
It's us!
ガタ
CLANK
Come on out!
ガタ
CLANK
Ah...
Oh...Sorry...
はっ
HUP

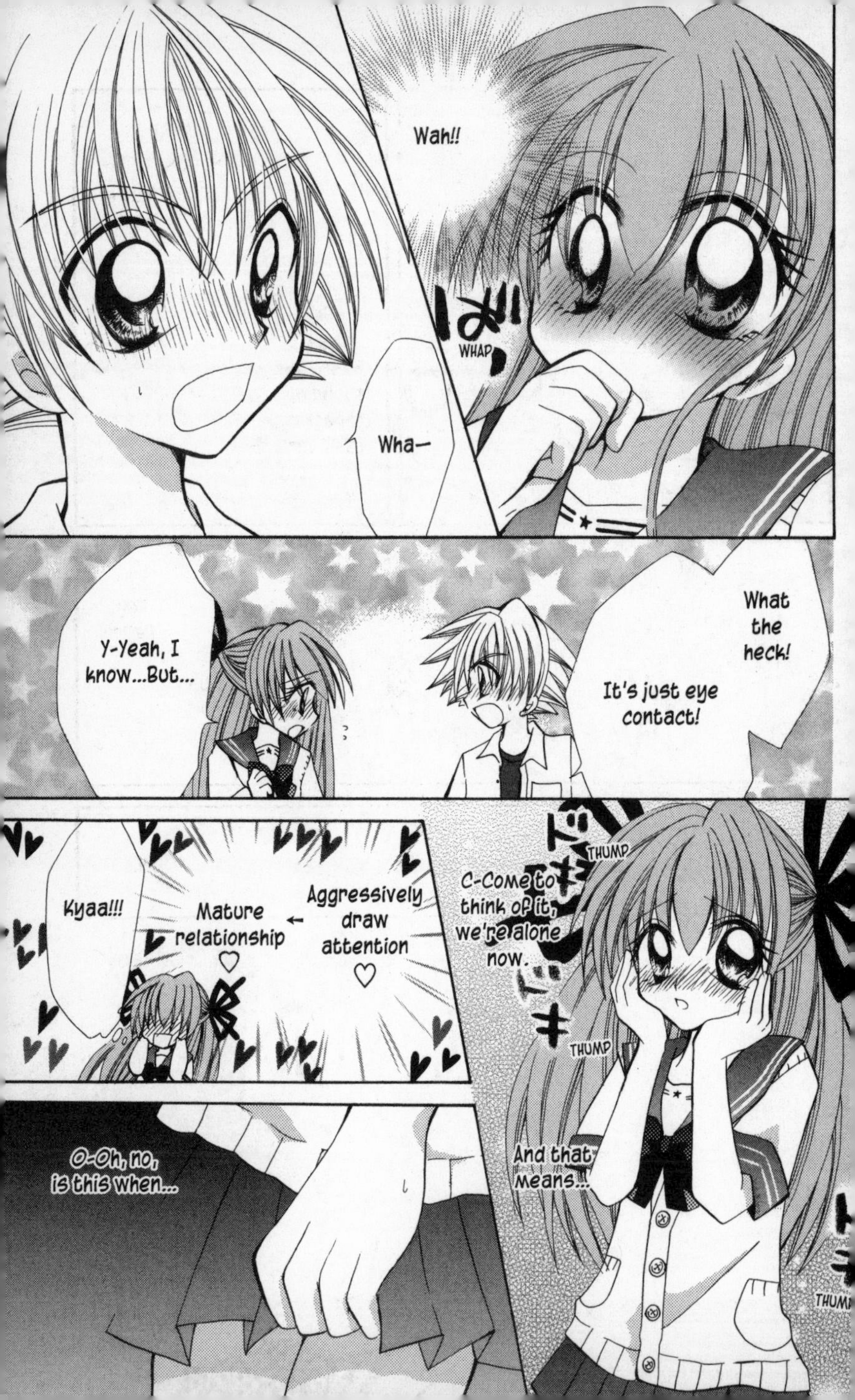
Wah!!
WHAP
Wha—
What the heck!
It's just eye contact!
Y-Yeah, I know...But...
THUMP
C-Come to think of it, we're alone now.
THUMP
And that means...
THUMP
Aggressively draw attention ♡
←
Mature relationship ♡
Kyaa!!!
O-Oh, no, is this when...

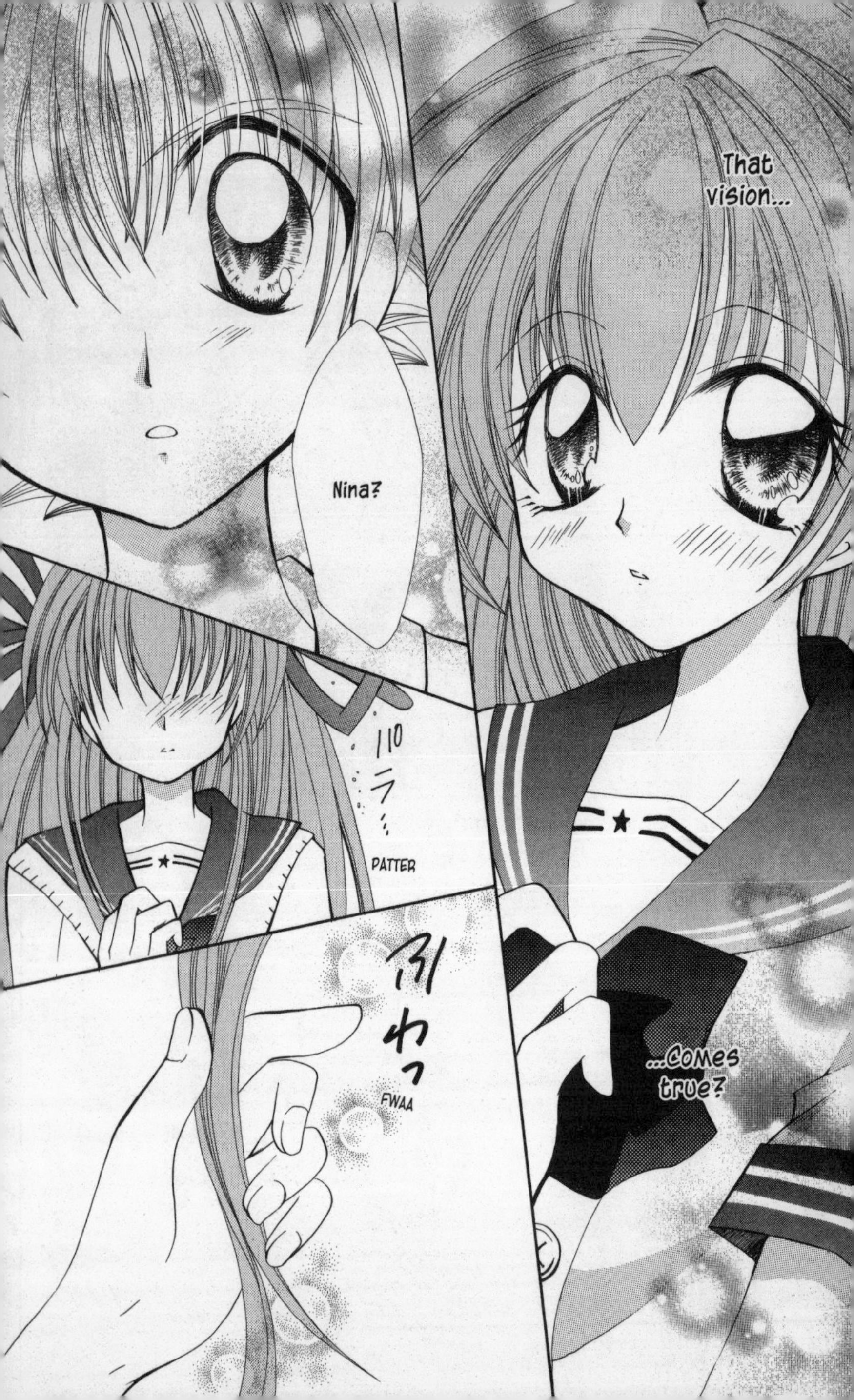
That vision...
...Comes true?
Nina?
パラ
PATTER
ふわっ
FWAA

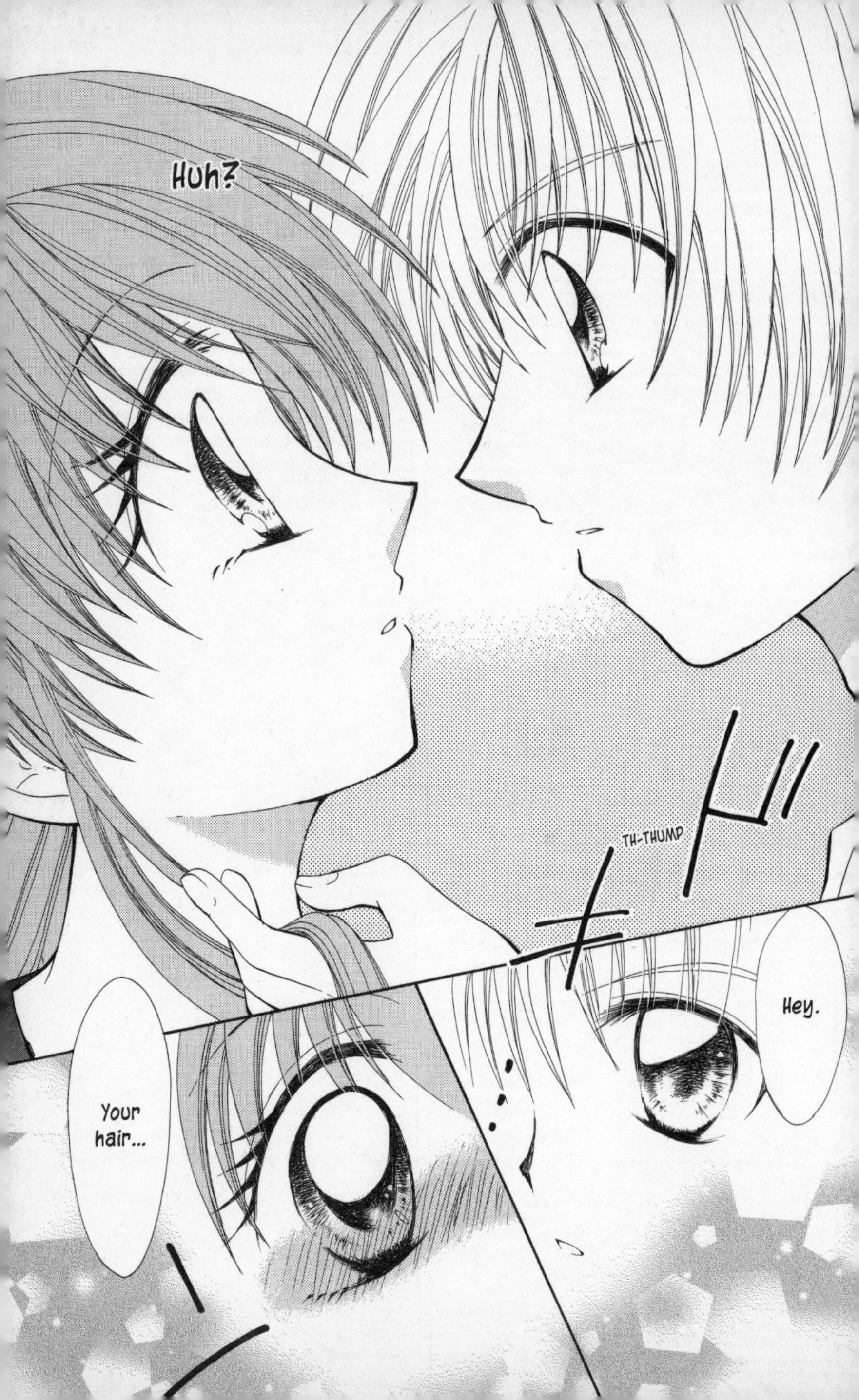
Huh?
TH-THUMP
Hey.
Your hair...

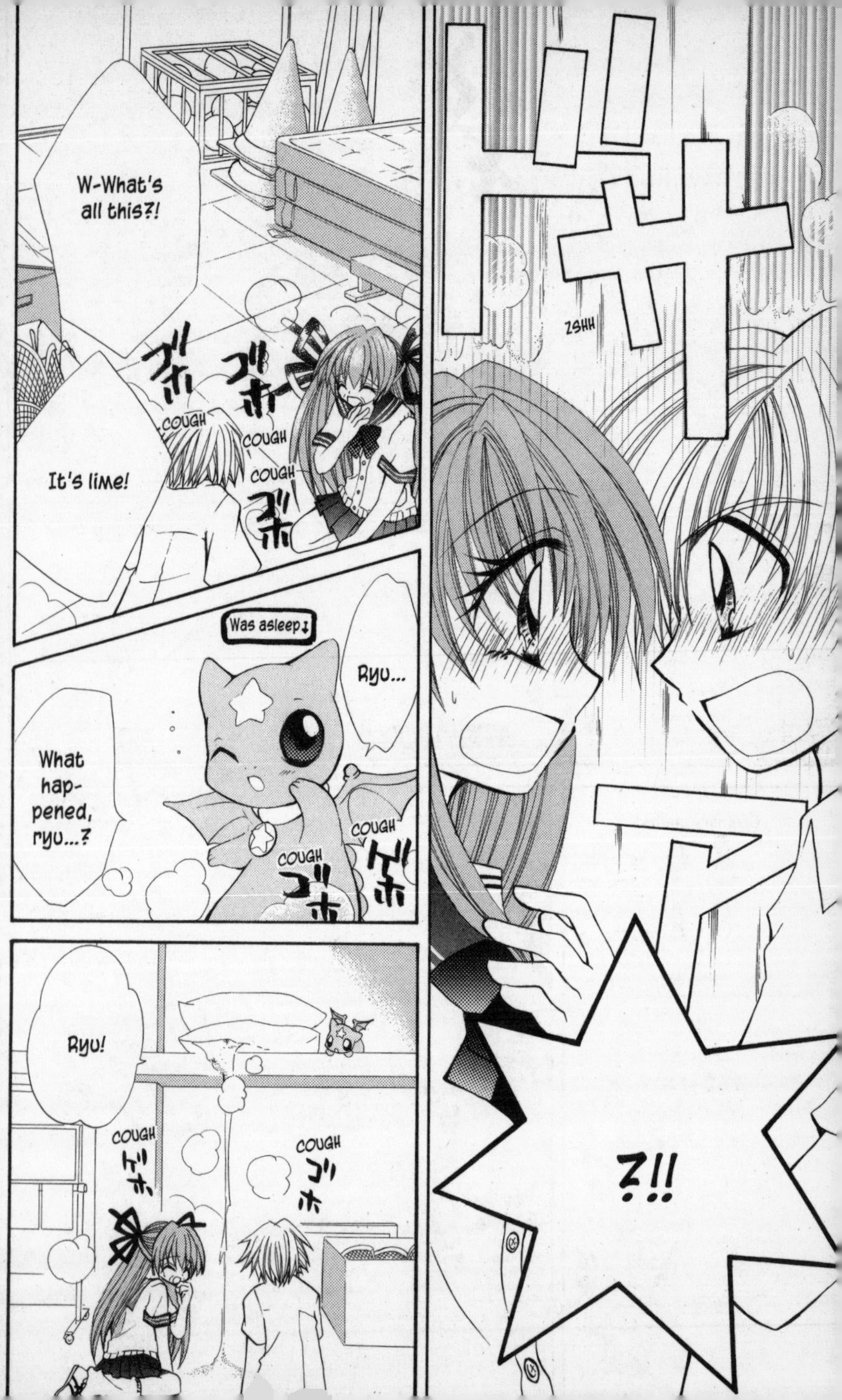
ZSHH
?!!
W-What's all this?!
COUGH
COUGH
COUGH
It's lime!
Was asleep↓
Ryu...
What hap-pened, ryu...?
COUGH
COUGH
Ryu!
COUGH
COUGH

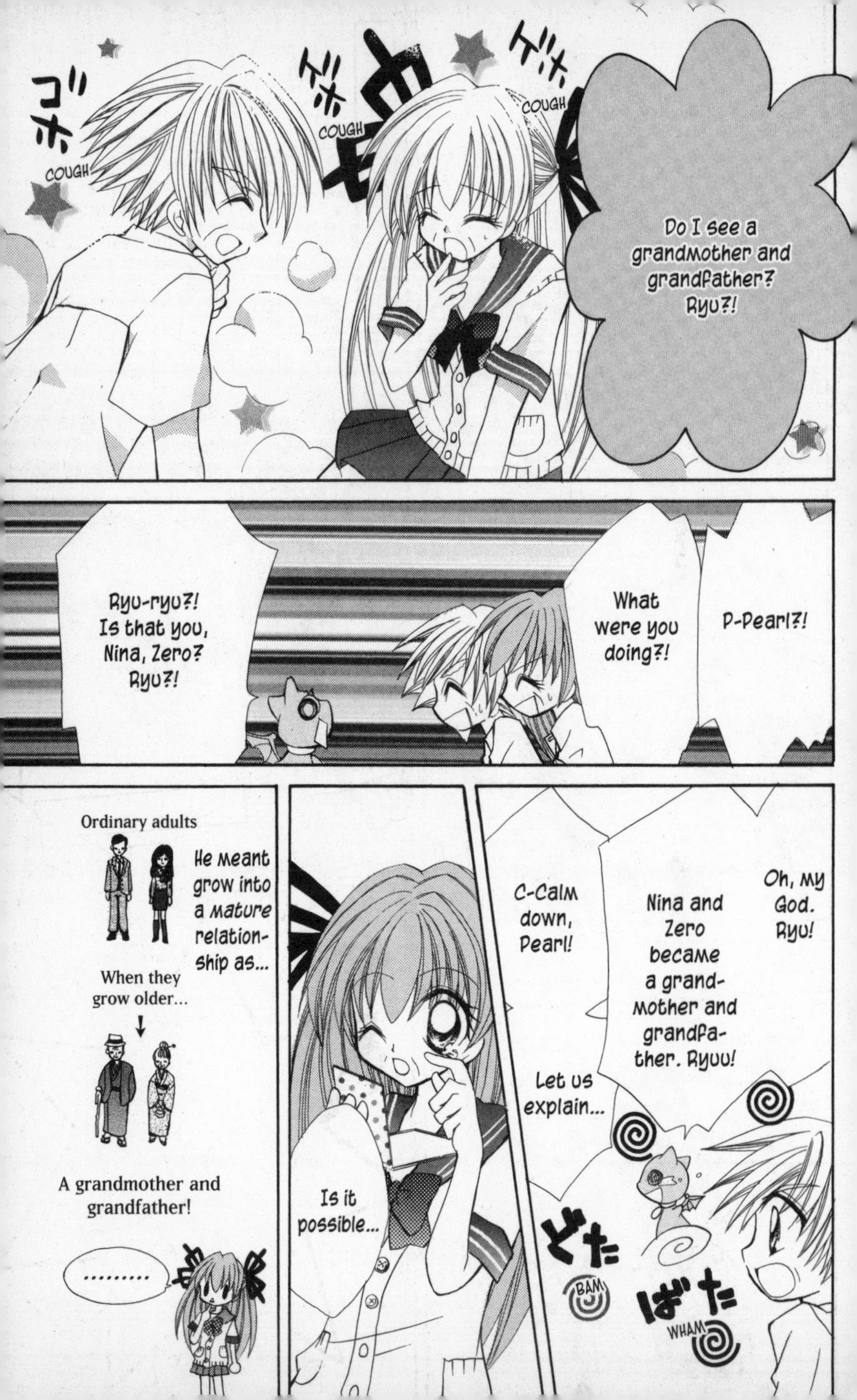
Do I see a grandmother and grandfather? Ryu?!
ゲホ
COUGH
ゲホ
COUGH
ゴホ
COUGH
P-Pearl?!
What were you doing?!
Ryu-ryu?! Is that you, Nina, Zero? Ryu?!
Oh, my God. Ryu!
Nina and Zero became a grand-mother and grandfa-ther. Ryuu!
C-Calm down, Pearl!
Let us explain...
どた
BAM
ばた
WHAM
Is it possible...
He meant grow into a mature relation-ship as...
Ordinary adults
When they grow older...
A grandmother and grandfather!
....

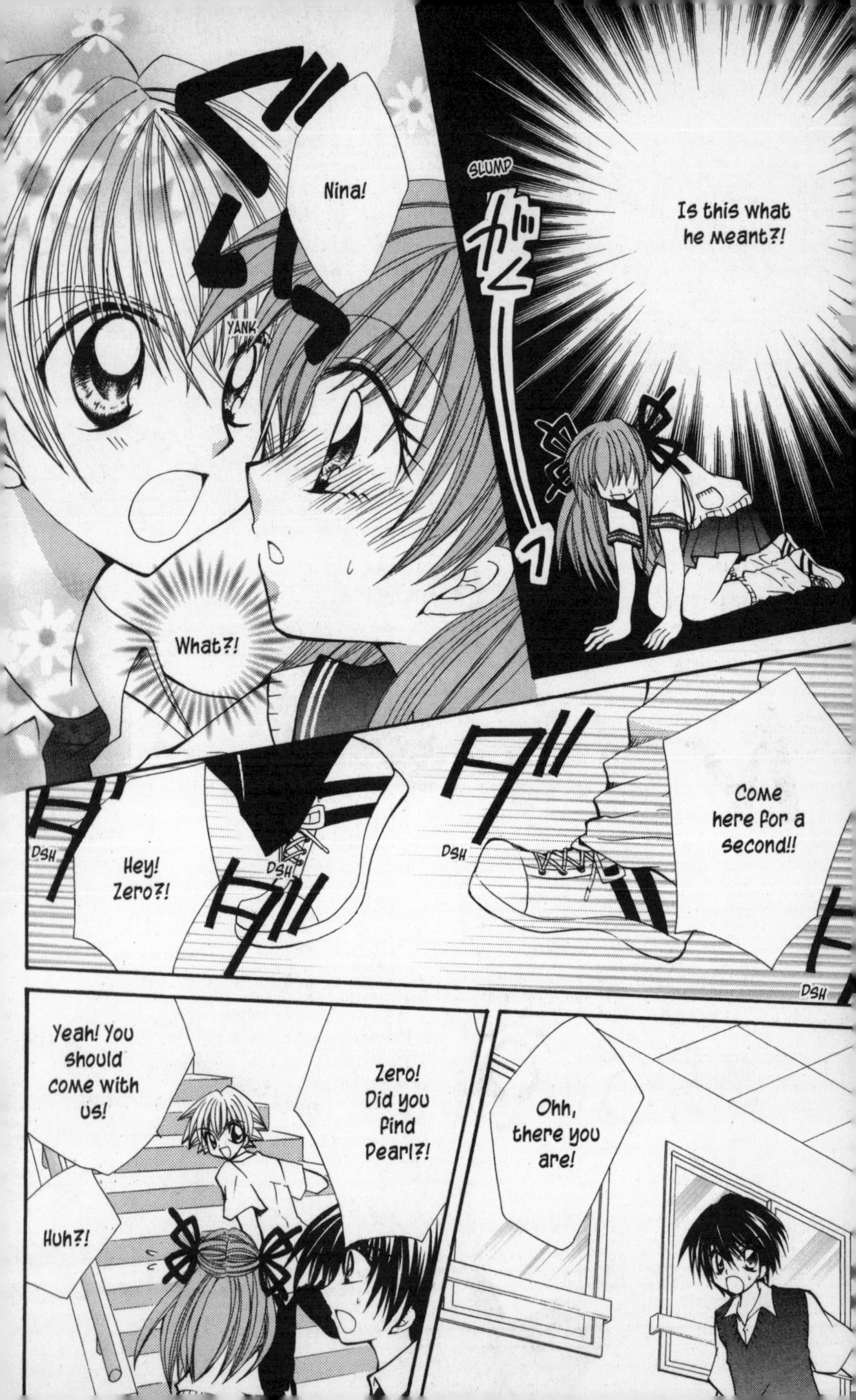
Is this what he meant?!
SLUMP
Nina!
YANK
What?!
Come here for a second!!
DSH
DSH
Hey! Zero?!
DSH
DSH
Ohh, there you are!
Zero! Did you find Pearl?!
Yeah! You should come with us!
Huh?!

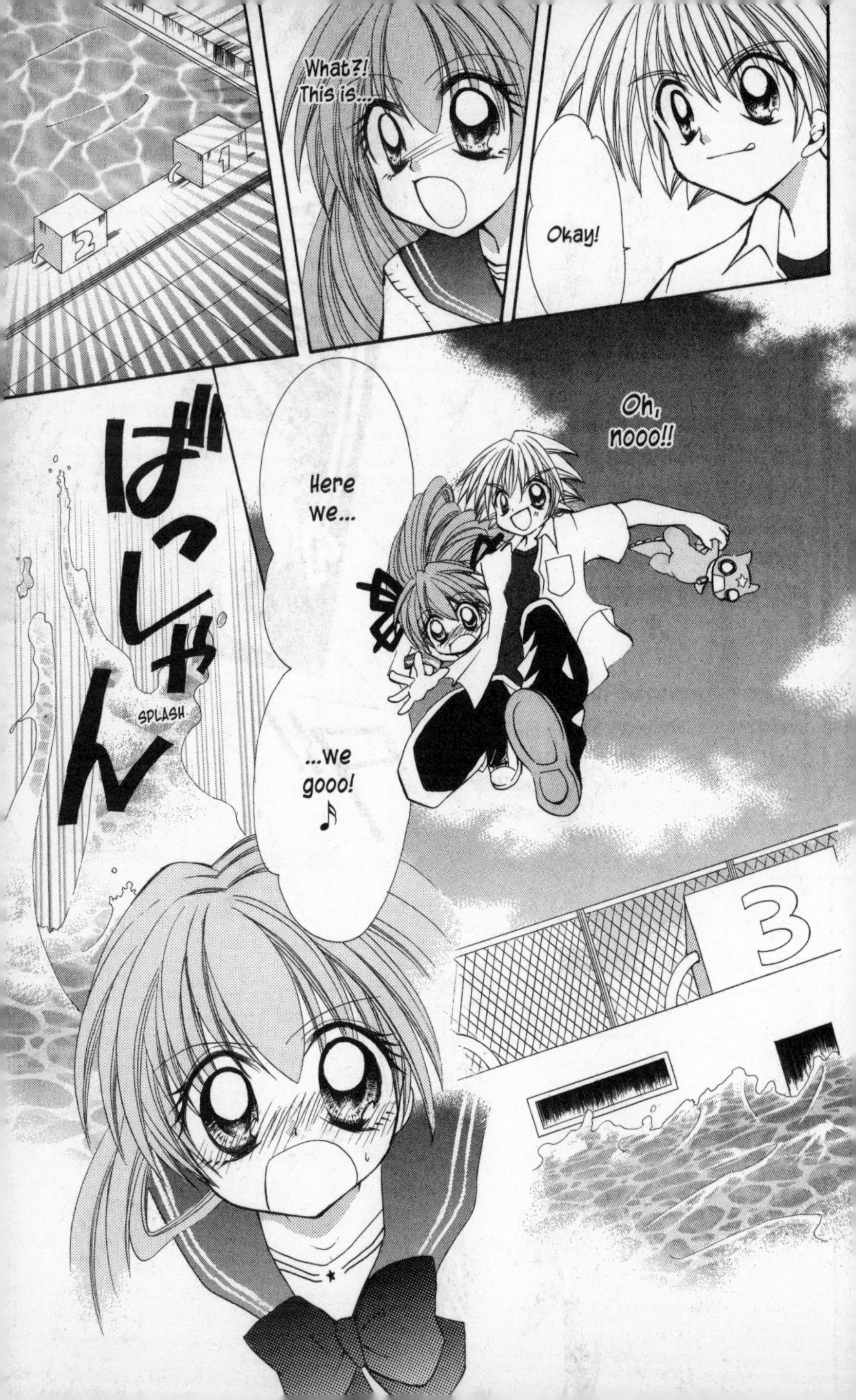
Okay!
What?! This is...
Oh, nooo!!
Here we...
...we gooo! ♪
ばっしゃん
SPLASH

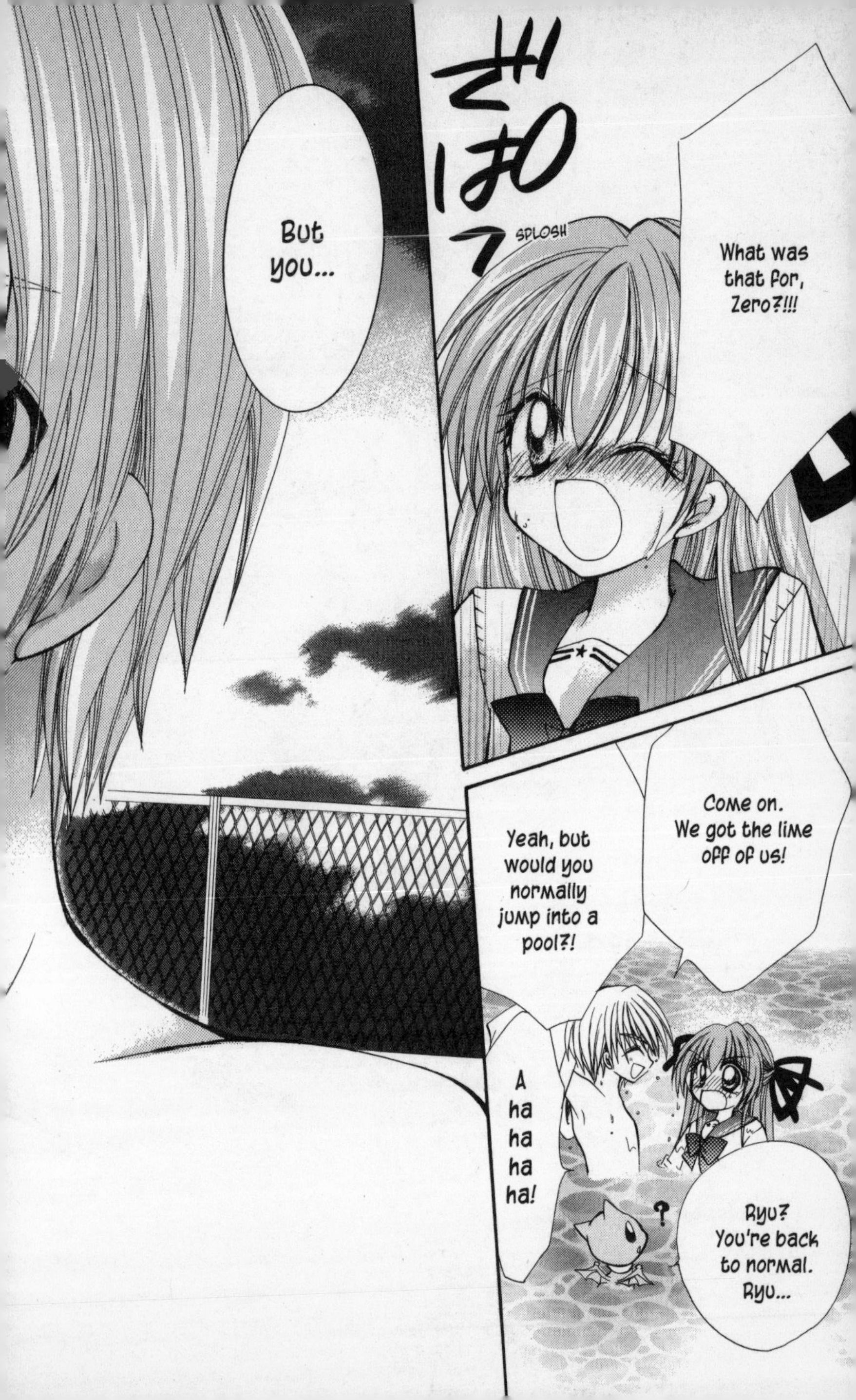
SPLOSH
What was that for, Zero?!!!
Come on. We got the lime off of us!
Yeah, but would you normally jump into a pool?!
A ha ha ha ha!
Ryu? You're back to normal. Ryu...
But you...

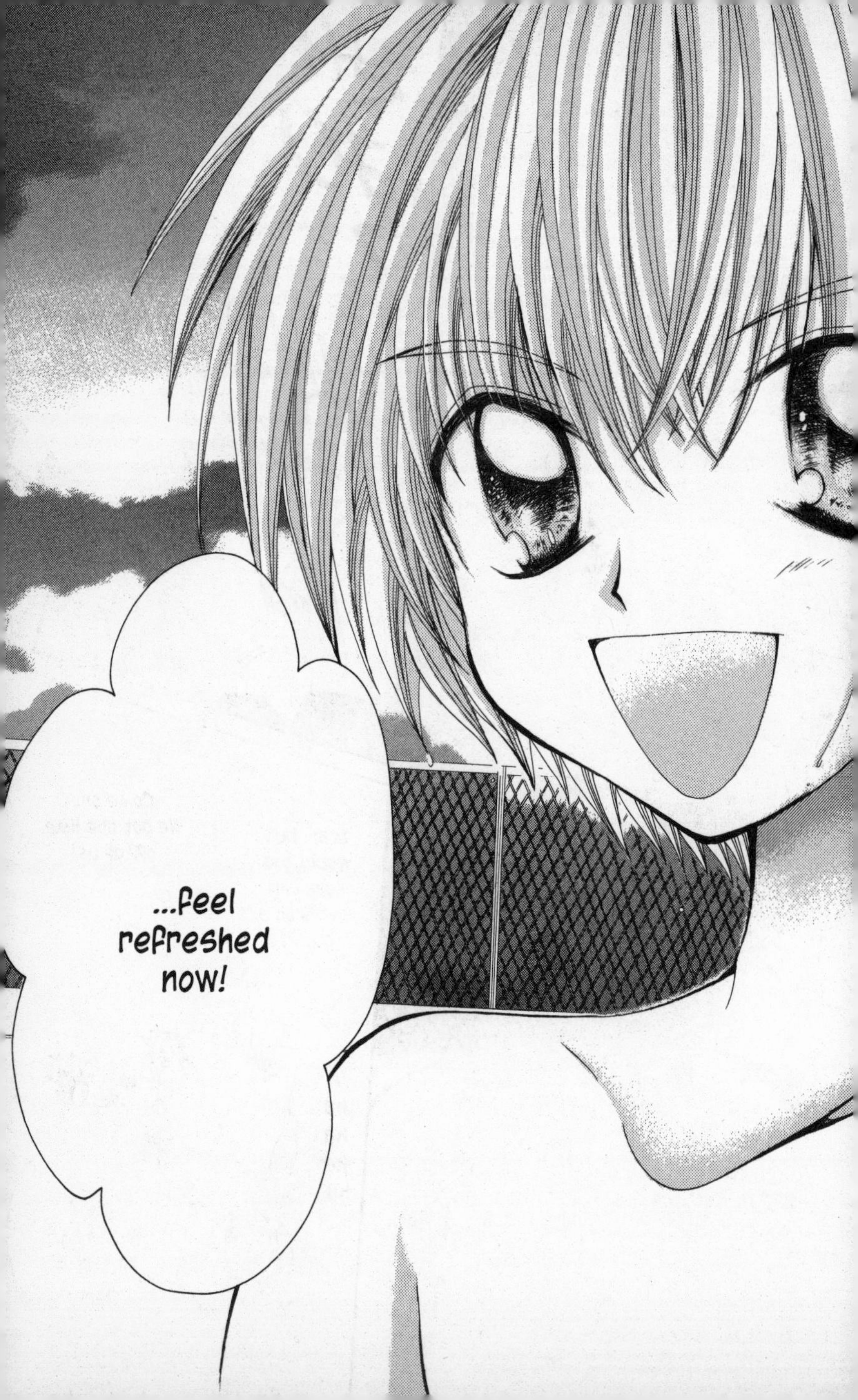
...feel refreshed now!

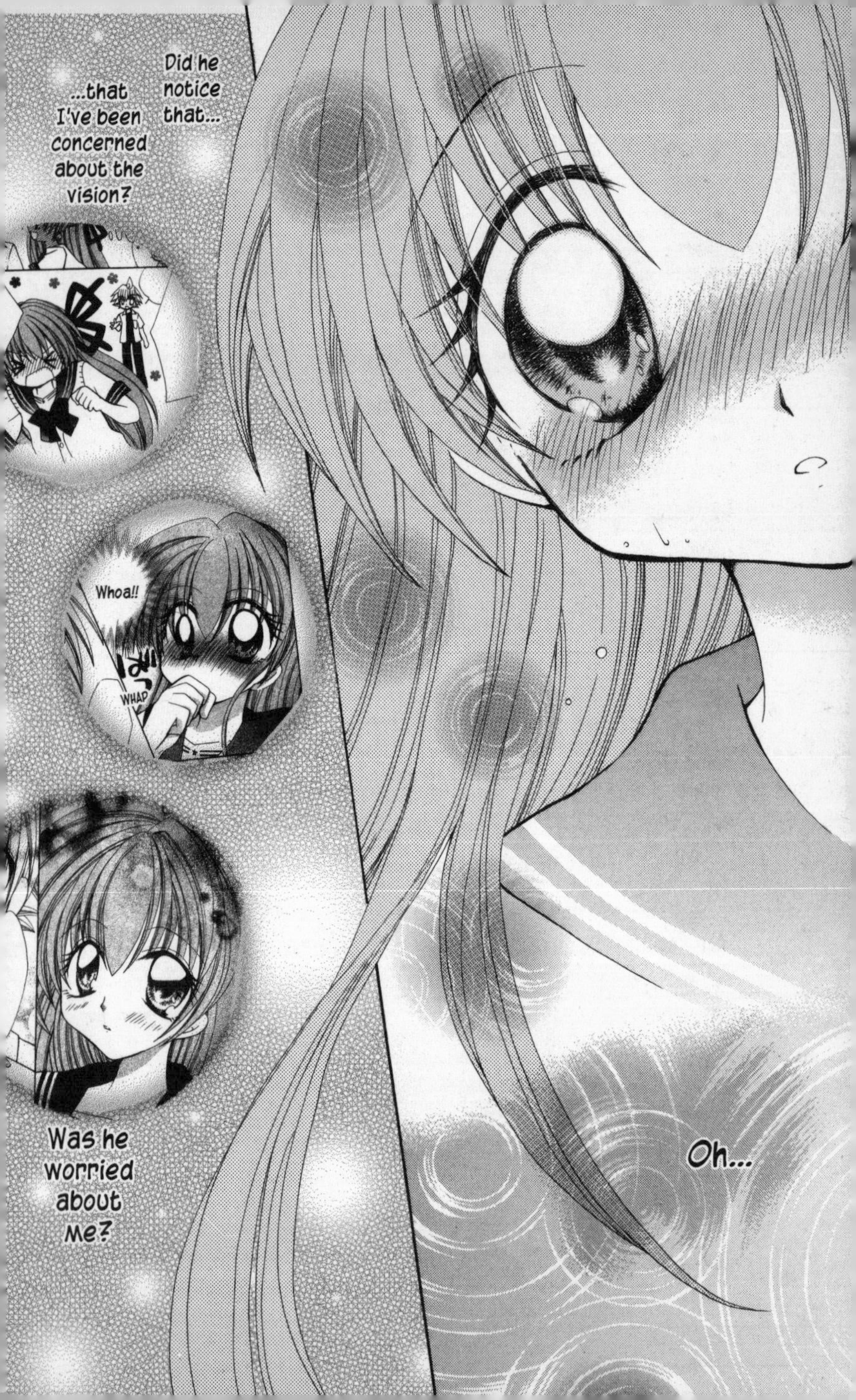
Oh...
Did he notice that...
...that I've been concerned about the vision?
Whoa!!
WHAP
Was he worried about me?

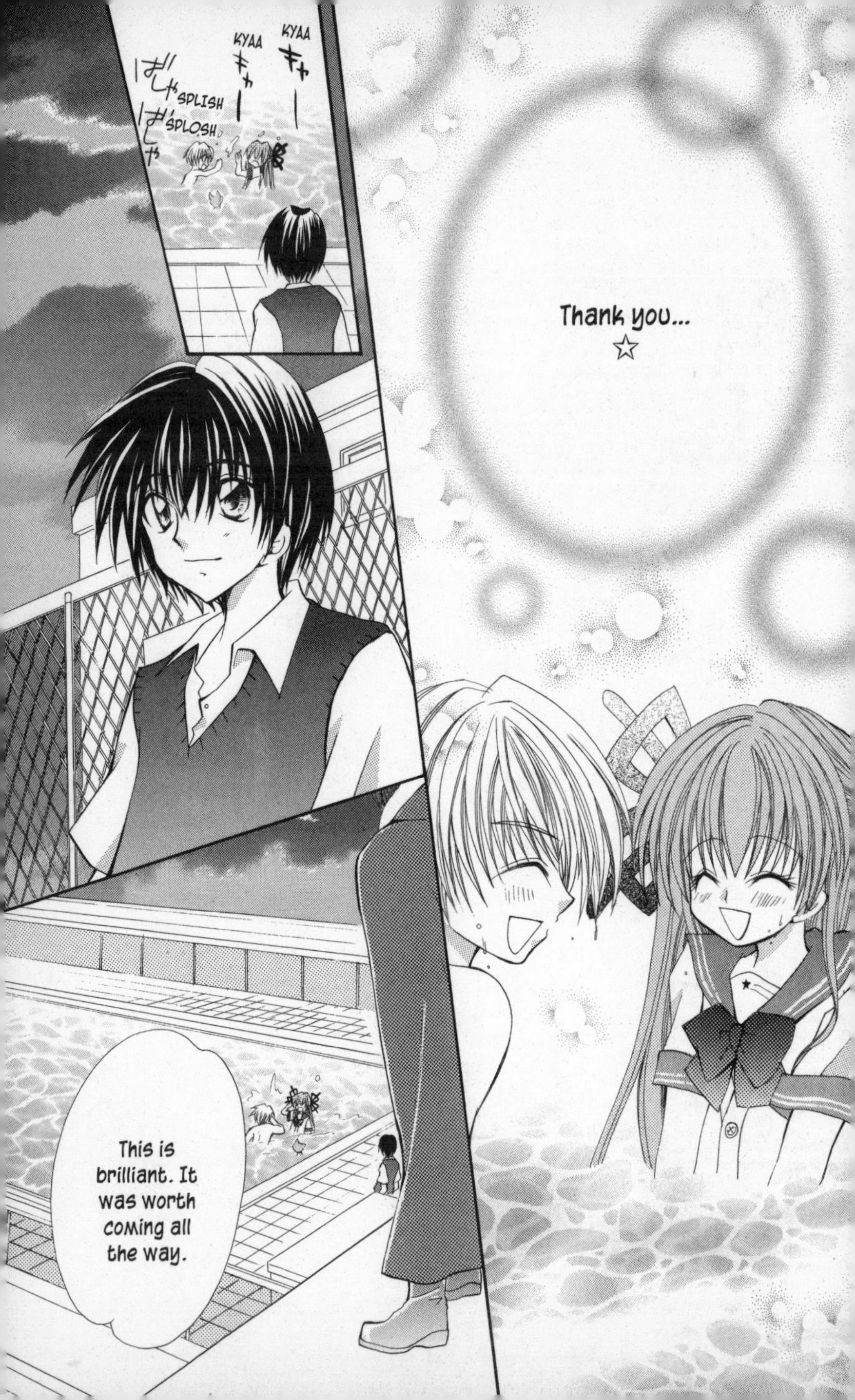
Thank you... ☆
KYAA キャー
KYAA キャー
ばしゃ SPLISH
ばしゃ SPLOSH
This is brilliant. It was worth coming all the way.

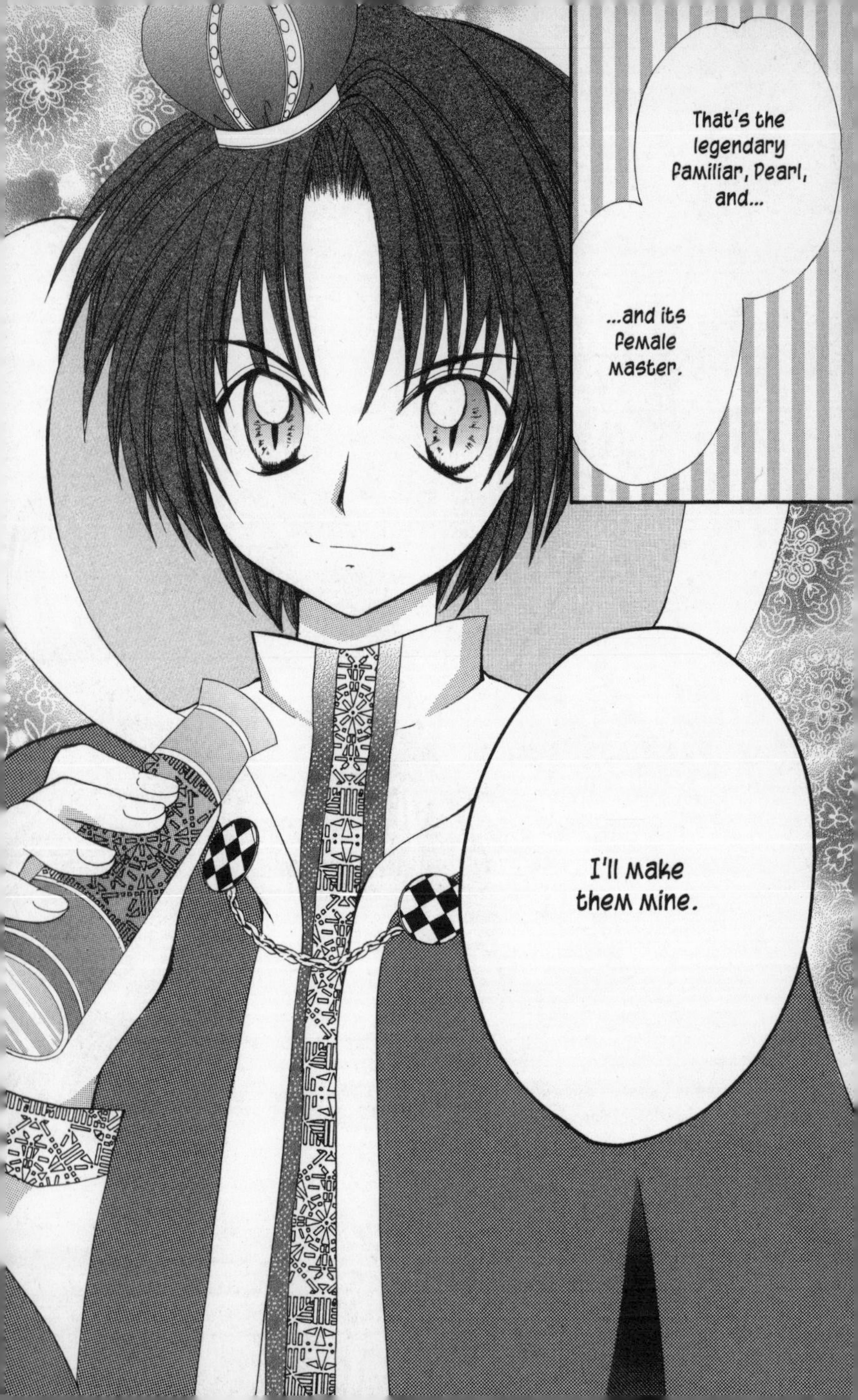
That's the legendary familiar, Pearl, and...
...and its female master.
I'll make them mine.

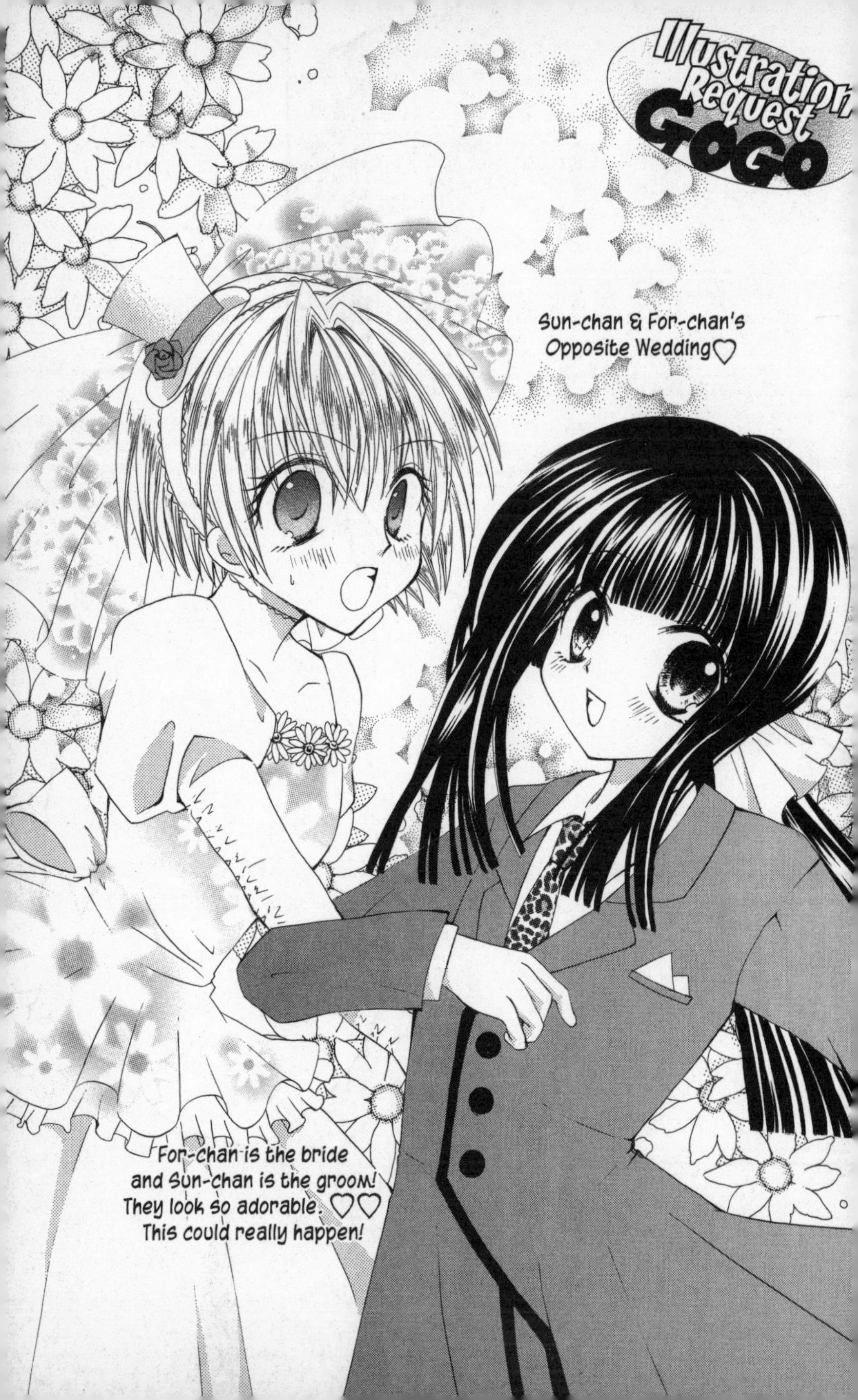
Illustration Request GoGo
Sun-chan & For-chan's Opposite Wedding♡
For-chan is the bride and Sun-chan is the groom! They look so adorable. ♡♡ This could really happen!

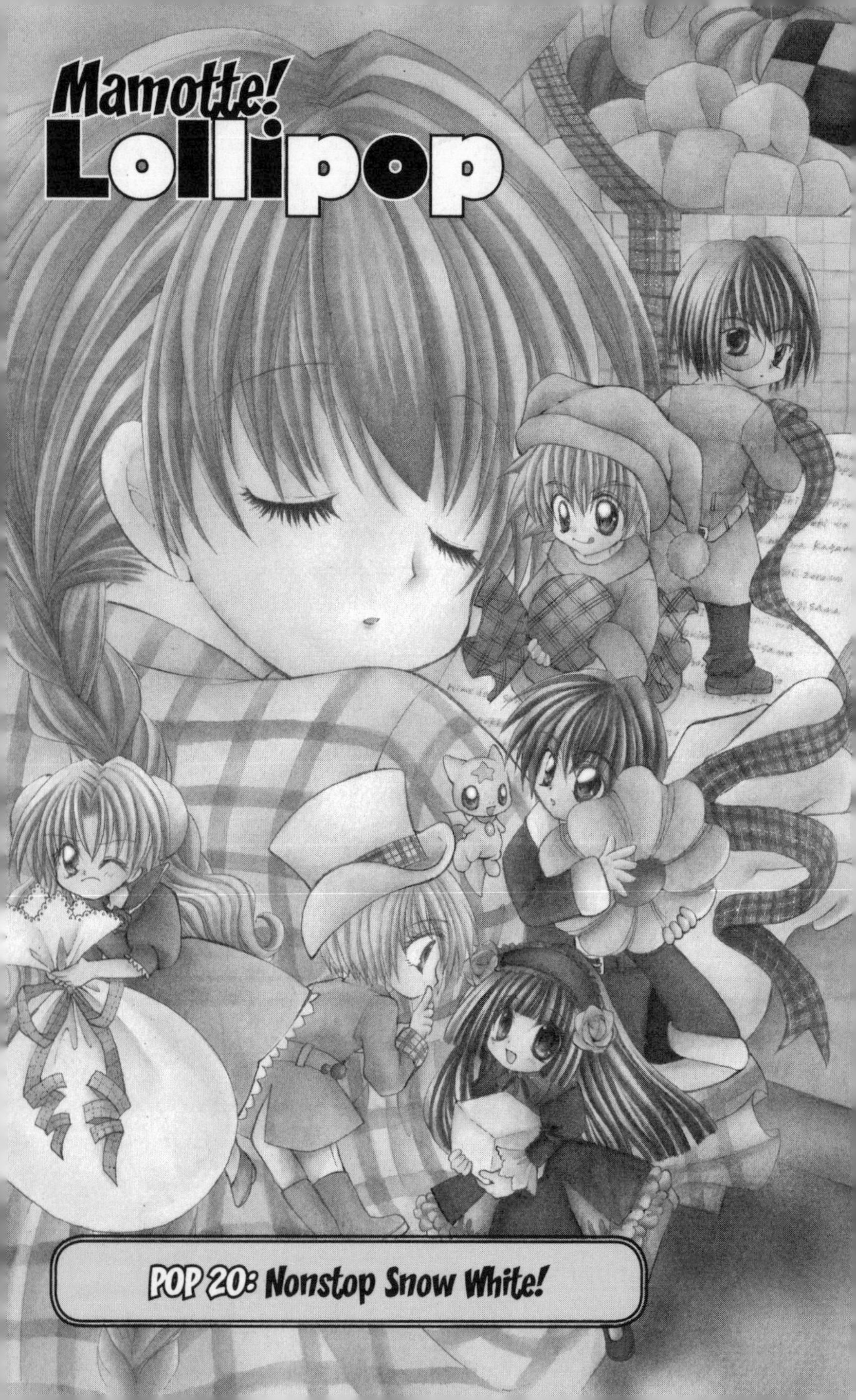
Mamotte! Lollipop
POP 20: Nonstop Snow White!

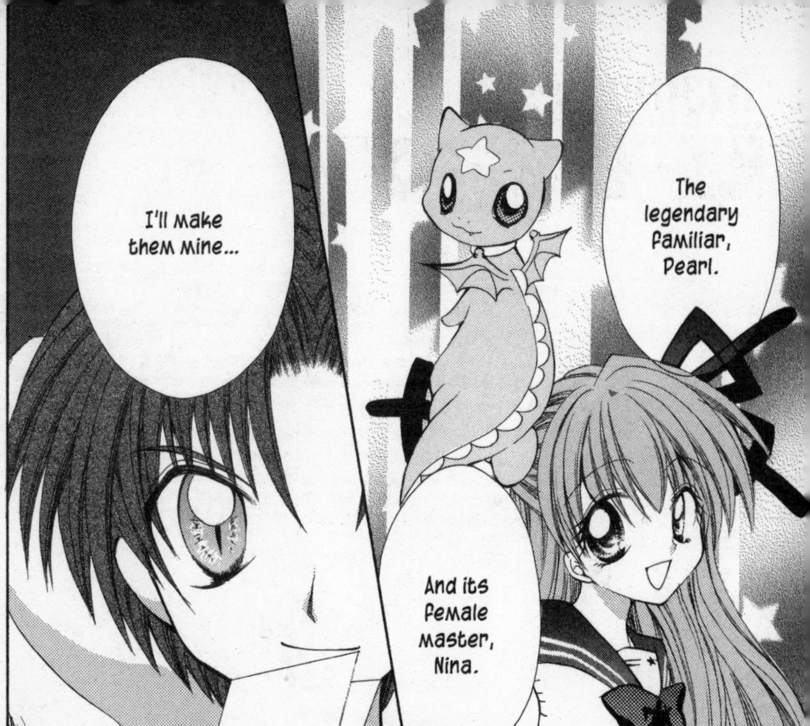
The legendary familiar, Pearl.
And its female master, Nina.
I'll make them mine...

PoP 20 Nonstop Snow White!

I drew the splash page with a fairy tale image. It's supposed to be the dwarfs sneaking candies out while Nina is asleep.

The new characters are here! I really love King and his followers!! I'd like to see them talk about a lot of things. Would *love* to. I personally enjoyed drawing this episode for a chance to dress up the characters differently.

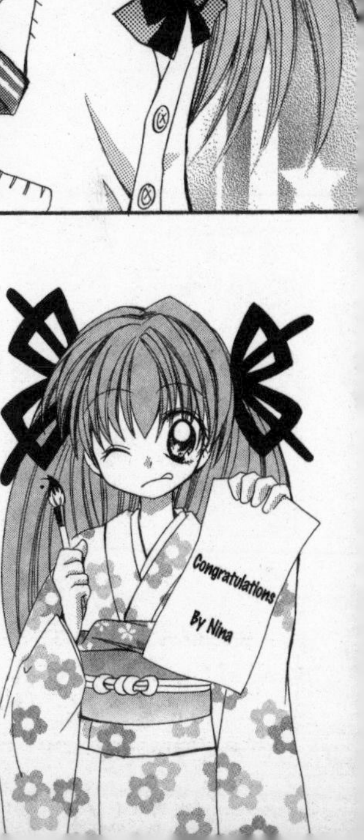
Congratulations
By Nina

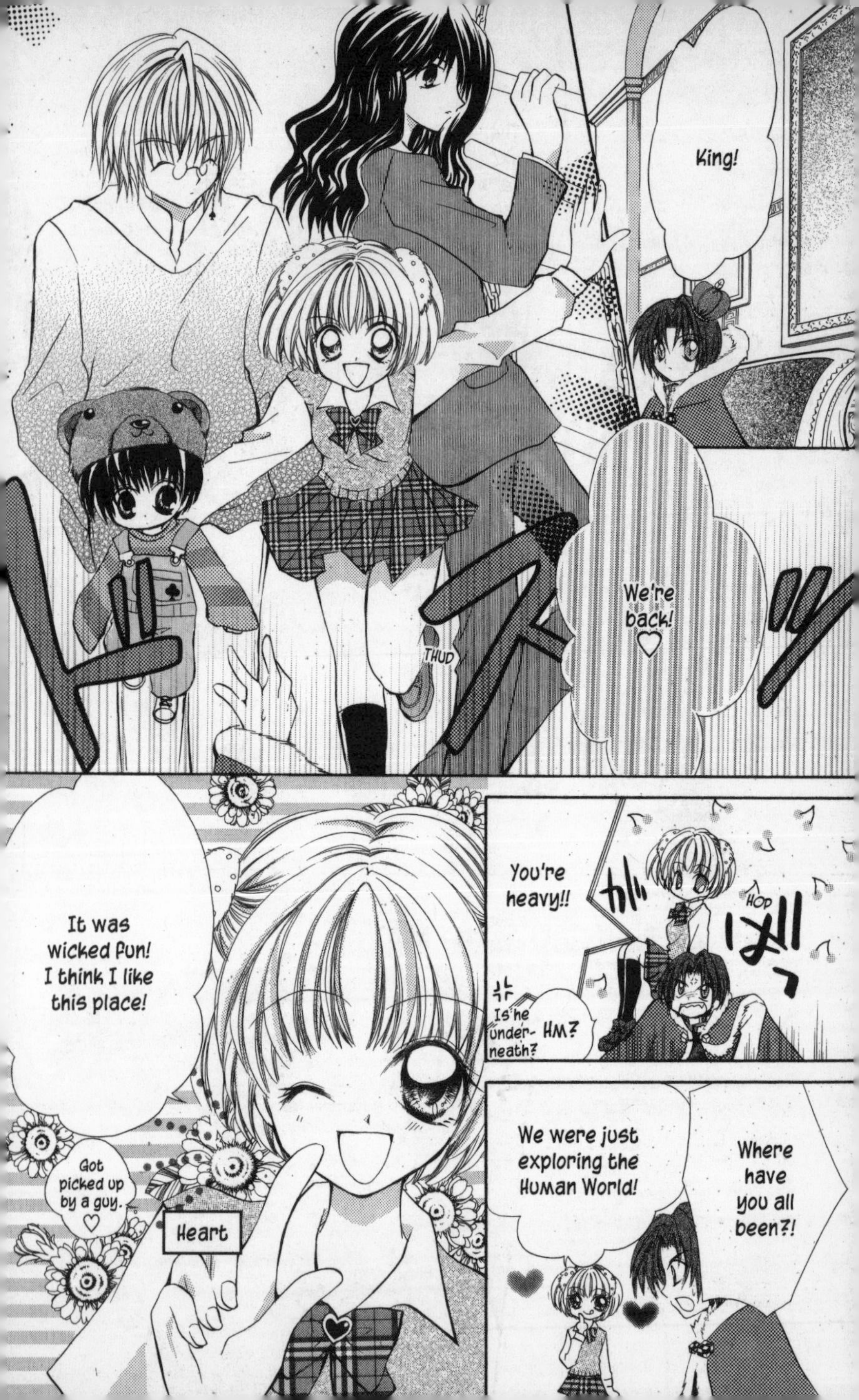

King!
We're back! ♡
THUD
HOP
You're heavy!!
HM?
Is he under-neath?
Where have you all been?!
We were just exploring the Human World!
It was wicked fun! I think I like this place!
Heart
Got picked up by a guy. ♡

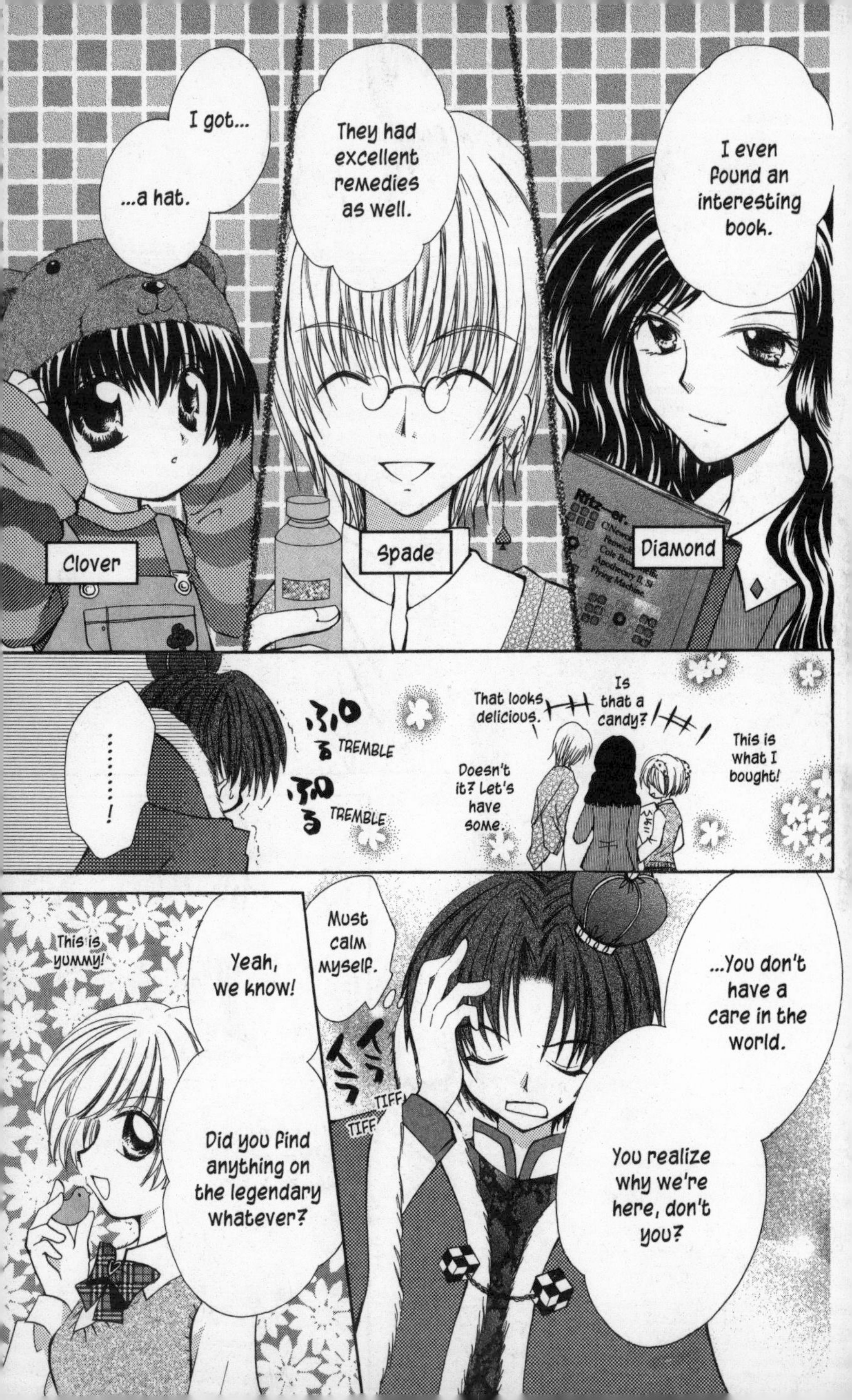
I even found an interesting book.
Diamond
They had excellent remedies as well.
Spade
I got...
...a hat.
Clover
This is what I bought!
Is that a candy?
That looks delicious.
Doesn't it? Let's have some.
TREMBLE
TREMBLE
........!
...You don't have a care in the world.
You realize why we're here, don't you?
Must calm myself.
TIFF
TIFF
Yeah, we know!
Did you find anything on the legendary whatever?
This is yummy!

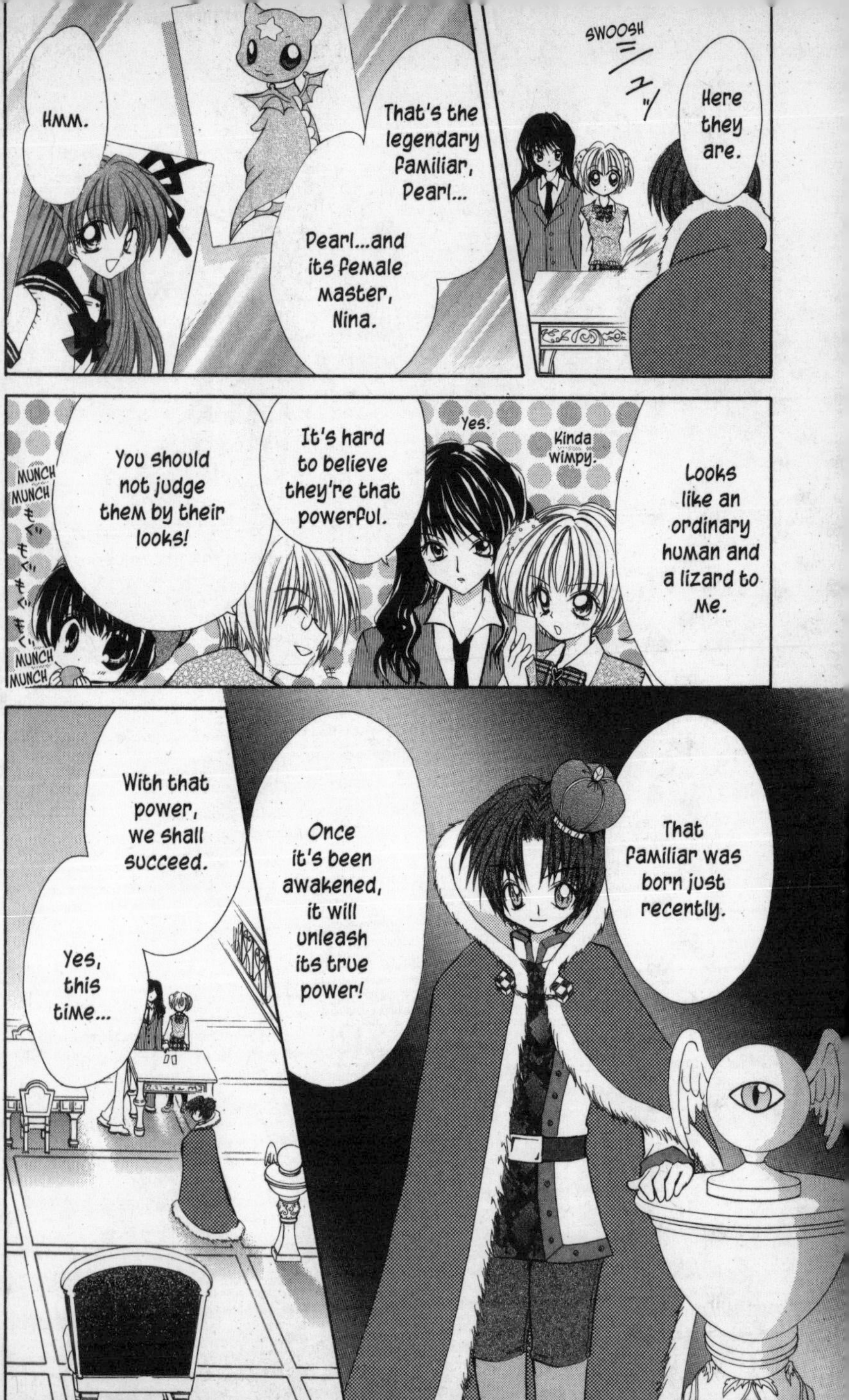
SWOOSH
Here they are.
That's the legendary familiar, Pearl...
Pearl...and its female master, Nina.
Hmm.
Looks like an ordinary human and a lizard to me.
Kinda wimpy.
Yes.
It's hard to believe they're that powerful.
You should not judge them by their looks!
MUNCH MUNCH
MUNCH MUNCH
That familiar was born just recently.
Once it's been awakened, it will unleash its true power!
With that power, we shall succeed.
Yes, this time...

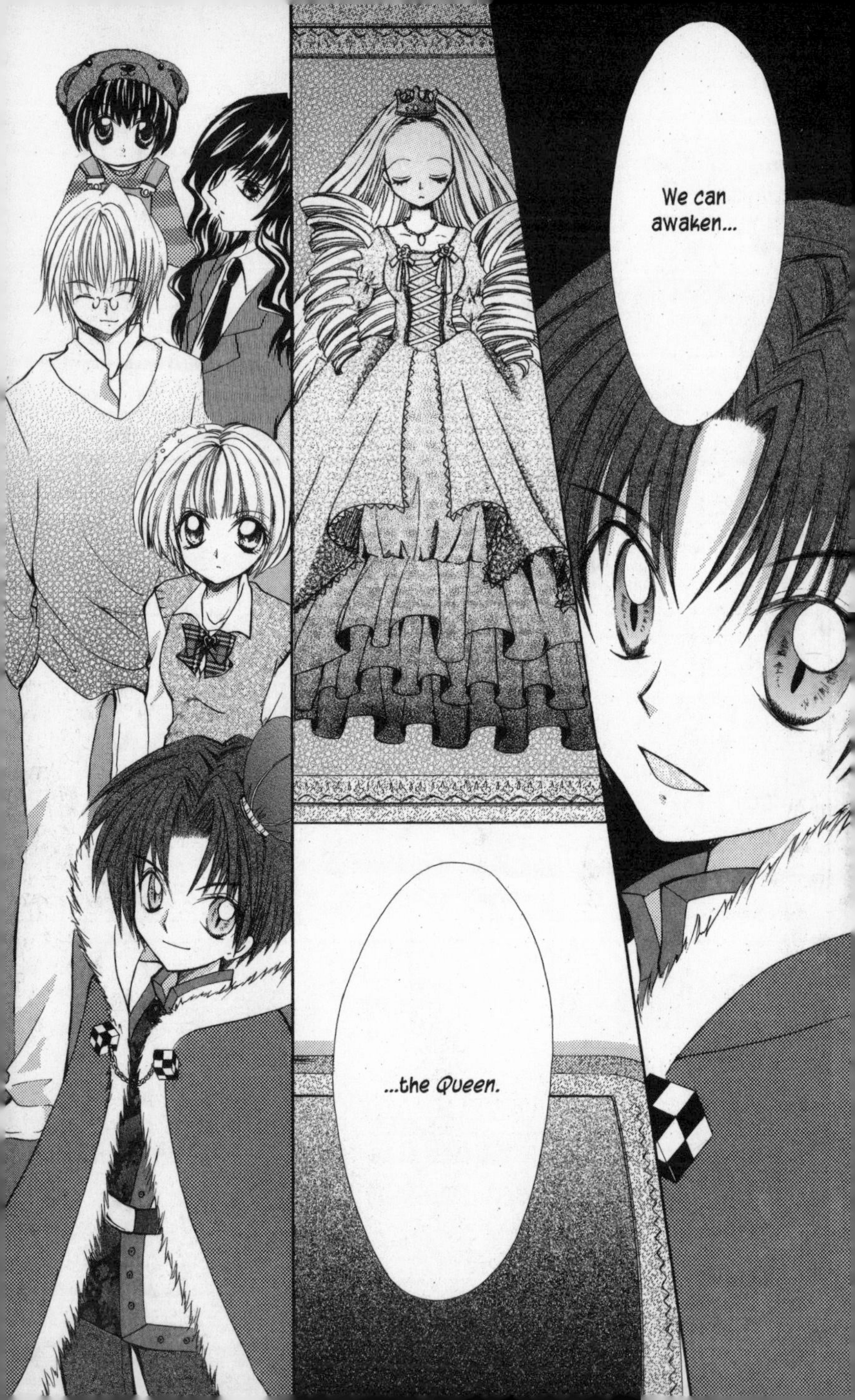
We can awaken...
...the Queen.

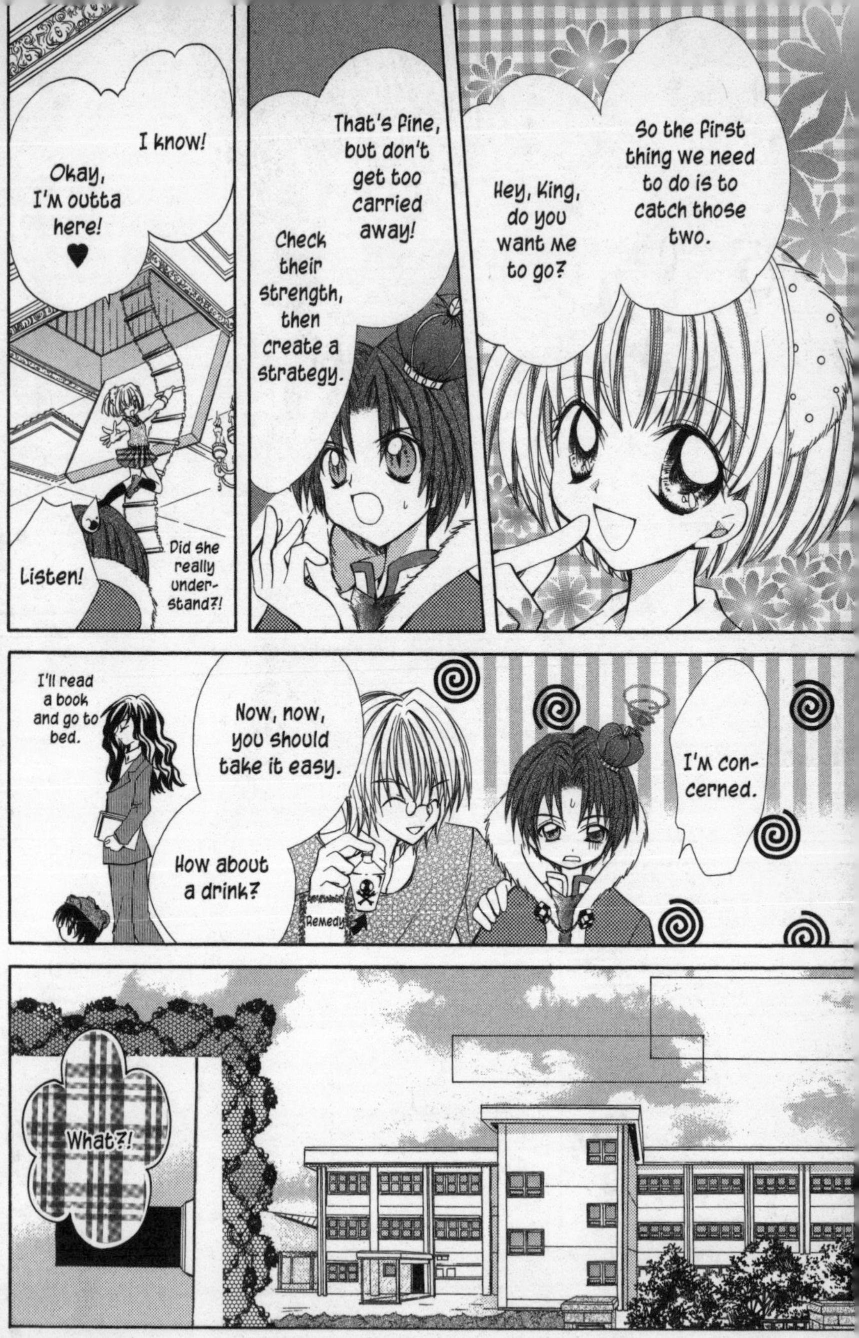
So the first thing we need to do is to catch those two.
Hey, King, do you want me to go?
That's fine, but don't get too carried away!
Check their strength, then create a strategy.
I know!
Okay, I'm outta here! ♥
Listen!
Did she really under-stand?!
I'm con-cerned.
Now, now, you should take it easy.
How about a drink?
Remedy
I'll read a book and go to bed.
What?!

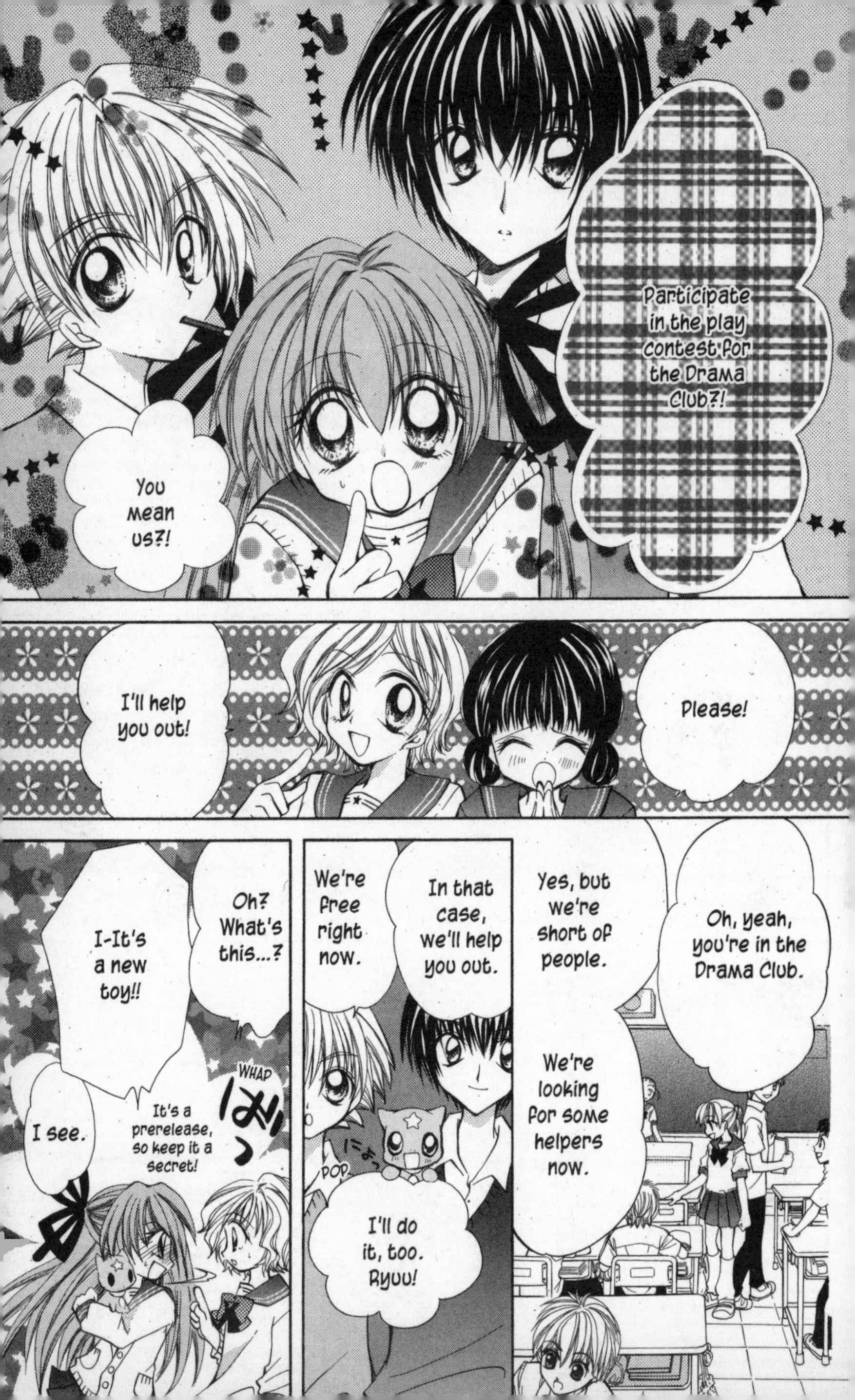
Participate in the play contest for the Drama Club?!
You mean us?!
Please!
I'll help you out!
Oh, yeah, you're in the Drama Club.
Yes, but we're short of people.
We're looking for some helpers now.
In that case, we'll help you out.
We're free right now.
POP
I'll do it, too. Ryuu!
Oh? What's this...?
I-It's a new toy!!
WHAP
It's a prerelease, so keep it a secret!
I see.

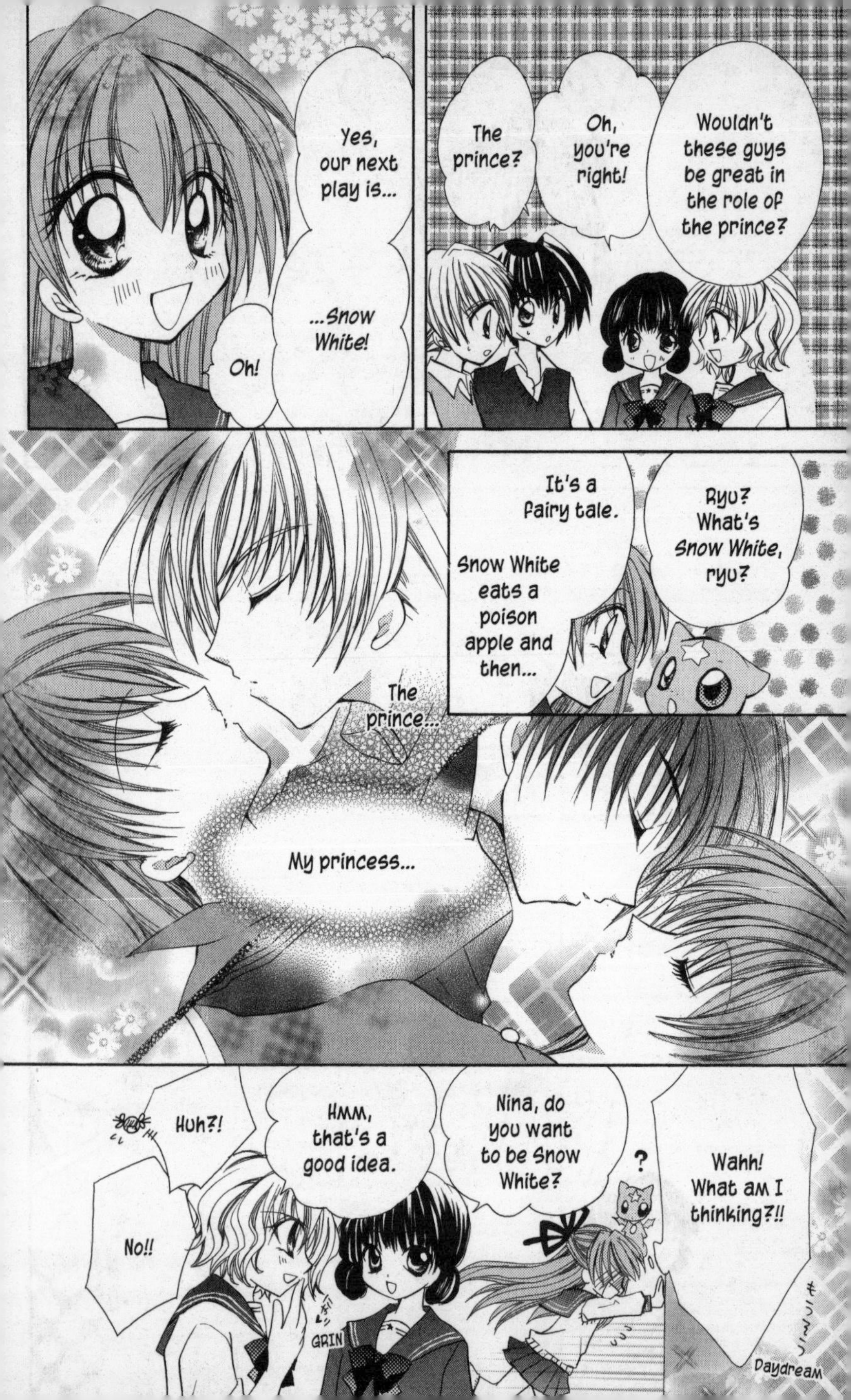

Wouldn't these guys be great in the role of the prince?
Oh, you're right!
The prince?
Yes, our next play is...
...Snow White!
Oh!
Ryu? What's Snow White, ryu?
It's a fairy tale.
Snow White eats a poison apple and then...
The prince...
My princess...
Wahh! What am I thinking?!!
Daydream
?
Nina, do you want to be Snow White?
Hmm, that's a good idea.
GRIN
Huh?!
No!!

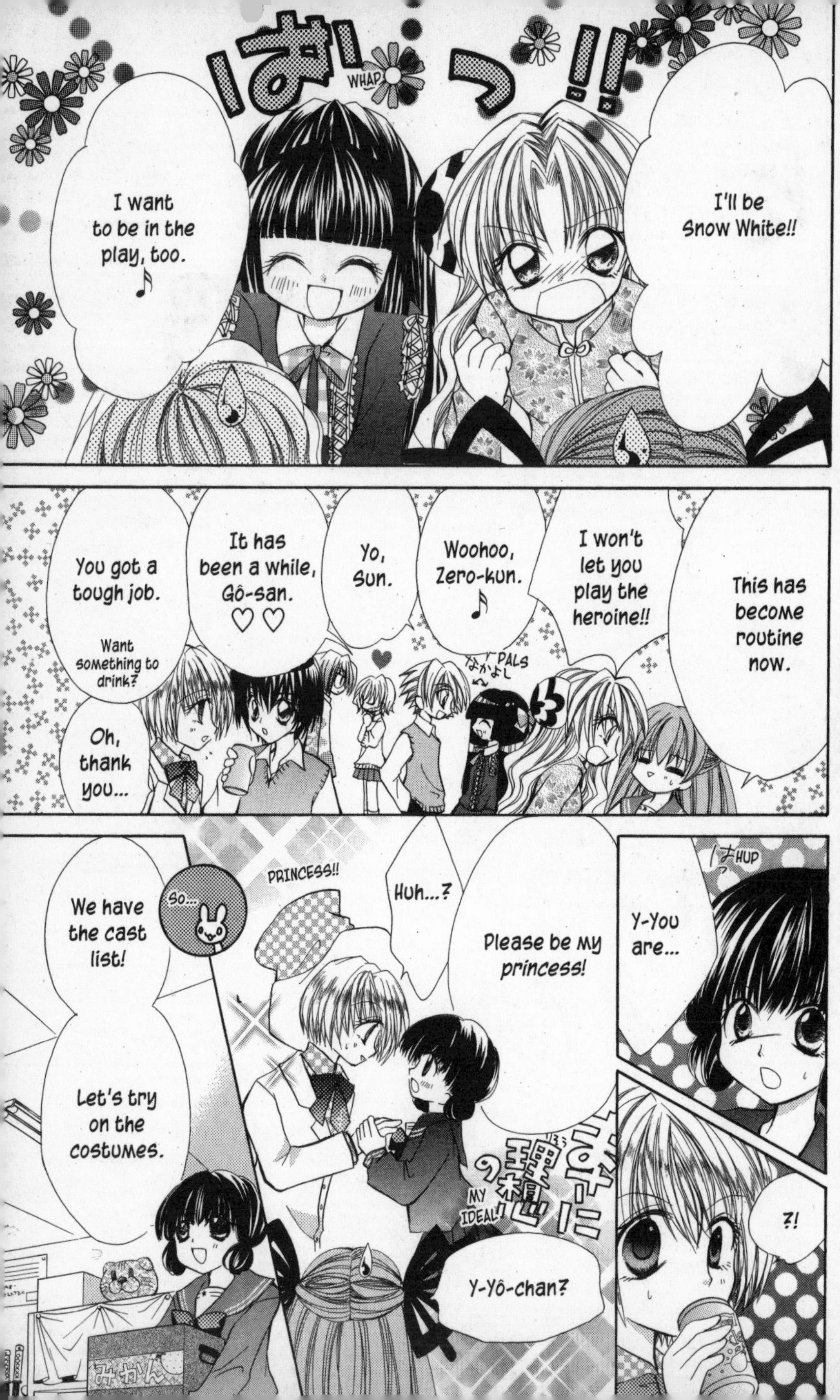
ばっ!!
WHAP
I'll be Snow White!!
I want to be in the play, too. ♪
This has become routine now.
I won't let you play the heroine!!
PALS
なかよし
Woohoo, Zero-kun. ♪
Yo, Sun.
It has been a while, Gô-san. ♡ ♡
You got a tough job.
Want something to drink?
Oh, thank you...
HUP
Y-You are...
?!
Please be my princess!
Huh...?
PRINCESS!!
MY IDEAL!
Y-Yô-chan?
So...
We have the cast list!
Let's try on the costumes.

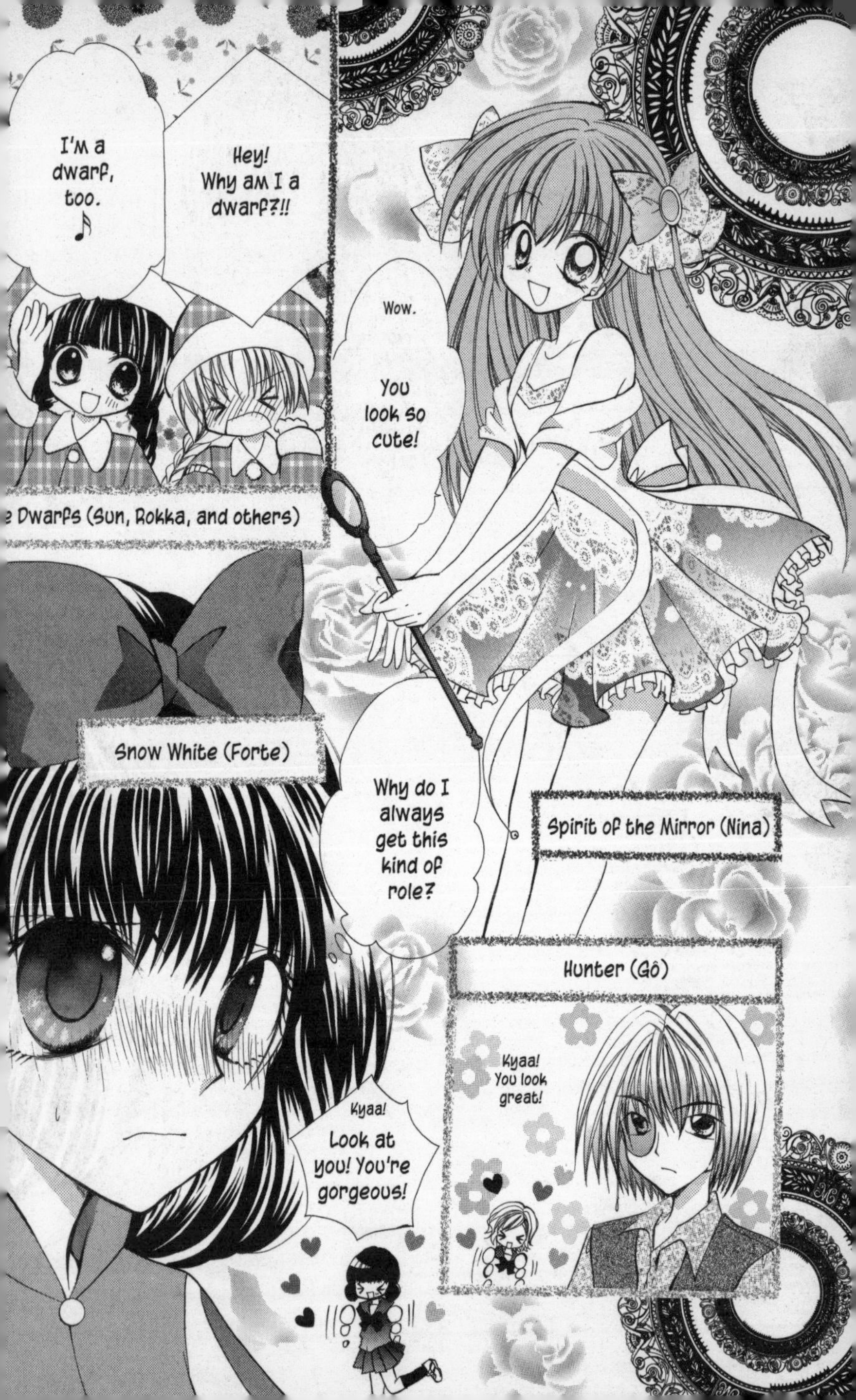
Wow.
You look so cute!
Why do I always get this kind of role?
Spirit of the Mirror (Nina)
Hunter (Gô)
Kyaa! You look great!
Hey! Why am I a dwarf?!!
I'm a dwarf, too. ♪
e Dwarfs (Sun, Rokka, and others)
Snow White (Forte)
Kyaa!
Look at you! You're gorgeous!

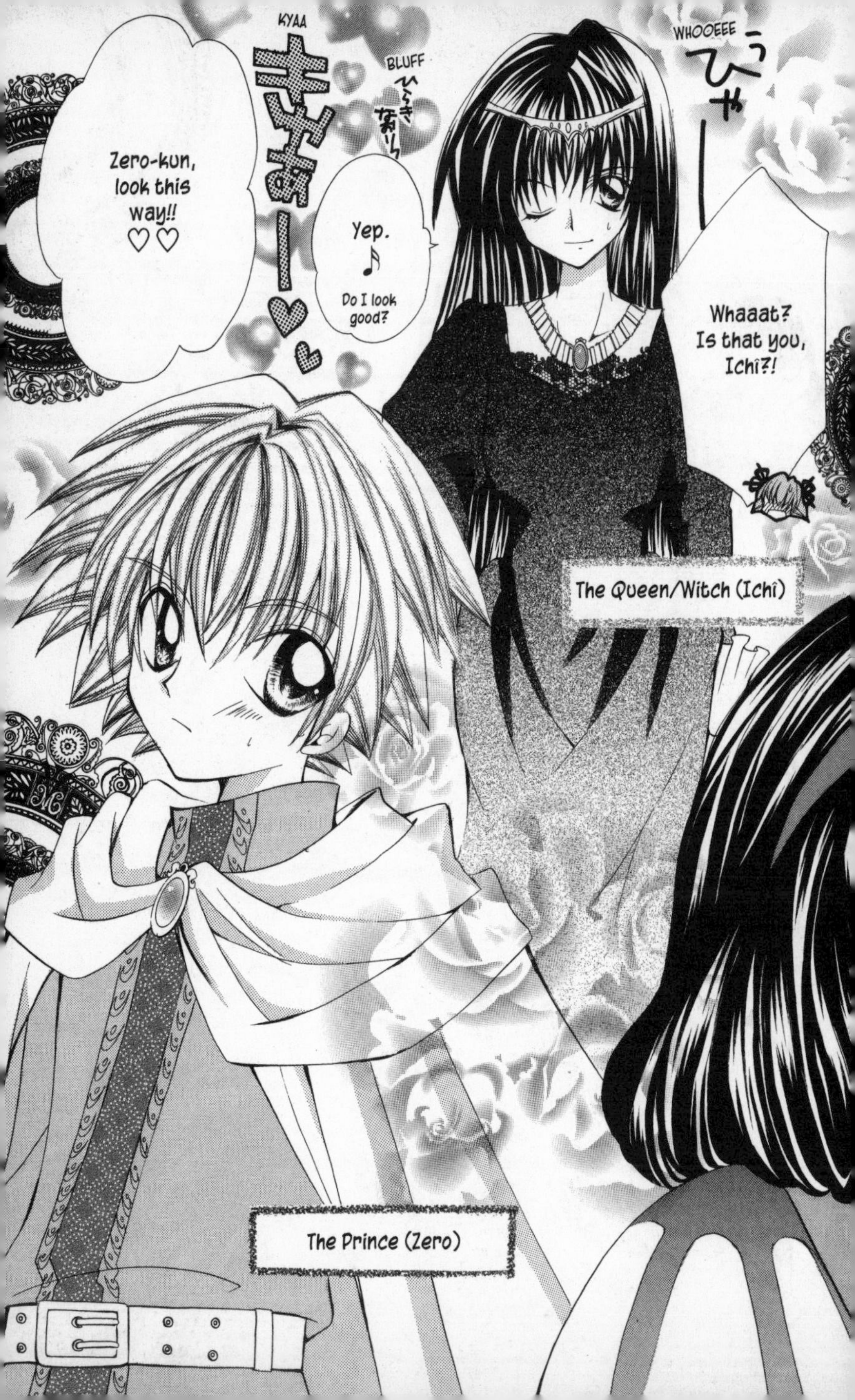

WHOOEEE
Whaaat? Is that you, Ichî?!
Yep. ♪ Do I look good?
BLUFF
KYAA
Zero-kun, look this way!! ♡ ♡
The Queen/Witch (Ichî)
The Prince (Zero)

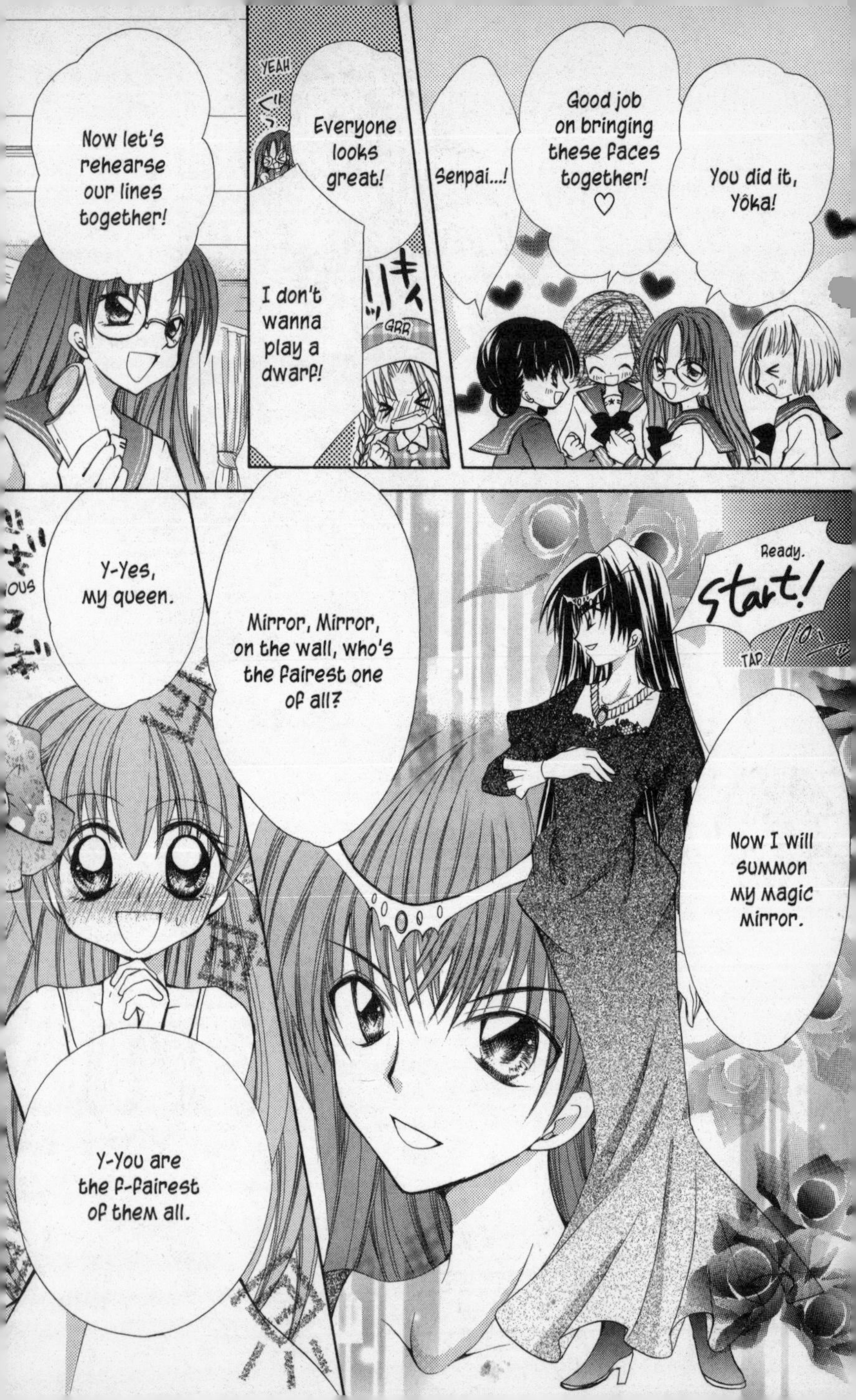
You did it, Yôka!
Good job on bringing these faces together! ♡
Senpai...!
YEAH
Everyone looks great!
I don't wanna play a dwarf!
GRR
Now let's rehearse our lines together!
Ready.
Start!
TAP
Now I will summon my magic mirror.
Mirror, Mirror, on the wall, who's the fairest one of all?
Y-Yes, my queen.
Y-You are the f-fairest of them all.

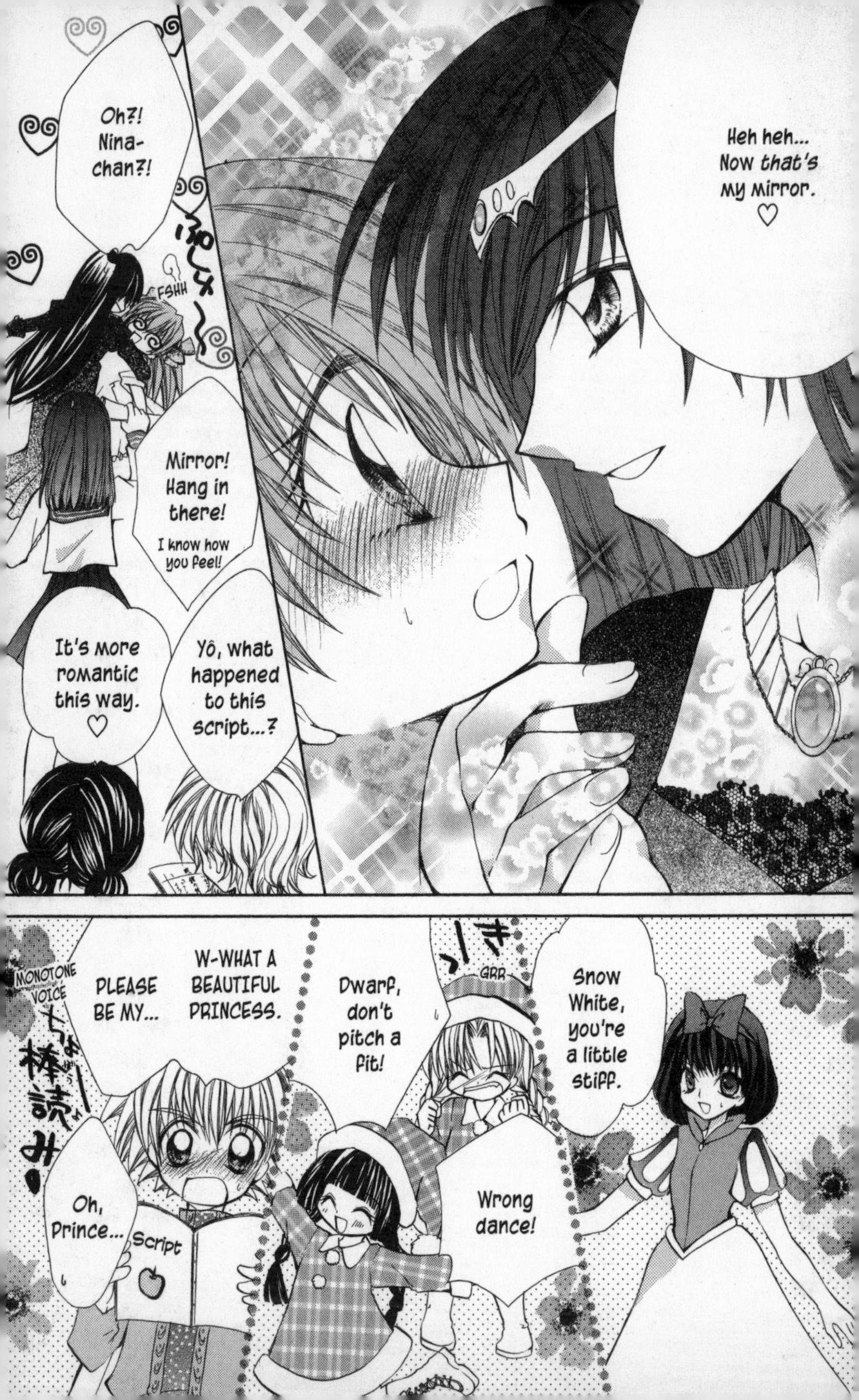
Heh heh... Now that's my mirror. ♡
Oh?! Nina-chan?!
FSHH
Mirror! Hang in there!
I know how you feel!
Yô, what happened to this script...?
It's more romantic this way. ♡
Snow White, you're a little stiff.
GRR
Dwarf, don't pitch a fit!
W-WHAT A BEAUTIFUL PRINCESS.
PLEASE BE MY...
MONOTONE VOICE
Wrong dance!
Oh, Prince...
Script

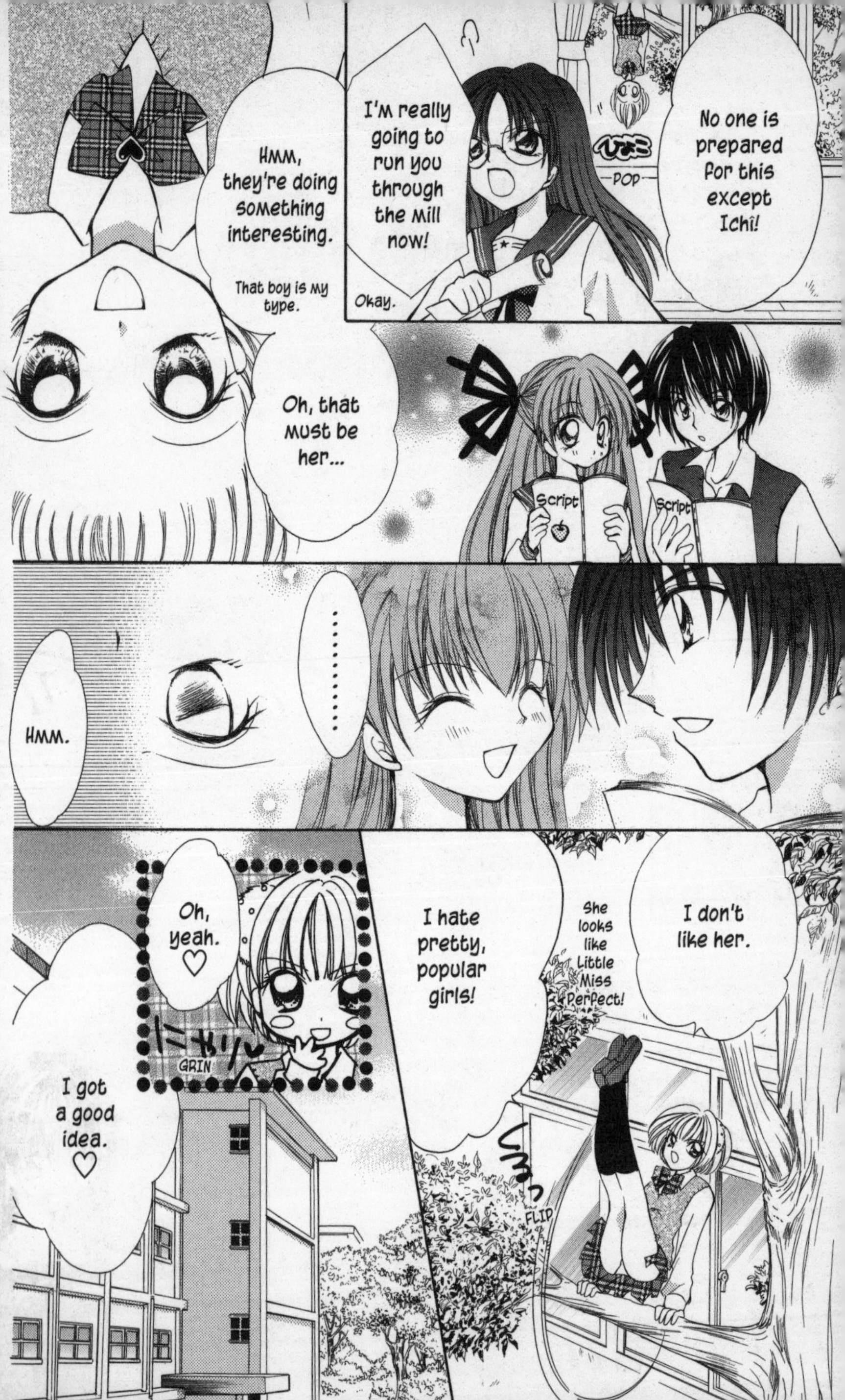
No one is prepared for this except Ichi!
POP
I'm really going to run you through the mill now!
Okay.
Script
Script
Hmm, they're doing something interesting.
That boy is my type.
Oh, that must be her...
......
Hmm.
I don't like her.
She looks like Little Miss Perfect!
I hate pretty, popular girls!
FLIP
Oh, yeah. ♡
GRIN
I got a good idea. ♡

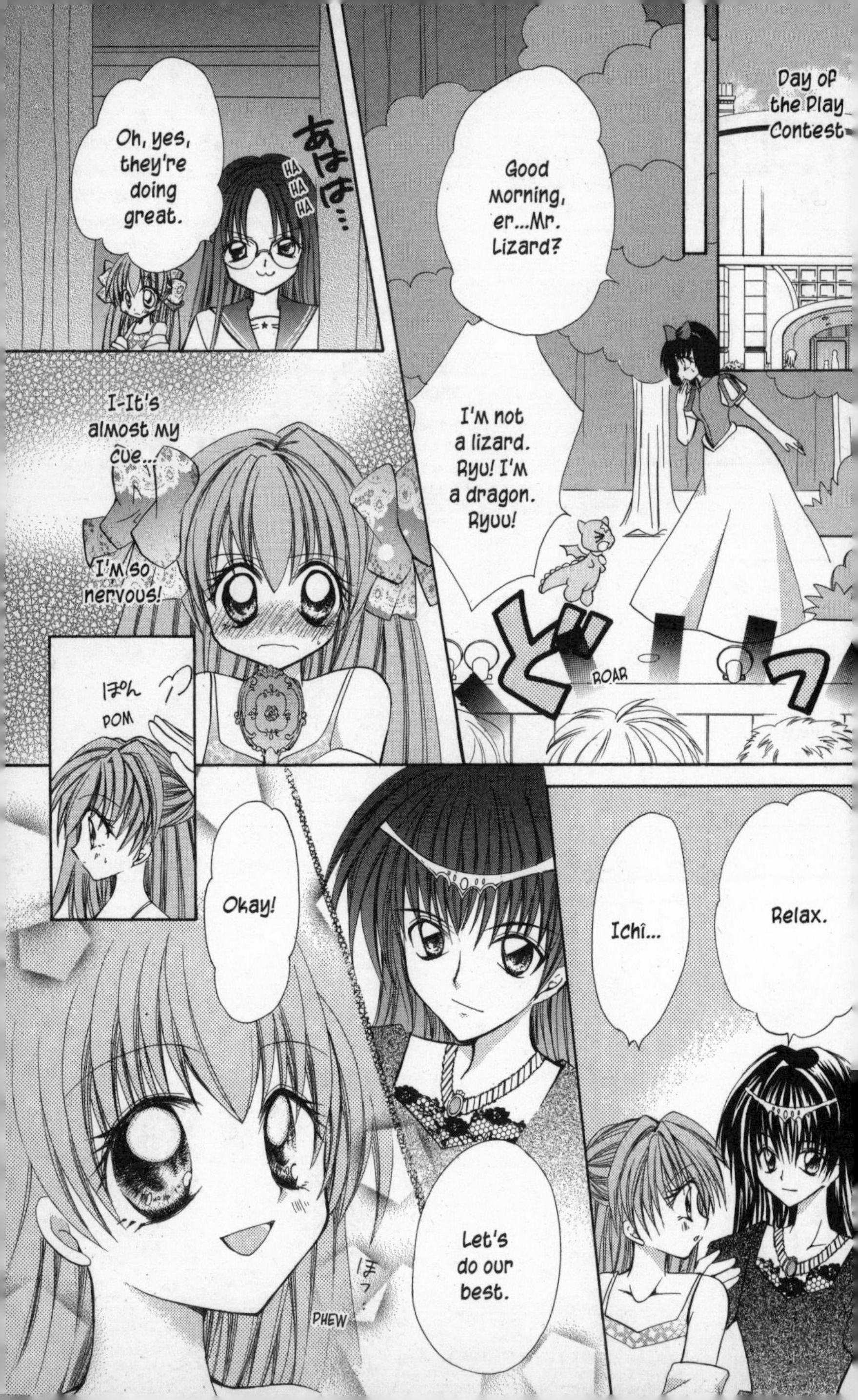

Day of the Play Contest
Good morning, er...Mr. Lizard?
I'm not a lizard. Ryu! I'm a dragon. Ryuu!
どーーっ
ROAR
あははは…
HA HA HA
Oh, yes, they're doing great.
I-It's almost my cue...
I'm so nervous!
ぽん
POM
Relax.
Ichi...
Okay!
Let's do our best.
ほっ
PHEW

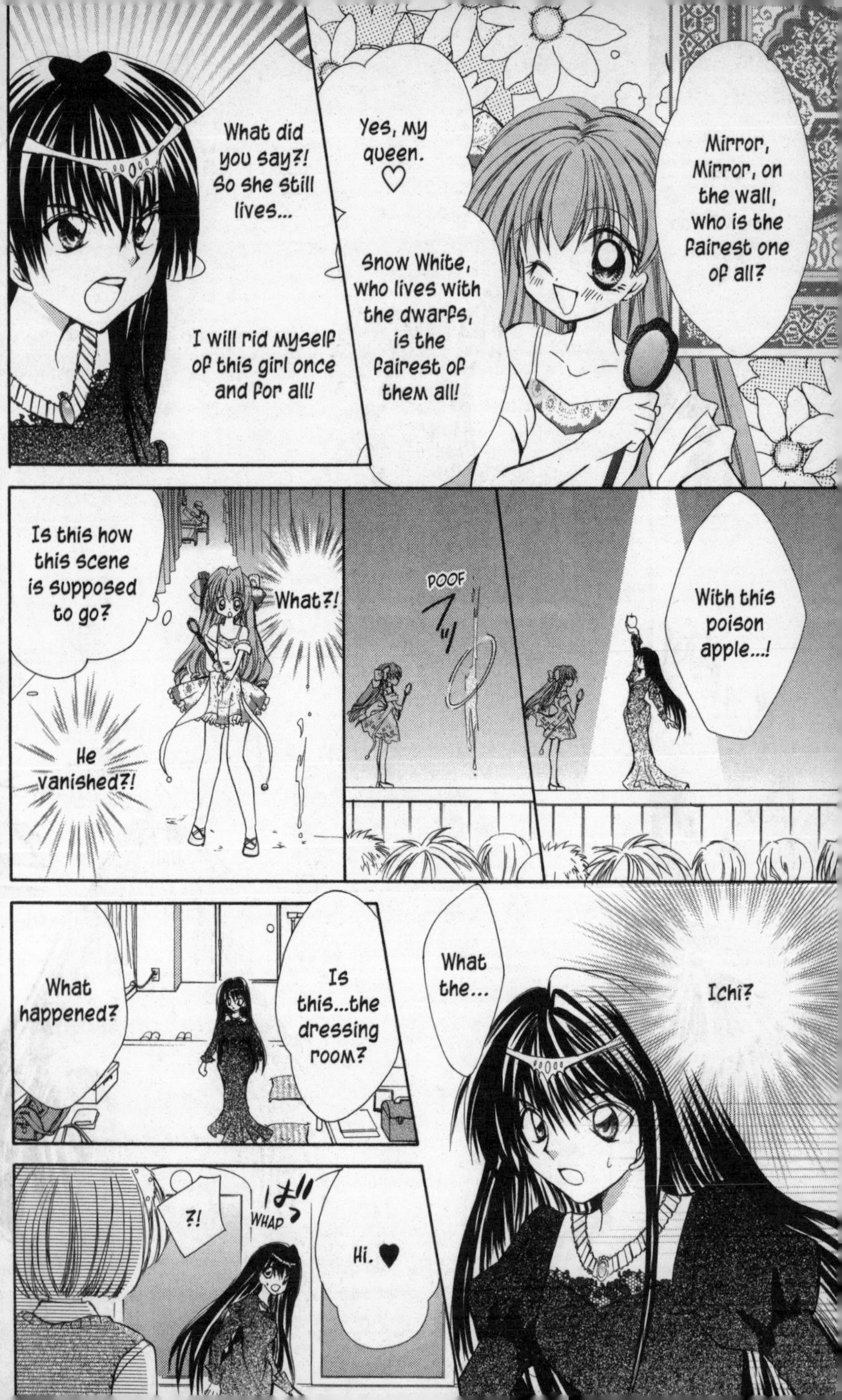
Mirror, Mirror, on the wall, who is the fairest one of all?
Yes, my queen. ♡
Snow White, who lives with the dwarfs, is the fairest of them all!
What did you say?! So she still lives...
I will rid myself of this girl once and for all!
With this poison apple...!
POOF
フッ
What?!
He vanished?!
Is this how this scene is supposed to go?
Ichi?
What the...
Is this...the dressing room?
What happened?
Hi. ♥
はっ!!
WHAP
?!

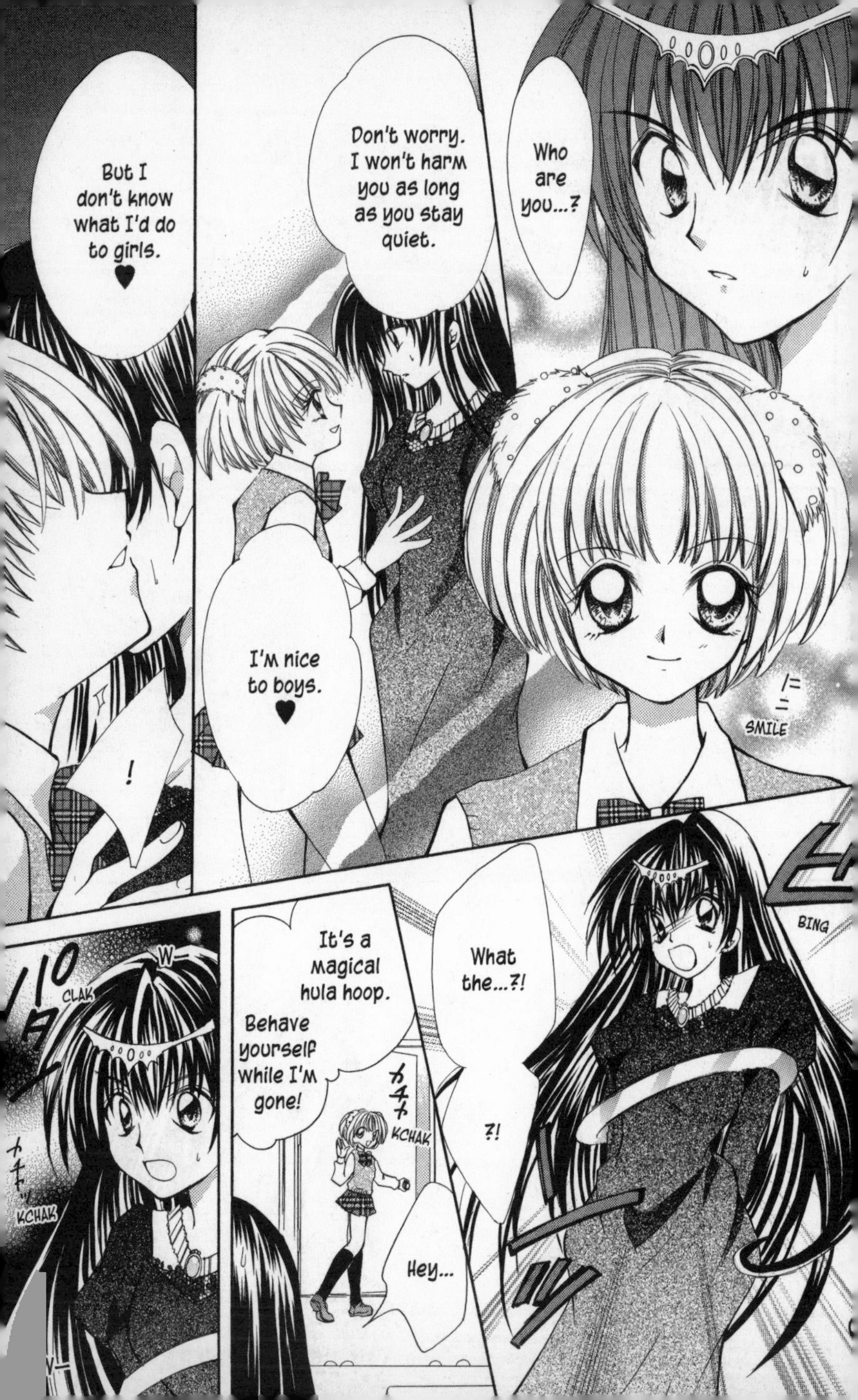

Who are you...?
SMILE
Don't worry. I won't harm you as long as you stay quiet.
I'm nice to boys. ♥
But I don't know what I'd do to girls. ♥
!
BING
What the...?!
?!
It's a magical hula hoop.
Behave yourself while I'm gone!
KCHAK
Hey...
CLAK
KCHAK

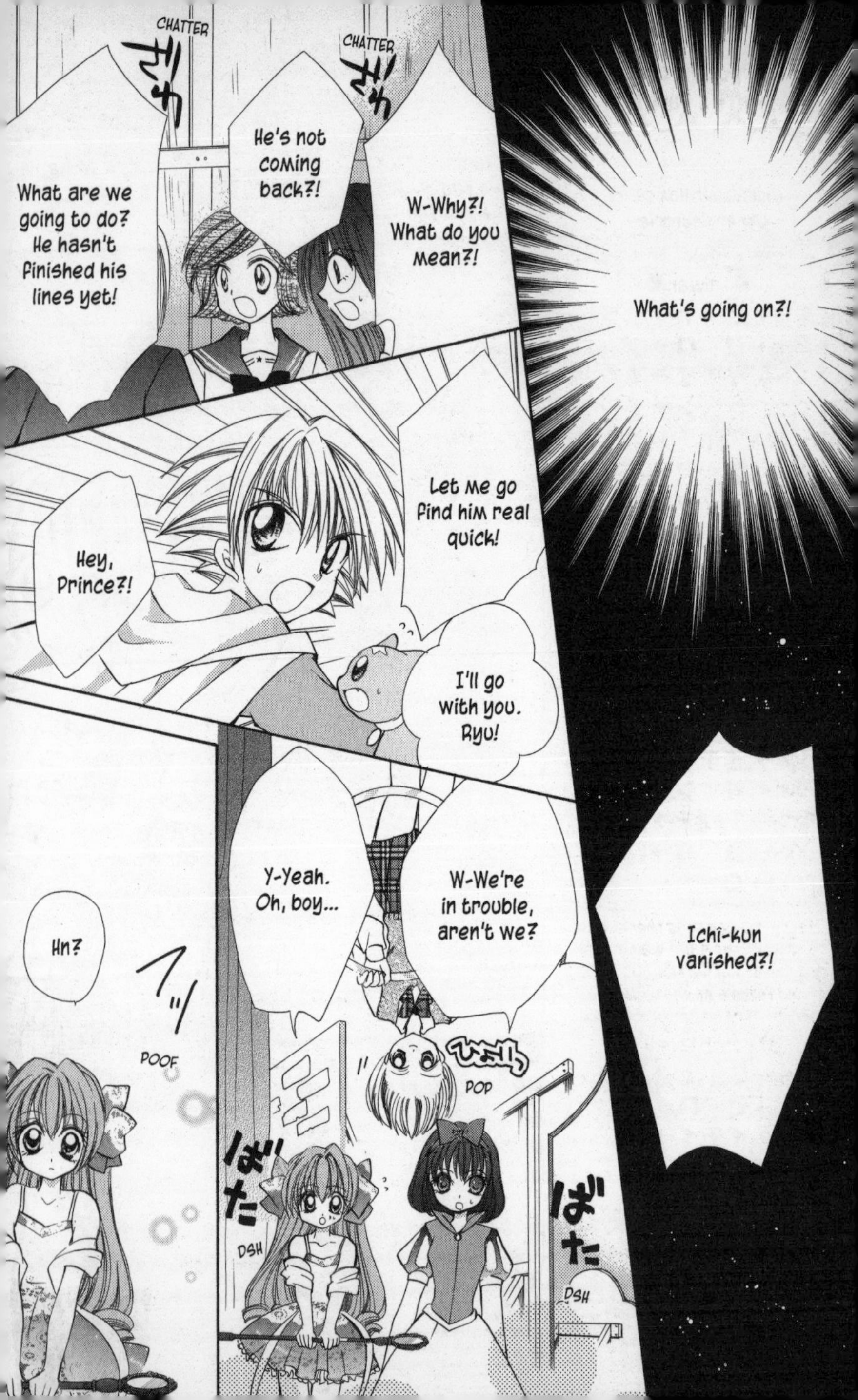
What's going on?!
Ichî-kun vanished?!
CHATTER
ざわ
CHATTER
ざわ
He's not coming back?!
W-Why?! What do you mean?!
What are we going to do? He hasn't finished his lines yet!
Let me go find him real quick!
Hey, Prince?!
I'll go with you. Ryu!
W-We're in trouble, aren't we?
Y-Yeah. Oh, boy...
POP
Hn?
POOF
ばた
DSH
ばた
DSH

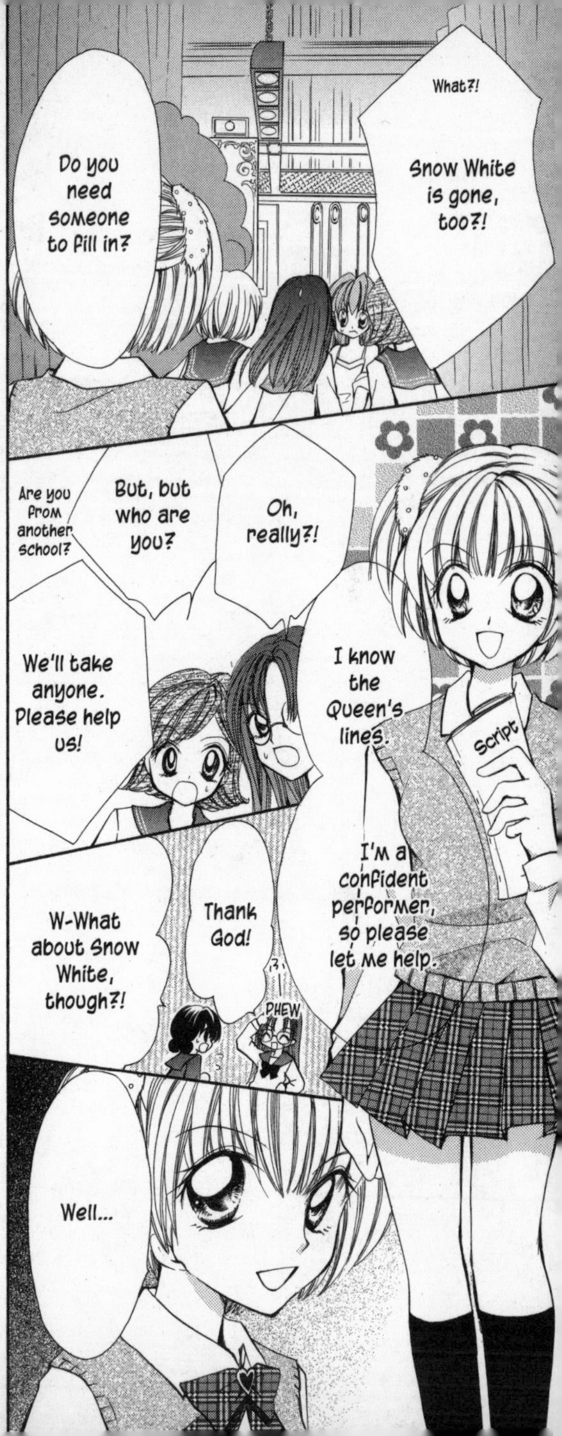
What?!
Snow White is gone, too?!
Do you need someone to fill in?
Oh, really?!
But, but who are you?
Are you from another school?
I know the Queen's lines.
Script
We'll take anyone. Please help us!
I'm a confident performer, so please let me help.
Thank God!
PHEW
W-What about Snow White, though?!
Well...

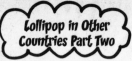

Lollipop in Other Countries Part Two

Character Names in Other Countries

●Taiwan●

Nina→	ニ　ナ→	二菜
Zero→	ゼ　ロ→	謝洛
Ichî→	イチイ→	伊奇
Sun→	サ　ン→	薩恩
Forte→	フォルテ→	弗羅迪
Gô→	ゴ　ウ→	葛烏
Rokka→	ロッカ→	羅佳

Their writing is hard. But can you sort of read them? I'm surprised at how Zero is written!

● Hong Kong ●

Nina→	ニ　ナ→	二菜
Zero→	ゼ　ロ→	零
Ichî→	イチイ→	一伊
Sun→	サ　ン→	小三
Forte→	フォルテ→	小四
Gô→	ゴ　ウ→	阿五
Rokka→	ロッカ→	六嘉

Maybe you can read these. Nina is written the same way in both countries. I get a kick out of Sun and Forte's names... (laugh)

● South Korea ●

Nina→	ニ　ナ→	니나
Zero→	ゼ　ロ→	제로
Ichî→	イチイ→	이지이

I have no clue whatsoever. I want to know how to read these.

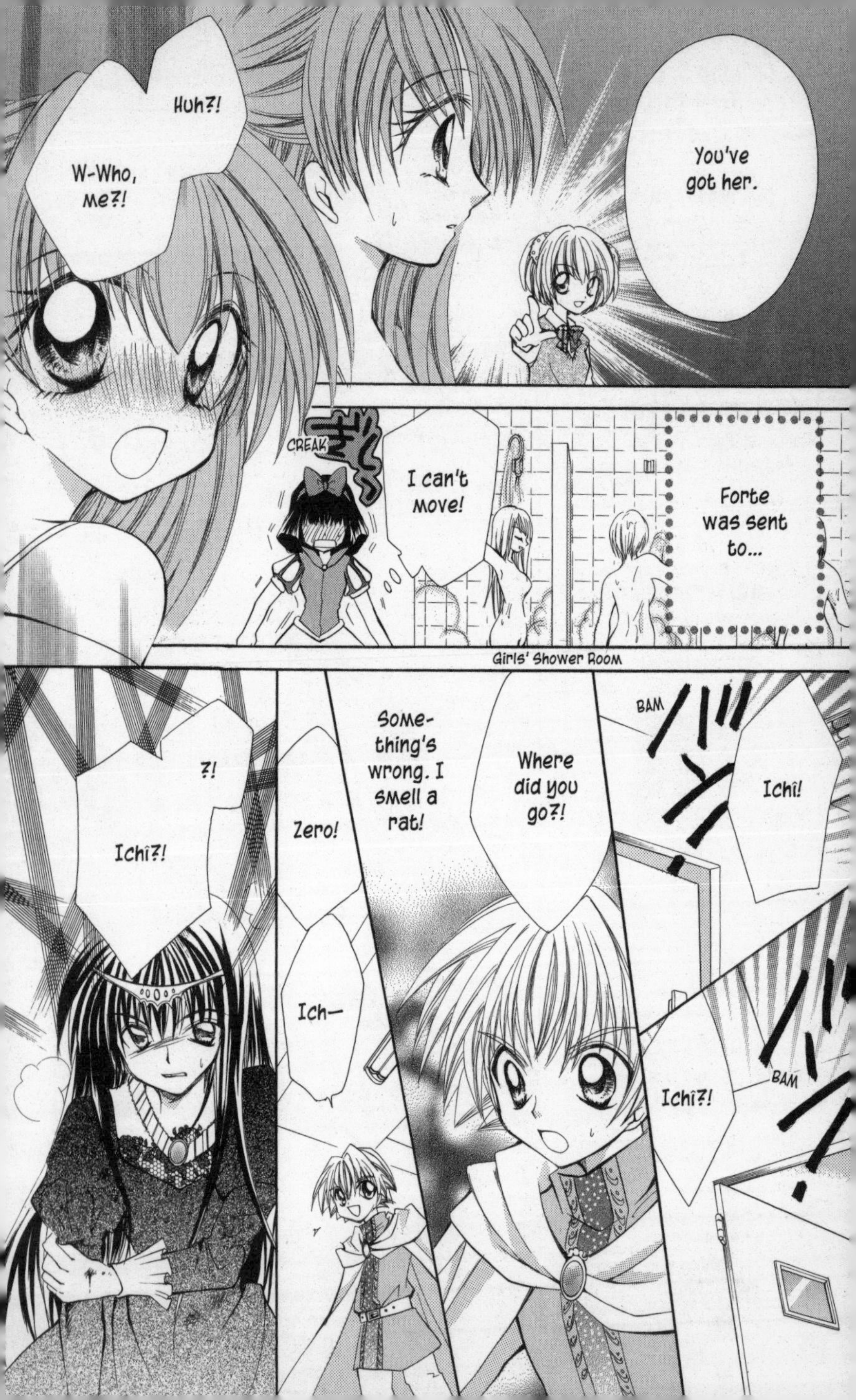
You've got her.
Forte was sent to...
Girls' Shower Room
CREAK
I can't move!
Huh?!
W-Who, me?!
BAM
Ichi!
BAM
Ichi?!
Where did you go?!
Some-thing's wrong. I smell a rat!
Zero!
Ich—
?!
Ichi?!

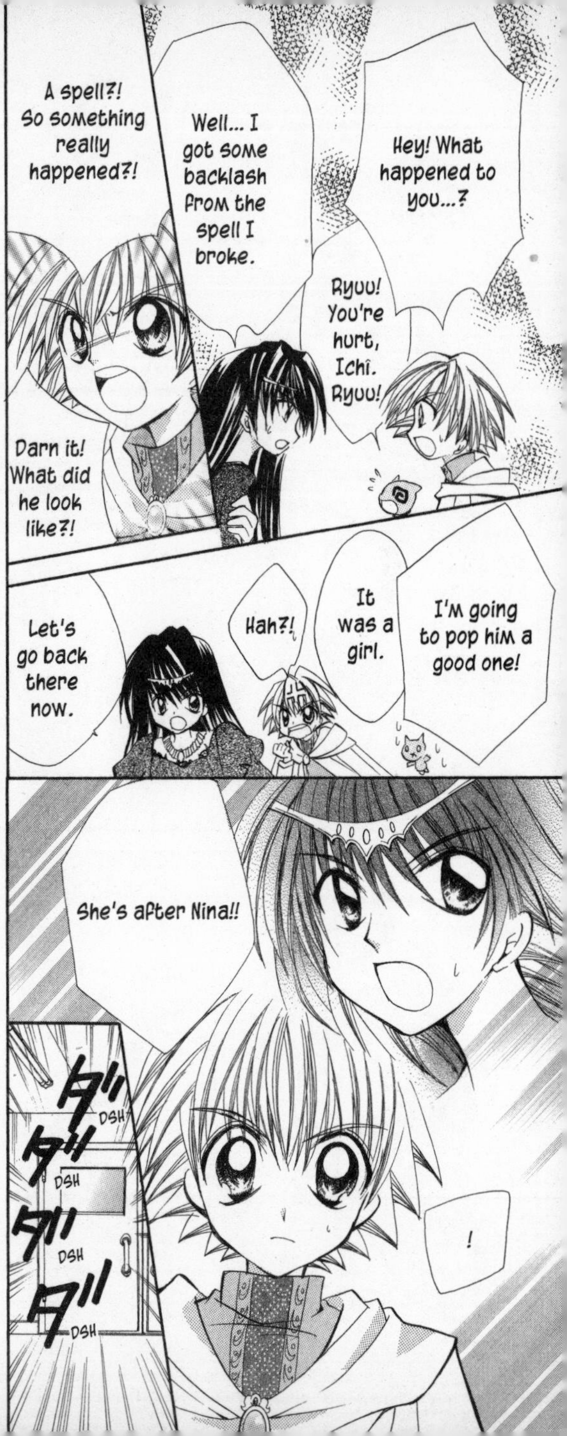
Hey! What happened to you...?
Ryuu! You're hurt, Ichi. Ryuu!
Well... I got some backlash from the spell I broke.
A spell?! So something really happened?!
Darn it! What did he look like?!
I'm going to pop him a good one!
It was a girl.
Hah?!
Let's go back there now.
She's after Nina!!
!
DSH
DSH
DSH
DSH

Masks

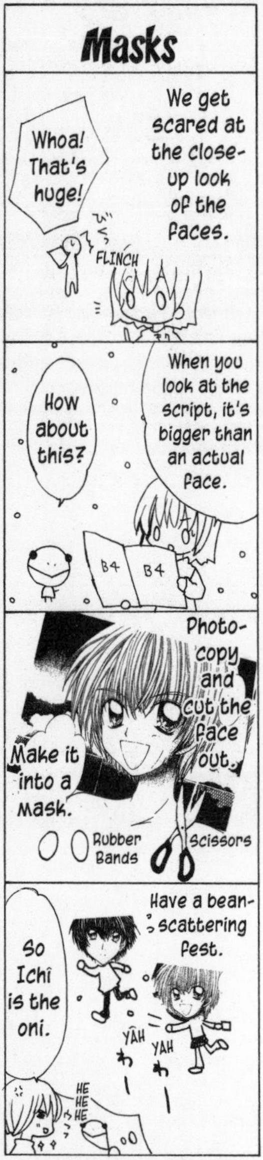
We get scared at the close-up look of the faces.
Whoa! That's huge!
FLINCH
When you look at the script, it's bigger than an actual face.
How about this?
B4
B4
Photocopy and cut the face out.
Make it into a mask.
Rubber Bands
Scissors
Have a bean-scattering fest.
So Ichi is the oni.
YAH
YAH
HE HE HE

Here's a close-up look of Ichi in volume 5.

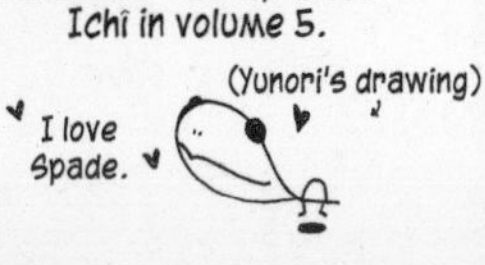
(Yunori's drawing)
I love Spade.

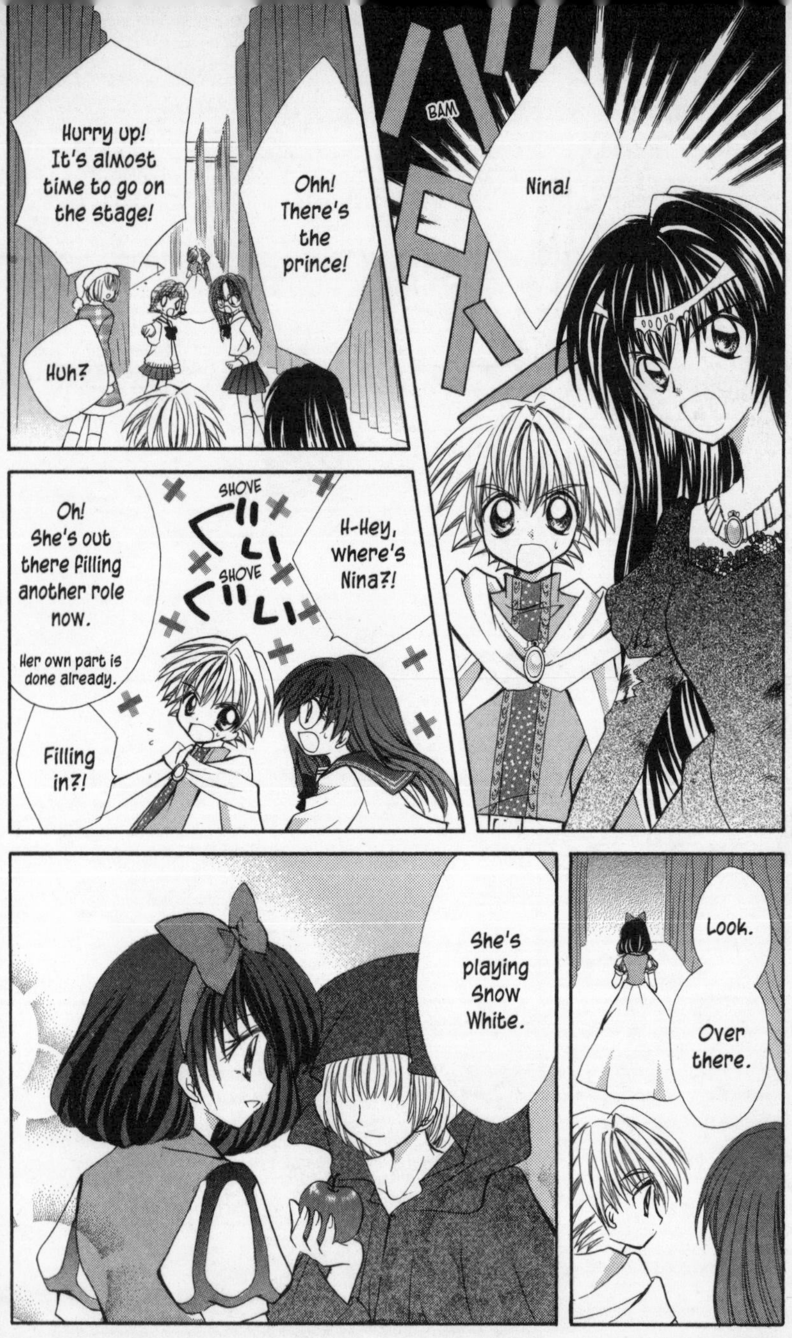
BAM
Nina!
Ohh! There's the prince!
Hurry up! It's almost time to go on the stage!
Huh?
H-Hey, where's Nina?!
SHOVE
SHOVE
Oh! She's out there filling another role now.
Her own part is done already.
Filling in?!
Look.
Over there.
She's playing Snow White.

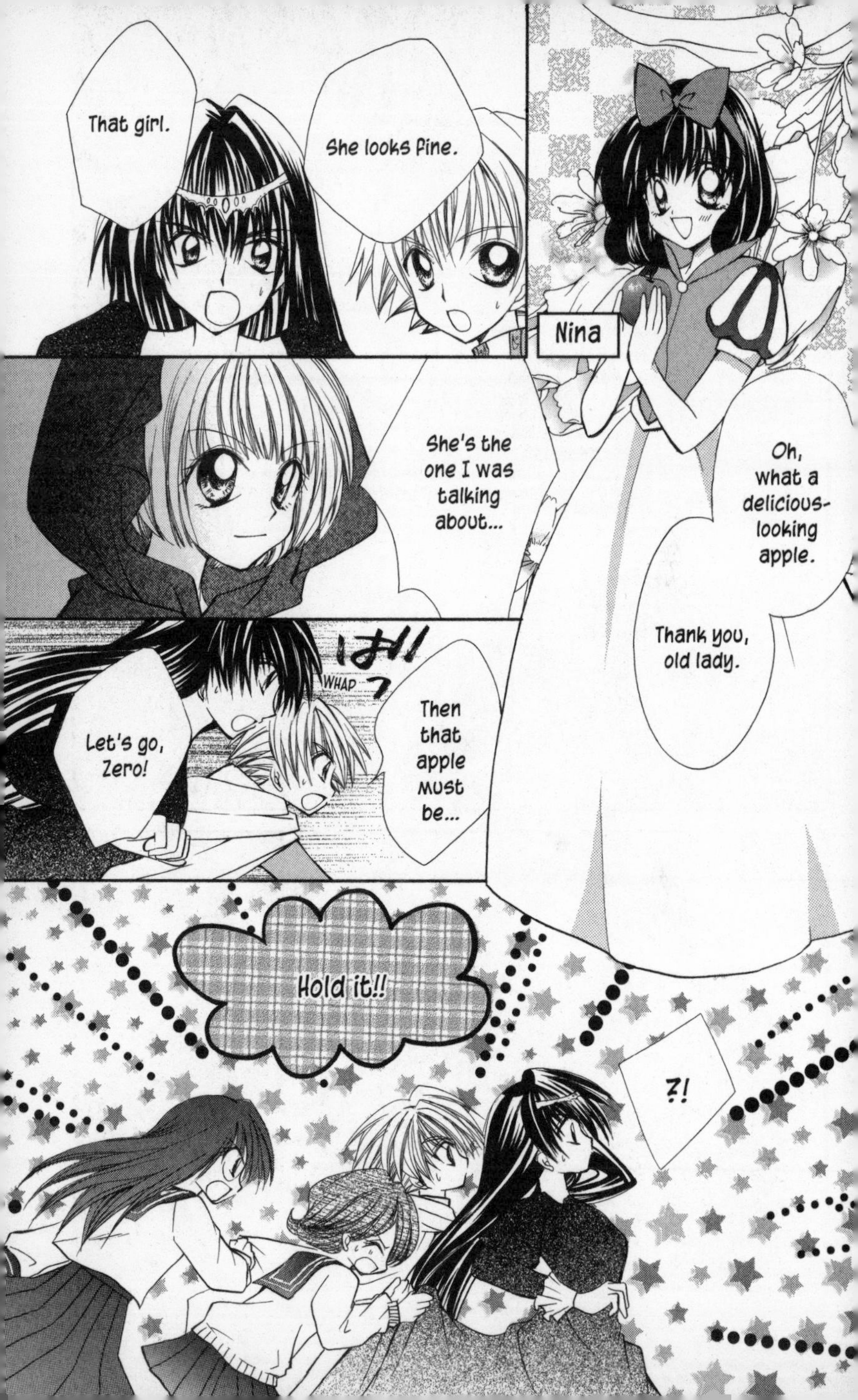
Nina
Oh, what a delicious-looking apple.
Thank you, old lady.
She looks fine.
That girl.
She's the one I was talking about...
Then that apple must be...
は!!
WHAP
Let's go, Zero!
Hold it!!
?!

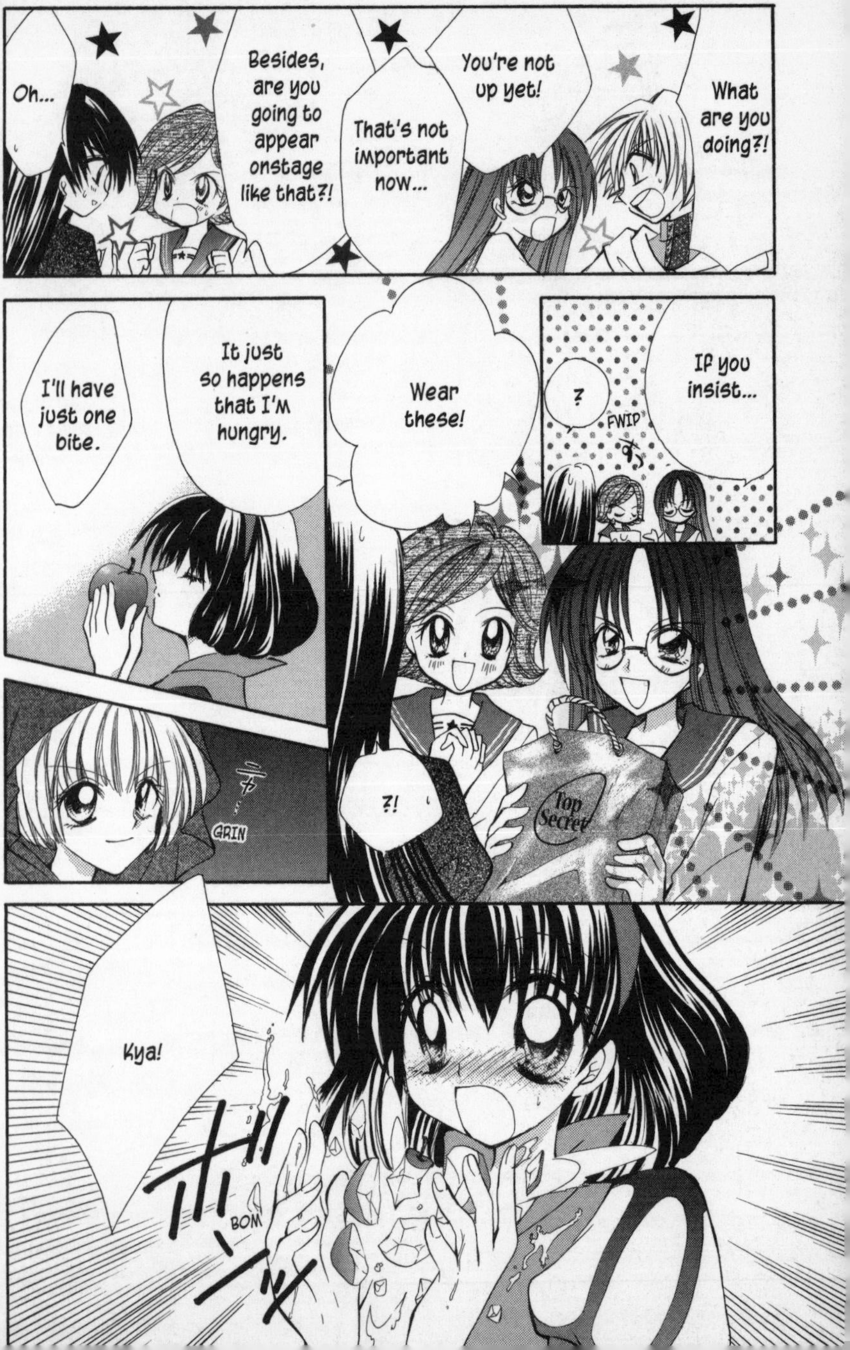

What are you doing?!
You're not up yet!
That's not important now...
Besides, are you going to appear onstage like that?!
Oh...
If you insist...
?
FWIP
Wear these!
?!
Top Secret
It just so happens that I'm hungry.
I'll have just one bite.
GRIN
Kya!
BOM

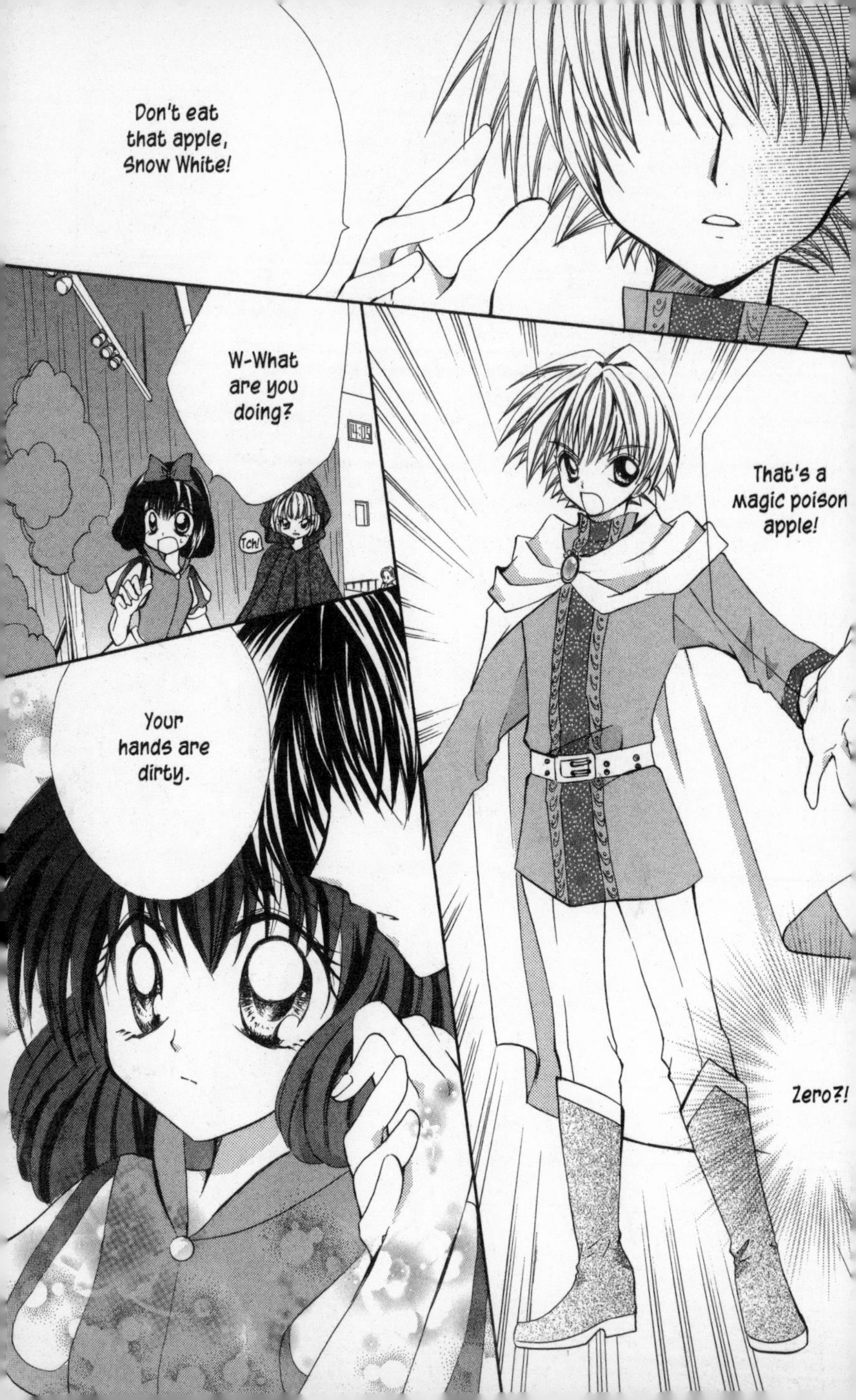
Don't eat that apple, Snow White!
That's a magic poison apple!
Zero?!
W-What are you doing?
Tch!
Your hands are dirty.

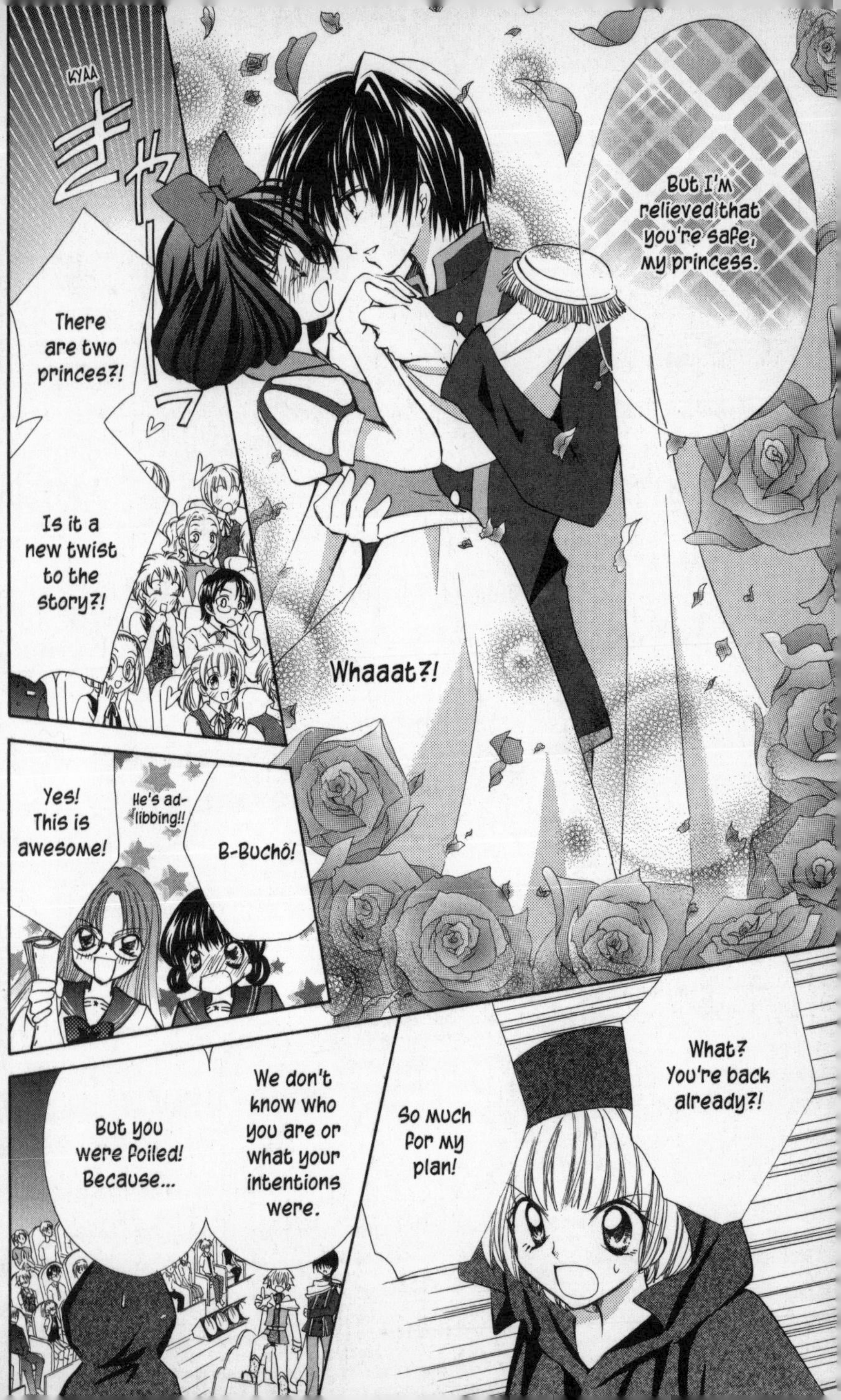

But I'm relieved that you're safe, my princess.
KYAA
Whaaat?!
There are two princes?!
Is it a new twist to the story?!
B-Buchô!
He's ad-libbing!!
Yes! This is awesome!
What? You're back already?!
So much for my plan!
We don't know who you are or what your intentions were.
But you were foiled! Because...

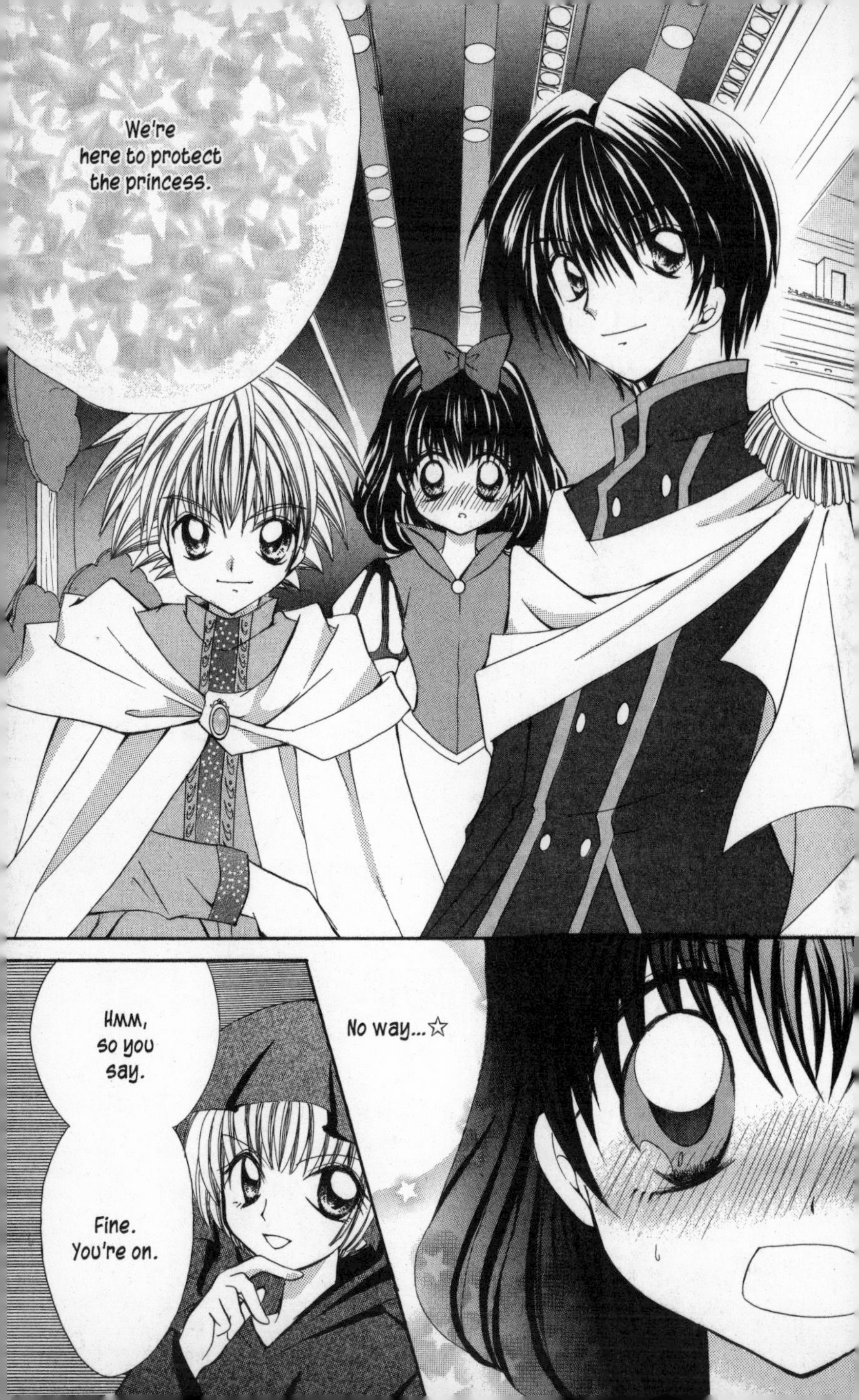
We're here to protect the princess.
No way...☆
Hmm, so you say.
Fine. You're on.

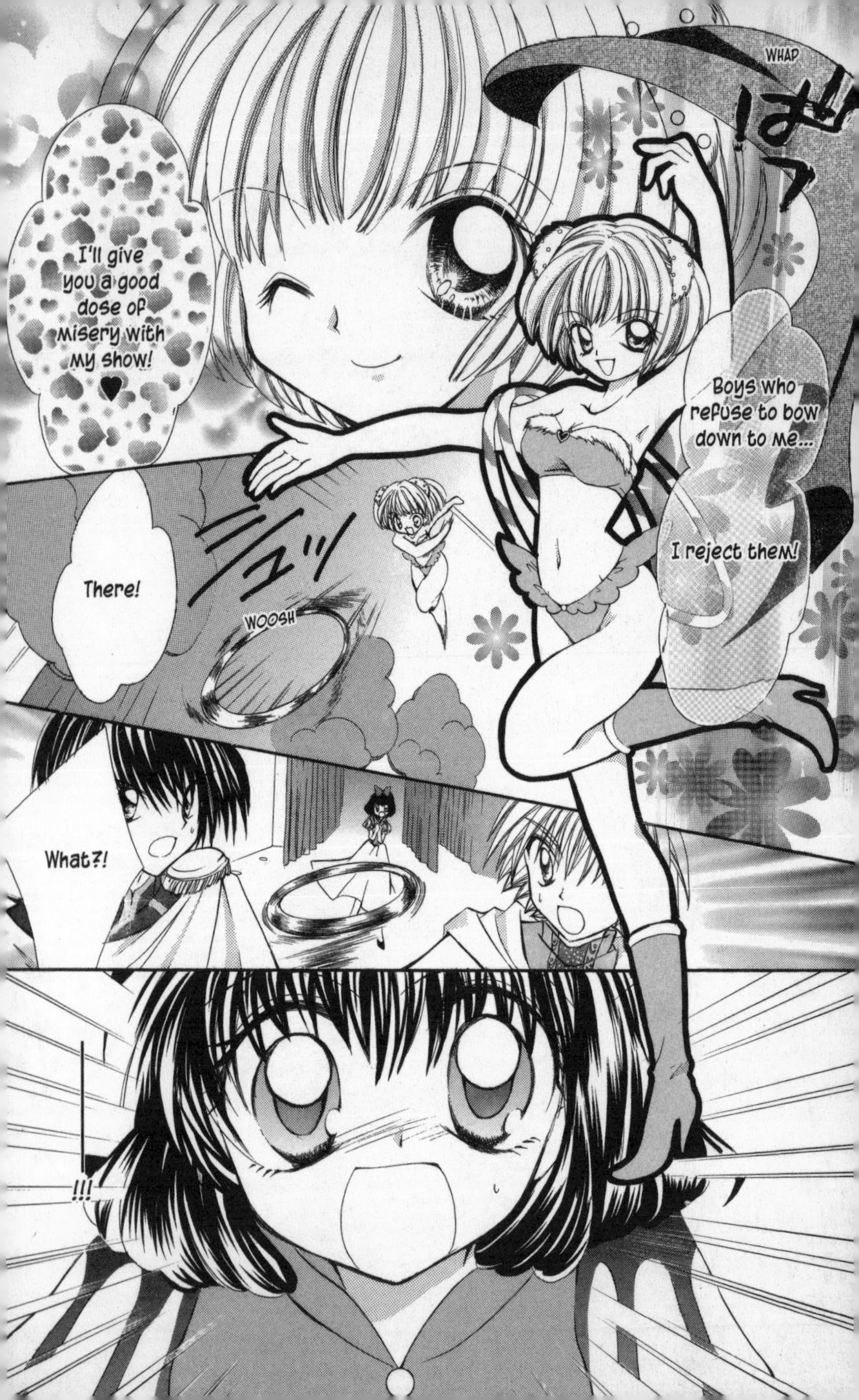
WHAP
Boys who refuse to bow down to me...
I reject them!
I'll give you a good dose of misery with my show! ♥
WOOSH
There!
What?!
!!!

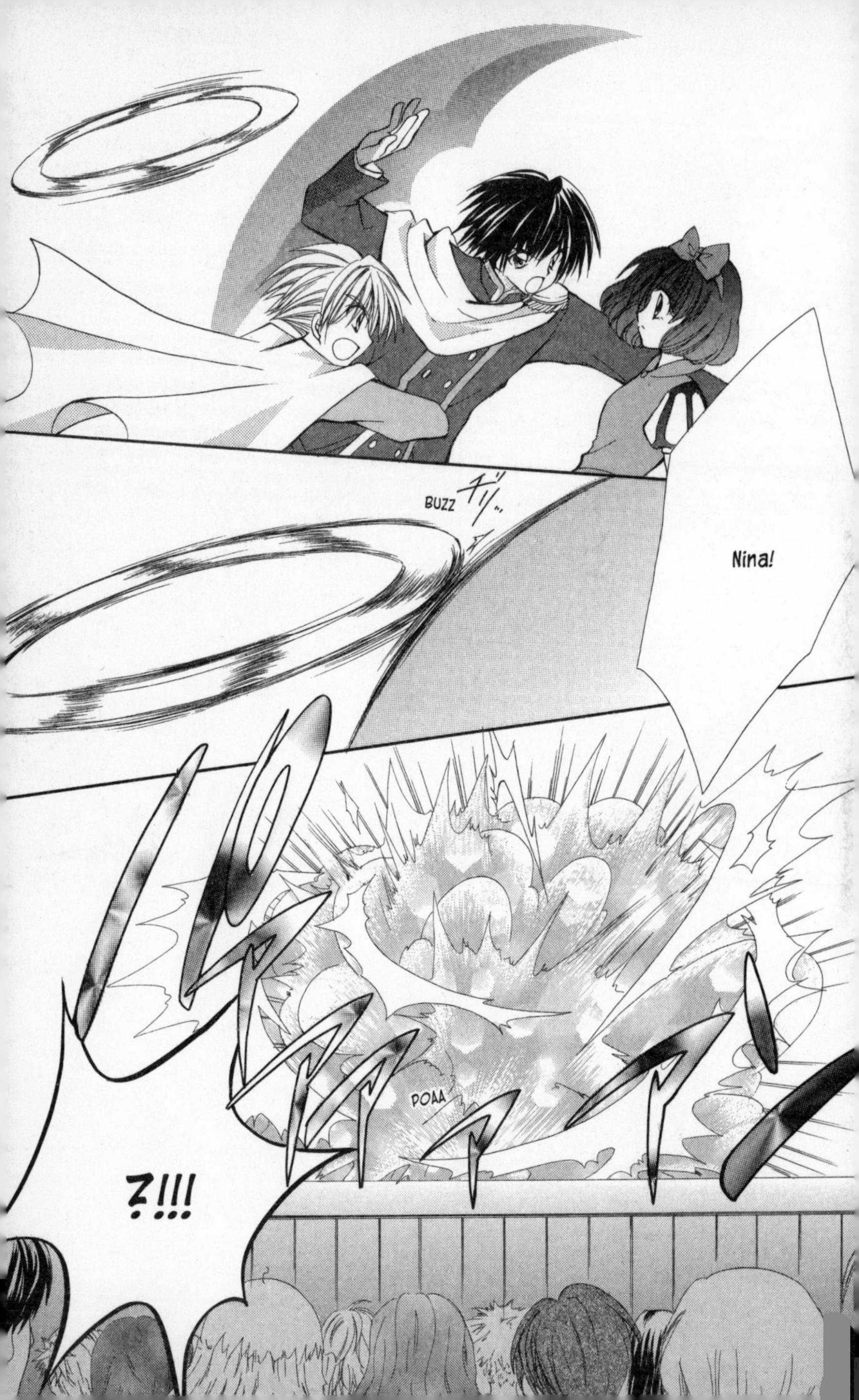
Nina!
BUZZ
POAA
?!!!

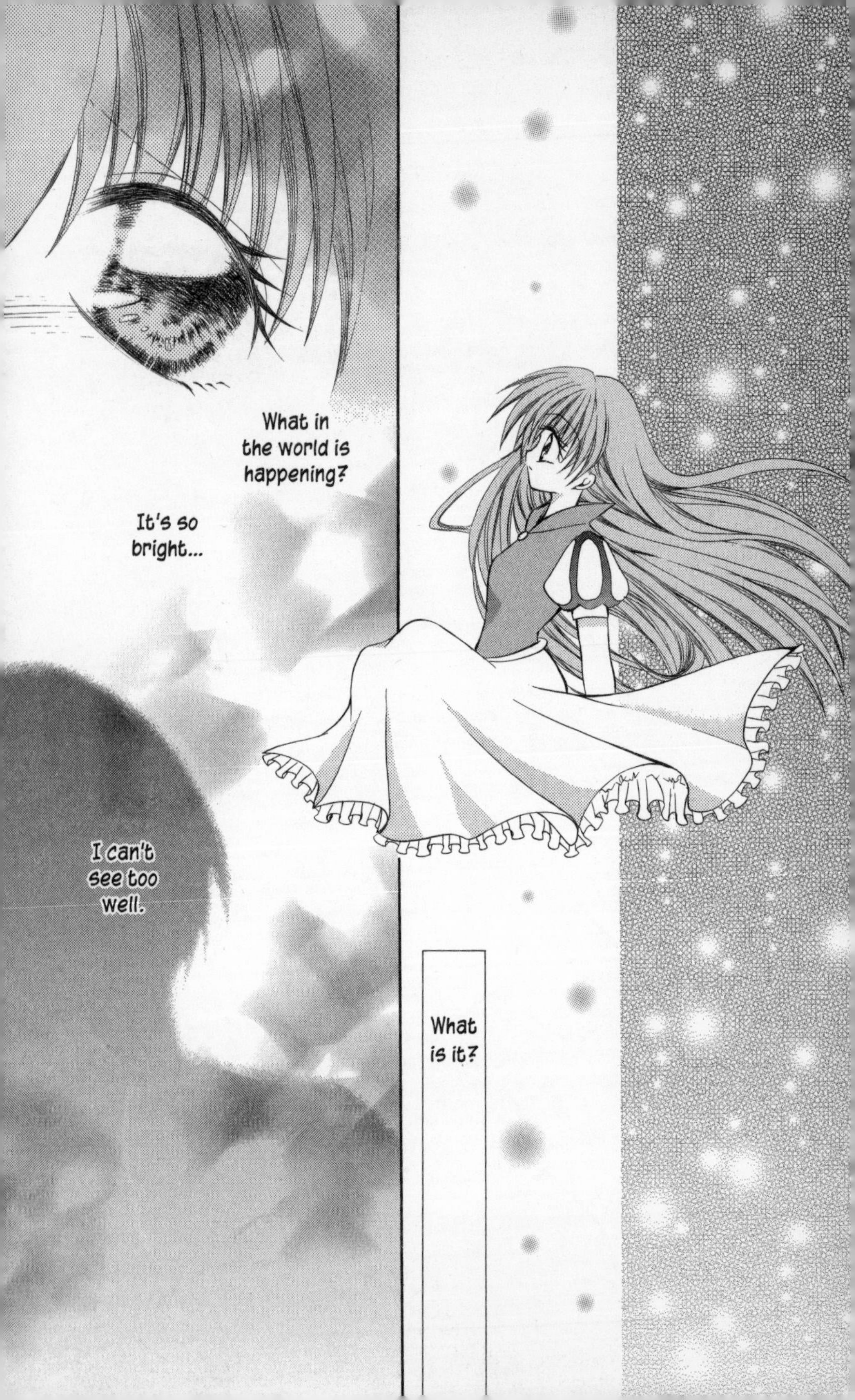
What is it?
What in the world is happening?
It's so bright...
I can't see too well.

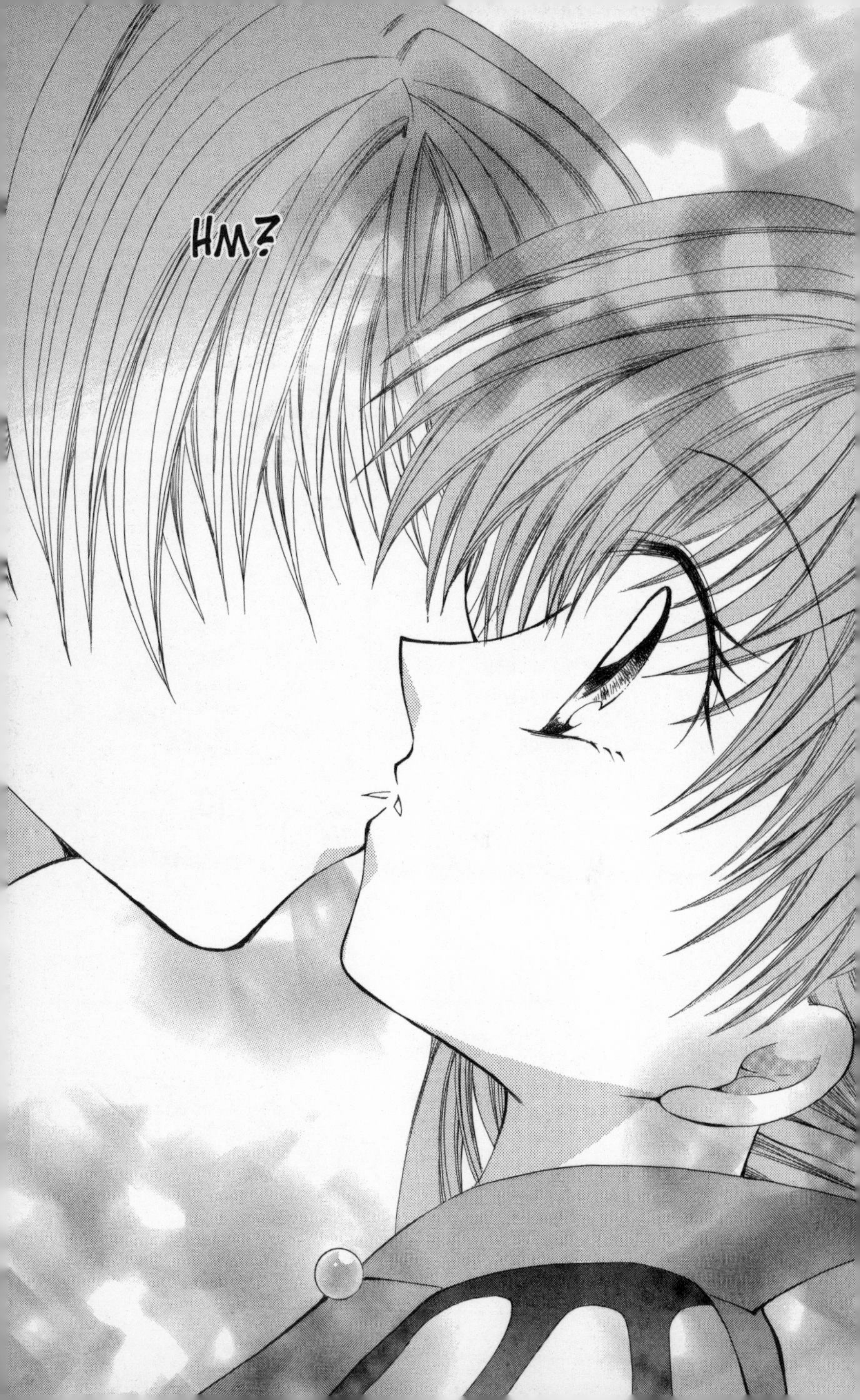
HM?

Tomorrow's Luck

Mini☆Theatre: TAKE 1

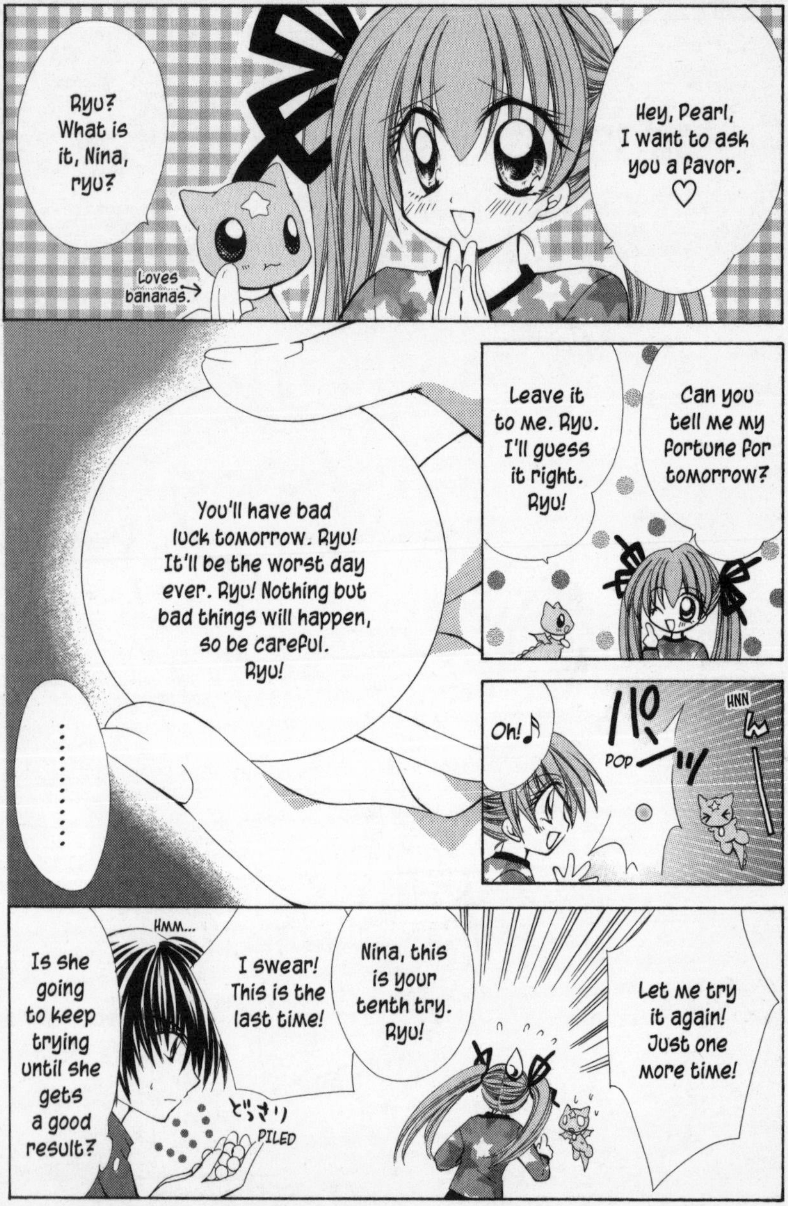
Hey, Pearl, I want to ask you a favor. ♡
Ryu? What is it, Nina, ryu?
Loves bananas.
Can you tell me my fortune for tomorrow?
Leave it to me. Ryu. I'll guess it right. Ryu!
HNN
POP
Oh!♪
You'll have bad luck tomorrow. Ryu! It'll be the worst day ever. Ryu! Nothing but bad things will happen, so be careful. Ryu!
....
Let me try it again! Just one more time!
Nina, this is your tenth try. Ryu!
I swear! This is the last time!
HMM...
Is she going to keep trying until she gets a good result?
どっさり
PILED

Is It a Horn or an Ear?

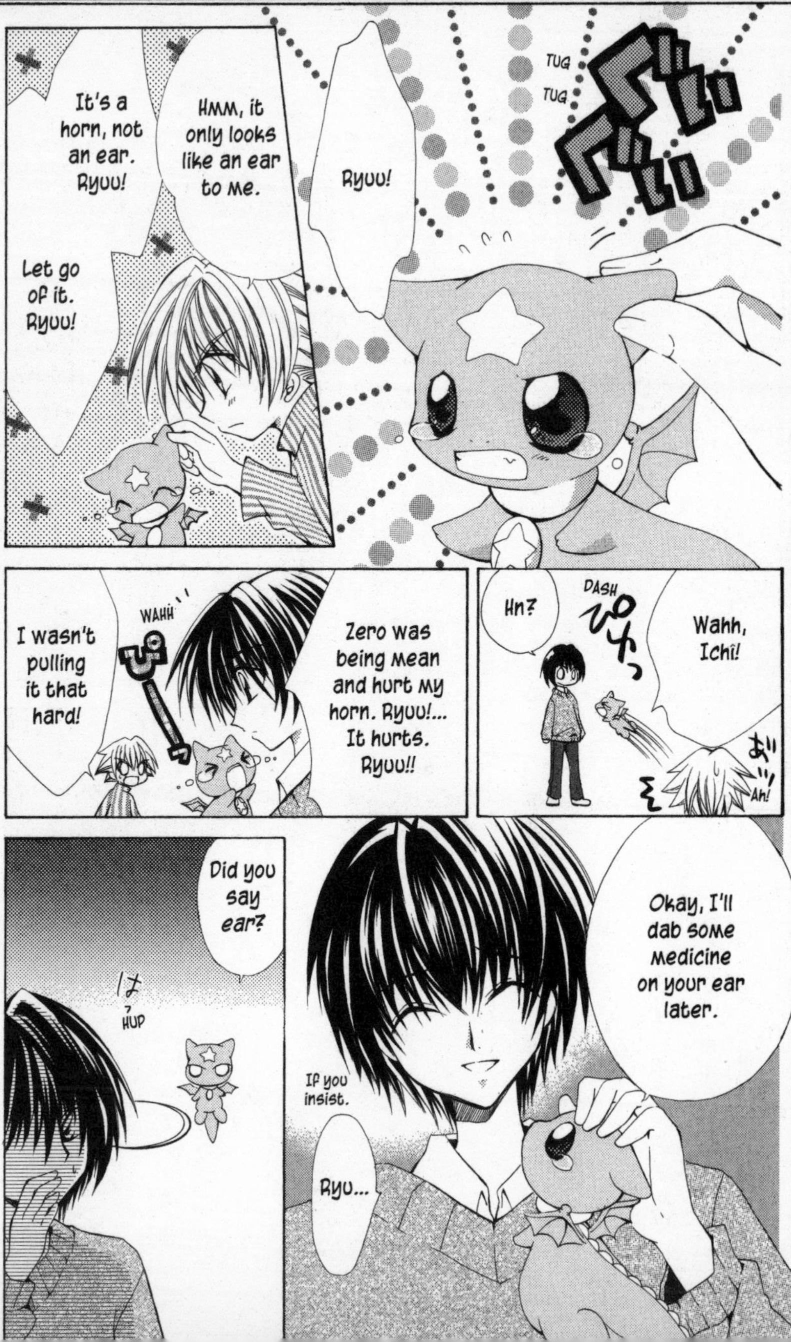
TUG
TUG
Ryuu!
Hmm, it only looks like an ear to me.
It's a horn, not an ear. Ryuu!
Let go of it. Ryuu!
Wahh, Ichi!
DASH
Hn?
Ah!
Zero was being mean and hurt my horn. Ryuu!... It hurts. Ryuu!!
WAHH
I wasn't pulling it that hard!
Okay, I'll dab some medicine on your ear later.
If you insist.
Ryu...
Did you say ear?
HUP

Sun-chan Goes Shopping

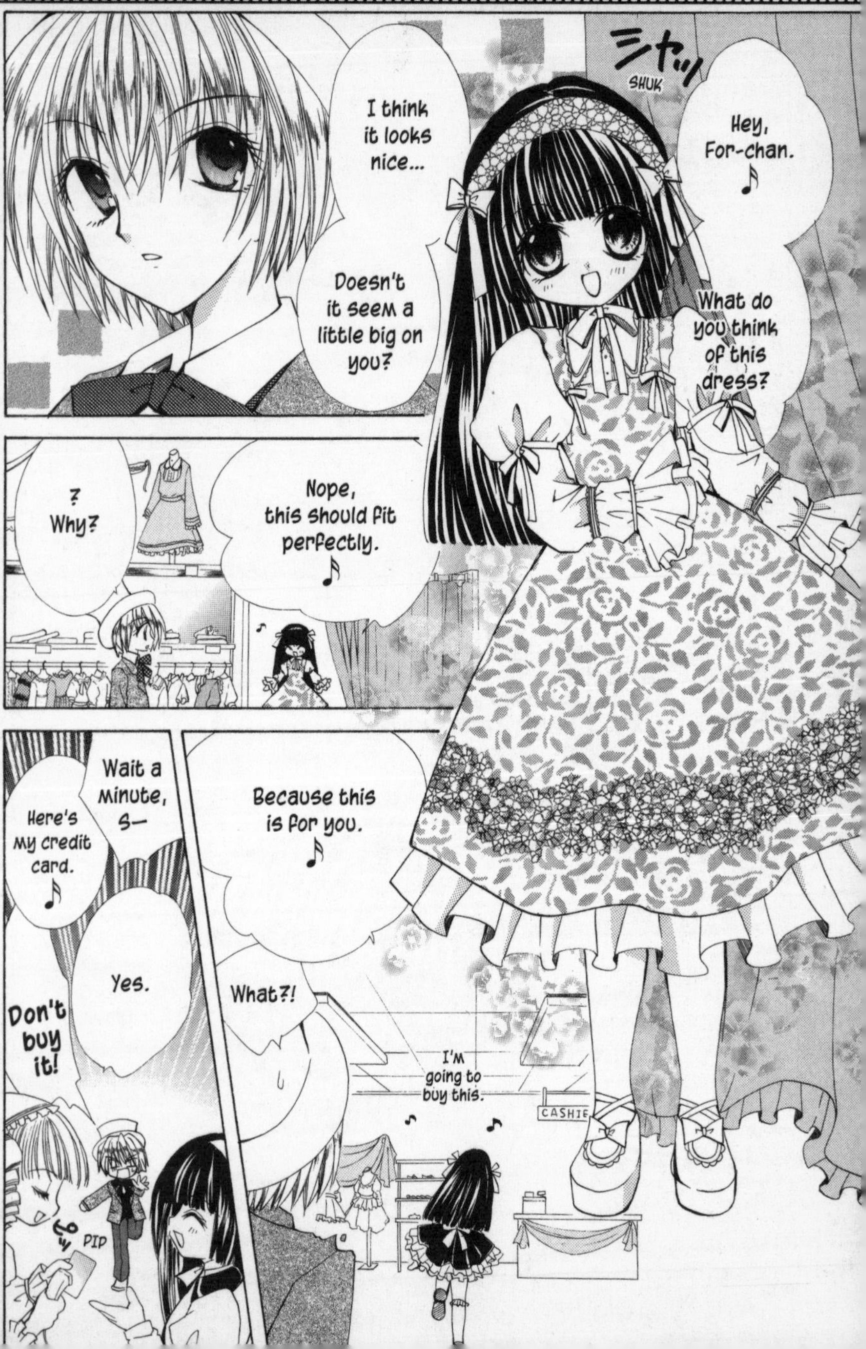

シャッ
SHUK
Hey, For-chan. ♪
What do you think of this dress?
I think it looks nice...
Doesn't it seem a little big on you?
Nope, this should fit perfectly. ♪
? Why?
Because this is for you. ♪
What?!
I'm going to buy this.
CASHIE
Wait a minute, S—
Here's my credit card. ♪
Yes.
Don't buy it!
PIP

The Drama Club's Secret

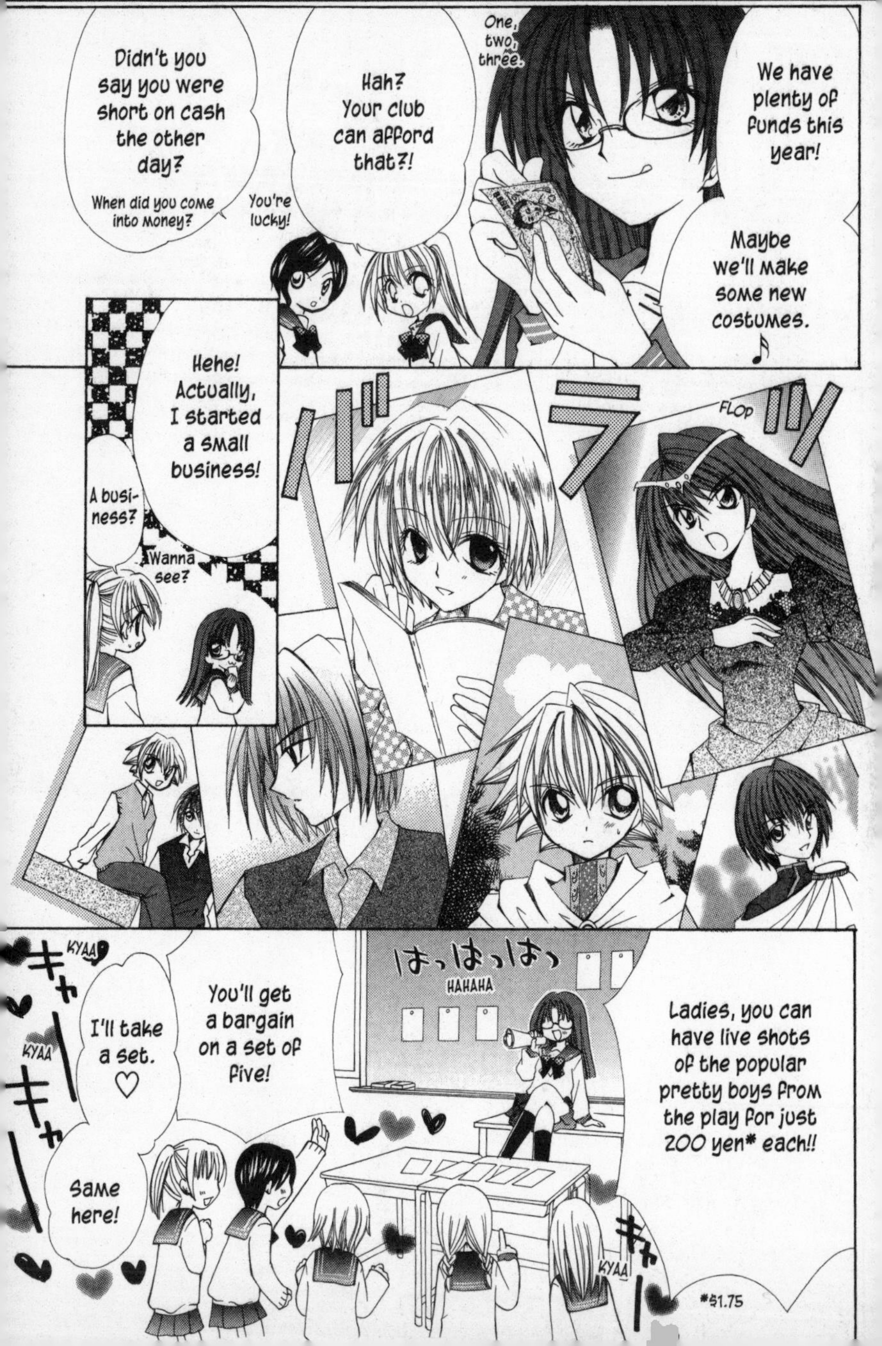
One, two, three.
We have plenty of funds this year!
Maybe we'll make some new costumes. ♪
Hah? Your club can afford that?!
You're lucky!
Didn't you say you were short on cash the other day?
When did you come into money?
FLOP
Hehe! Actually, I started a small business!
A business?
Wanna see?
Ladies, you can have live shots of the popular pretty boys from the play for just 200 yen* each!!
はっはっはっ
HAHAHA
You'll get a bargain on a set of five!
I'll take a set. ♡
Same here!
KYAA
KYAA
KYAA
*$1.75

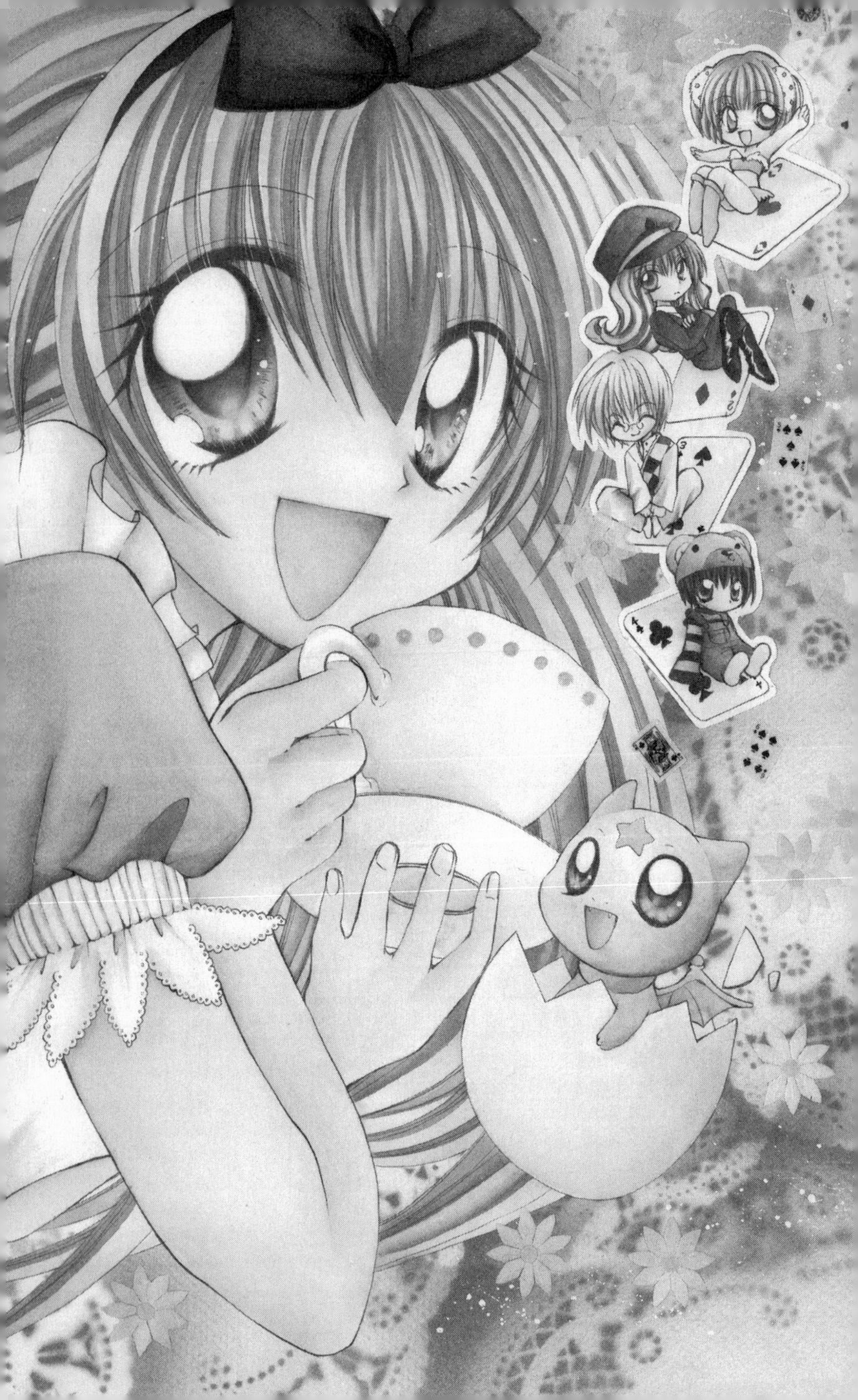

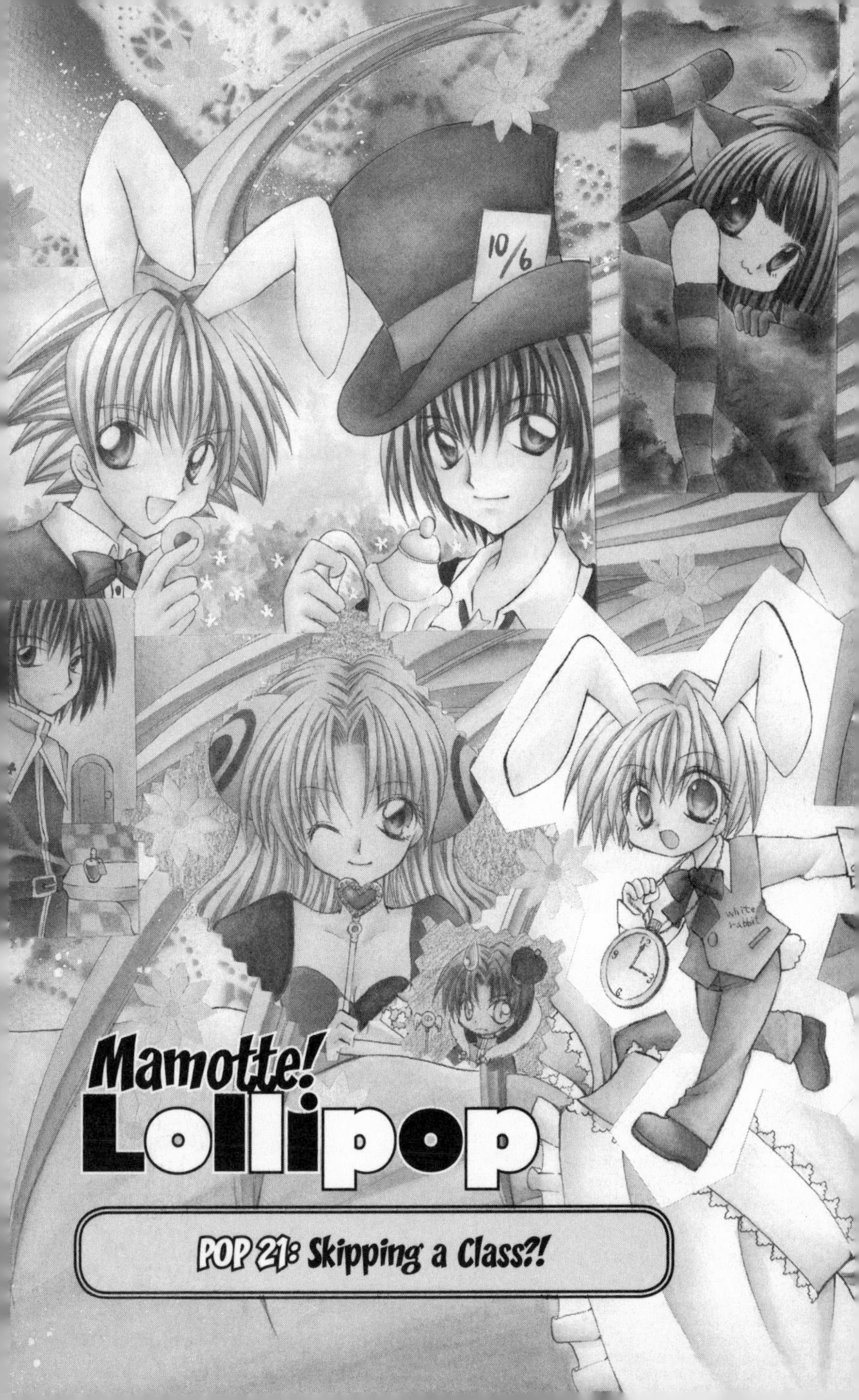
10/6
White Rabbit
Mamotte! Lollipop
POP 21: Skipping a Class?!

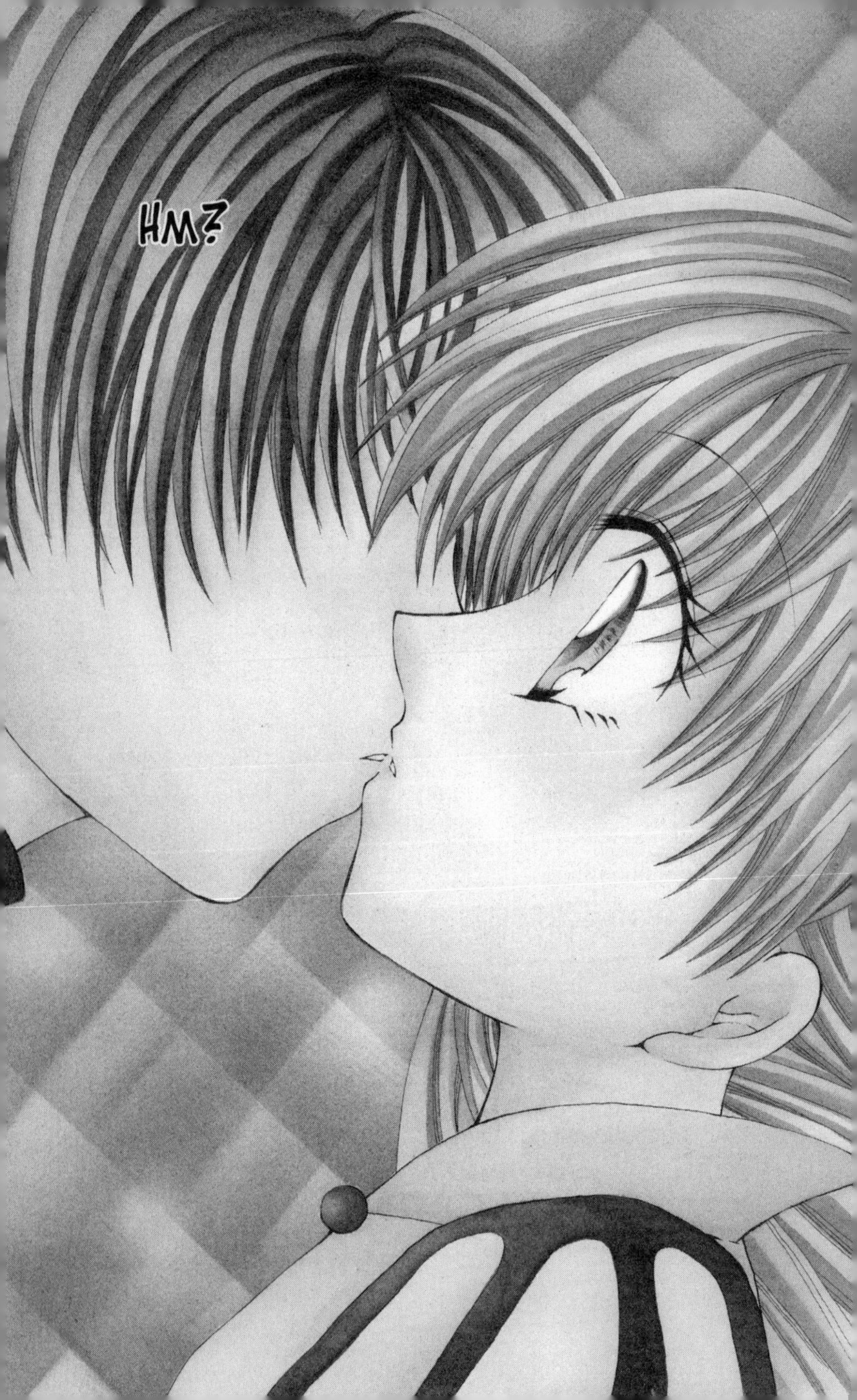
HM?

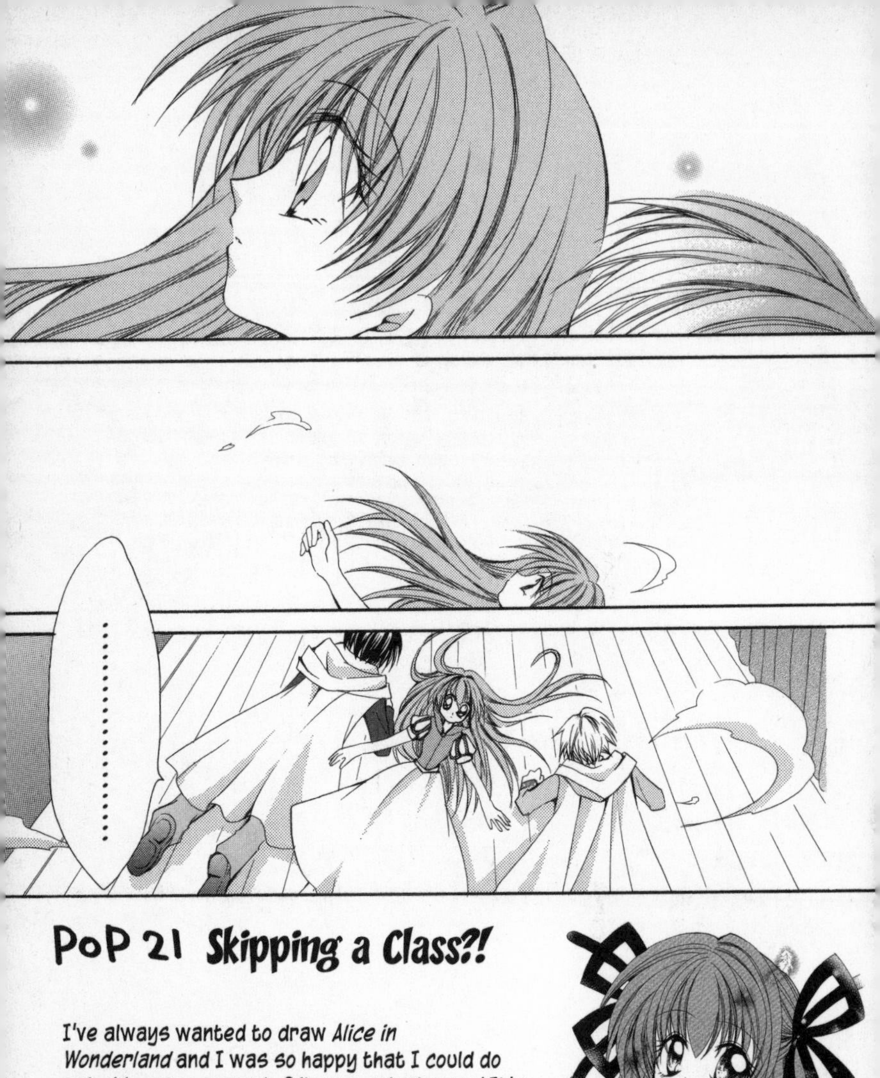
......

PoP 21 Skipping a Class?!

I've always wanted to draw *Alice in Wonderland* and I was so happy that I could do a double-page spread of it as a splash page! It's one of my favorite illustrations in all of *Mamotte! Lollipop.*

This episode is all about Ichi! It was the most romantic story I've ever done, and I even had fun drawing it. Since I used a crow quill pen for this entire episode, the lines appear finer than usual.

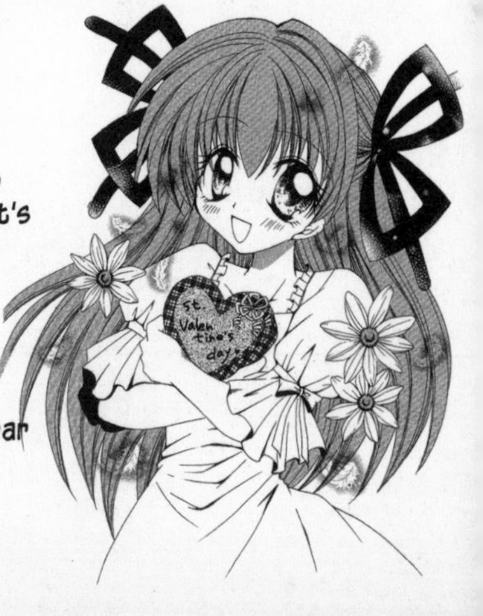
St. Valentine's day

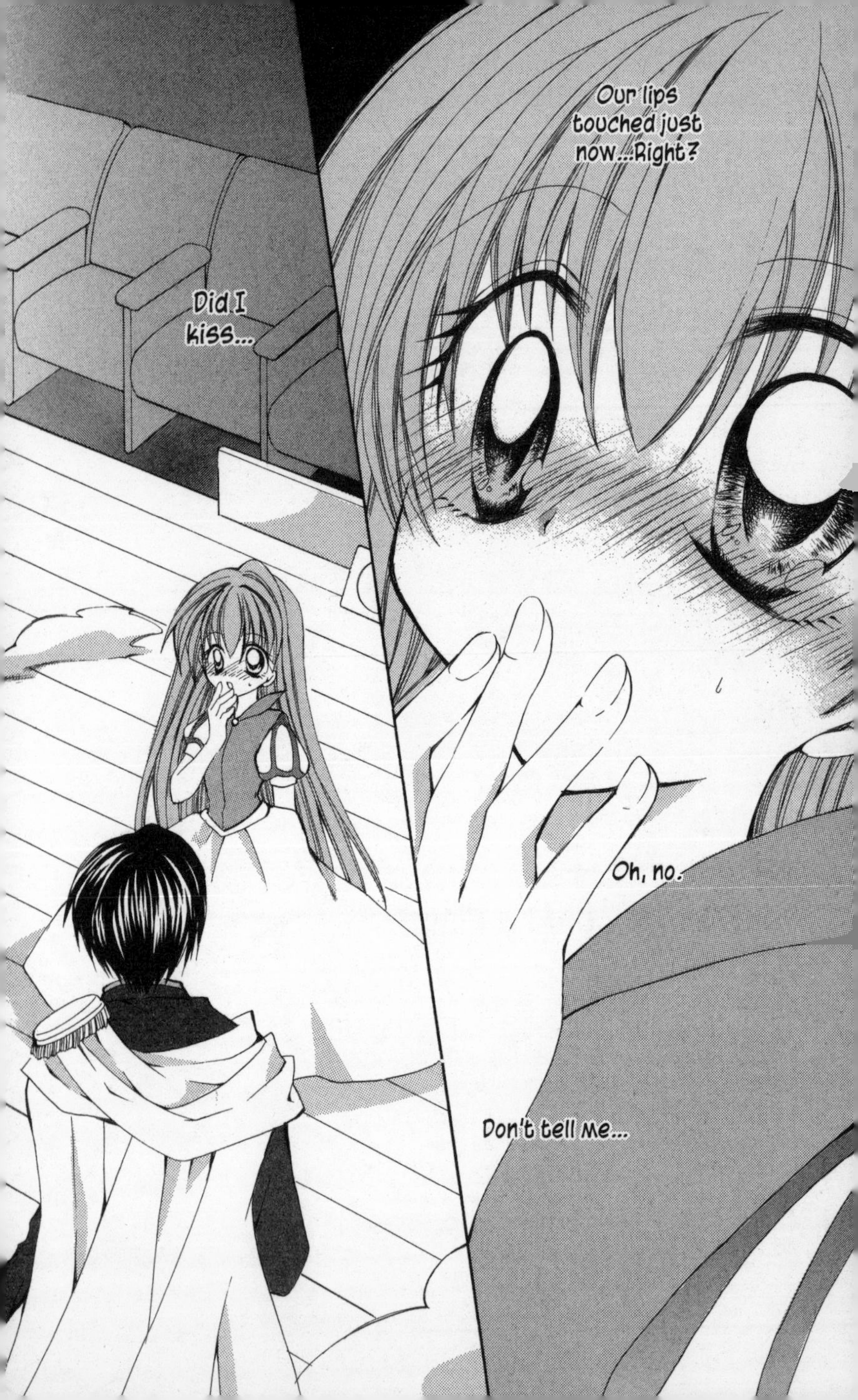
Our lips touched just now...Right?
Oh, no.
Don't tell me...
Did I kiss...

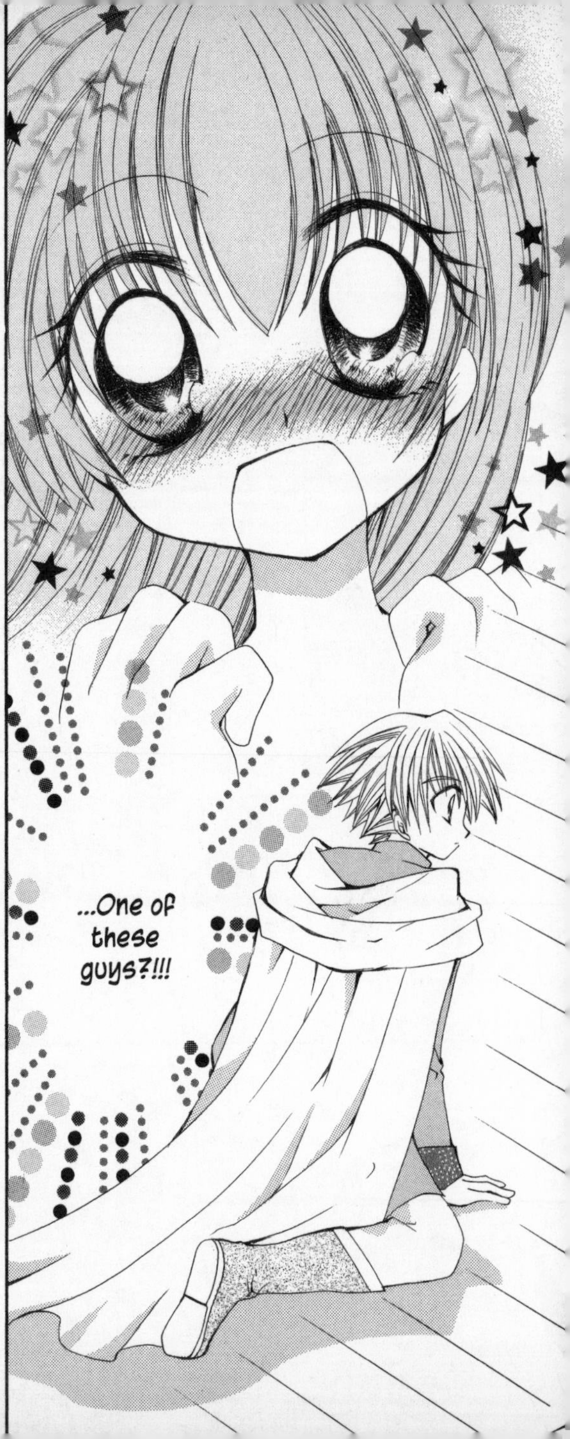
...One of these guys?!!!

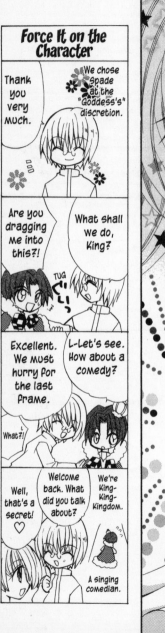

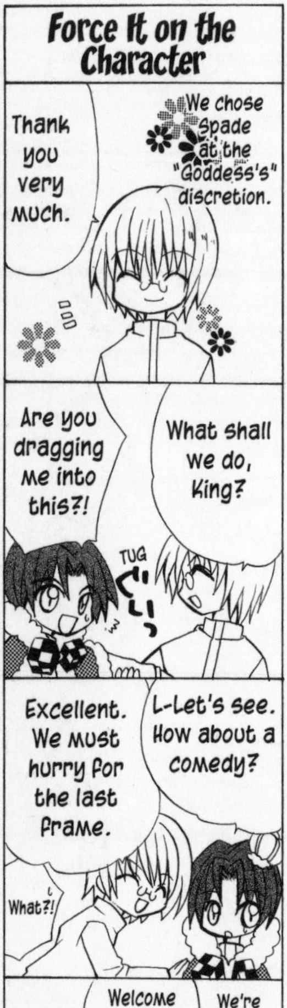
Force It on the Character
We chose Spade at the "Goddess's" discretion.
Thank you very much.
What shall we do, King?
Are you dragging me into this?!
TUG
L-Let's see. How about a comedy?
Excellent. We must hurry for the last frame.
What?!
We're King-King-Kingdom.
Welcome back. What did you talk about?
Well, that's a secret! ♡
A singing comedian.

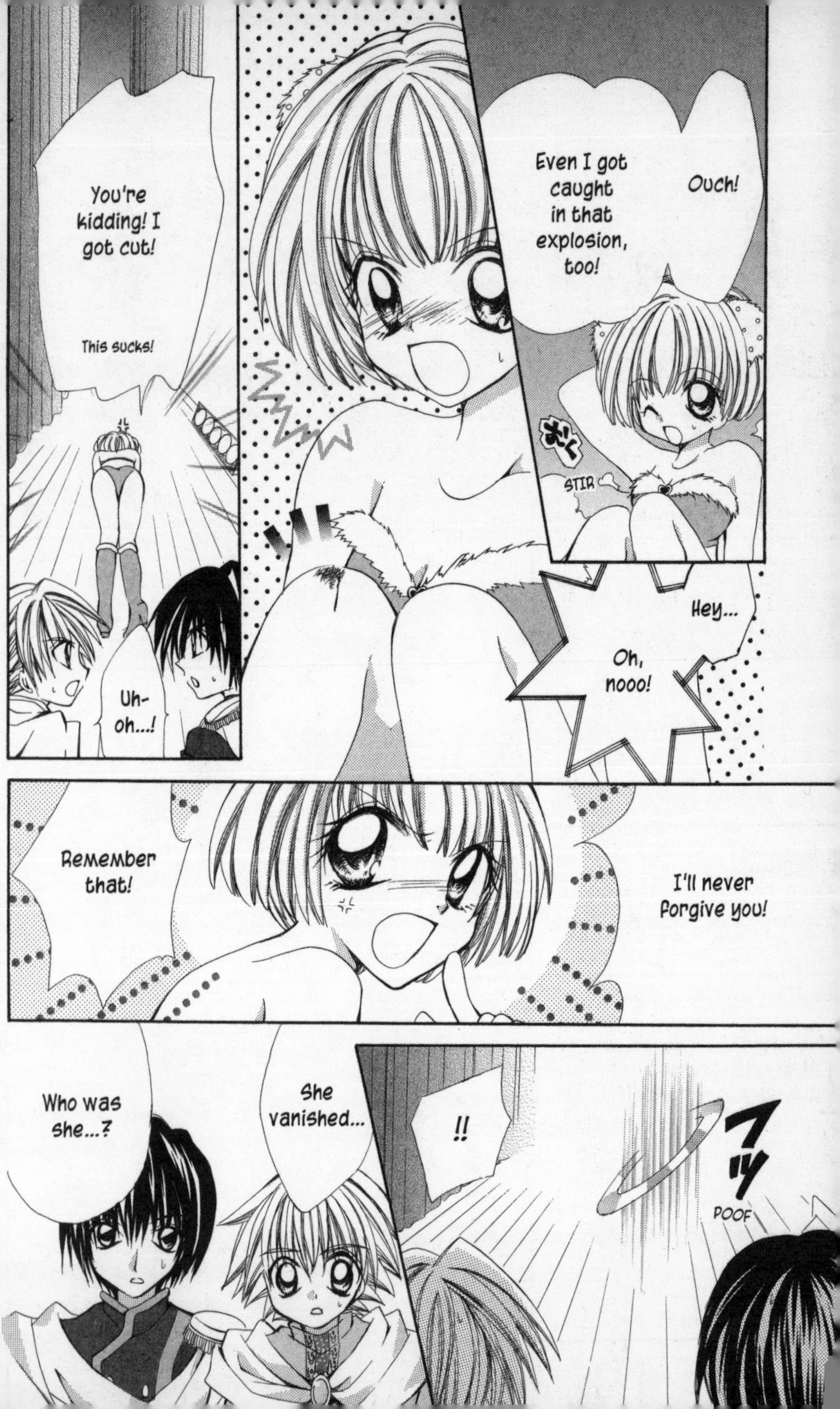
Ouch!
Even I got caught in that explosion, too!
STIR
Hey...
Oh, nooo!
You're kidding! I got cut!
This sucks!
Uh-oh...!
I'll never forgive you!
Remember that!
フッ
POOF
!!
She vanished...
Who was she...?

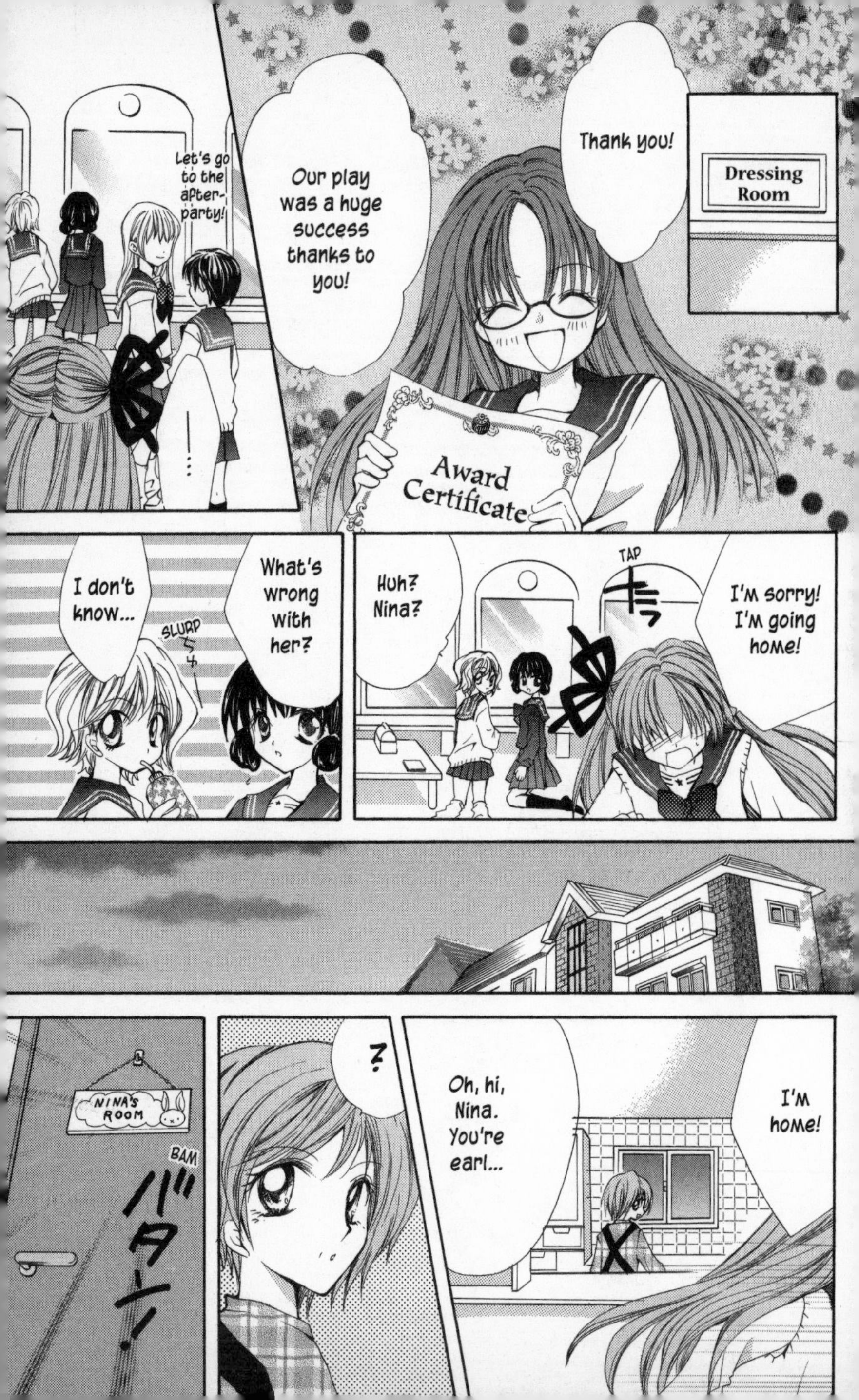
Dressing Room
Thank you!
Our play was a huge success thanks to you!
Award Certificate
Let's go to the after-party!
…
I'm sorry! I'm going home!
TAP
Huh? Nina?
What's wrong with her?
SLURP
I don't know...
I'm home!
Oh, hi, Nina. You're earl...
?
NINA'S ROOM
BAM
バターン!

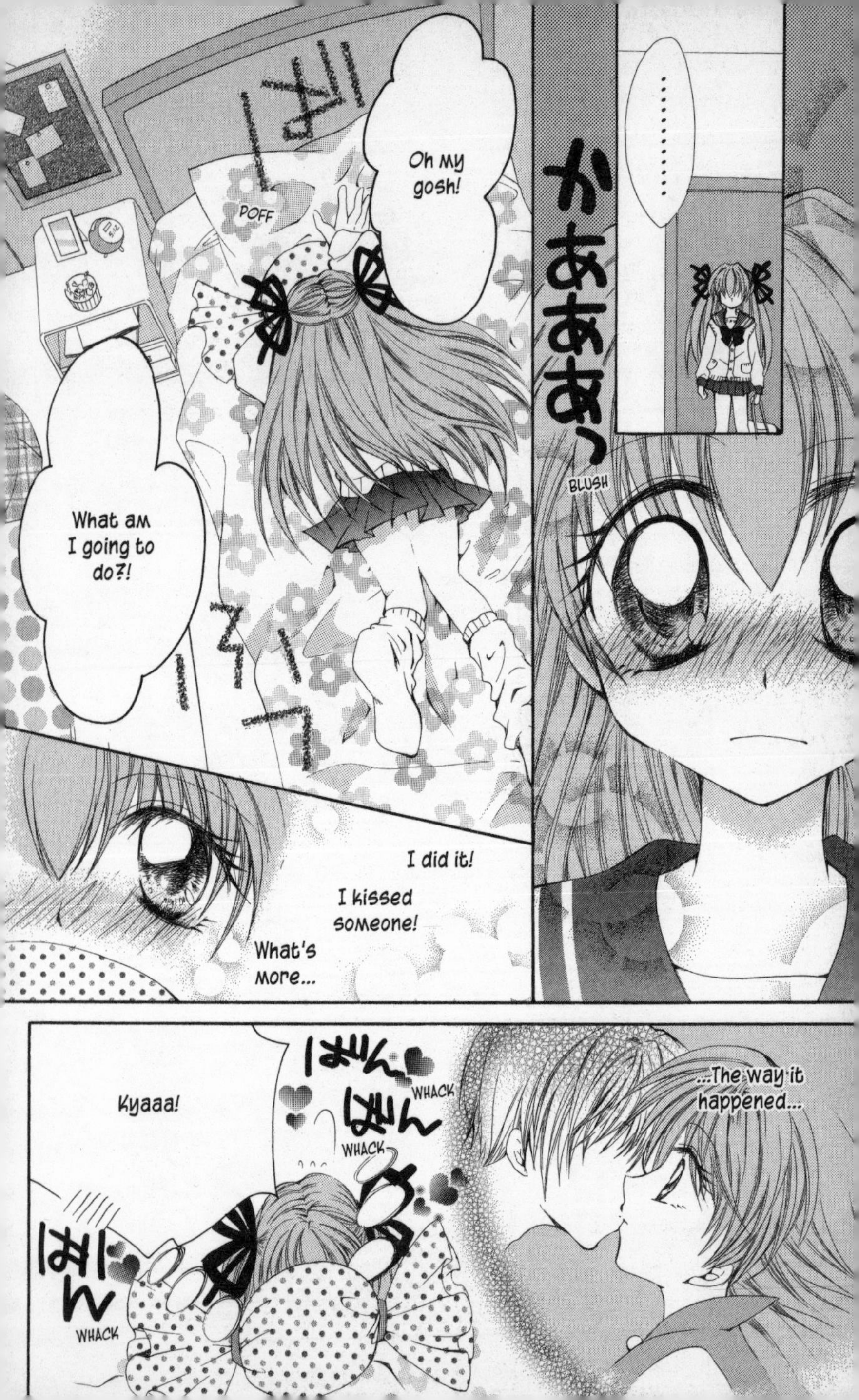
......
かあああっ
BLUSH
Oh my gosh!
POFF
What am I going to do?!
I did it!
I kissed someone!
What's more...
...The way it happened...
WHACK
WHACK
Kyaaa!
WHACK

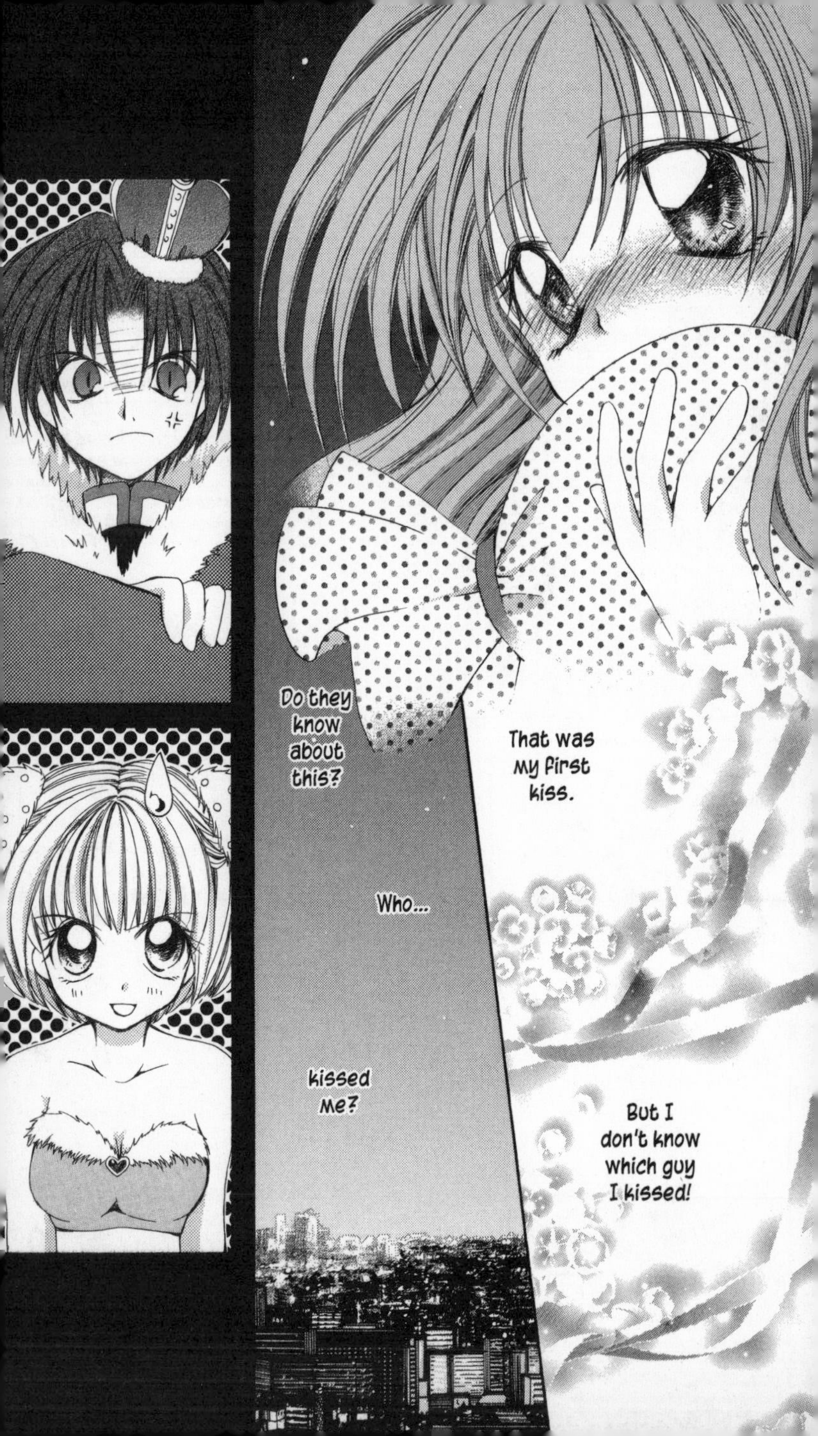
That was my first kiss.
But I don't know which guy I kissed!
Do they know about this?
Who...
kissed me?

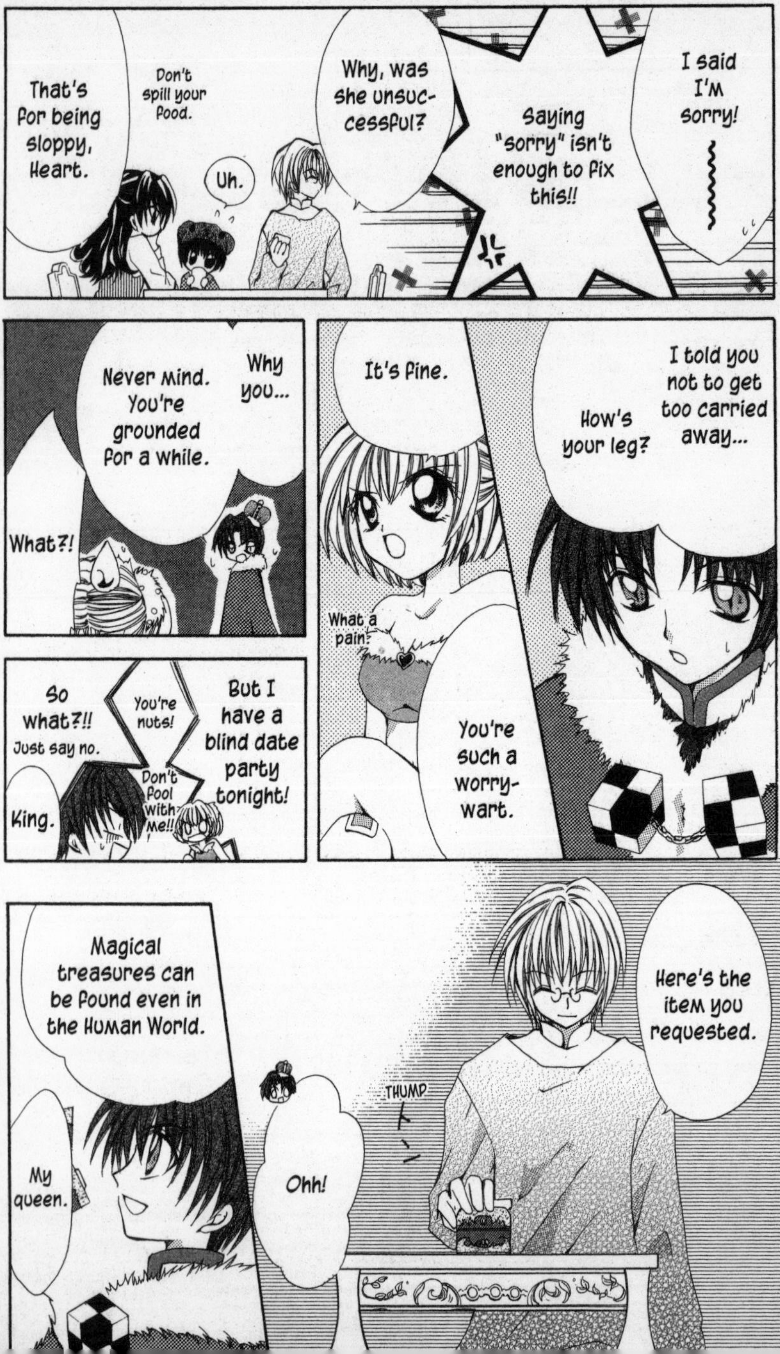
I said I'M sorry!
Saying "sorry" isn't enough to fix this!!
Why, was she unsuccessful?
Uh.
Don't spill your food.
That's for being sloppy, Heart.
I told you not to get too carried away...
How's your leg?
It's fine.
What a pain.
You're such a worry-wart.
Why you...
Never mind. You're grounded for a while.
What?!
But I have a blind date party tonight!
You're nuts!
Don't fool with me!!
So what?!! Just say no.
King.
Here's the item you requested.
THUMP
Magical treasures can be found even in the Human World.
Ohh!
My queen.

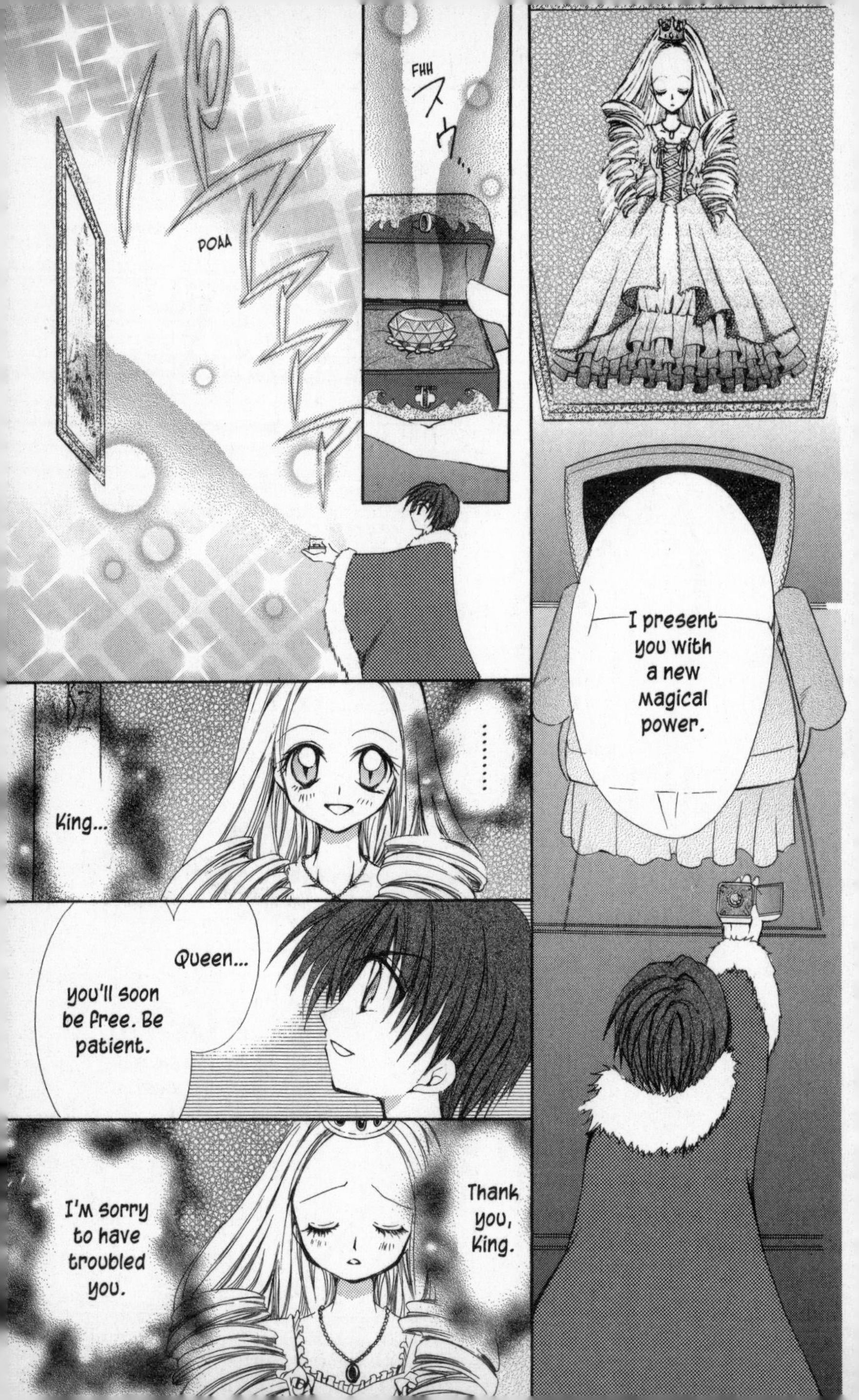
I present you with a new magical power.
FHH
スゥ…
POAA
......
King...
Queen...
you'll soon be free. Be patient.
Thank you, King.
I'm sorry to have troubled you.

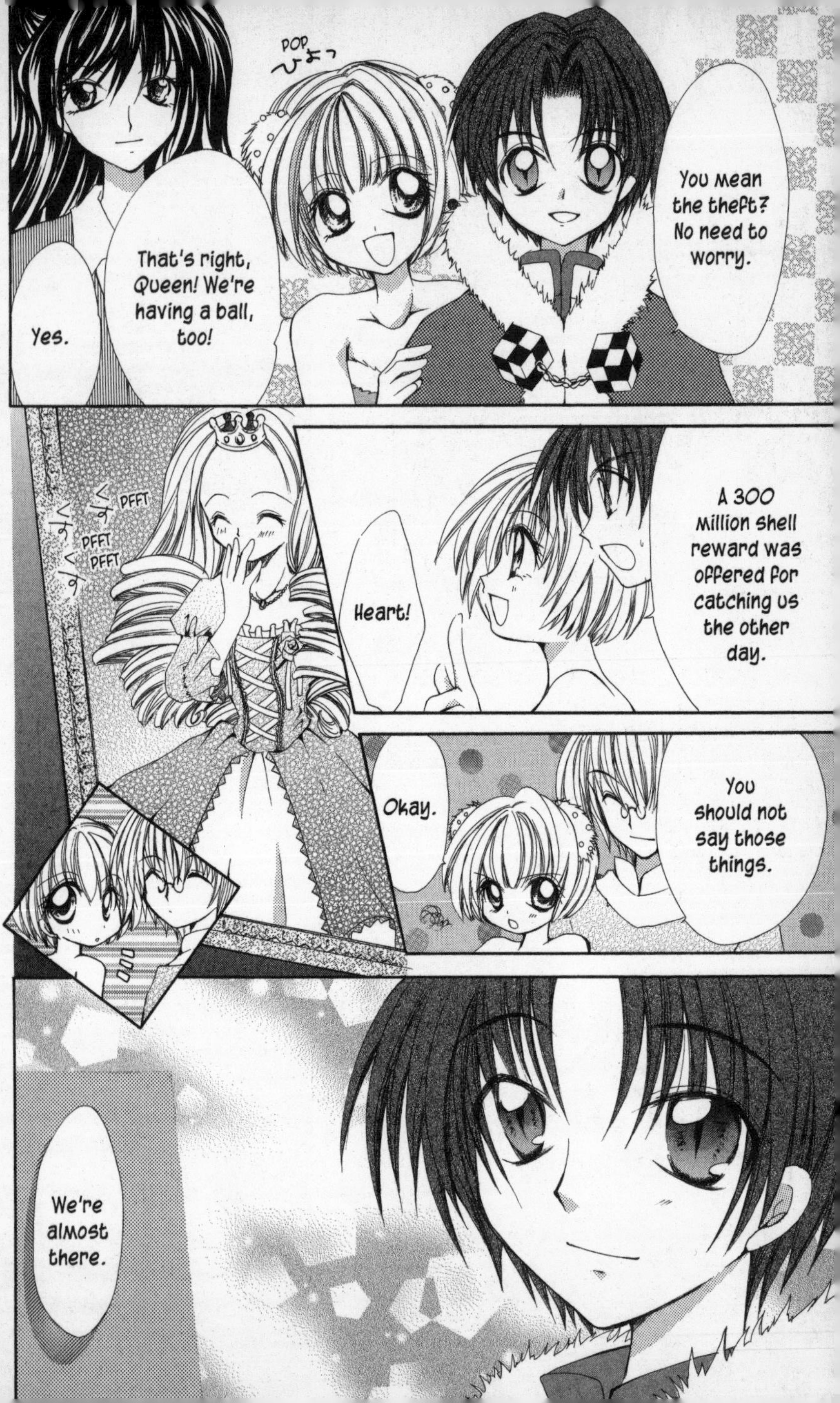

You mean the theft? No need to worry.
POP ぴよっ
That's right, Queen! We're having a ball, too!
Yes.
A 300 million shell reward was offered for catching us the other day.
Heart!
You should not say those things.
Okay.
くすくす PFFT
くすくす PFFT PFFT
We're almost there.

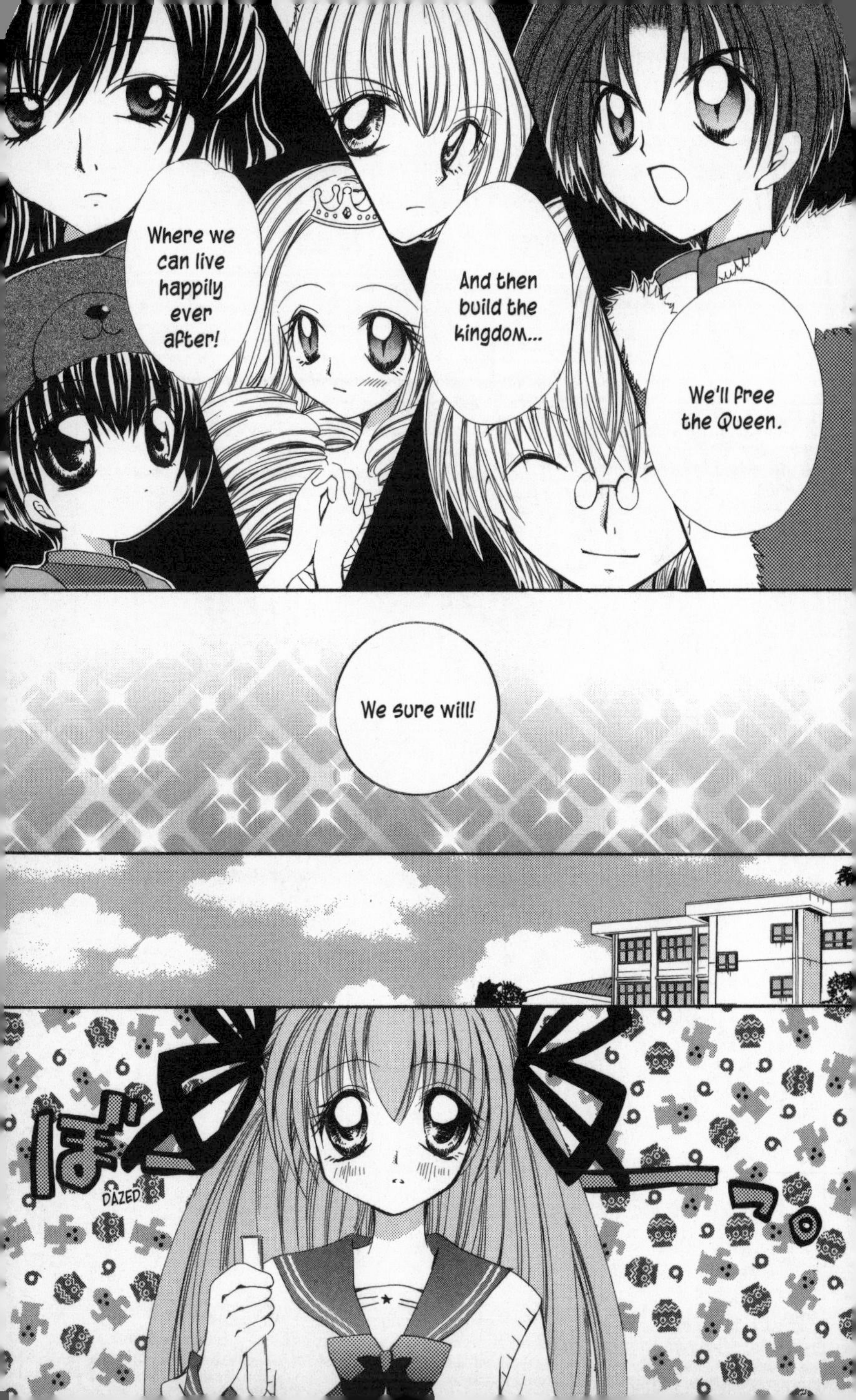
We'll free the Queen.
And then build the kingdom...
Where we can live happily ever after!
We sure will!
ぼーっ。
DAZED

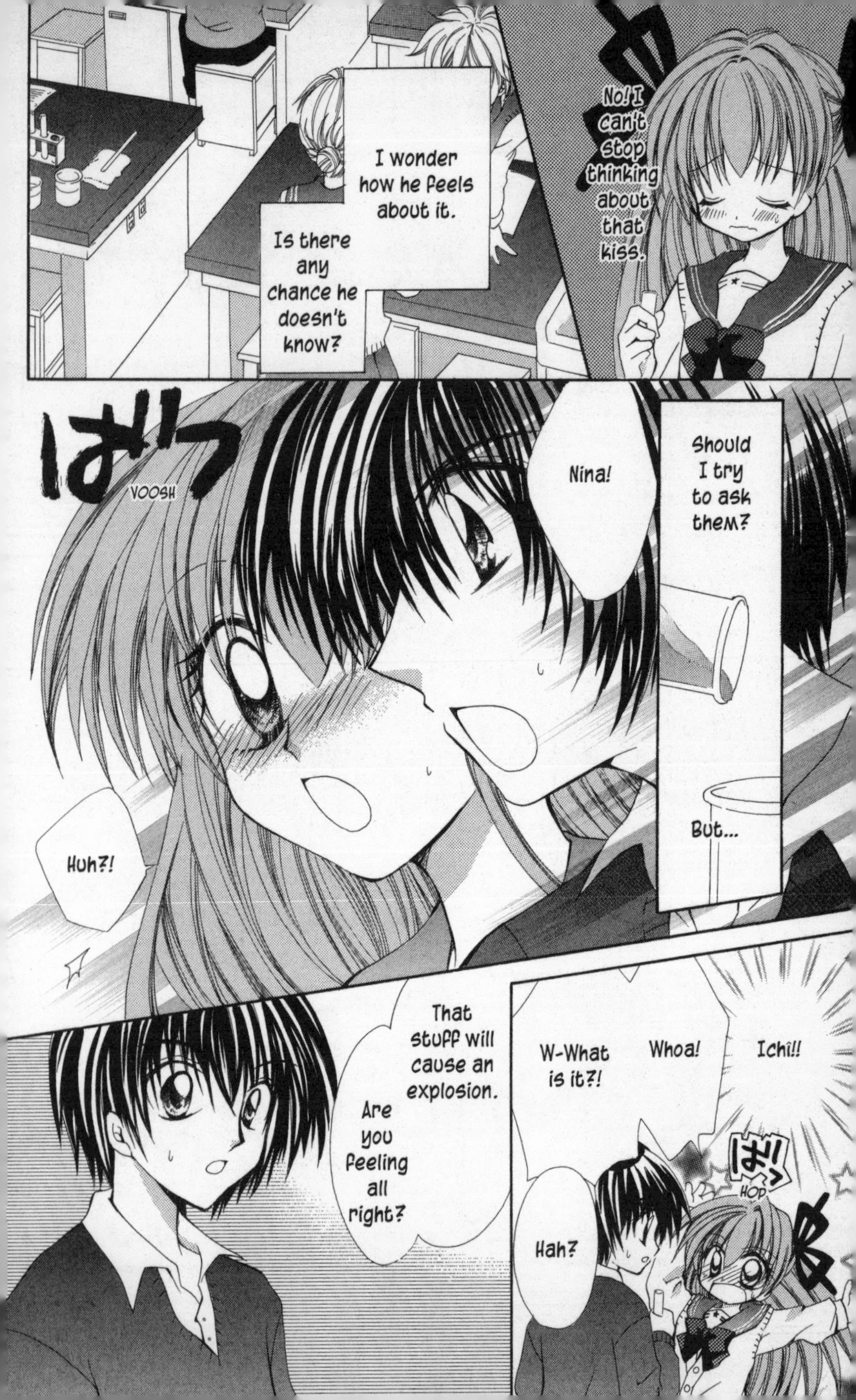
No! I can't stop thinking about that kiss.
I wonder how he feels about it.
Is there any chance he doesn't know?
Should I try to ask them?
But...
Nina!
はっ
VOOSH
Huh?!
Ichi!!
Whoa!
W-What is it?!
ぱ!
HOP
Hah?
That stuff will cause an explosion.
Are you feeling all right?

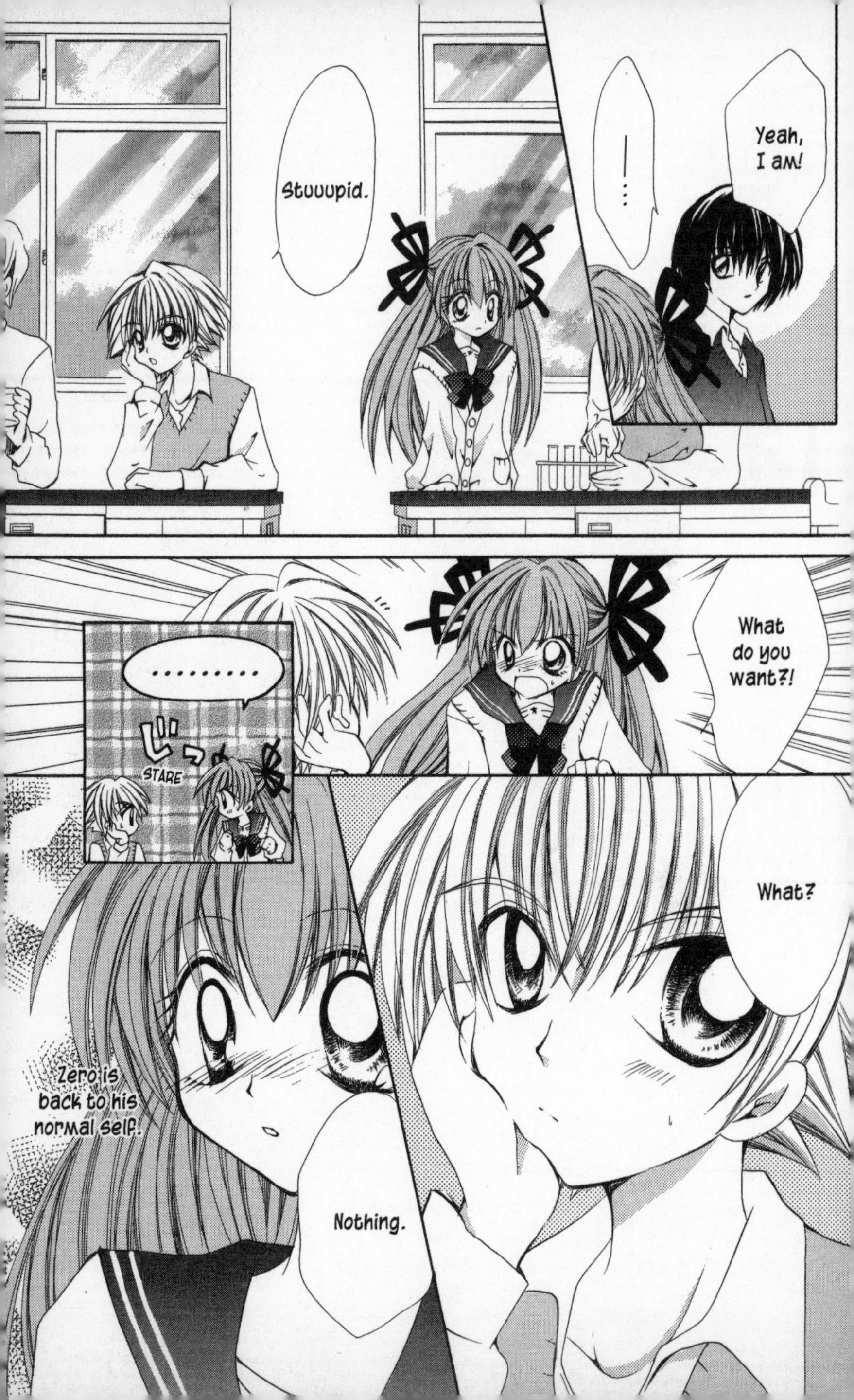
Yeah, I am!
!…
Stuuupid.
What do you want?!
....
STARE
What?
Nothing.
Zero is back to his normal self.

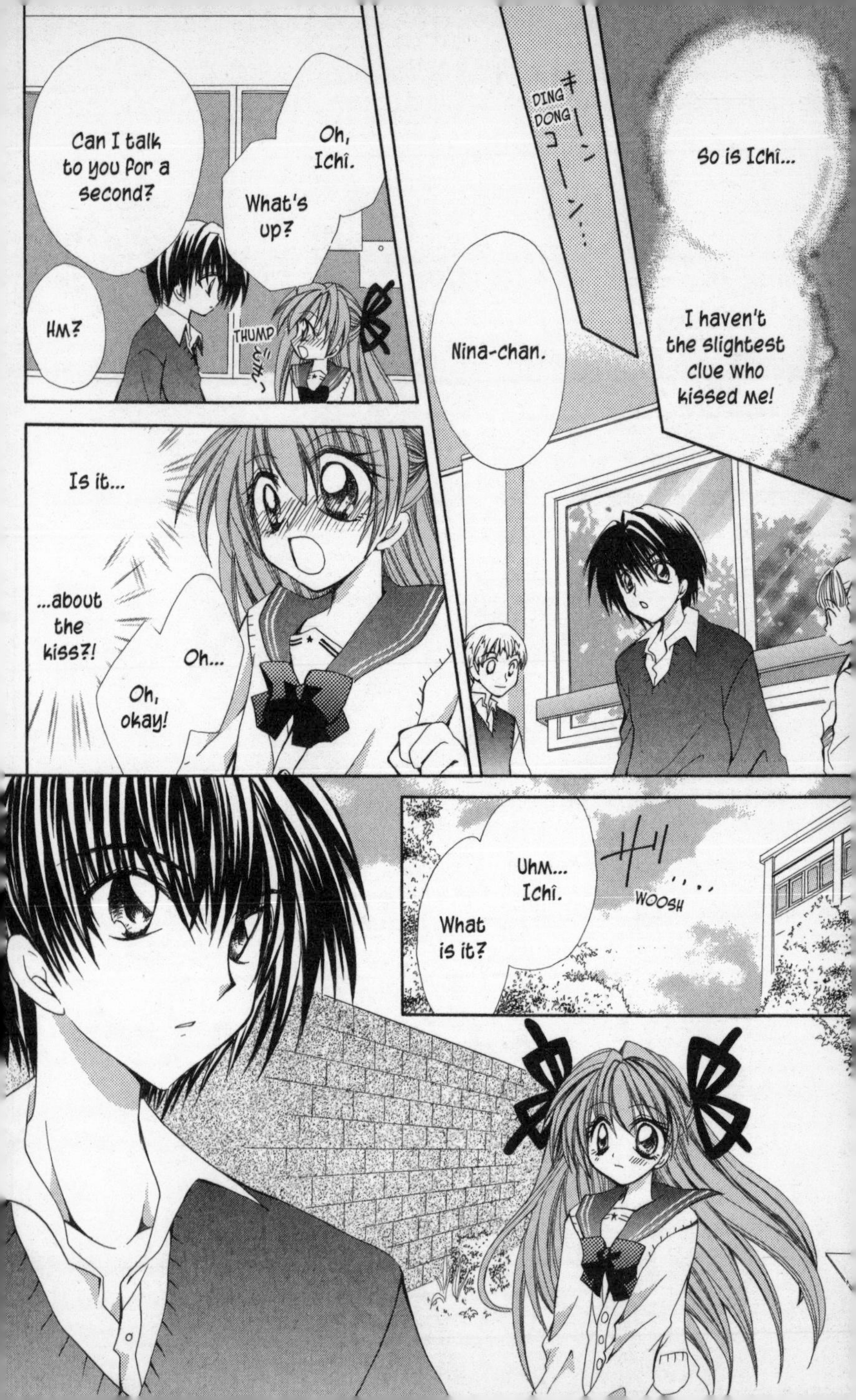
So is Ichî...
I haven't the slightest clue who kissed me!
DING DONG
Nina-chan.
Oh, Ichî.
What's up?
Can I talk to you for a second?
Hm?
THUMP
Is it...
...about the kiss?!
Oh...
Oh, okay!
Uhm... Ichî.
What is it?
WOOSH

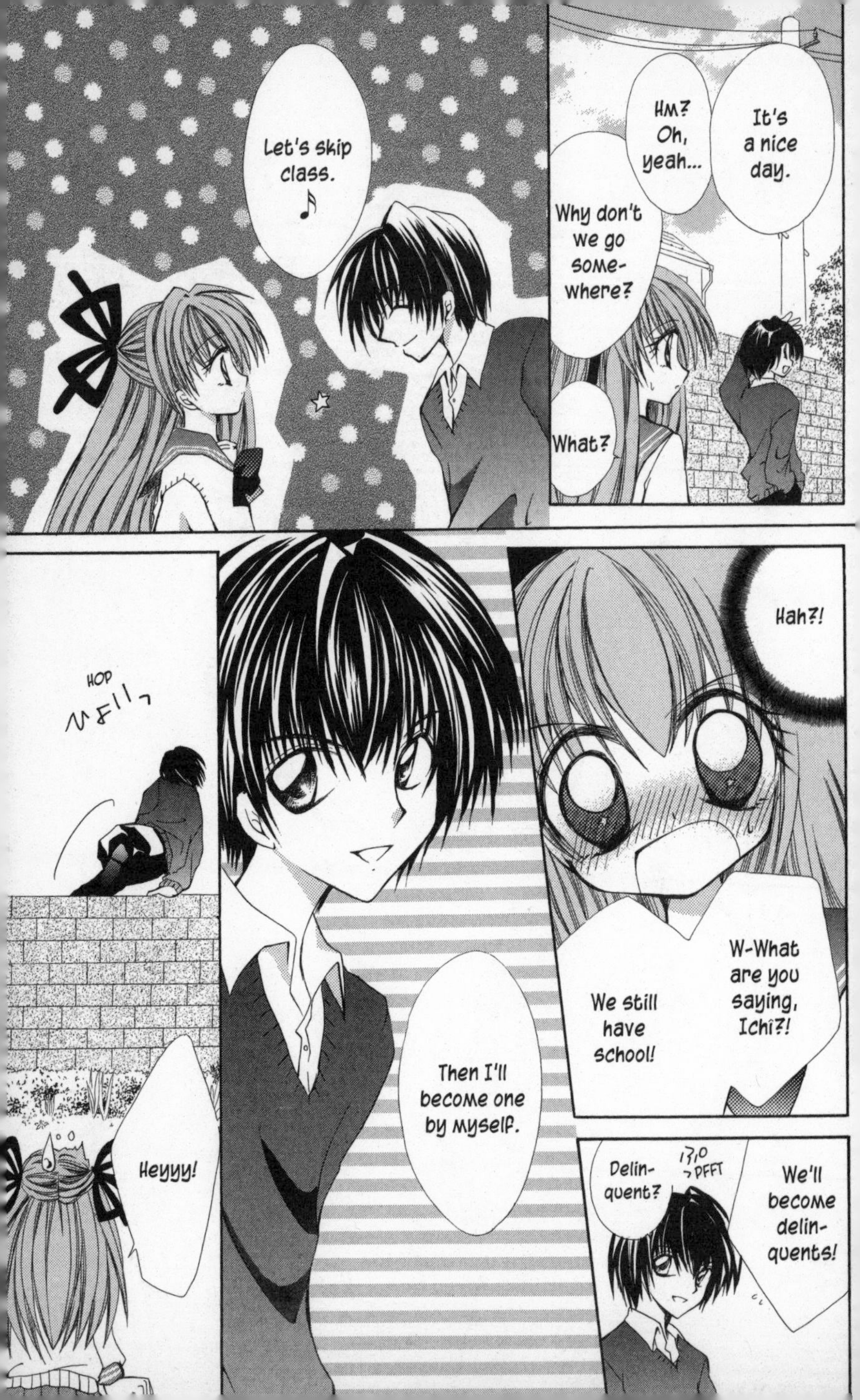
It's a nice day.
Hm? Oh, yeah...
Why don't we go somewhere?
What?
Let's skip class. ♪
Hah?!
W-What are you saying, Ichi?!
We still have school!
We'll become delinquents!
PFFT
Delinquent?
Then I'll become one by myself.
HOP
Heyyy!

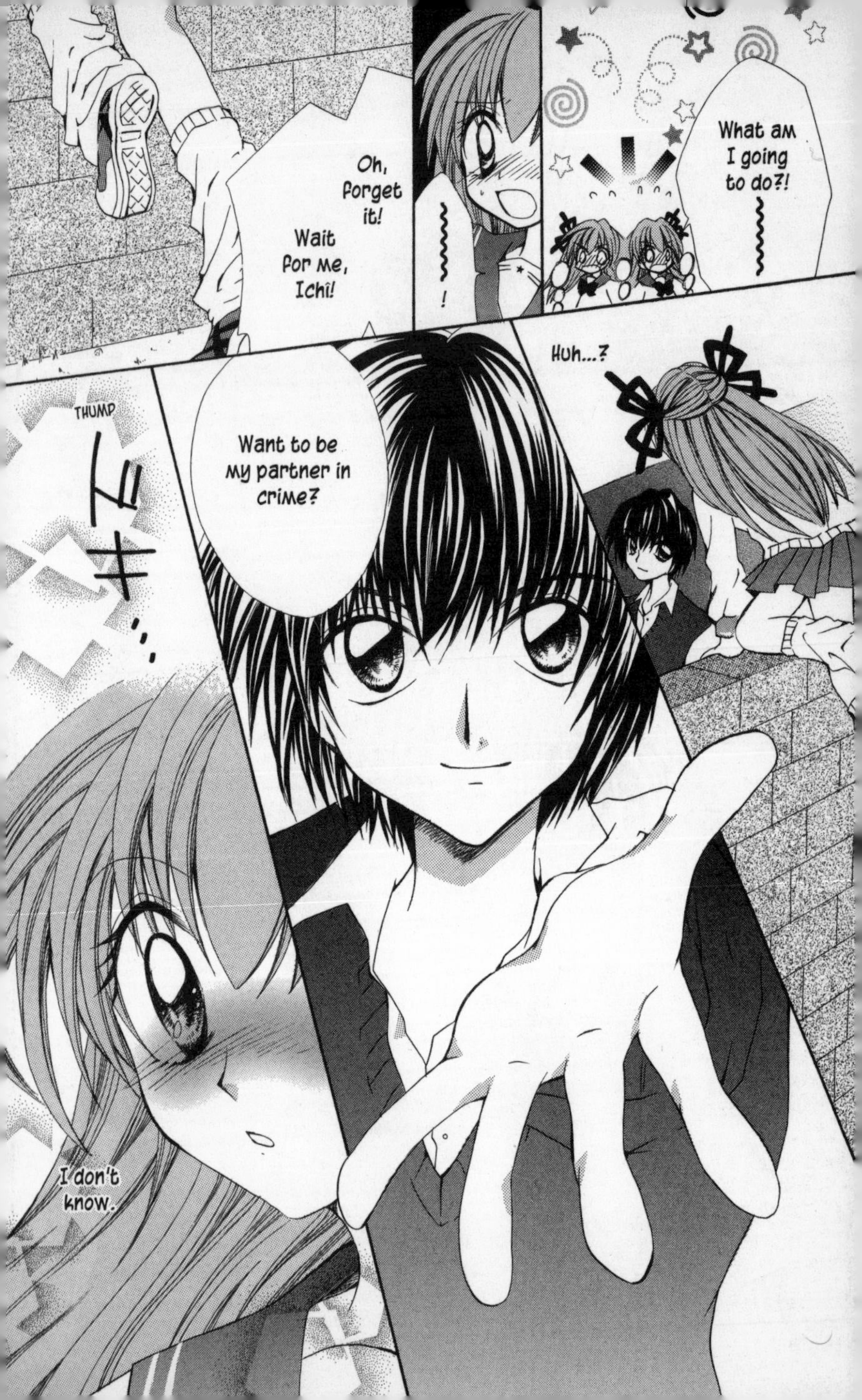
What am I going to do?!
!
Oh, forget it!
Wait for me, Ichi!
Huh...?
Want to be my partner in crime?
THUMP
ドキ...
I don't know.

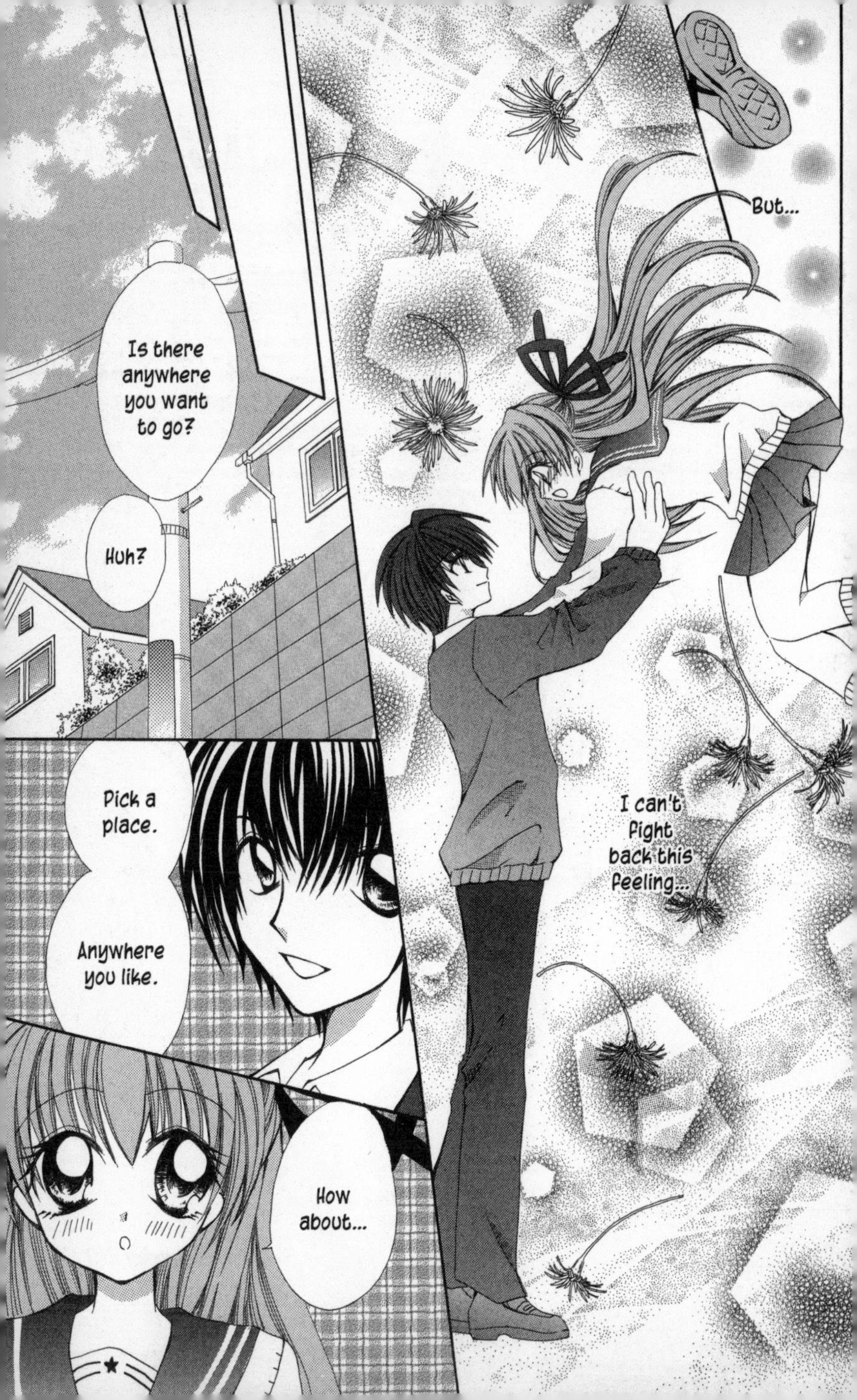
But...
I can't fight back this feeling...
Is there anywhere you want to go?
Huh?
Pick a place.
Anywhere you like.
How about...

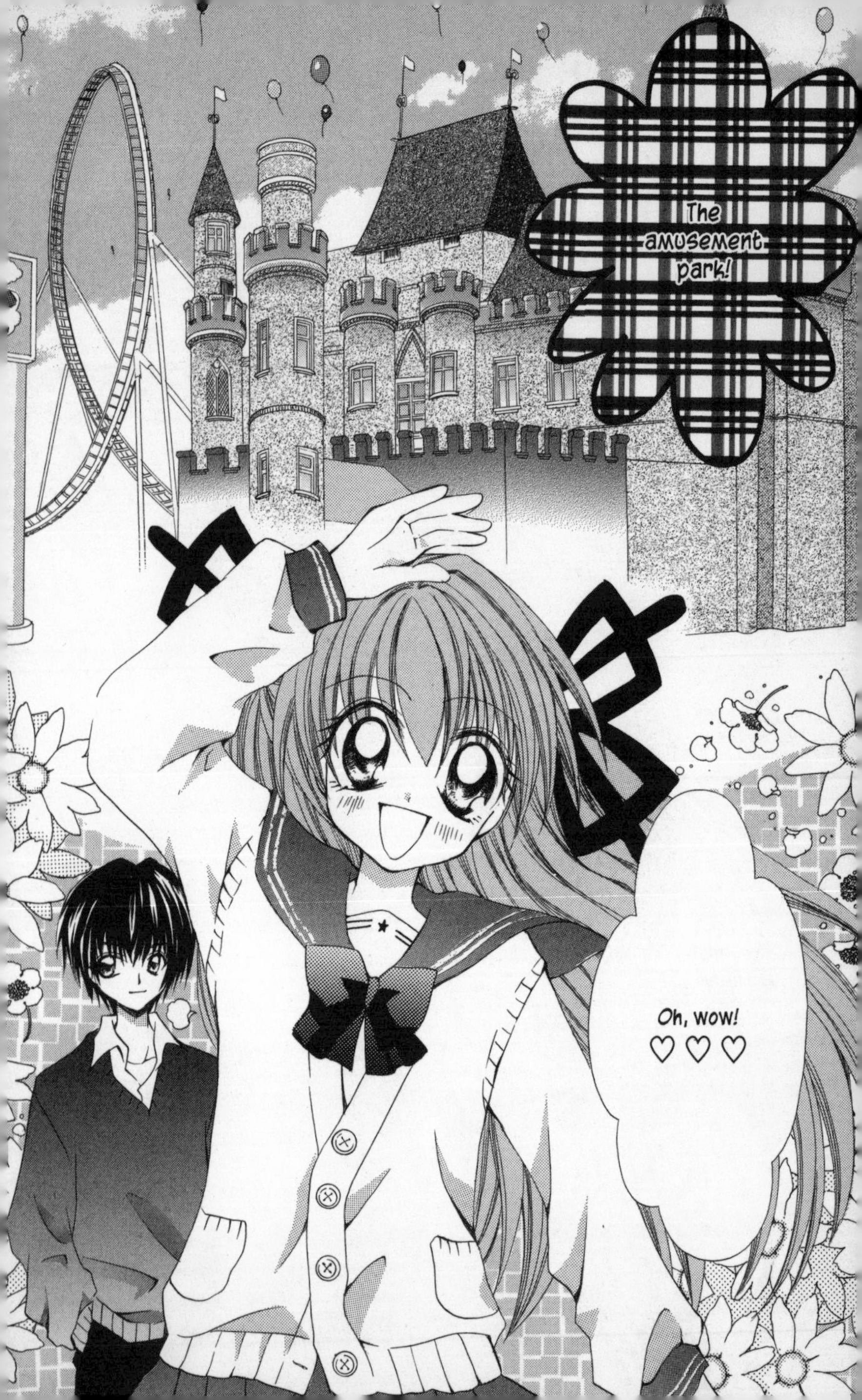
The amusement park!
Oh, wow! ♡♡♡

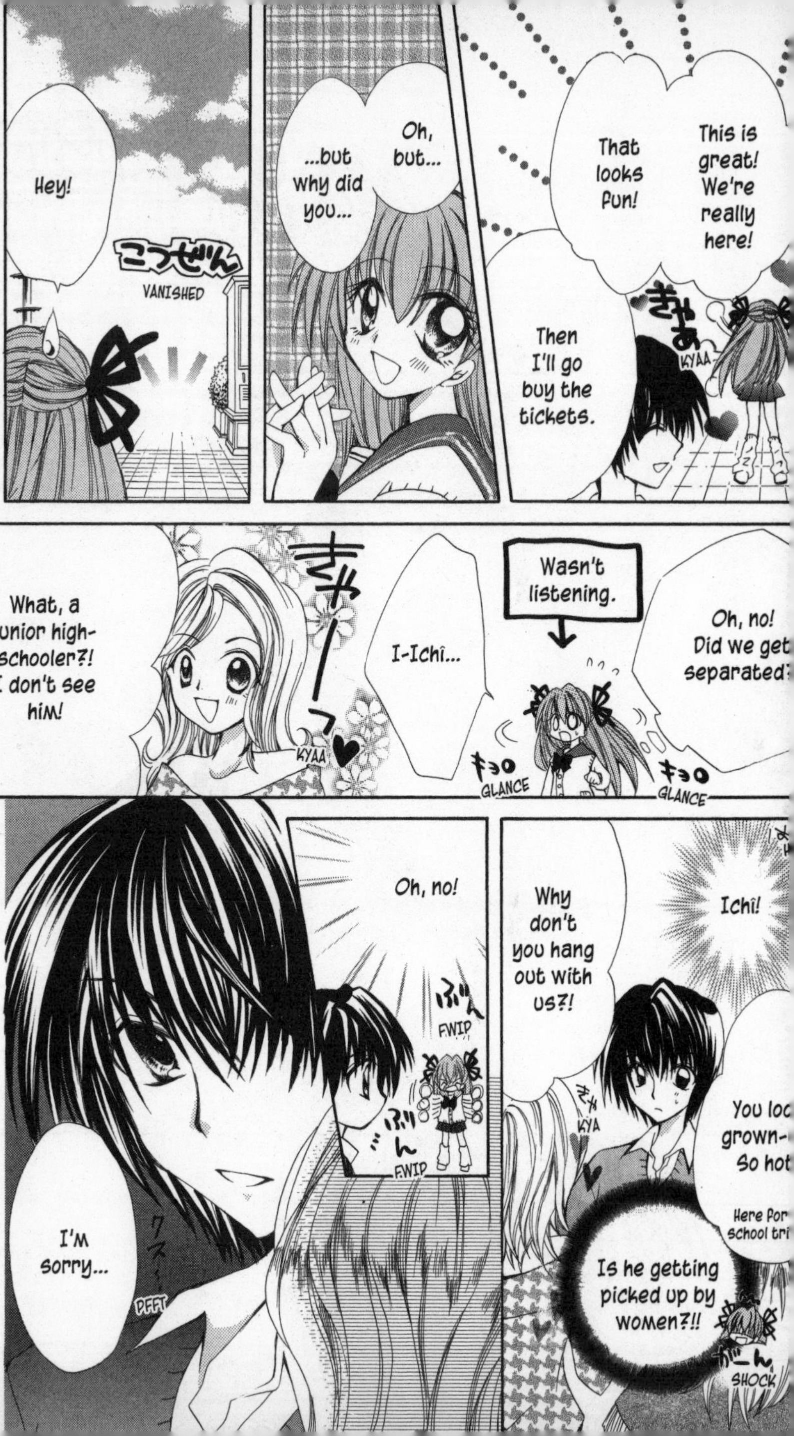
This is great! We're really here!
That looks fun!
KYAA
Then I'll go buy the tickets.
Oh, but...
...but why did you...
こつぜん
VANISHED
Hey!
Oh, no! Did we get separated?!
Wasn't listening.
GLANCE
GLANCE
I-Ichi...
KYAA
What, a junior high-schooler?! I don't see him!
Ichi!
You loo
grown-
So hot
Here for
school tri
Why don't you hang out with us?!
KYA
Is he getting picked up by women?!!
SHOCK
Oh, no!
FWIP
FWIP
I'm sorry...
PFFT

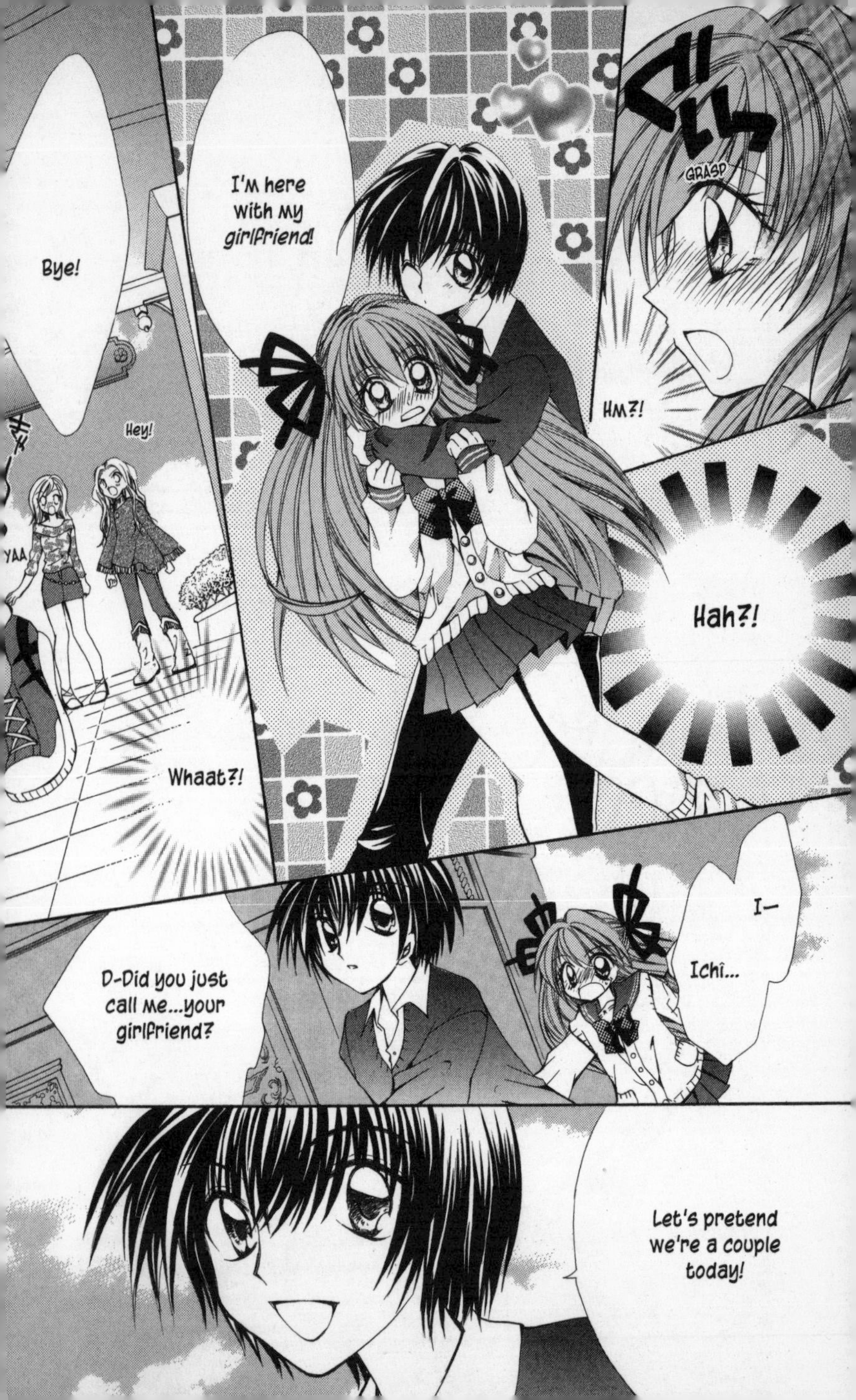
GRASP
HM?!
Hah?!
I'm here with my girlfriend!
Bye!
Hey!
YAA
Whaat?!
I—
Ichi...
D-Did you just call me...your girlfriend?
Let's pretend we're a couple today!

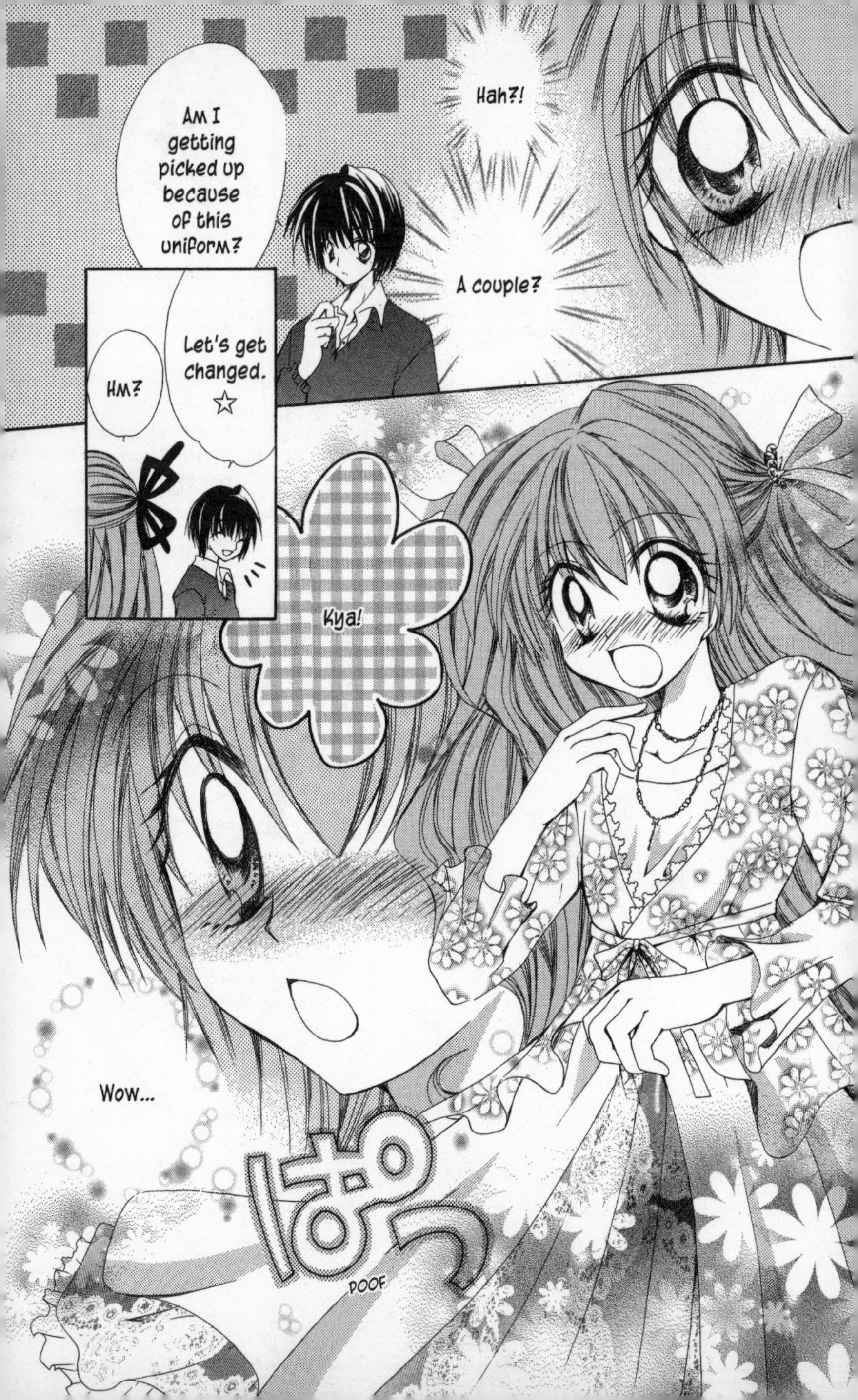
Hah?!
A couple?
Am I getting picked up because of this uniform?
Let's get changed. ☆
Hm?
Kya!
Wow...
ぱっ
POOF

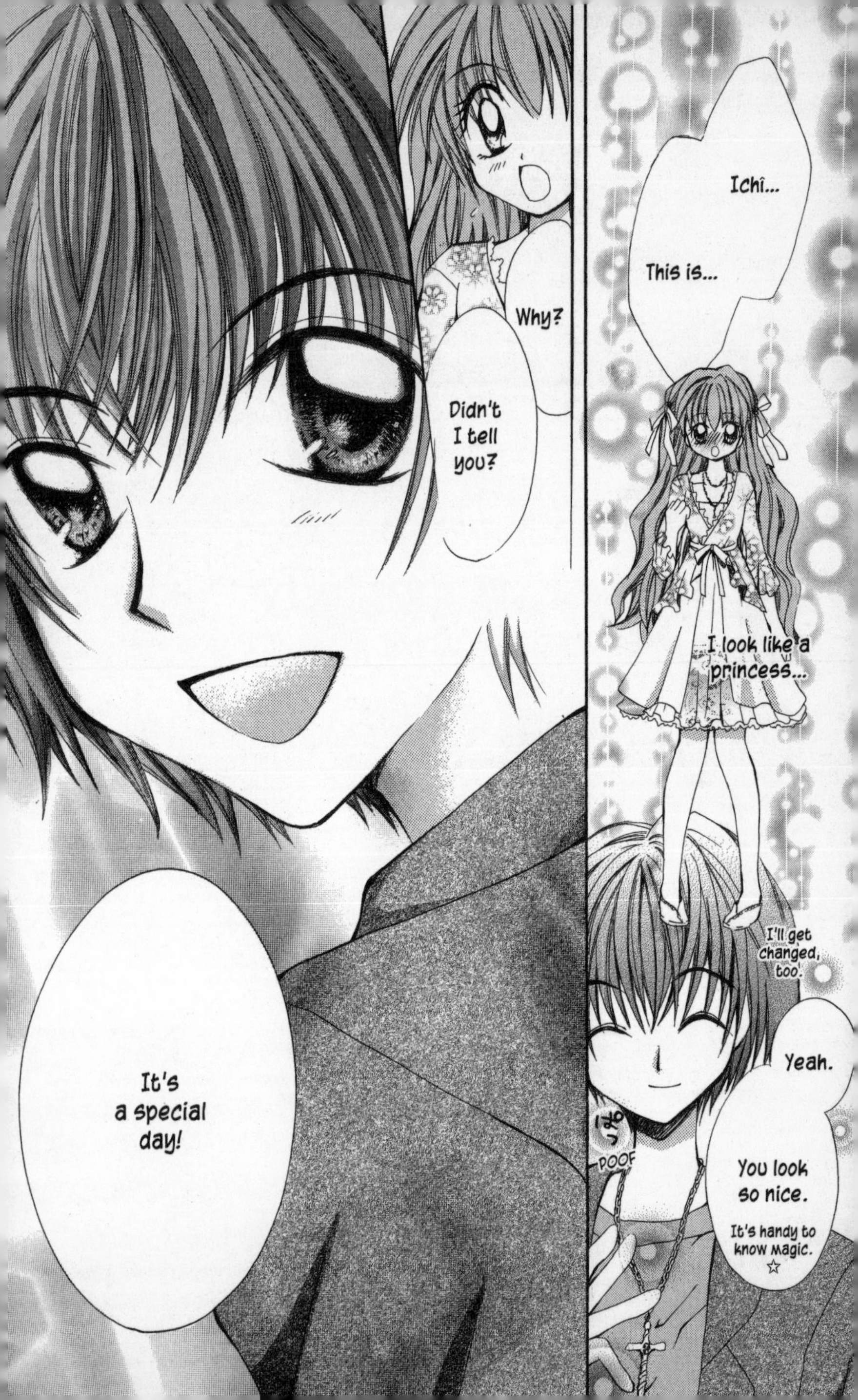
Ichi...
This is...
I look like a princess...
I'll get changed, too.
POOF
Yeah.
You look so nice.
It's handy to know magic. ☆
Why?
Didn't I tell you?
It's a special day!

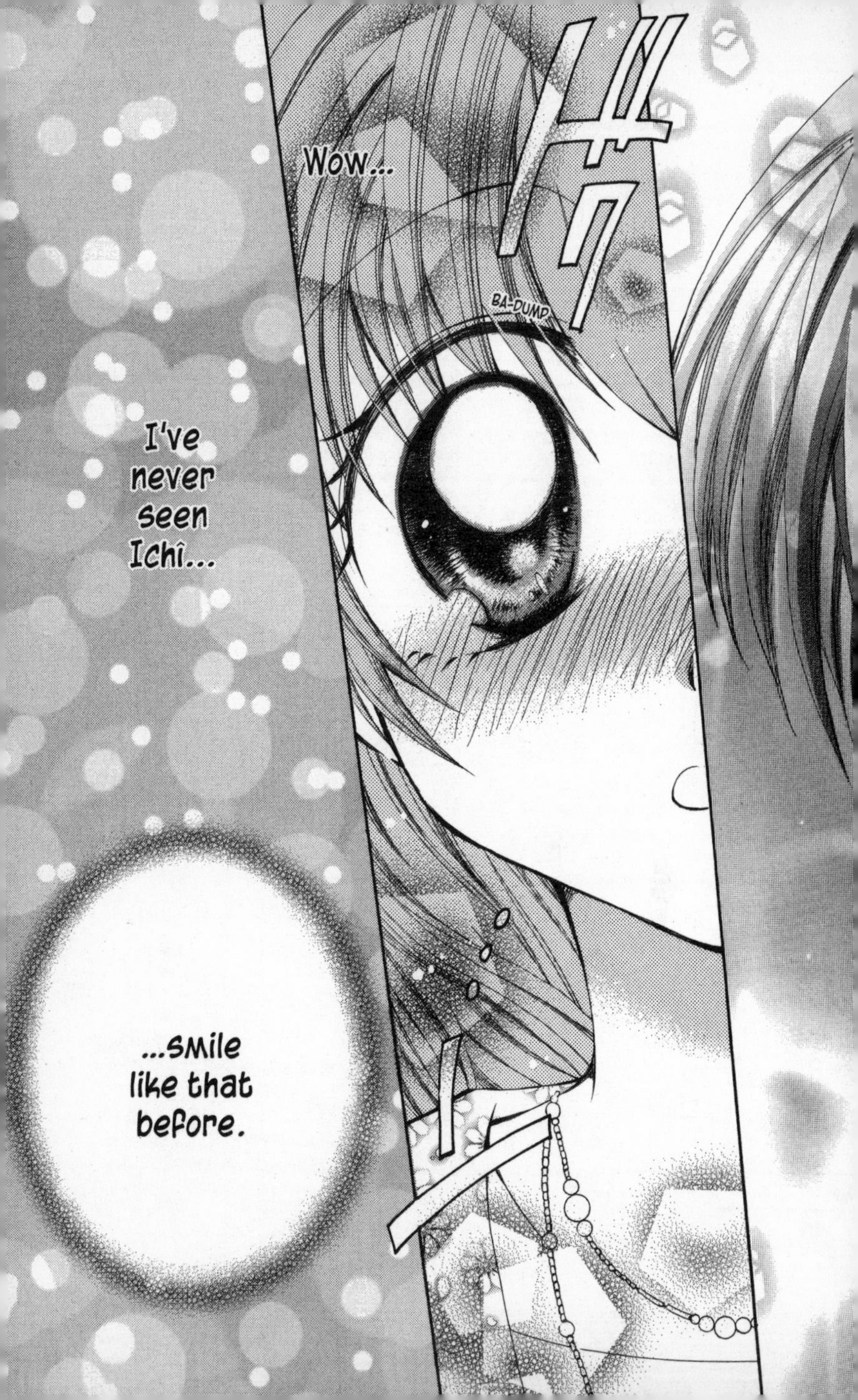
Wow...
BA-DUMP
I've never seen Ichi...
...smile like that before.

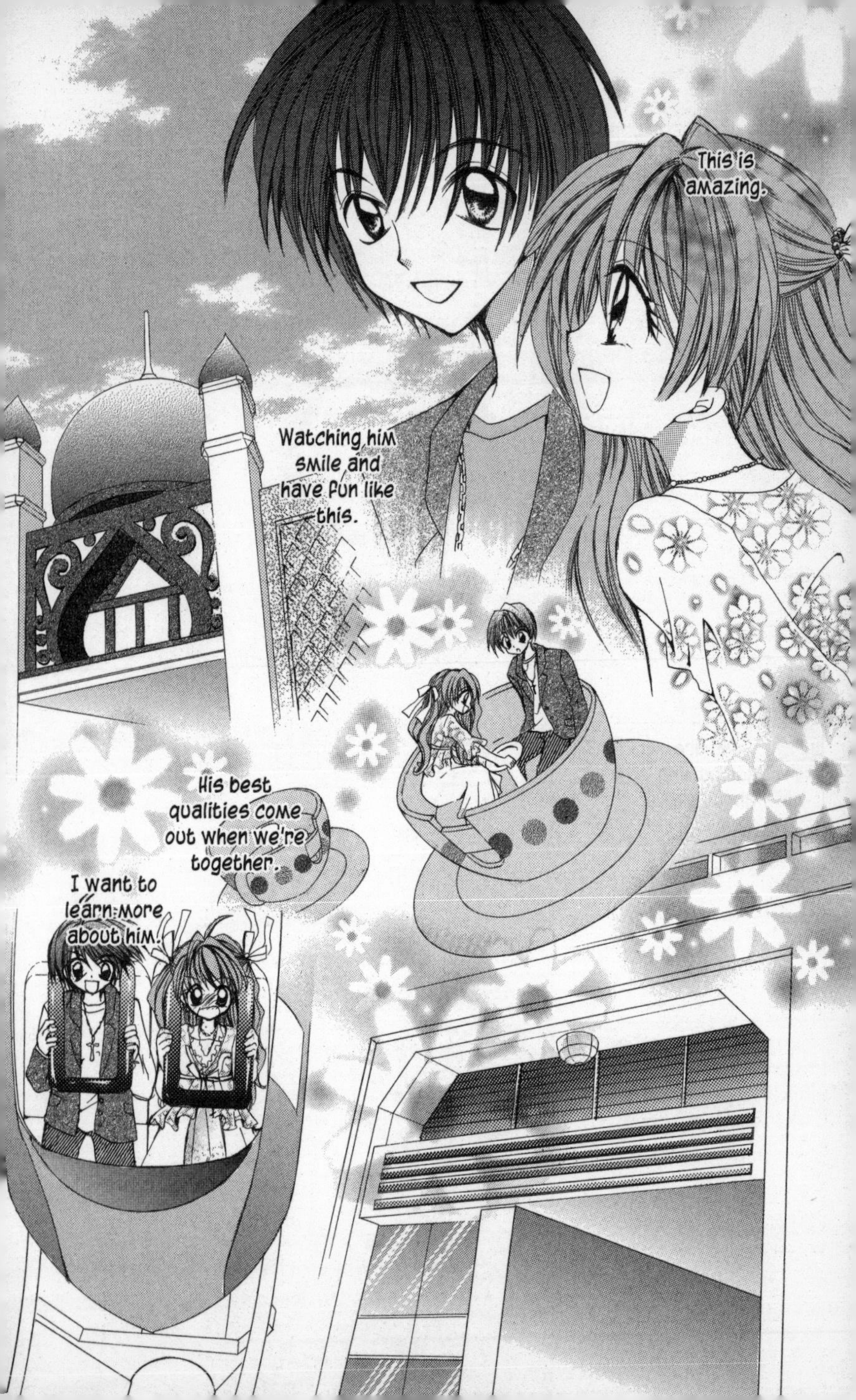
This is amazing.
Watching him smile and have fun like this.
His best qualities come out when we're together.
I want to learn more about him.

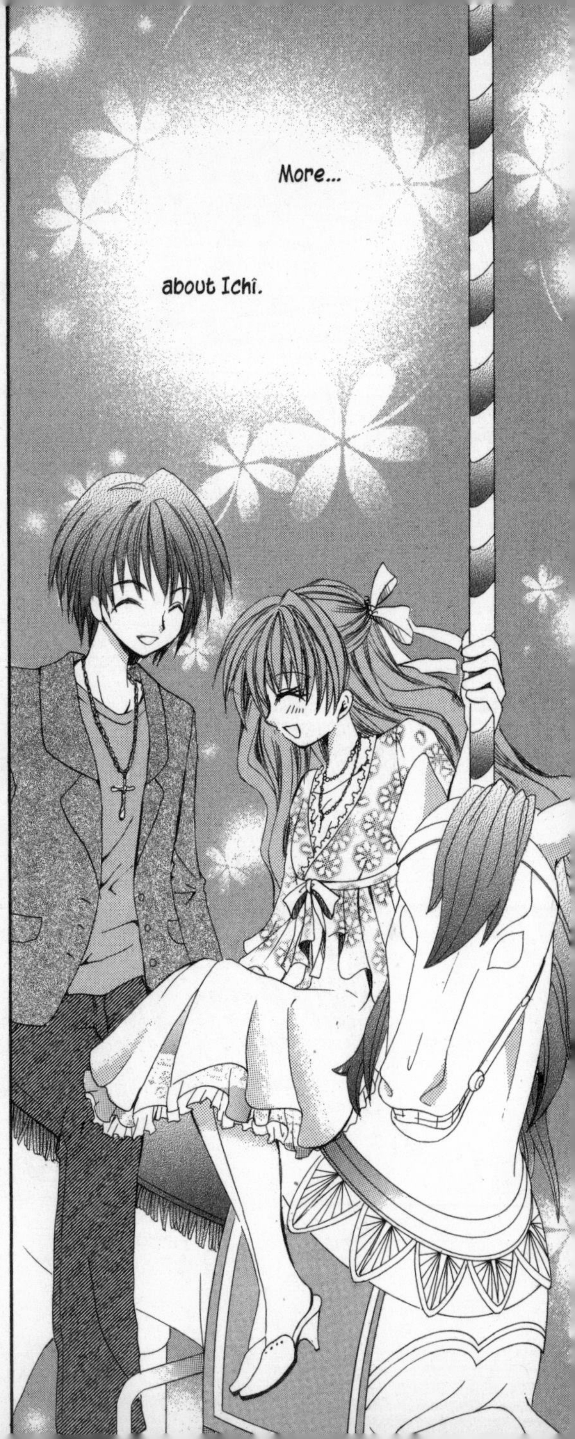
More...
about Ichi.

Force It on the Character

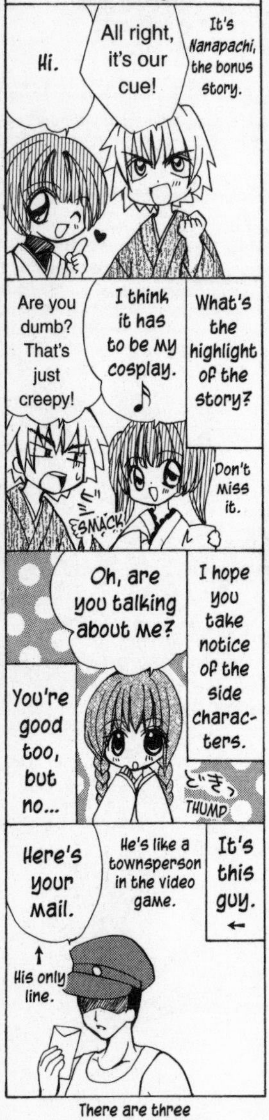
It's Nanapachi, the bonus story.
All right, it's our cue!
Hi.
What's the highlight of the story?
I think it has to be my cosplay. ♪
Are you dumb? That's just creepy!
Don't miss it.
SMACK
I hope you take notice of the side characters.
Oh, are you talking about me?
You're good too, but no...
THUMP
It's this guy. ←
He's like a townsperson in the video game.
Here's your mail.
↑ His only line.

There are three characters altogether.

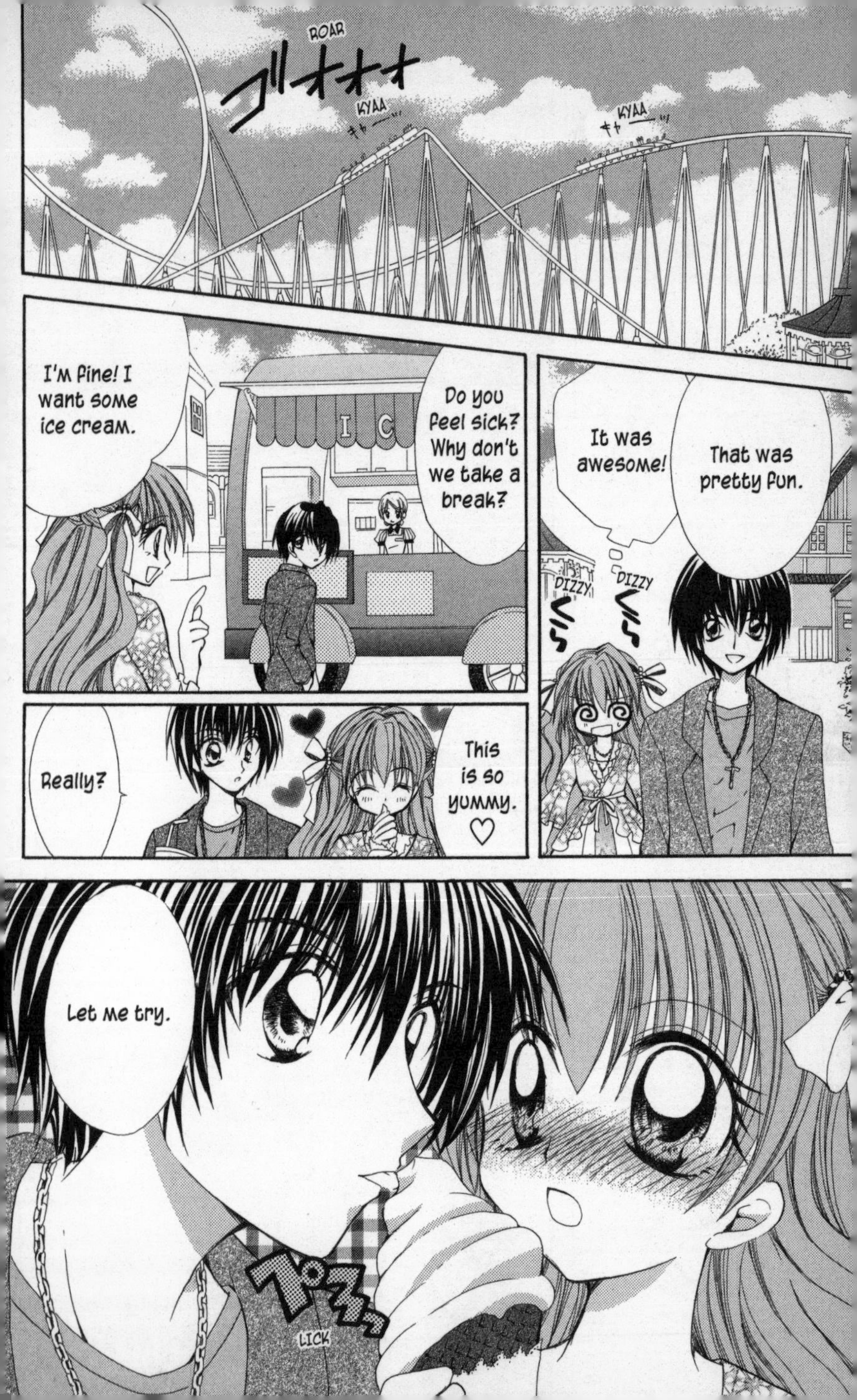
ROAR
KYAA
KYAA
That was pretty fun.
It was awesome!
DIZZY
DIZZY
Do you feel sick? Why don't we take a break?
I'm fine! I want some ice cream.
This is so yummy. ♡
Really?
Let me try.
LICK

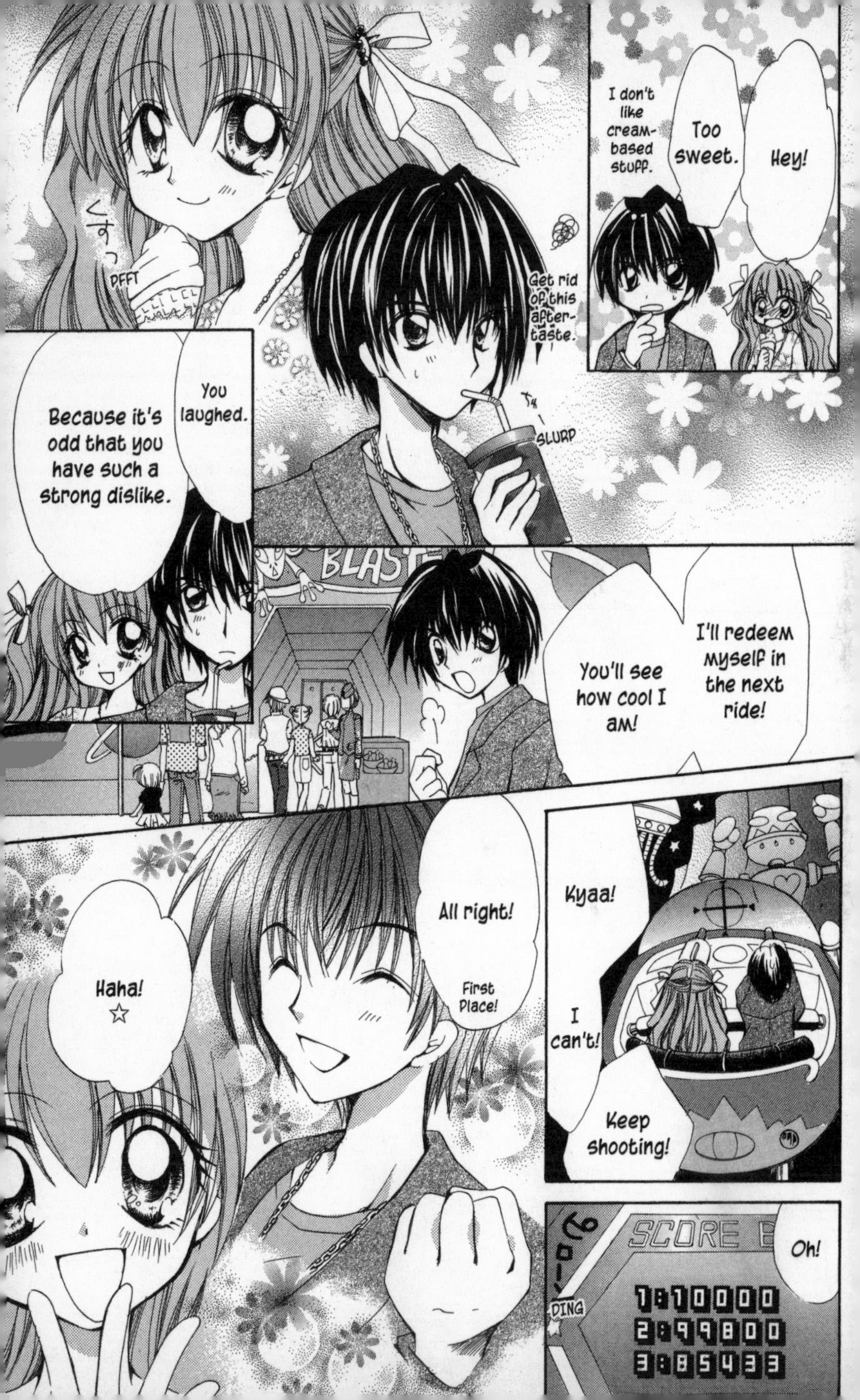
Hey!
Too sweet.
I don't like cream-based stuff.
くすっ
PFFT
Get rid of this after-taste.
SLURP
You laughed.
Because it's odd that you have such a strong dislike.
BLAST
I'll redeem myself in the next ride!
You'll see how cool I am!
Kyaa!
I can't!
Keep shooting!
SCORE B
Oh!
DING
1:10000
2:99800
3:85433
All right!
First Place!
Haha! ☆

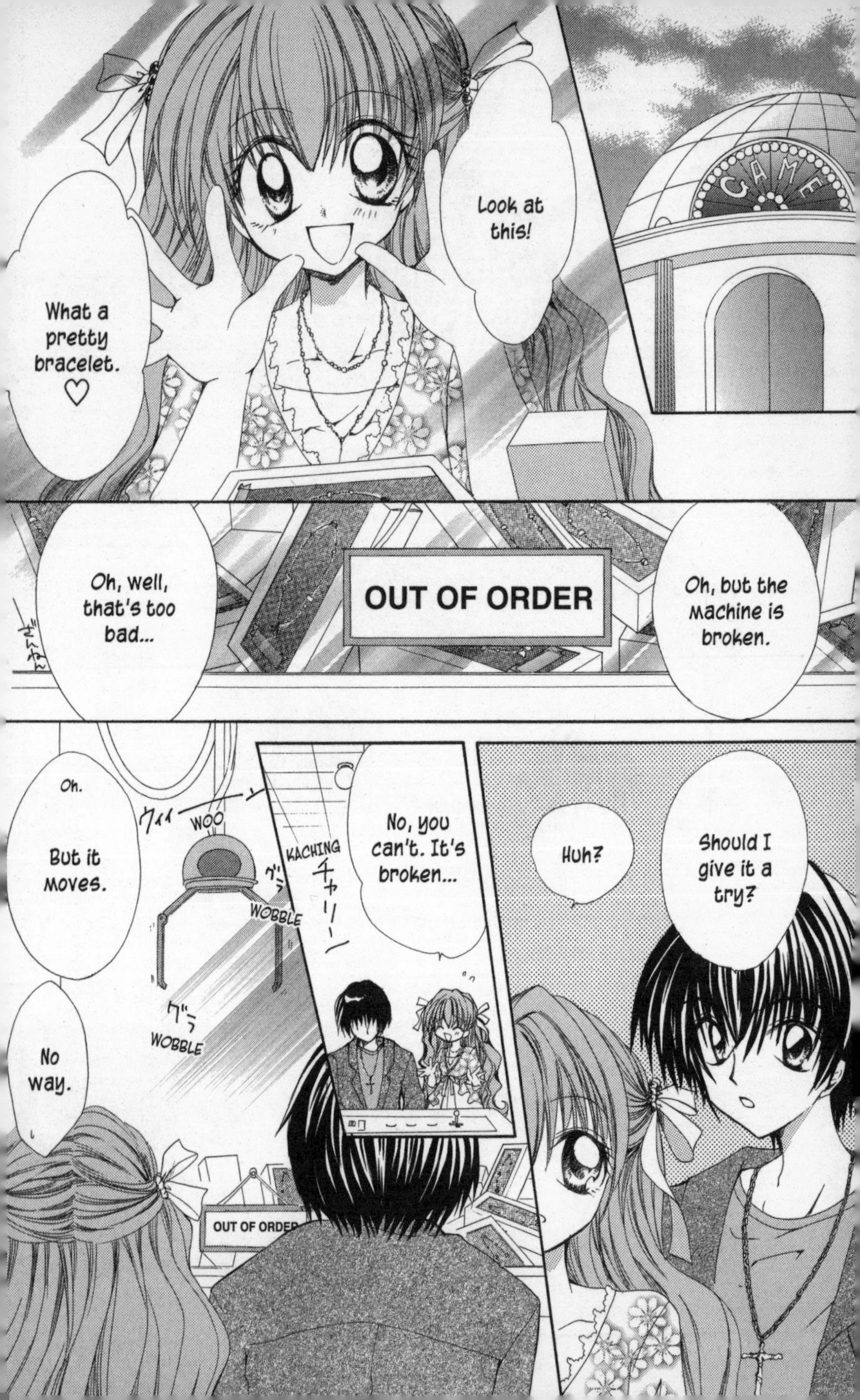
Look at this!
What a pretty bracelet. ♡
Oh, but the machine is broken.
OUT OF ORDER
Oh, well, that's too bad...
Should I give it a try?
Huh?
OUT OF ORDER
No, you can't. It's broken...
KACHING
Oh.
WOO
But it moves.
WOBBLE
WOBBLE
No way.

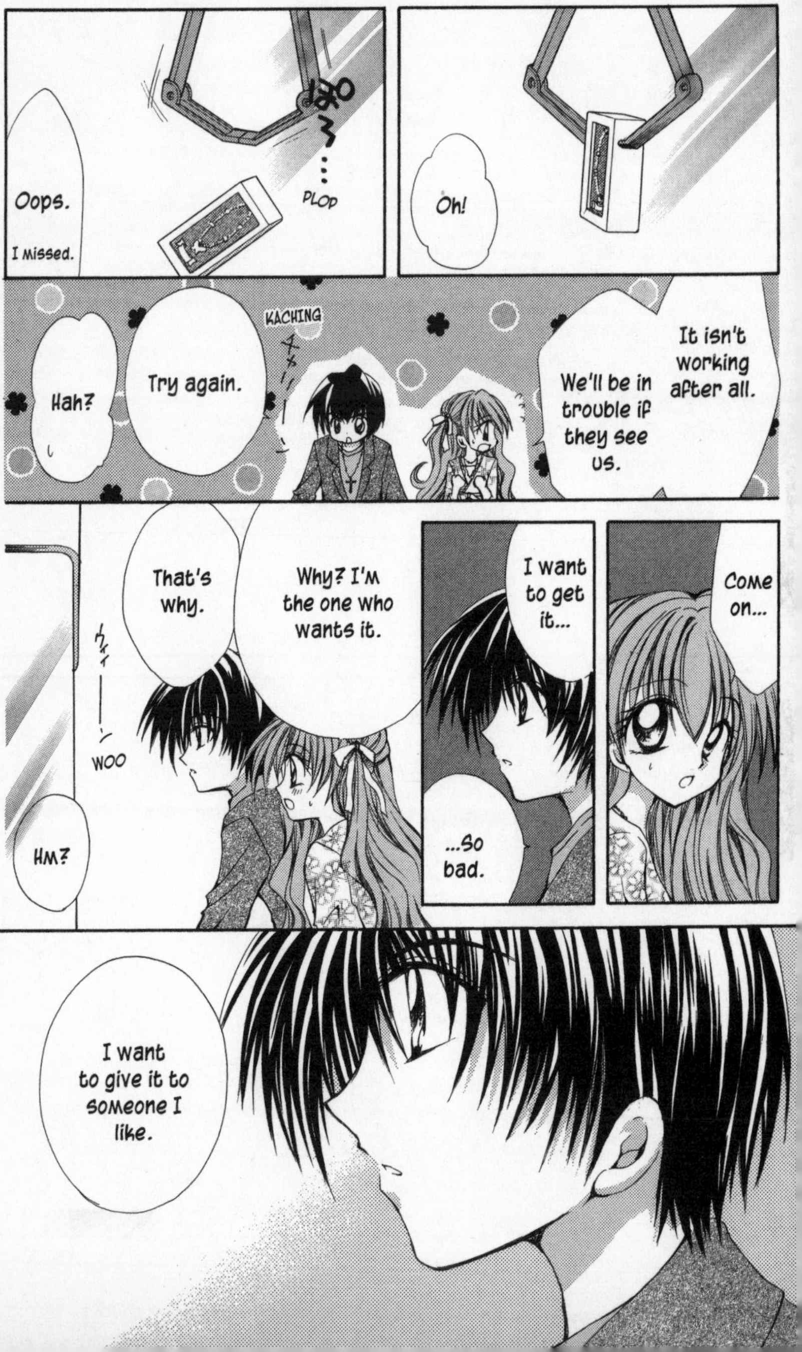
Oh!
PLOP
Oops.
I missed.
It isn't working after all.
We'll be in trouble if they see us.
KACHING
Try again.
Hah?
Come on...
I want to get it...
...So bad.
Why? I'm the one who wants it.
That's why.
WOO
Hm?
I want to give it to someone I like.

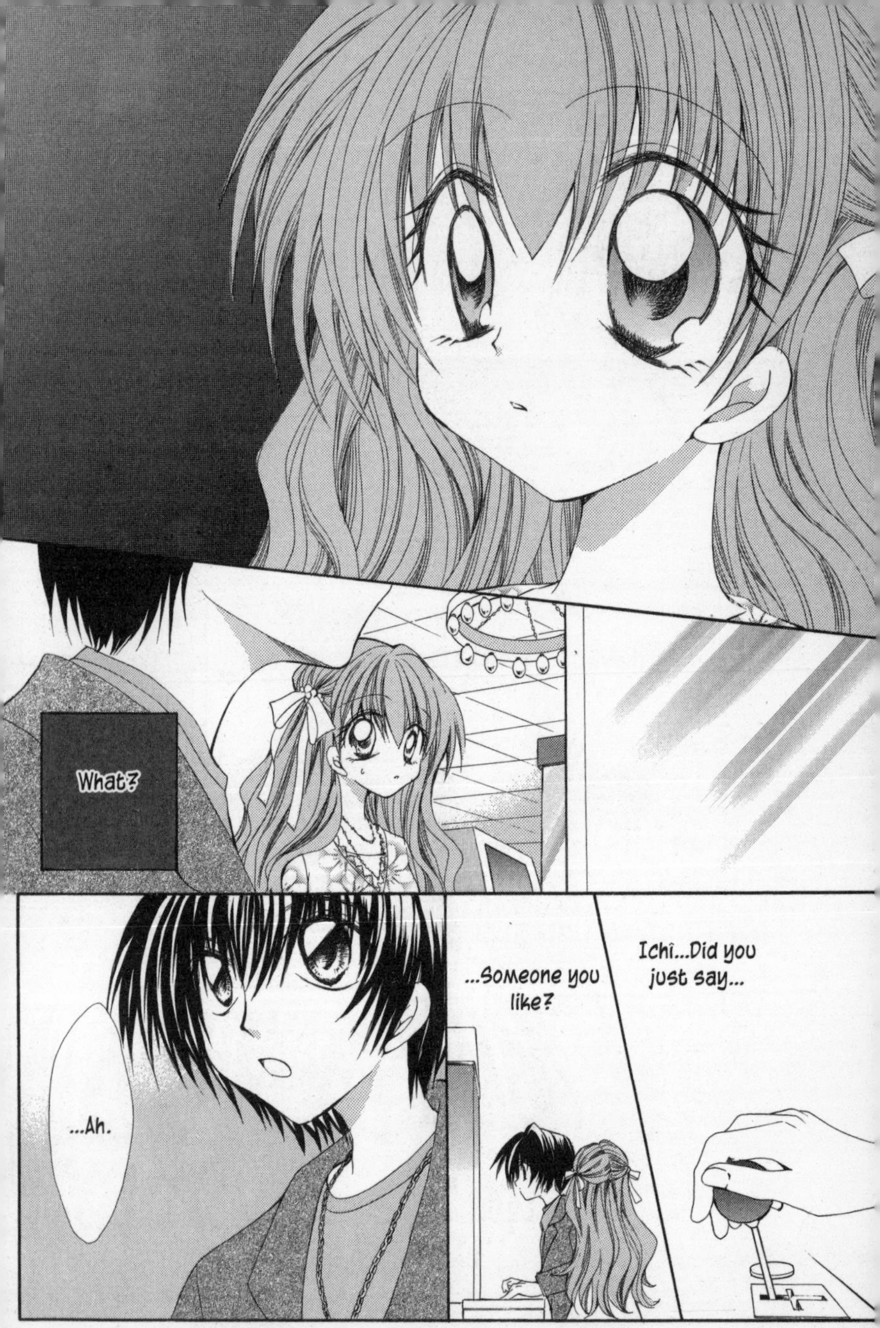
What?
Ichî...Did you just say...
...Someone you like?
...Ah.

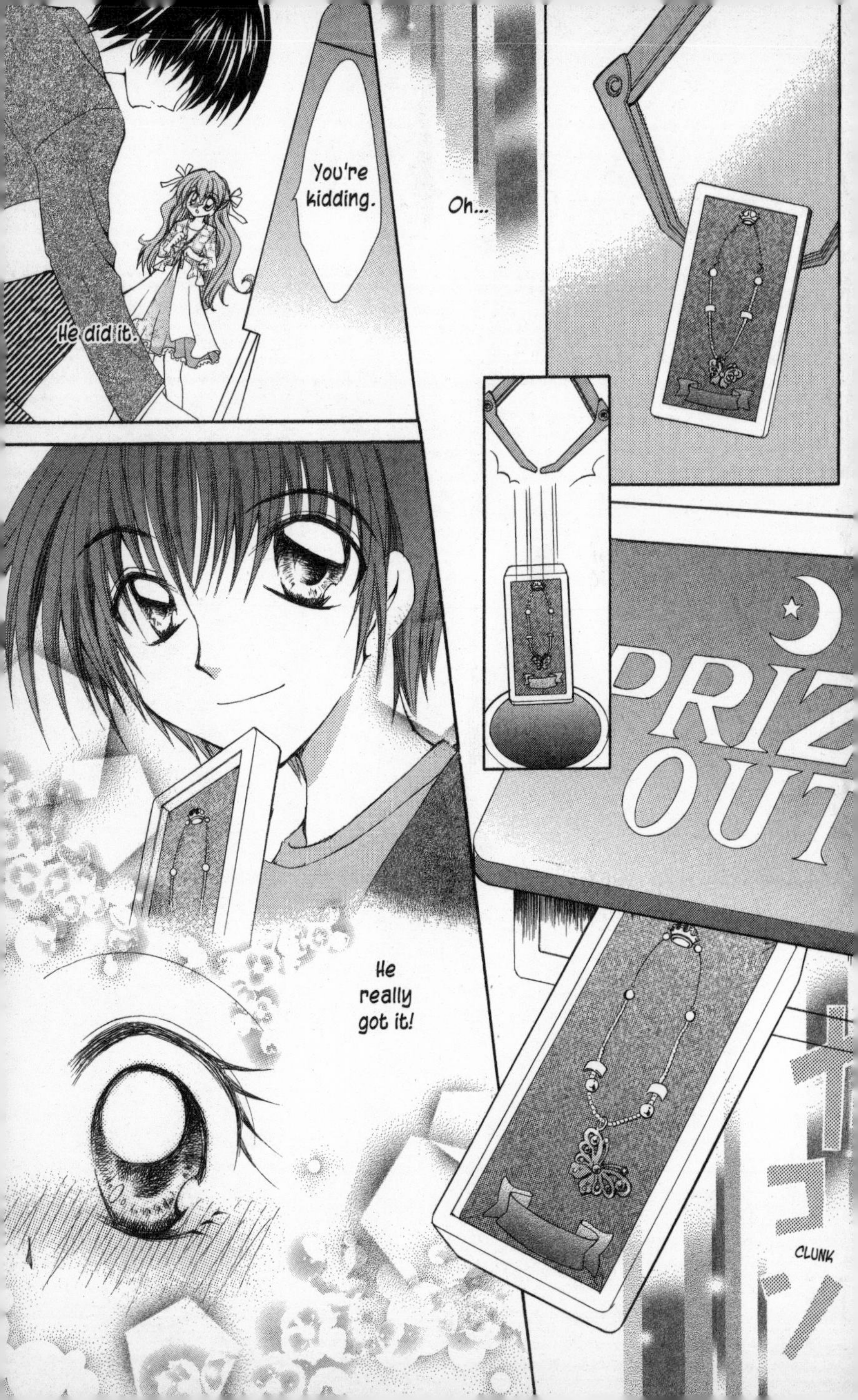
Oh...
You're kidding.
He did it.
PRIZ
OUT
CLUNK
He really got it!

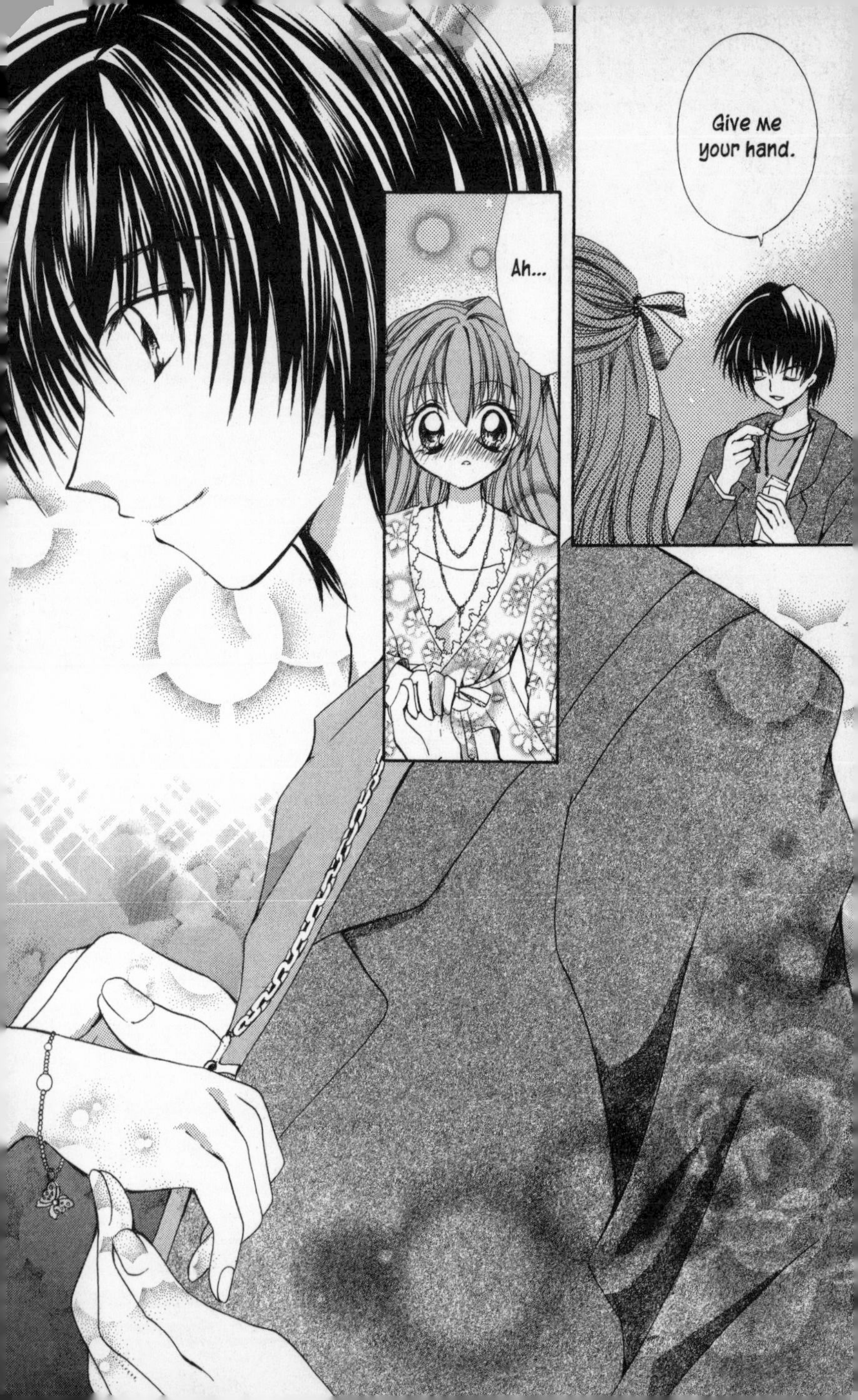
Give me your hand.
Ah...

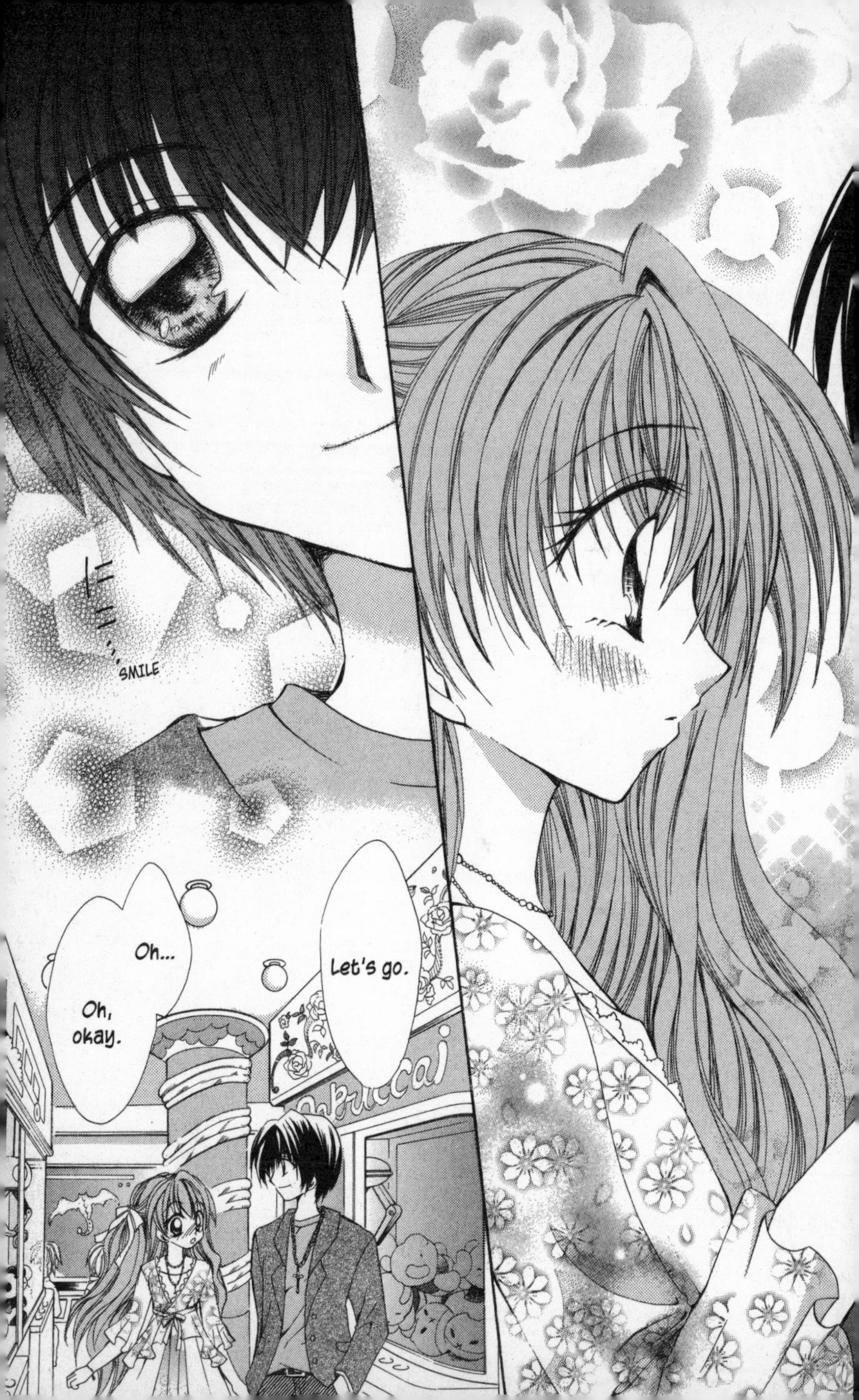
SMILE
Let's go.
Oh...
Oh, okay.

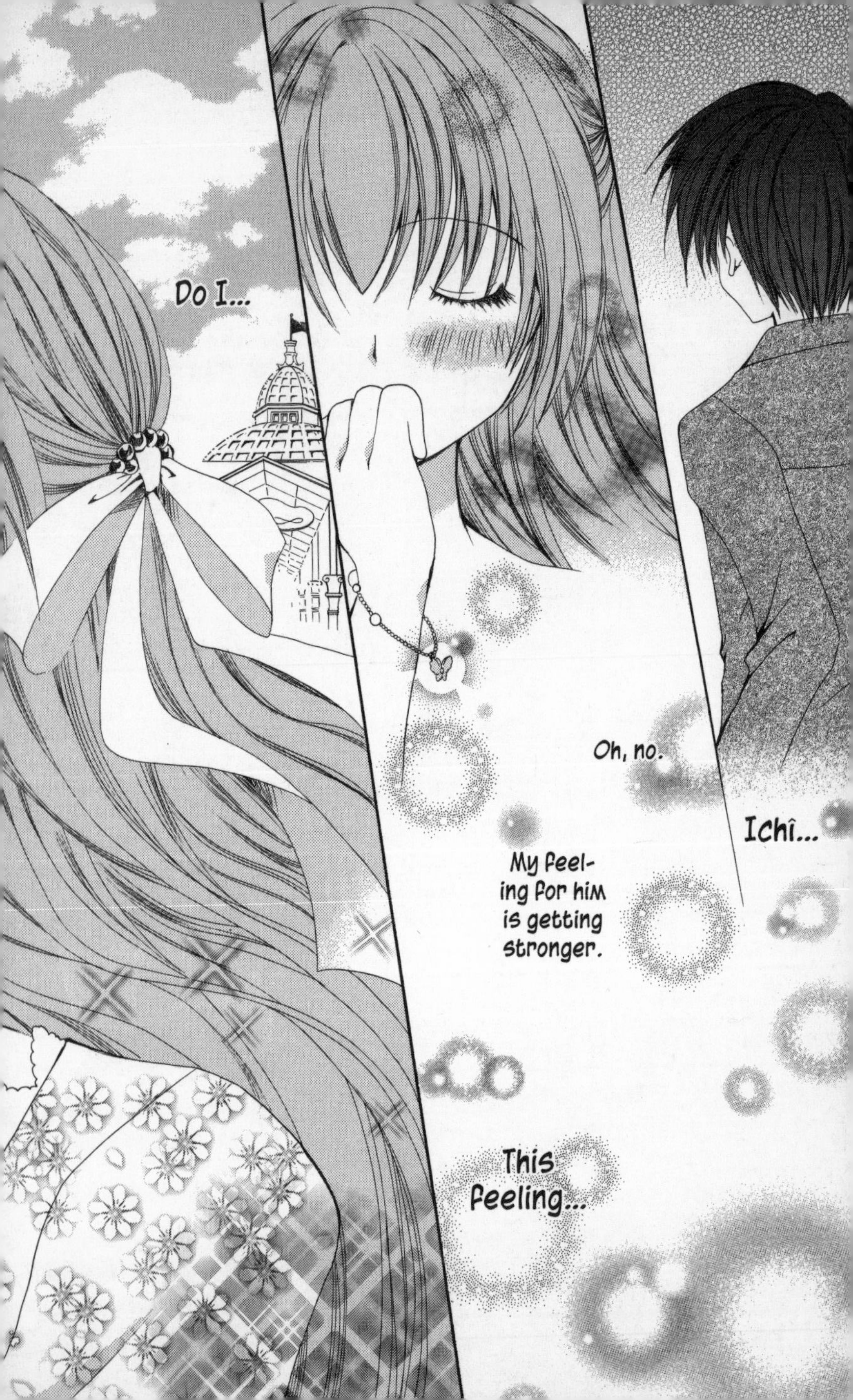
Ichi...
Oh, no.
My feeling for him is getting stronger.
This feeling...
Do I...

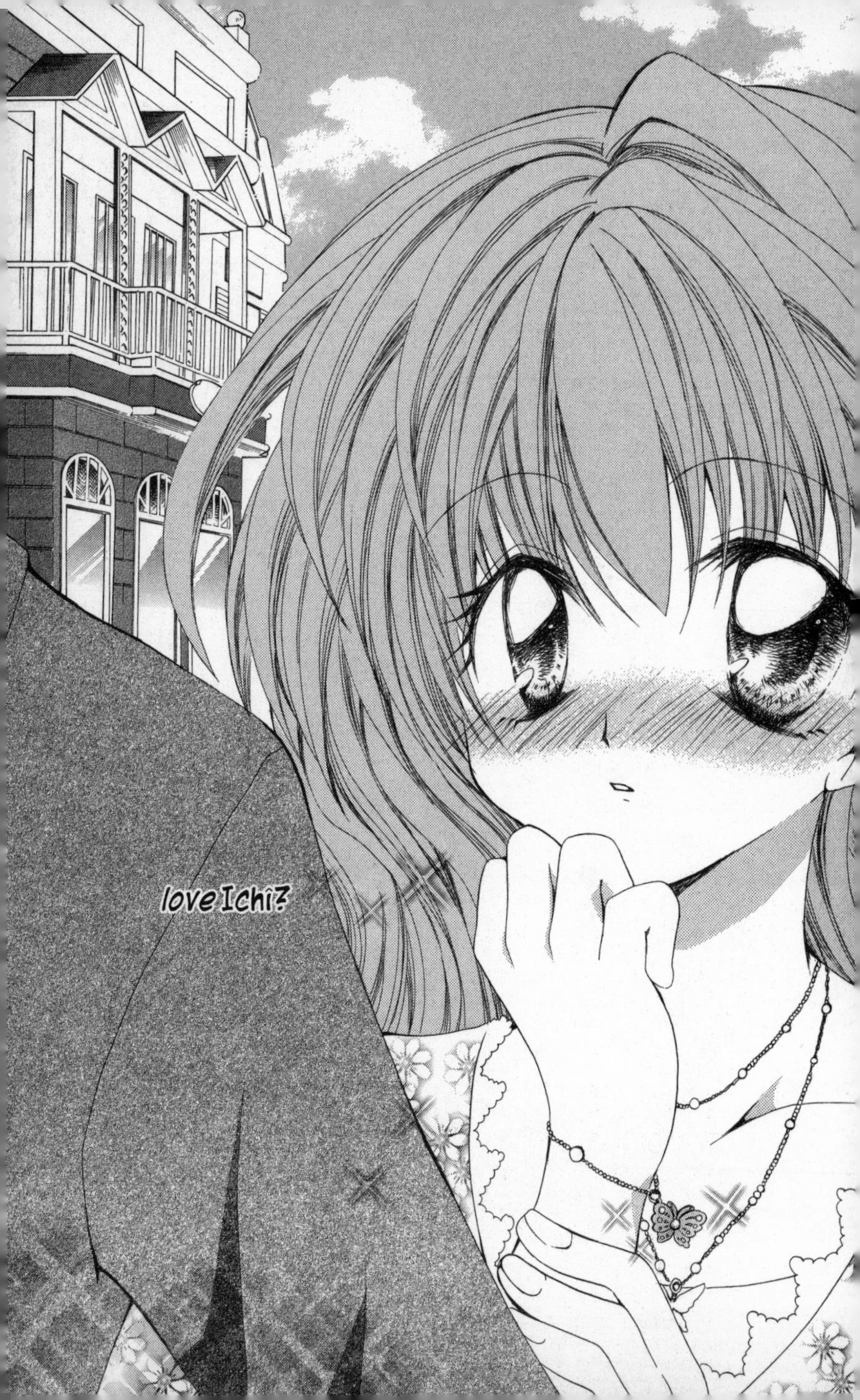
love Ichi?

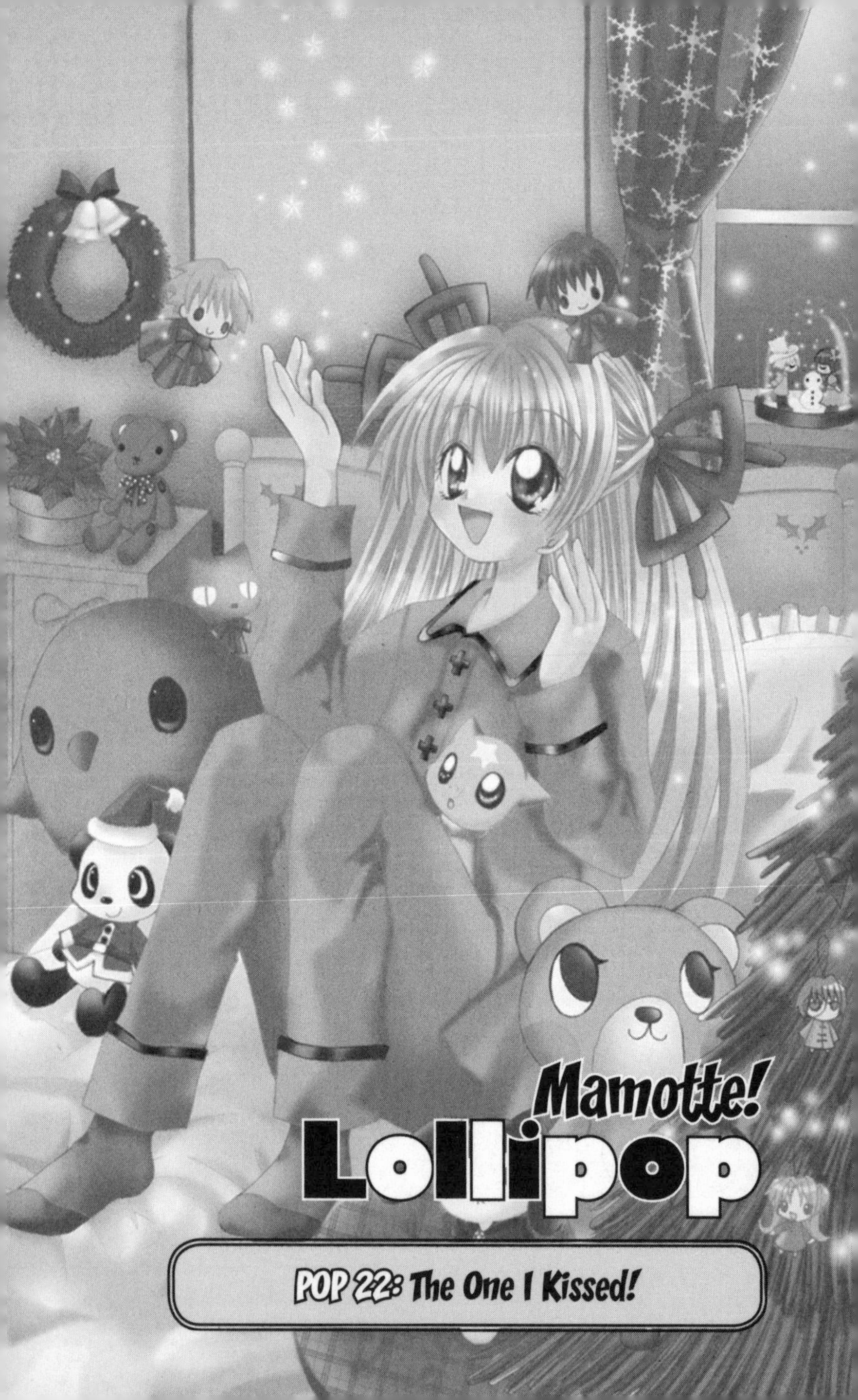
Mamotte! Lollipop
POP 22: The One I Kissed!

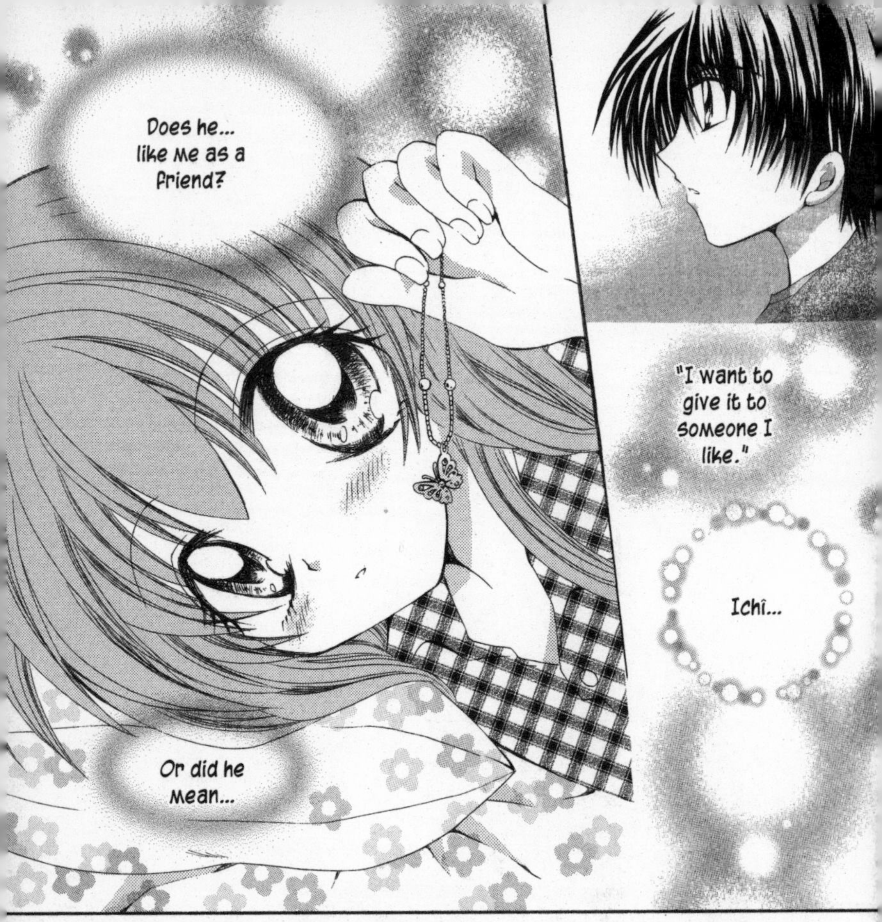
"I want to give it to someone I like."
Ichi...
Does he... like me as a friend?
Or did he mean...

PoP22 The One I Kissed!

This Christmas splash page was done in digital media. If you take a closer look, you can find all the characters in it.

I was pleased that I was able to explain King's past thoroughly. I hope I can reveal his whole backstory. It was nice being able to show some of Zero's inner feelings as well. He's probably changed since the beginning of the series. I think everyone is gradually maturing.

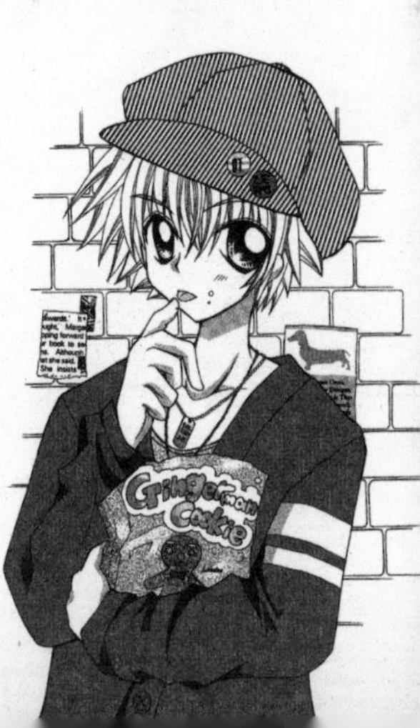

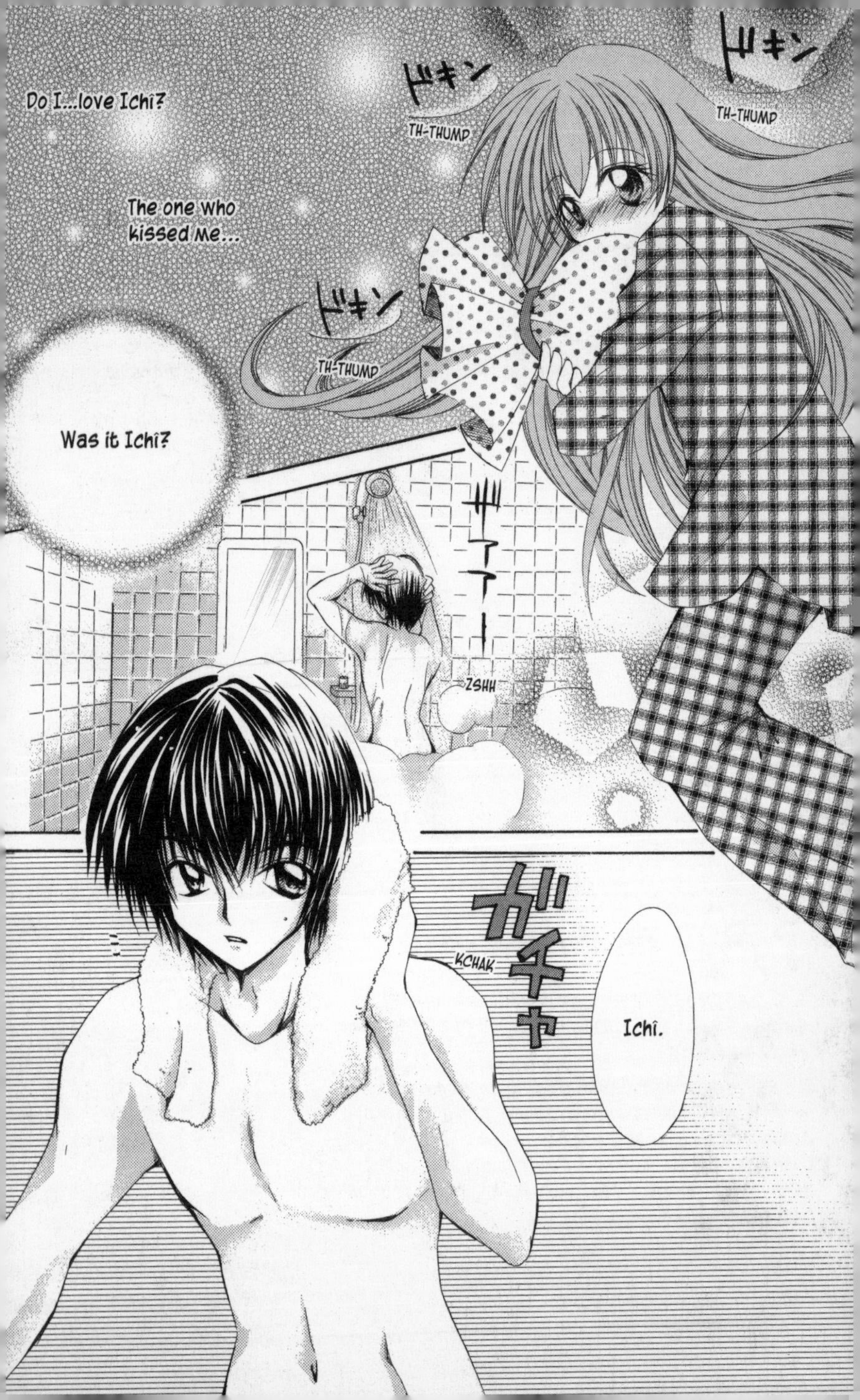

ドキン
TH-THUMP
ドキン
TH-THUMP
Do I...love Ichi?
The one who kissed me...
ドキン
TH-THUMP
Was it Ichi?
ザアアー
ZSHH
ガチャ
KCHAK
Ichi.

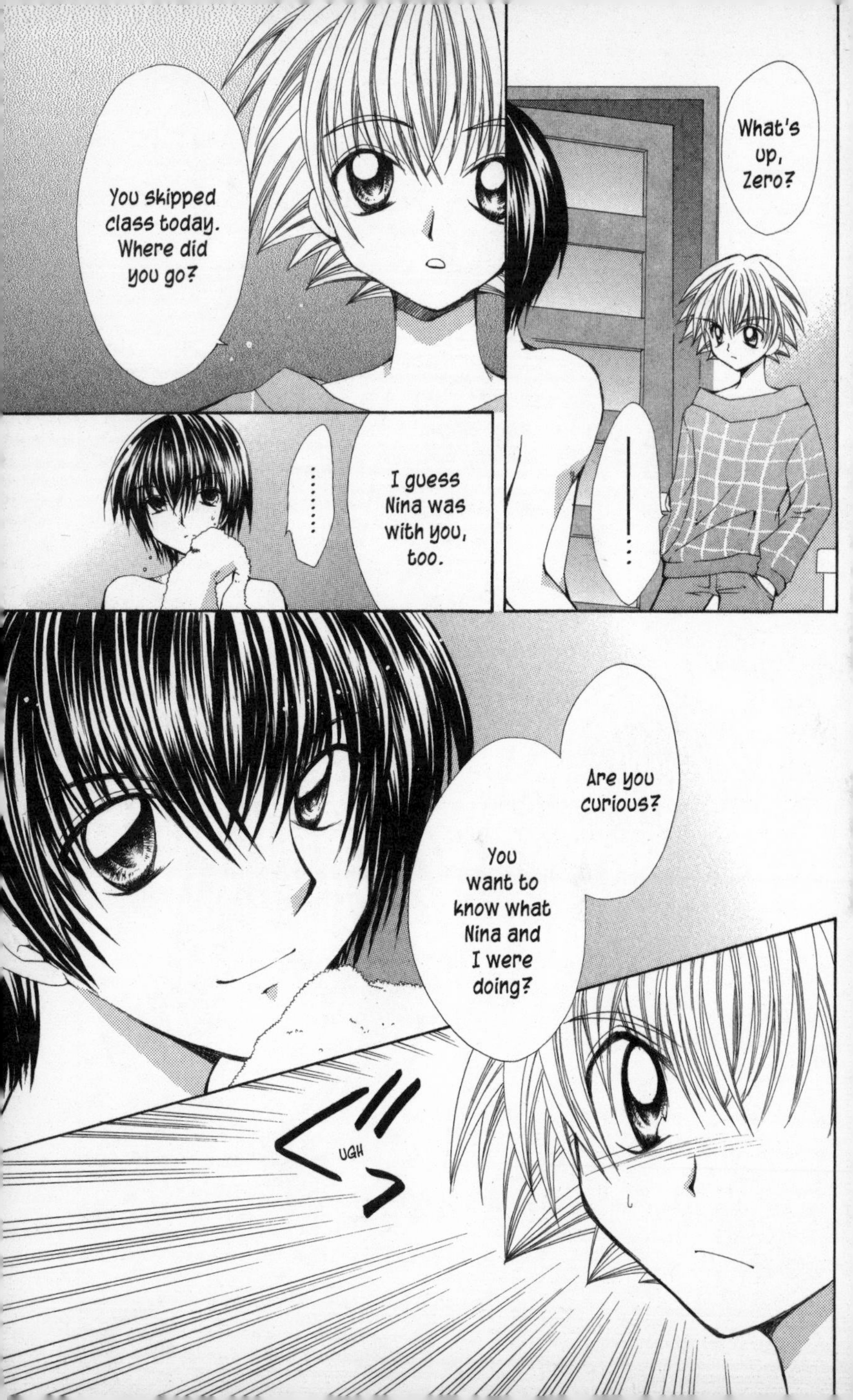
What's up, Zero?
......
You skipped class today. Where did you go?
I guess Nina was with you, too.
......
Are you curious?
You want to know what Nina and I were doing?
UGH

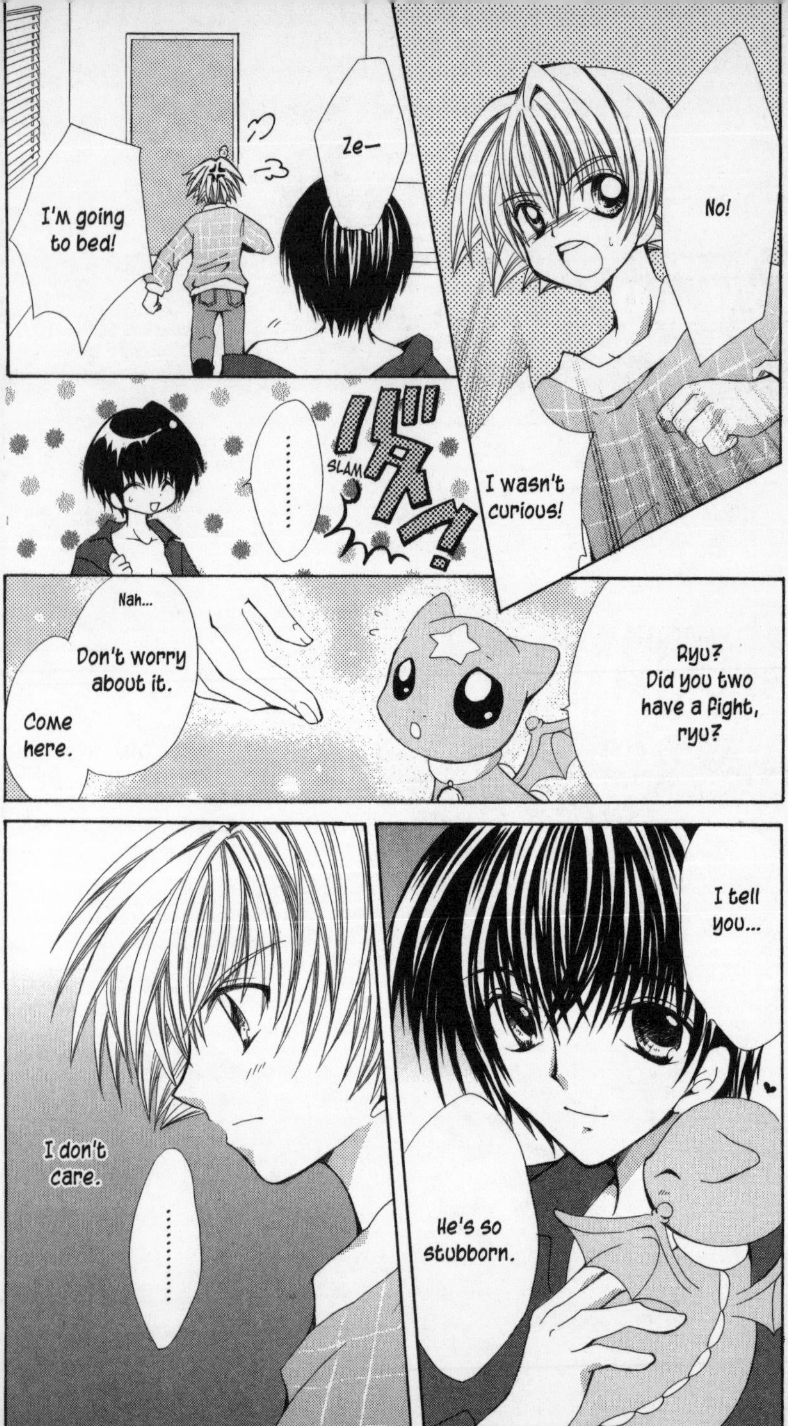
No!
I wasn't curious!
Ze—
I'm going to bed!
SLAM
......
Ryu? Did you two have a fight, ryu?
Nah...
Don't worry about it.
Come here.
I tell you...
He's so stubborn.
I don't care.
......

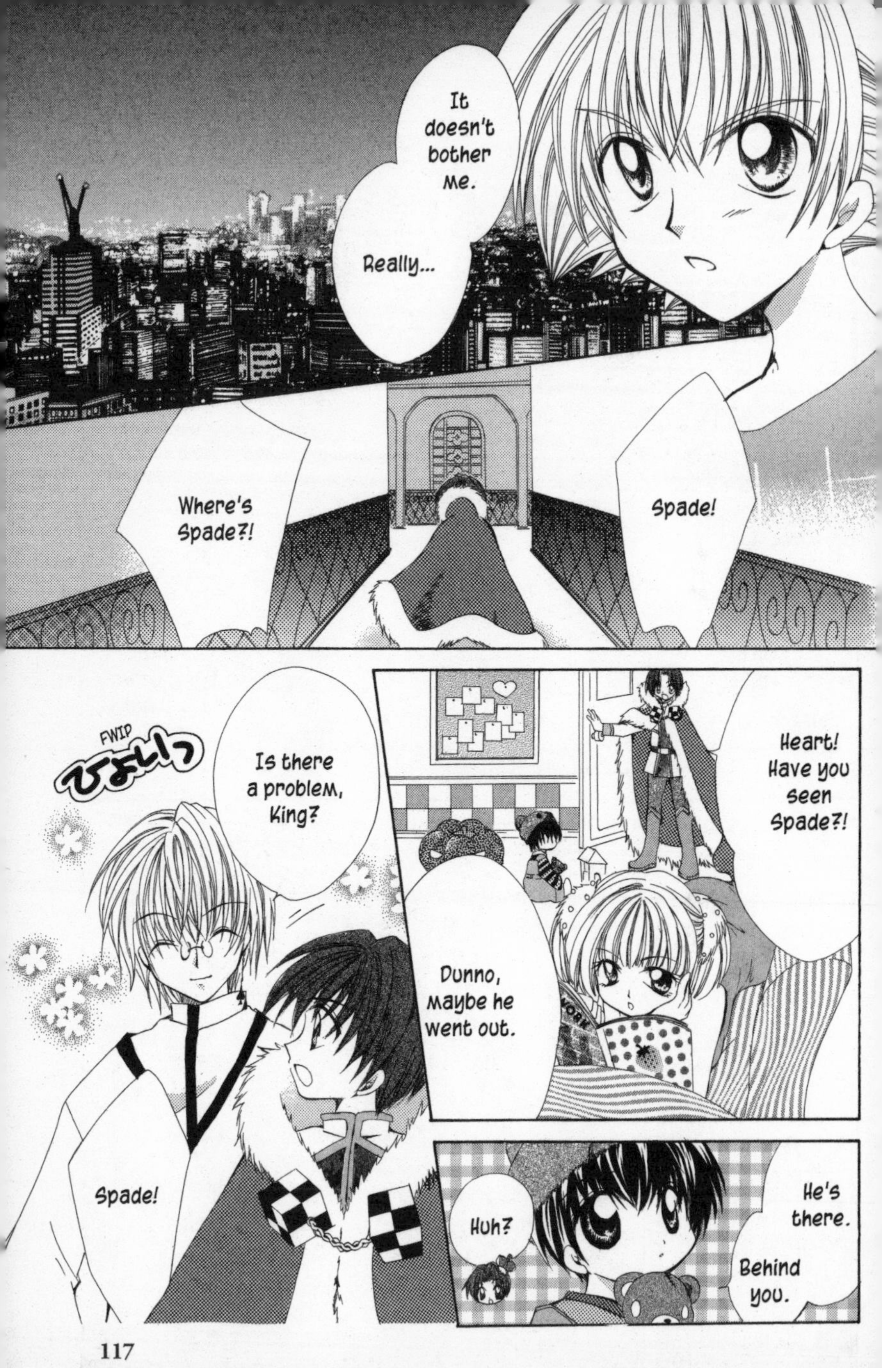
It doesn't bother me.
Really...
Spade!
Where's Spade?!
Heart! Have you seen Spade?!
Dunno, maybe he went out.
He's there.
Behind you.
Huh?
FWIP
ひょいっ
Is there a problem, King?
Spade!

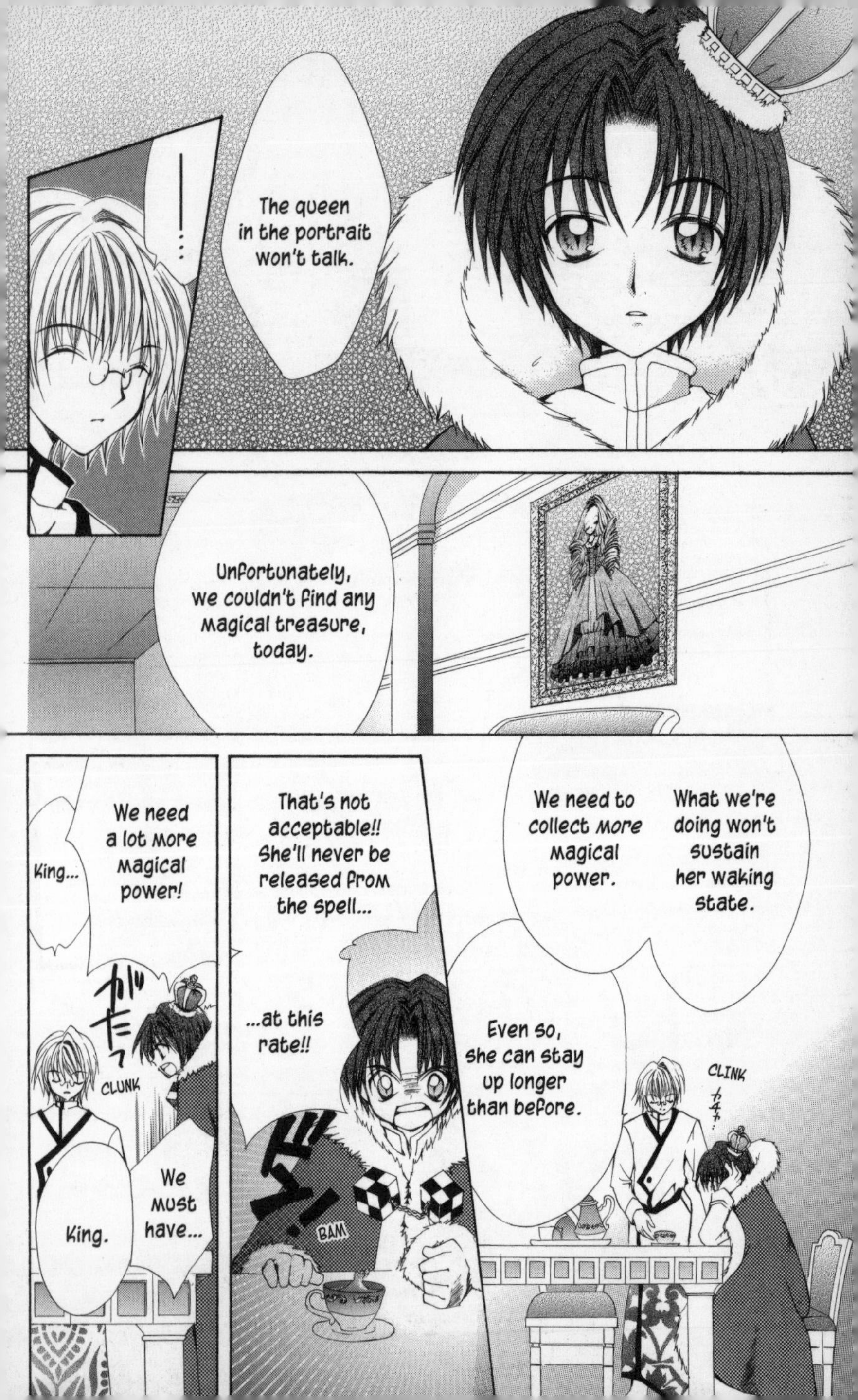
The queen in the portrait won't talk.
!...
Unfortunately, we couldn't find any magical treasure, today.
What we're doing won't sustain her waking state.
We need to collect more magical power.
Even so, she can stay up longer than before.
CLINK
That's not acceptable!! She'll never be released from the spell...
...at this rate!!
BAM
We need a lot more magical power!
King...
CLUNK
We must have...
King.

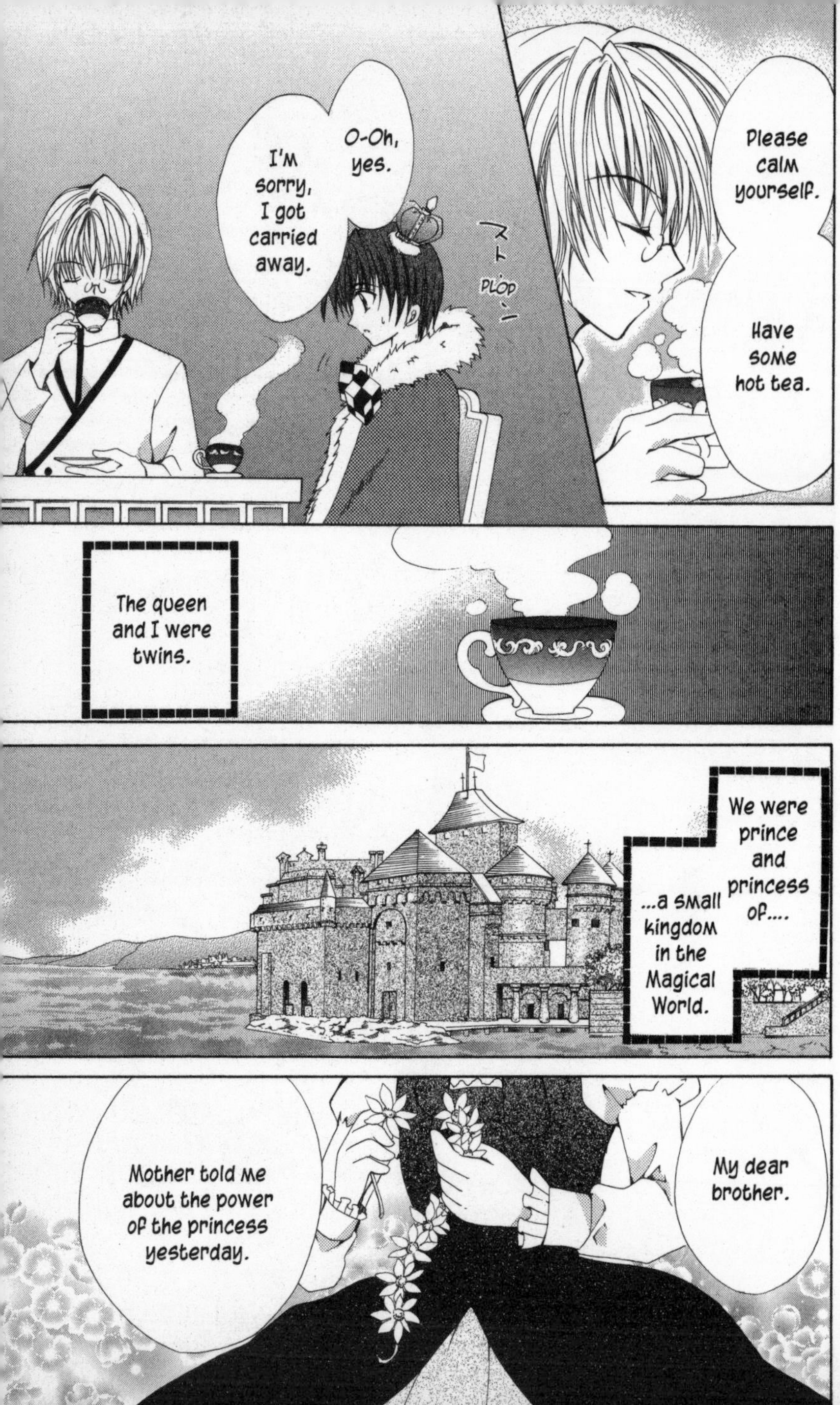
Please calm yourself.
Have some hot tea.
O-Oh, yes.
I'm sorry, I got carried away.
PLOP
The queen and I were twins.
We were prince and princess of....
...a small kingdom in the Magical World.
My dear brother.
Mother told me about the power of the princess yesterday.

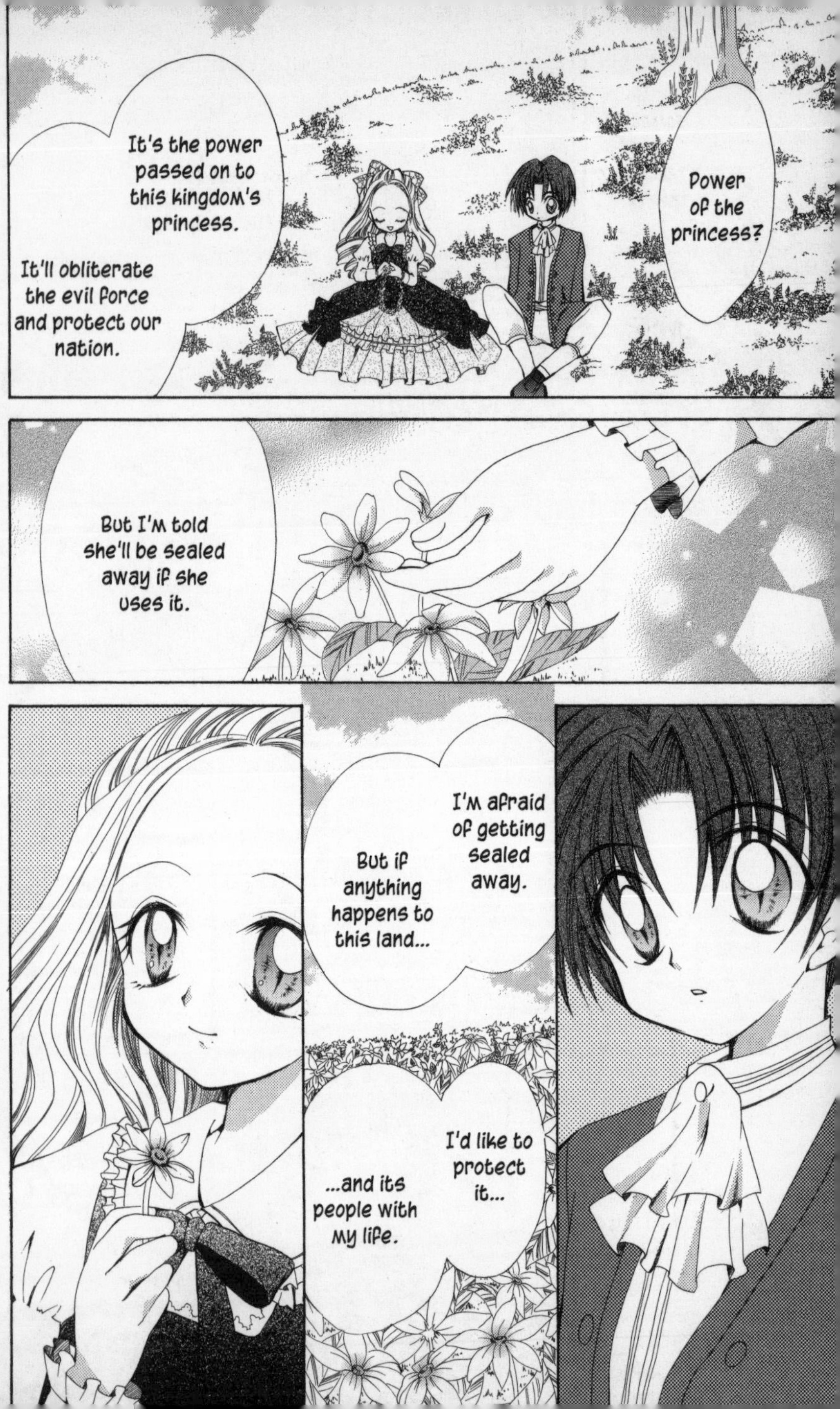

Power of the princess?
It's the power passed on to this kingdom's princess.
It'll obliterate the evil force and protect our nation.
But I'm told she'll be sealed away if she uses it.
I'm afraid of getting sealed away.
But if anything happens to this land...
I'd like to protect it...
...and its people with my life.

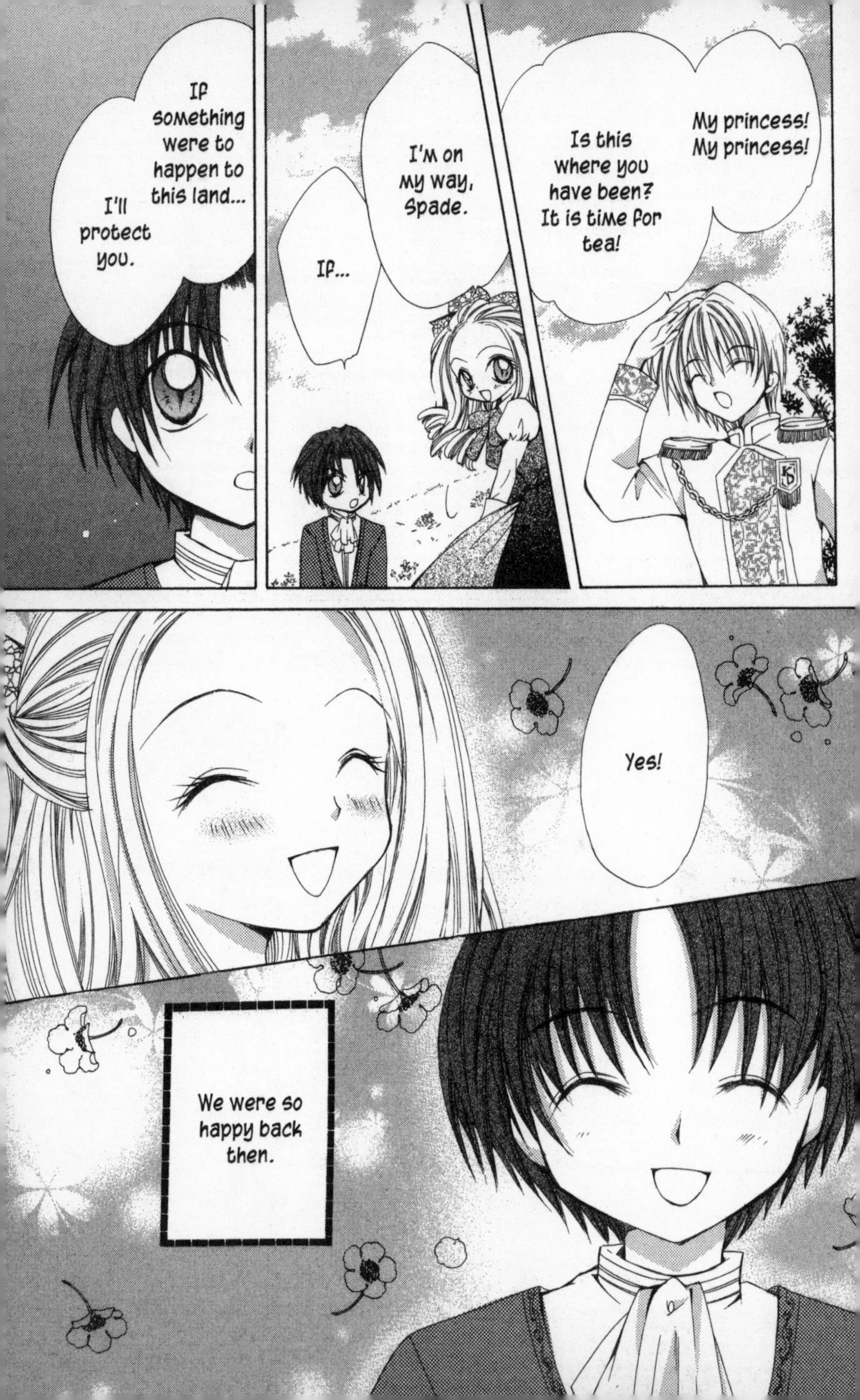
My princess! My princess!
Is this where you have been? It is time for tea!
I'm on my way, Spade.
If...
If something were to happen to this land...
I'll protect you.
Yes!
We were so happy back then.

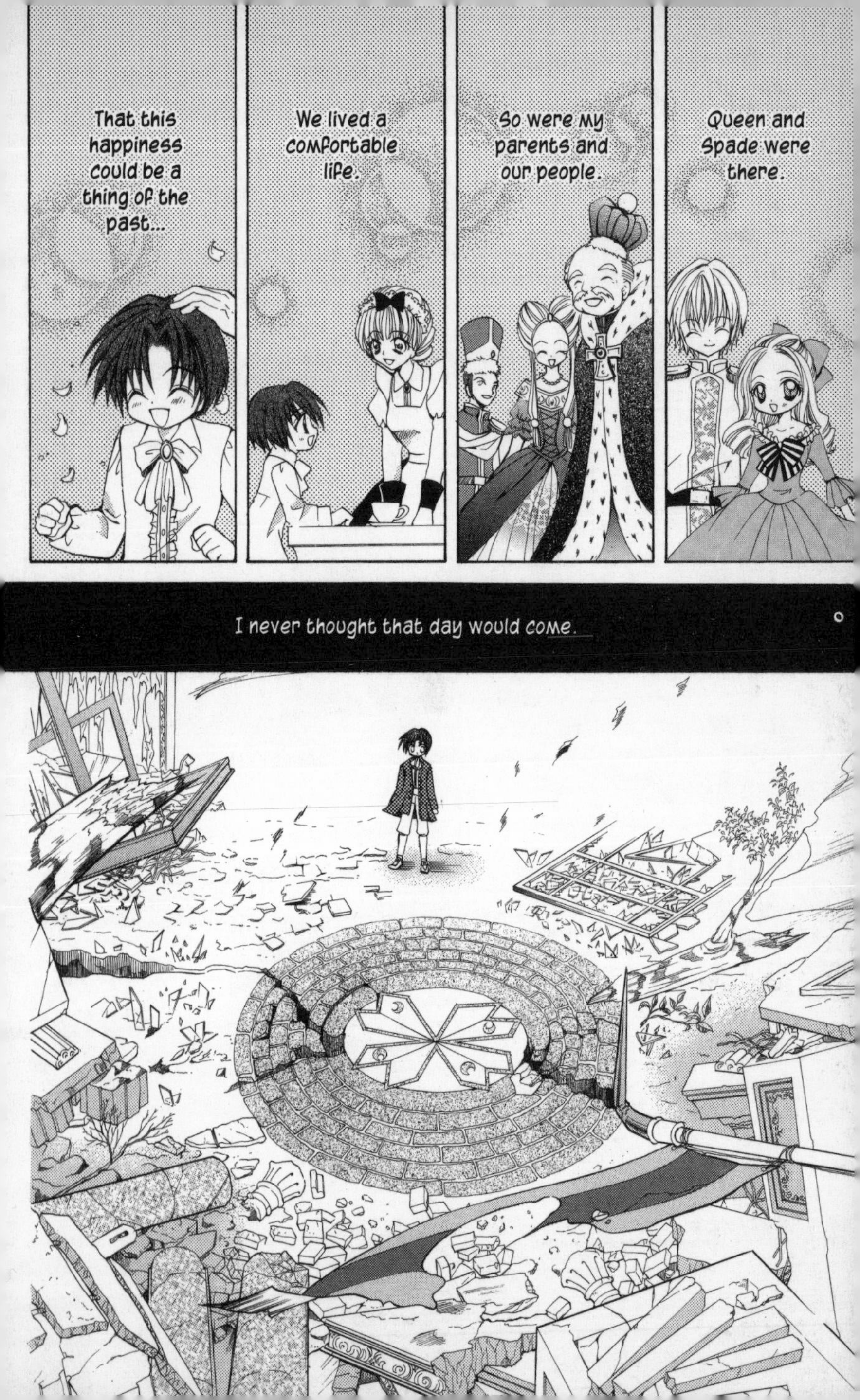
Queen and Spade were there.
So were my parents and our people.
We lived a comfortable life.
That this happiness could be a thing of the past...
I never thought that day would come.

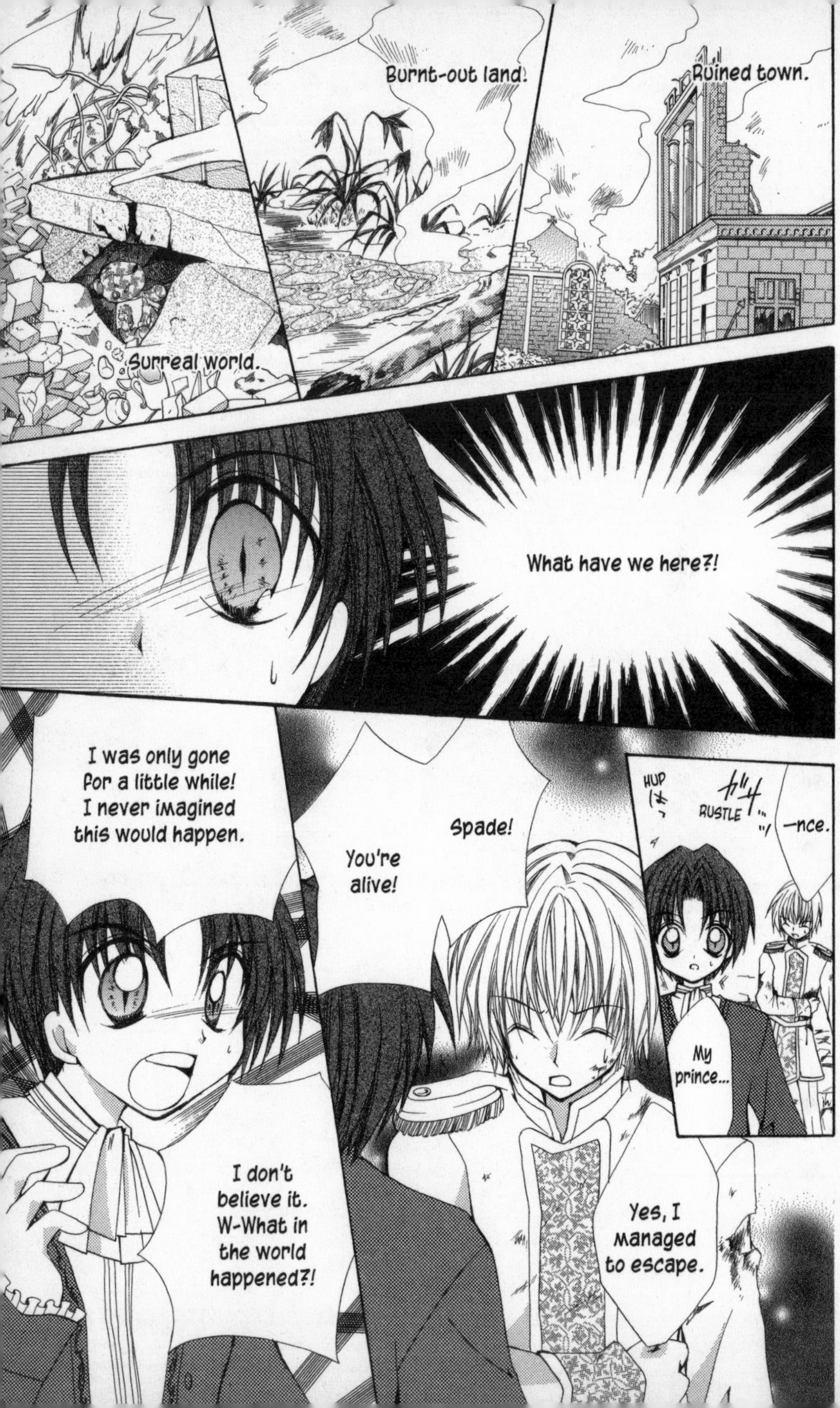

Ruined town.
Burnt-out land.
Surreal world.
What have we here?!
HUP
はっ
RUSTLE
ガサ
—nce.
My prince...
Spade!
You're alive!
Yes, I managed to escape.
I was only gone for a little while! I never imagined this would happen.
I don't believe it. W-What in the world happened?!

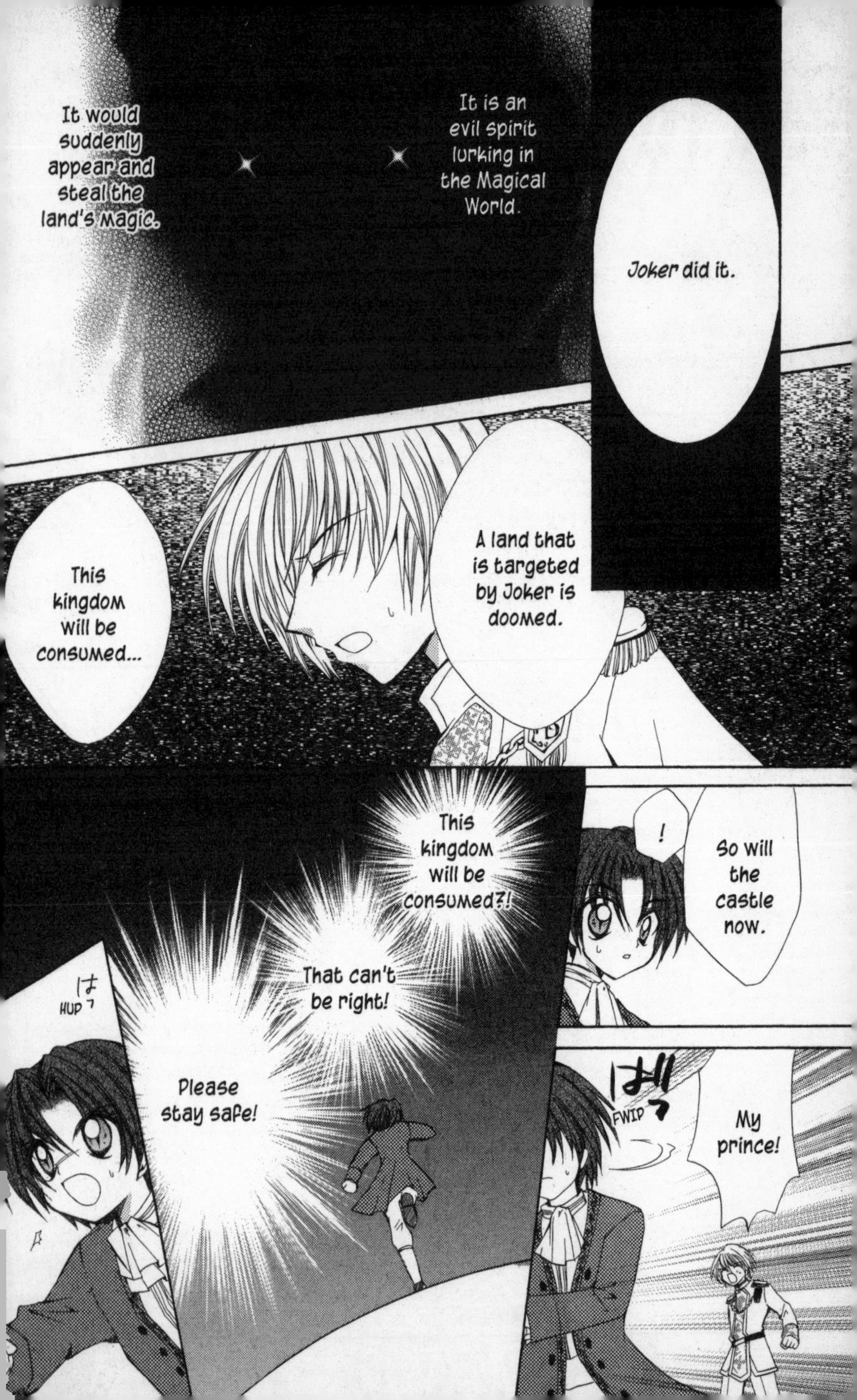
Joker did it.
It is an evil spirit lurking in the Magical World.
It would suddenly appear and steal the land's magic.
A land that is targeted by Joker is doomed.
This kingdom will be consumed...
!
So will the castle now.
FWIP
My prince!
This kingdom will be consumed?!
That can't be right!
Please stay safe!
HUP

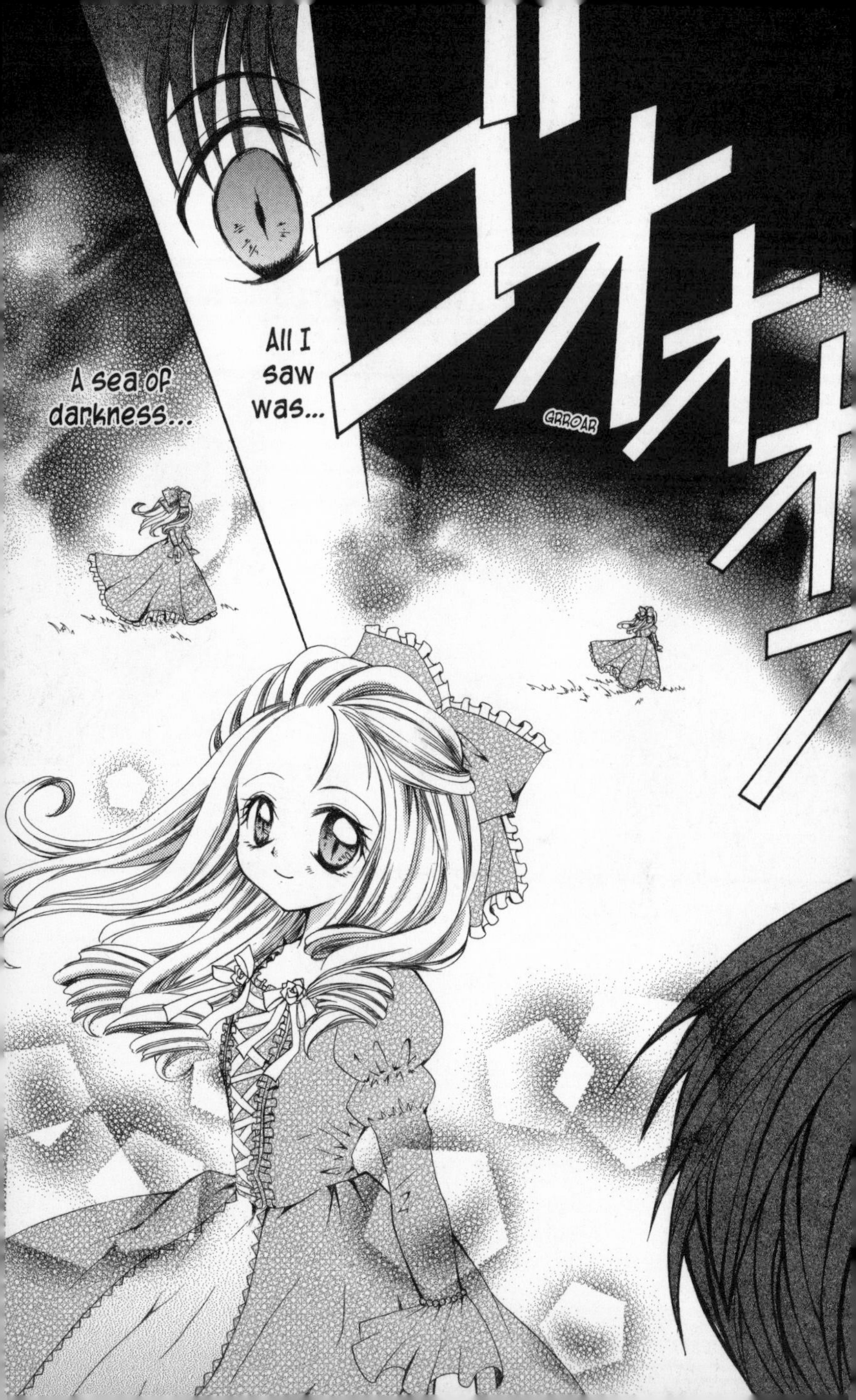
GRROAR
All I saw was...
A sea of darkness...

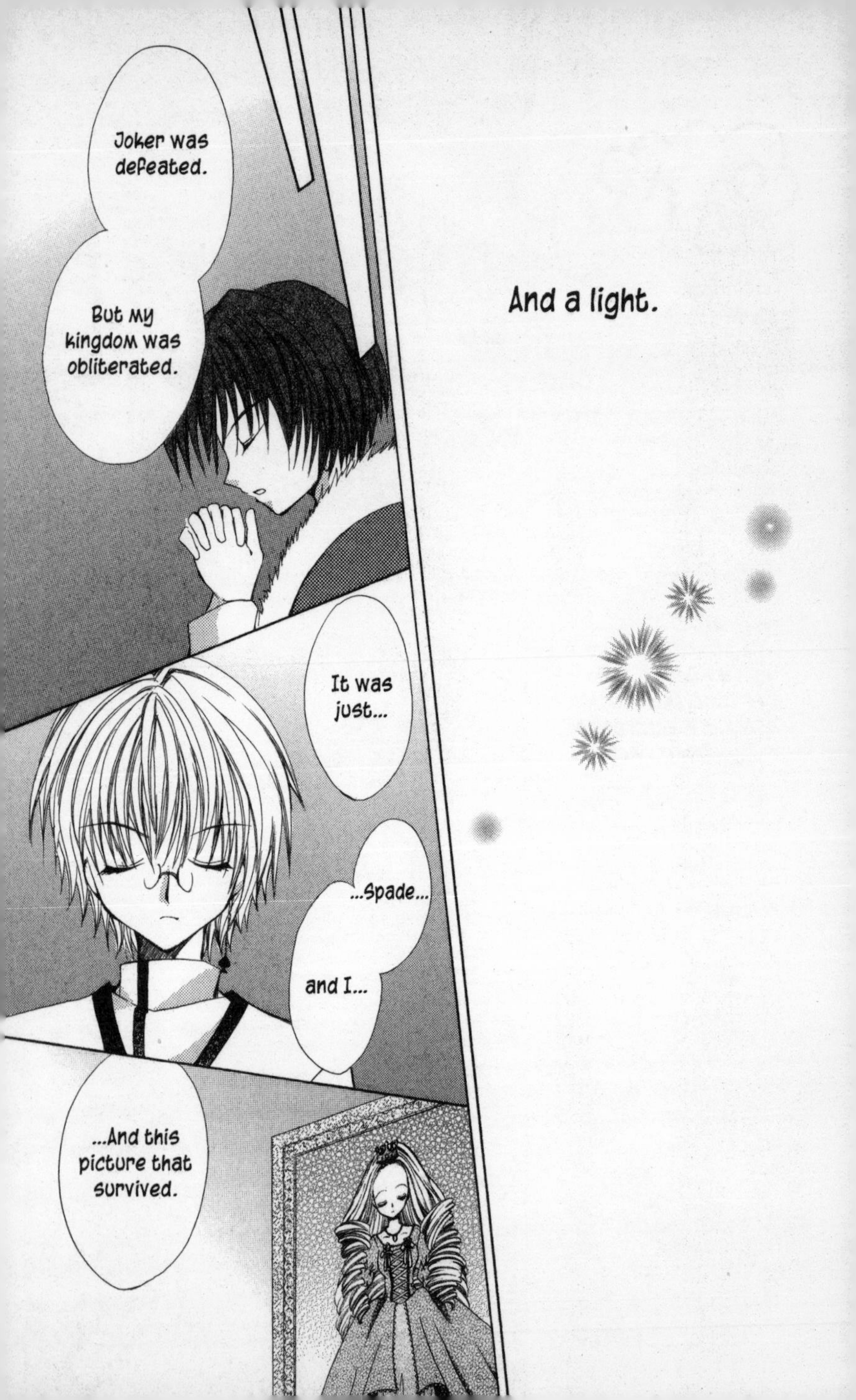
And a light.
Joker was defeated.
But my kingdom was obliterated.
It was just...
...Spade...
and I...
...And this picture that survived.

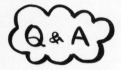

Q & A

Q. What's hard about drawing manga?

A. Well . . .it's rough when the deadlines draw near. Staying awake is hard. I also have a tough time when I can't get my storyboard approved.

Q. What do you enjoy about drawing manga?

A. Naturally, it makes me happy to have everyone read my manga in the magazine! And I like having the merchandise being made as well.

Q. Has Pearl gotten chubby lately? (By Goddess Y)

A. Oh, maybe you're right. Do you think he's had too many bananas? Should I put him on a diet?

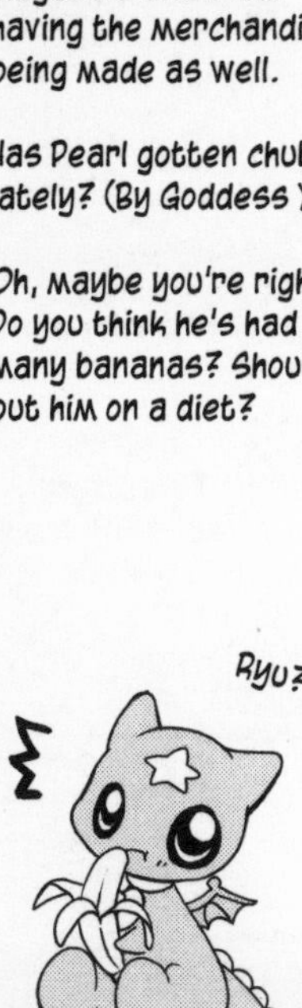
Ryu?!

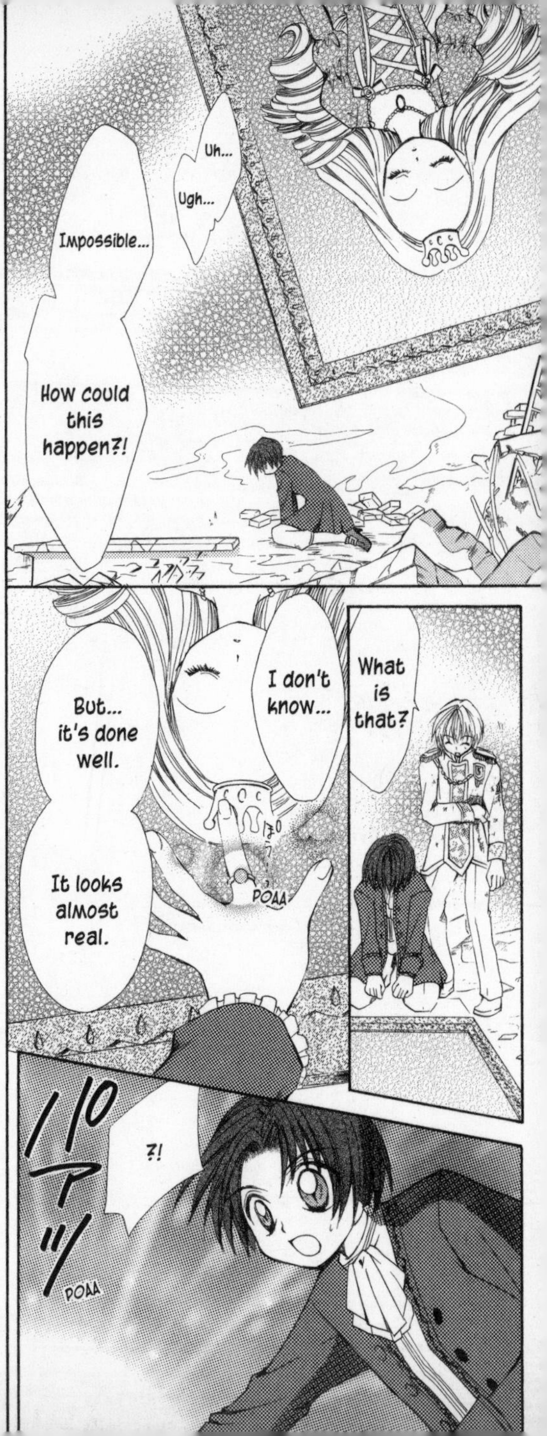
Uh...
Ugh...
Impossible...
How could this happen?!
What is that?
I don't know...
But... it's done well.
It looks almost real.
POAA
?!
POAA

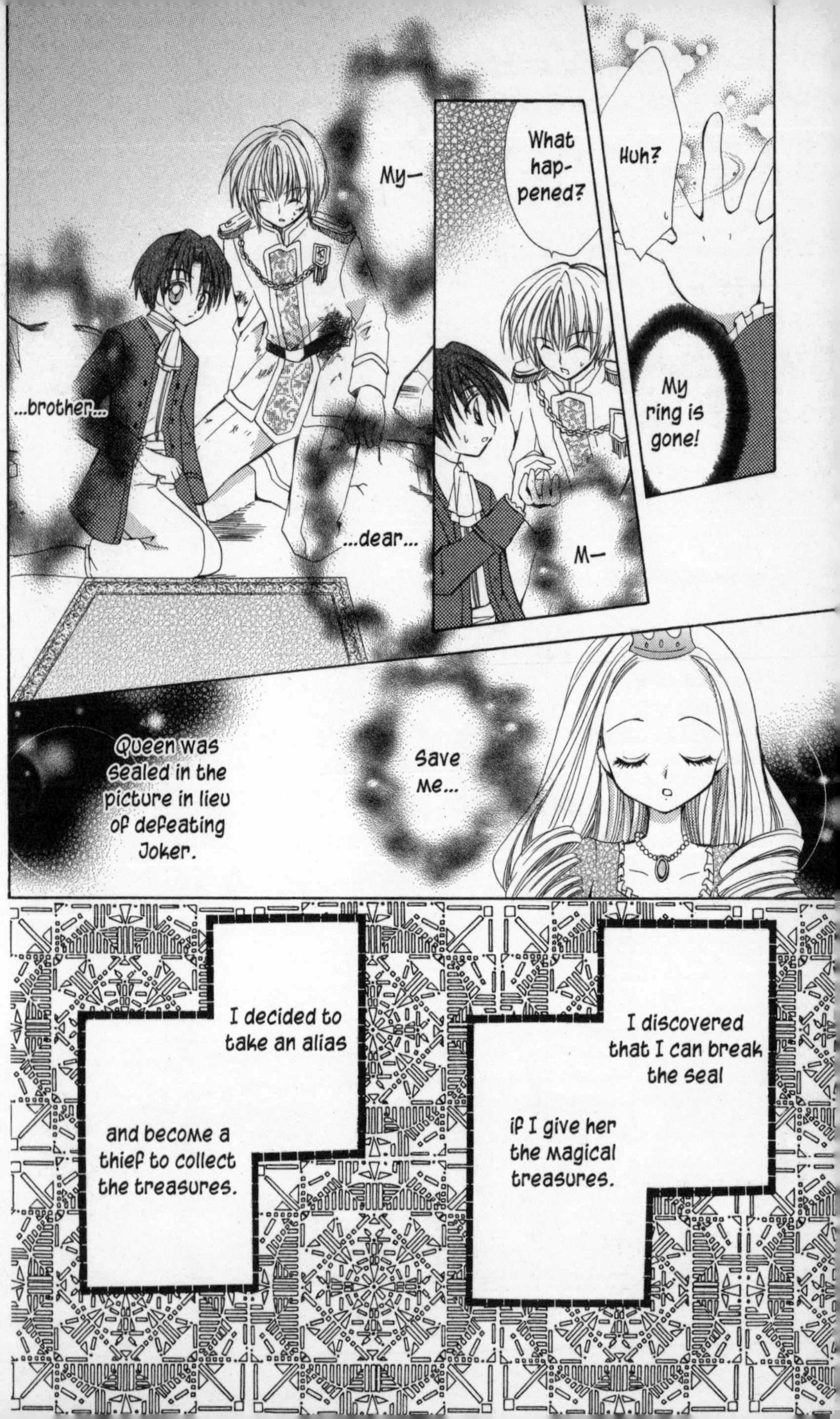
Huh?
My ring is gone!
What happened?
M—
My—
...dear...
...brother...
Save me...
Queen was sealed in the picture in lieu of defeating Joker.
I discovered that I can break the seal
if I give her the magical treasures.
I decided to take an alias
and become a thief to collect the treasures.

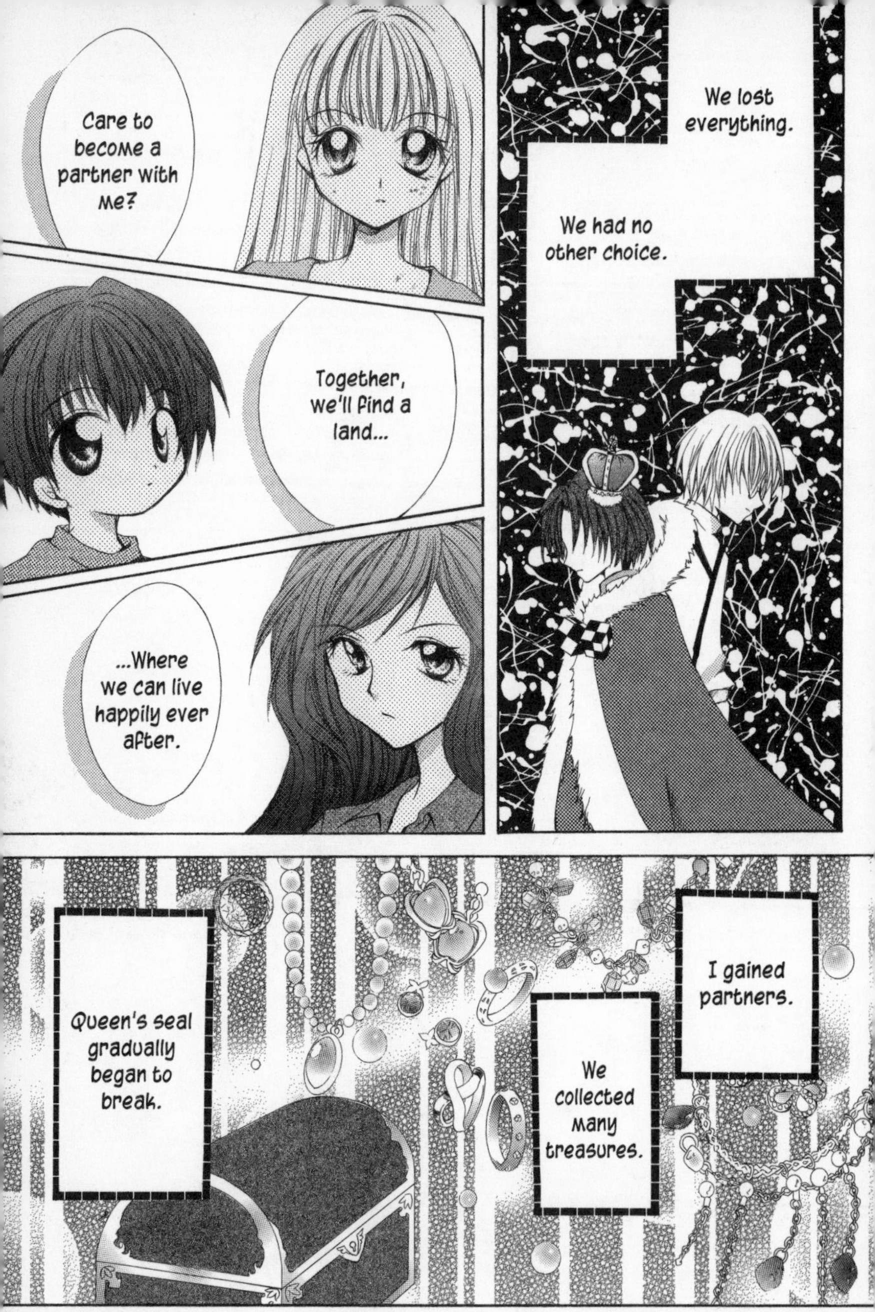
We lost everything.
We had no other choice.
Care to become a partner with me?
Together, we'll find a land...
...Where we can live happily ever after.
I gained partners.
We collected many treasures.
Queen's seal gradually began to break.

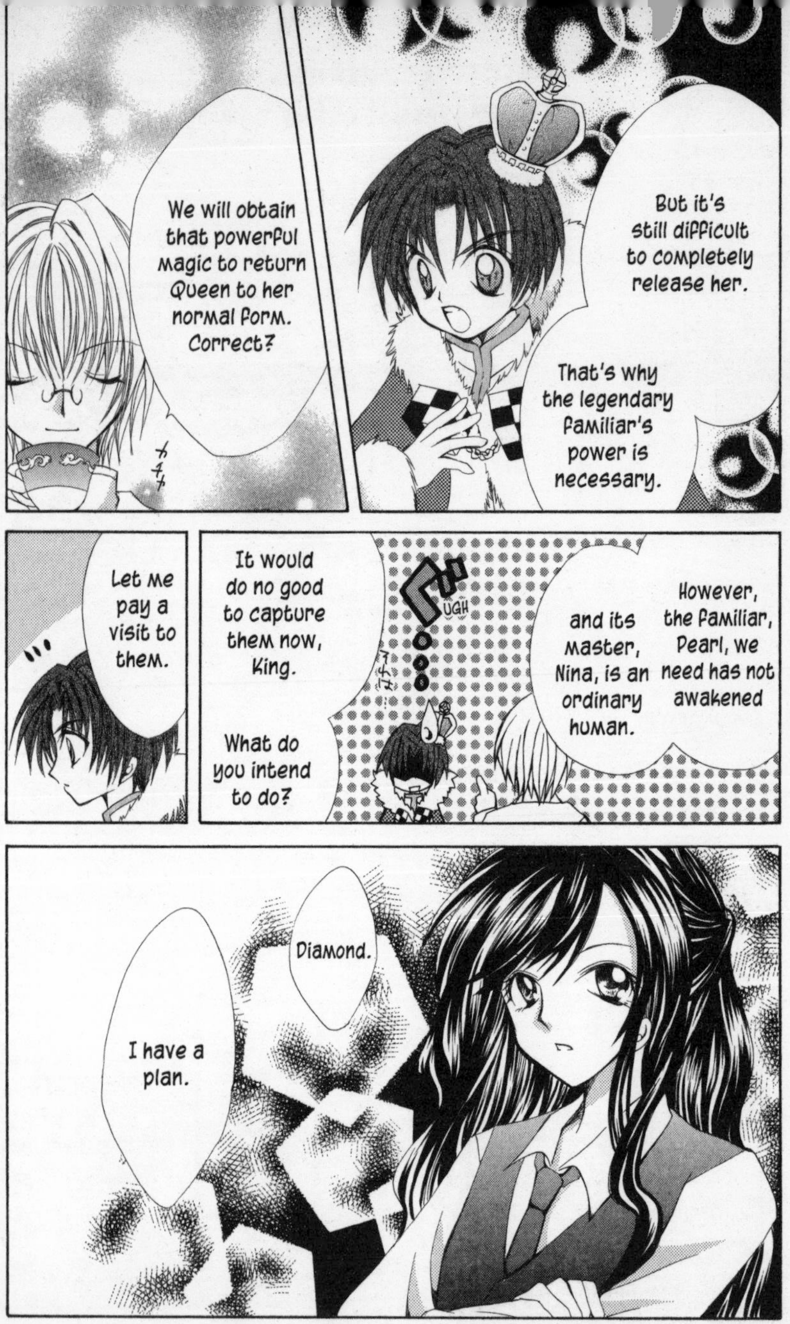
But it's still difficult to completely release her.
That's why the legendary familiar's power is necessary.
We will obtain that powerful magic to return Queen to her normal form. Correct?
However, the familiar, Pearl, we need has not awakened
and its master, Nina, is an ordinary human.
UGH
It would do no good to capture them now, King.
What do you intend to do?
Let me pay a visit to them.
Diamond.
I have a plan.

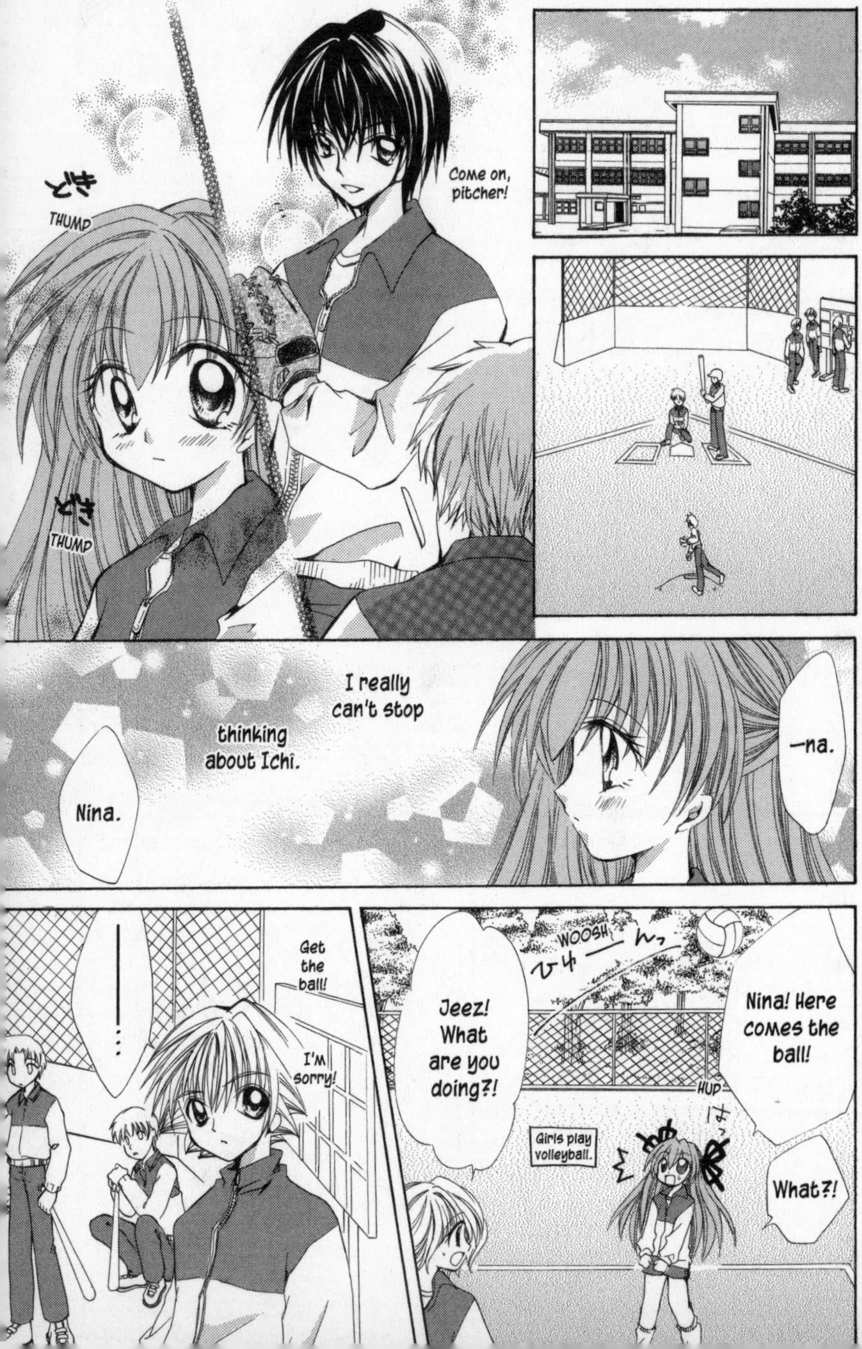
Come on, pitcher!
どき
THUMP
どき
THUMP
—na.
I really can't stop
thinking about Ichi.
Nina.
Nina! Here comes the ball!
ひゅーんっ
WOOSH
What?!
はっ
HUP
Jeez! What are you doing?!
Girls play volleyball.
Get the ball!
I'M sorry!
......

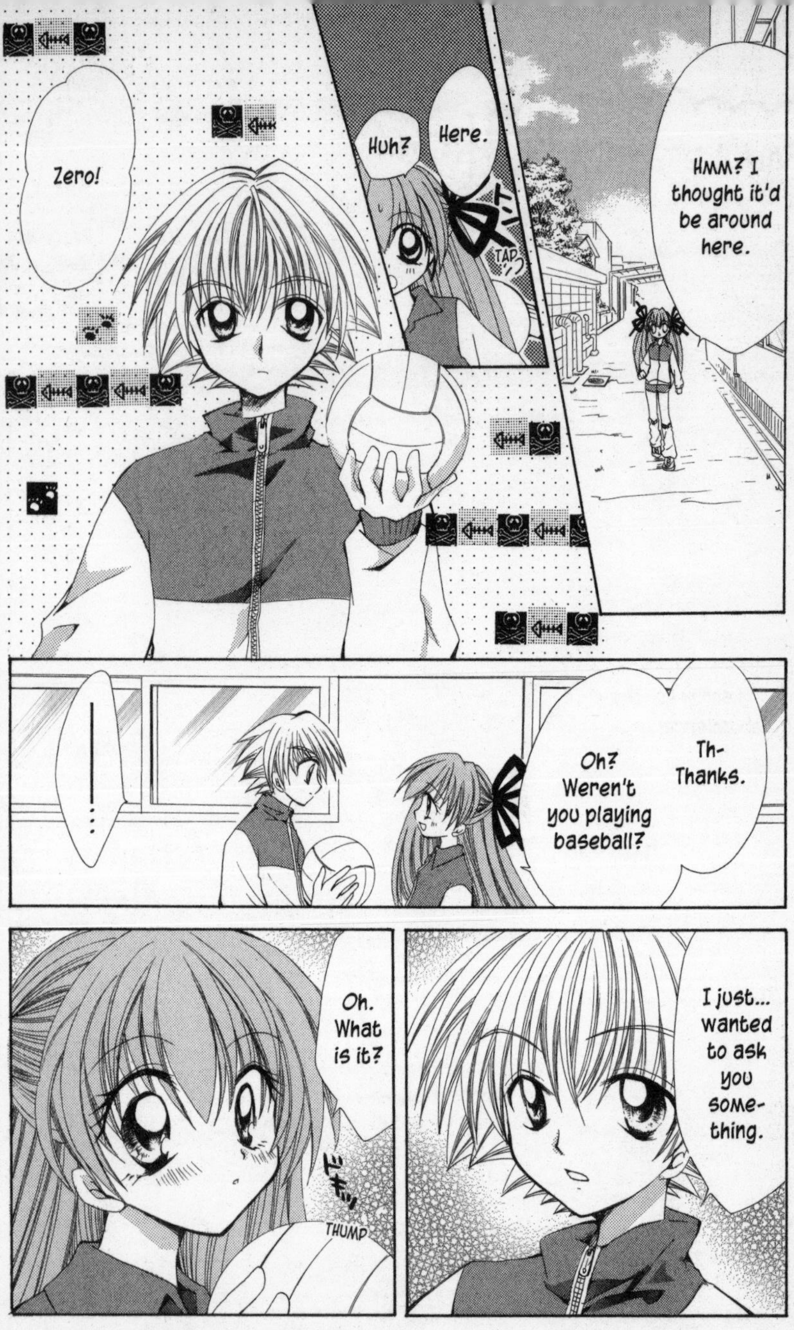
HMM? I thought it'd be around here.
Here.
Huh?
TAP
Zero!
Th- Thanks.
Oh? Weren't you playing baseball?
—...
I just... wanted to ask you something.
Oh. What is it?
ドキッ
THUMP

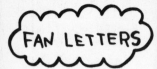

FAN LETTERS

Thank You for all the letters. It's nice to see the comments on the story and hear about the characters you like.♥

I'm sorry that I can't find time to reply to You. It'll be helpful if you could include a self-addressed envelope in the letter. I'm really sorry for the inconvenience! Thank you.

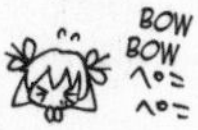
BOW
BOW
へこ
へこ

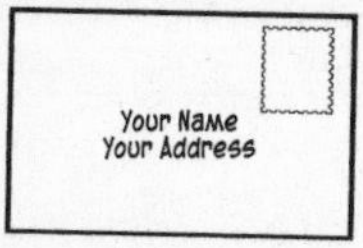
Your Name
Your Address

<Mailing Address for Fan Letters>
Nakayoshi Editorial Department
Michiyo Kikuta
P.O. Box 91
Akasaka Post Office
Tokyo, Japan 107-8652

<Official Website>
→http://tokyo.cool.ne.jp/michiyo-k-miracle/

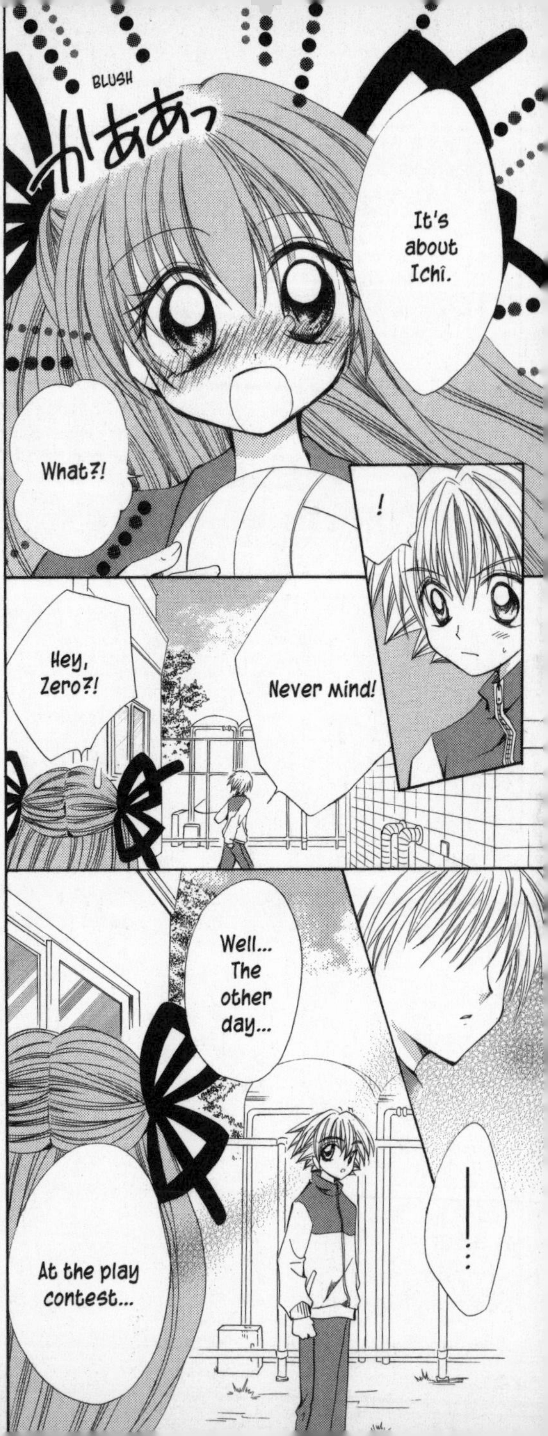
It's about Ichi.
BLUSH
かあぁっ
What?!
!
Never mind!
Hey, Zero?!
Well... The other day...
At the play contest...
!...

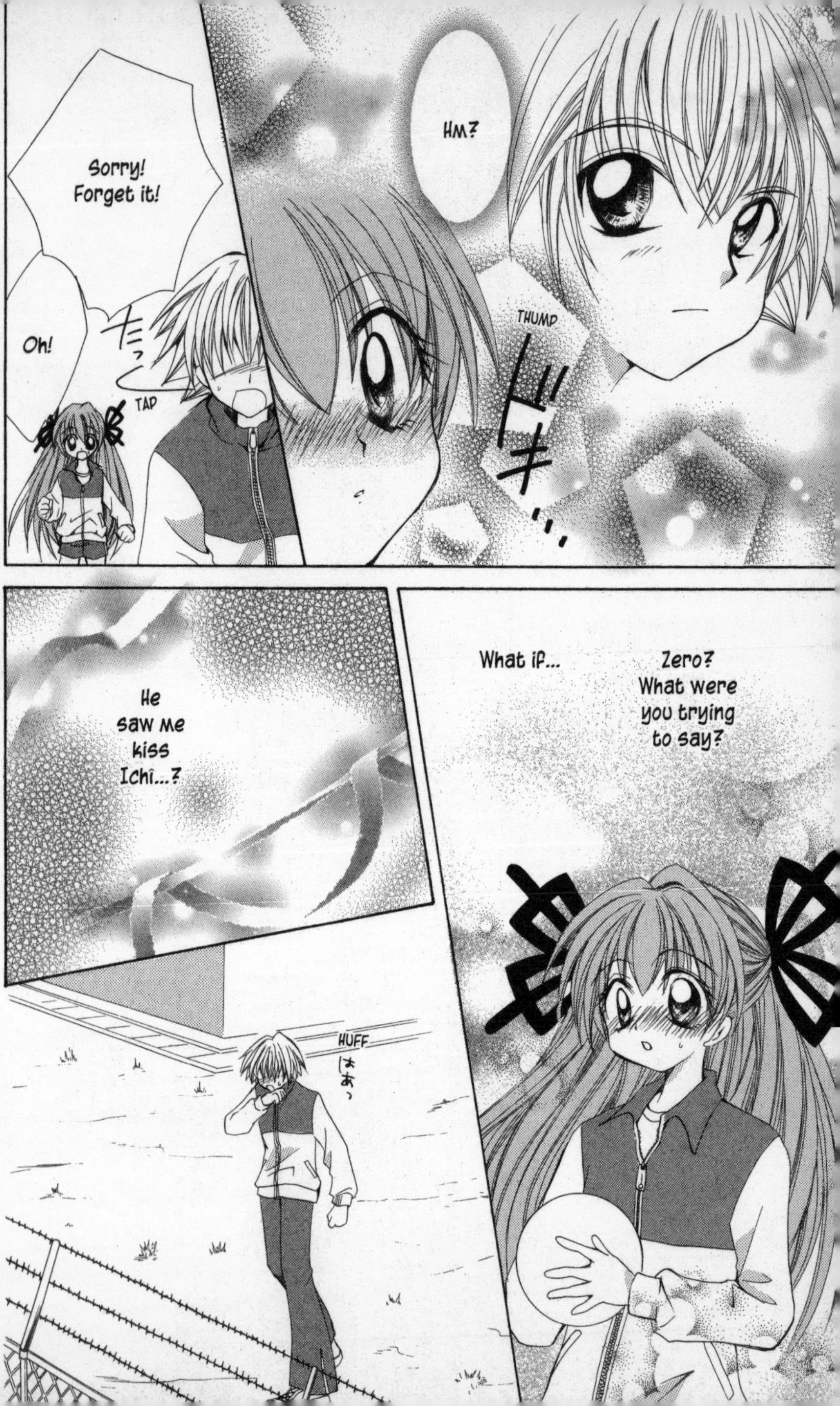
Hm?
THUMP
ドキ…
Sorry! Forget it!
Oh!
たっ
TAP
Zero? What were you trying to say?
What if...
He saw me kiss Ichi...?
HUFF
はあっ

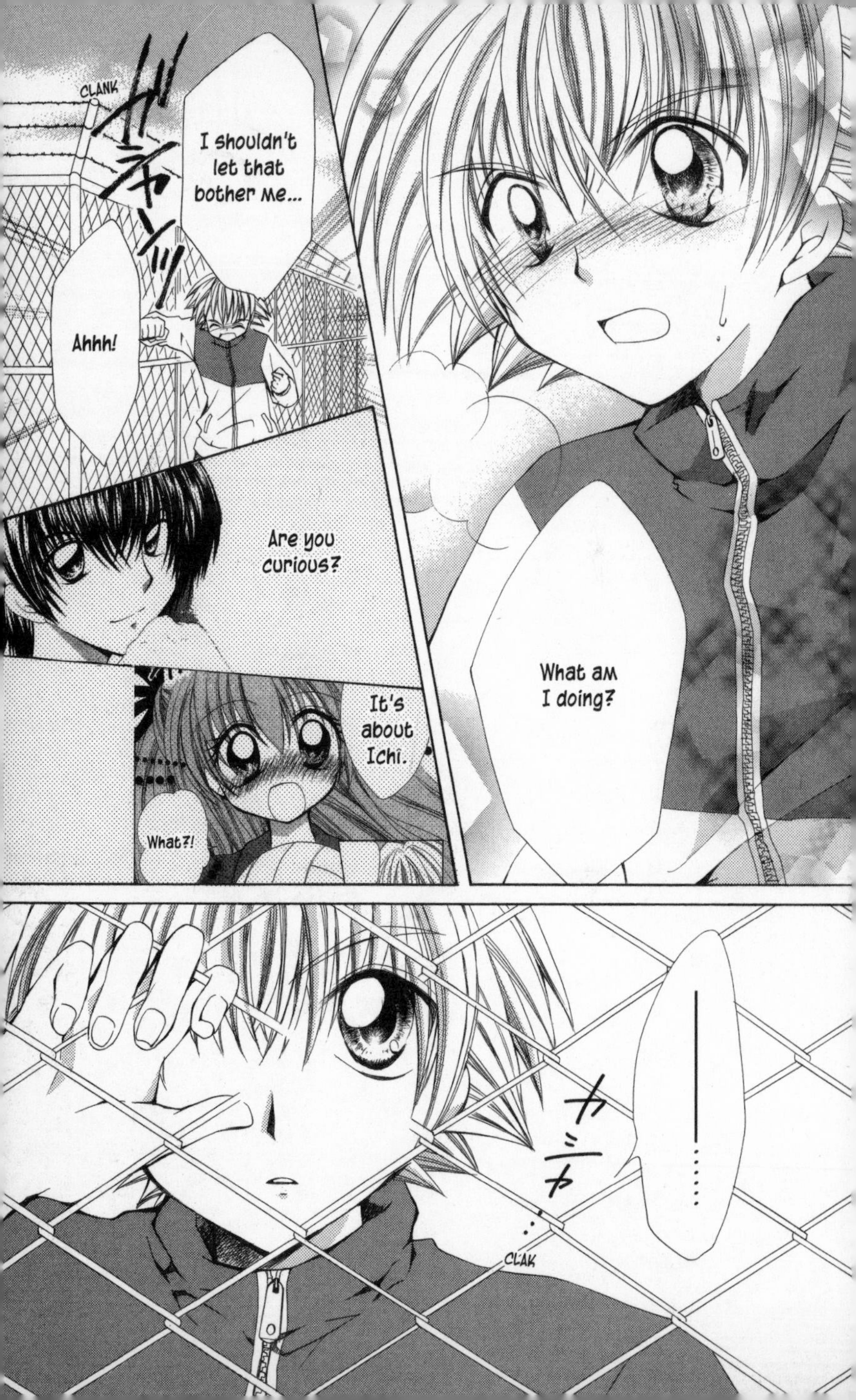
What am I doing?
I shouldn't let that bother me...
CLANK
Ahhh!
Are you curious?
It's about Ichi.
What?!
......
CLAK

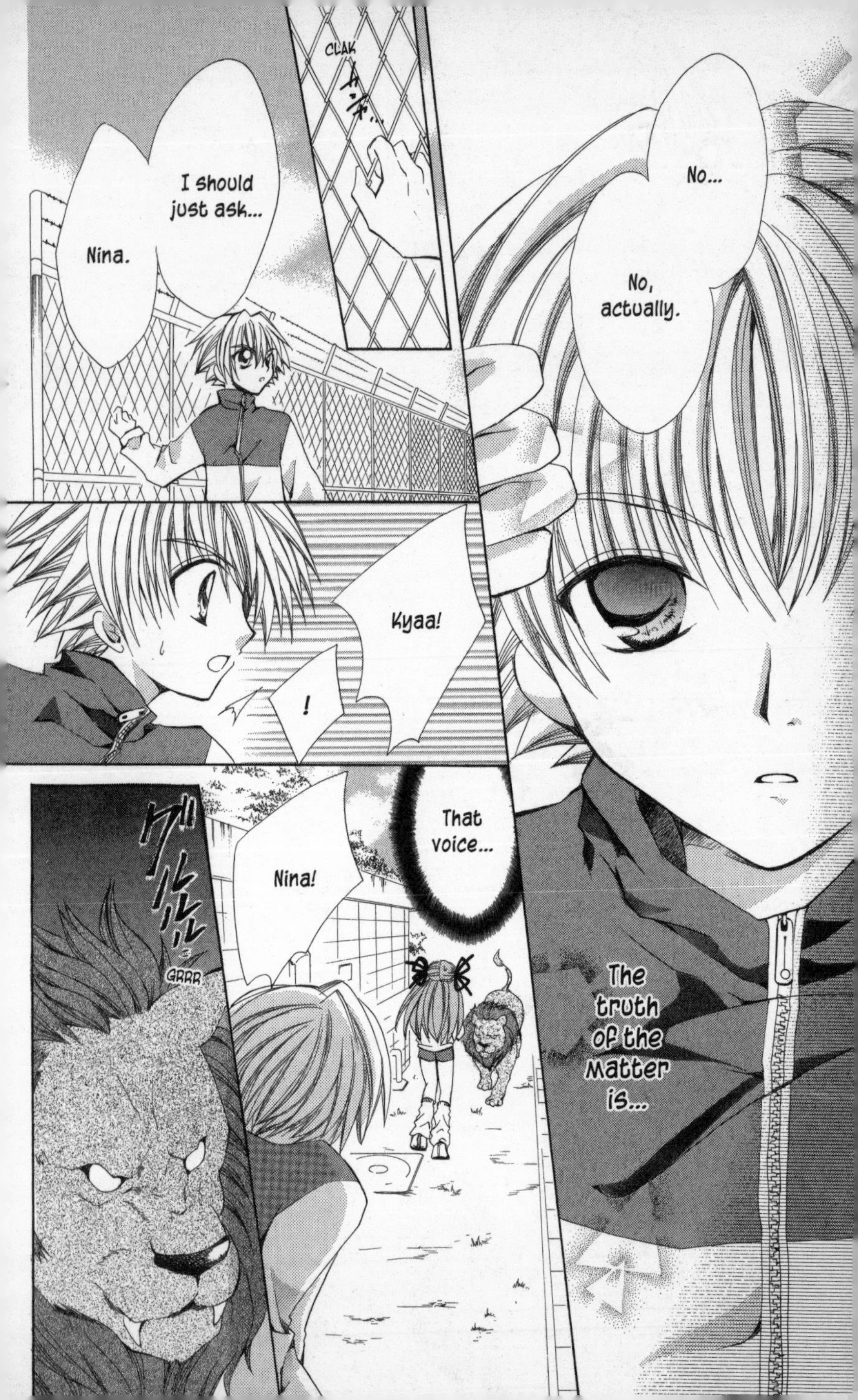
No...
No, actually.
The truth of the matter is...
CLAK
I should just ask...
Nina.
Kyaa!
!
That voice...
Nina!
GRRR

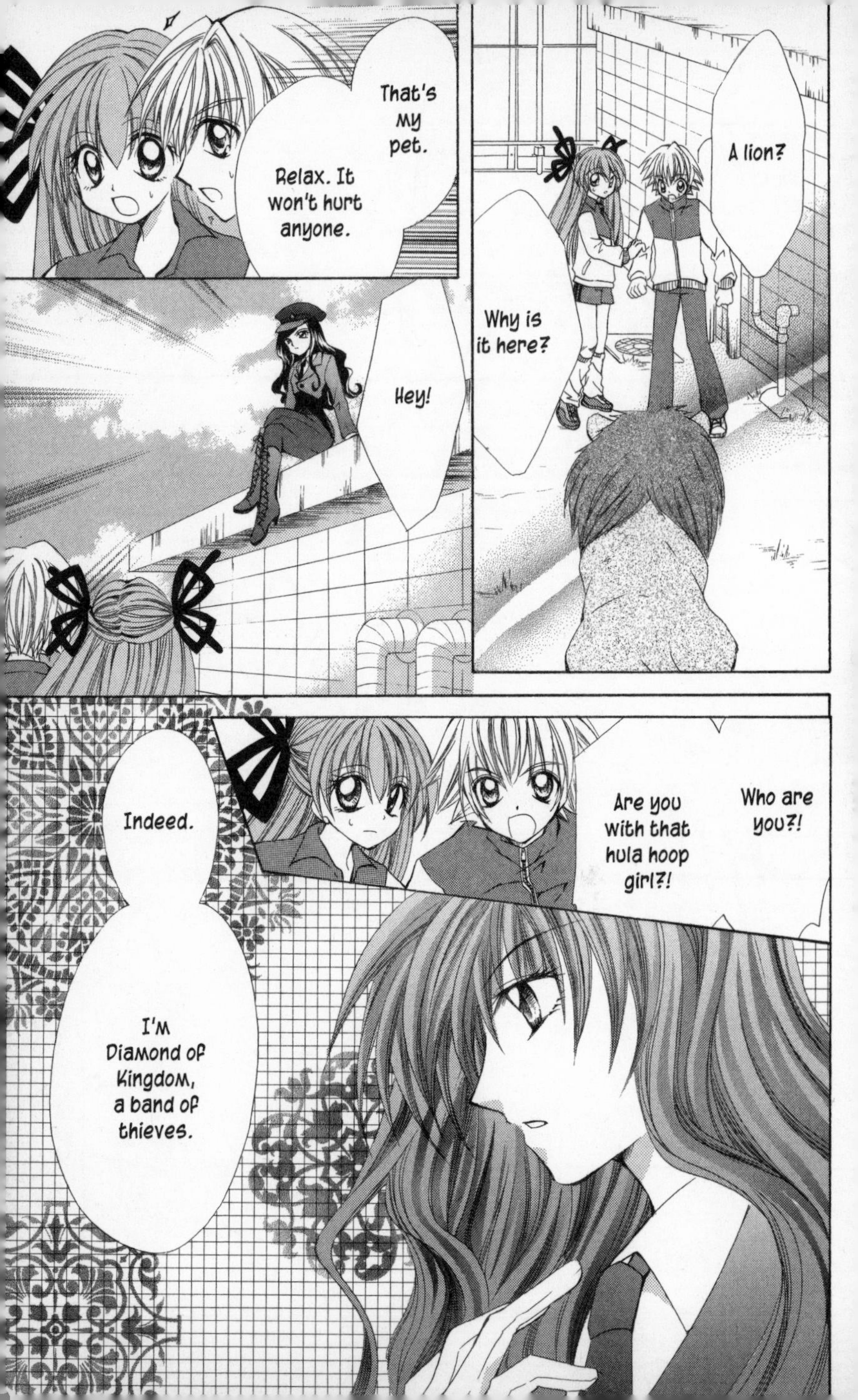
A lion?
Why is it here?
That's my pet.
Relax. It won't hurt anyone.
Hey!
Who are you?!
Are you with that hula hoop girl?!
Indeed.
I'm Diamond of Kingdom, a band of thieves.

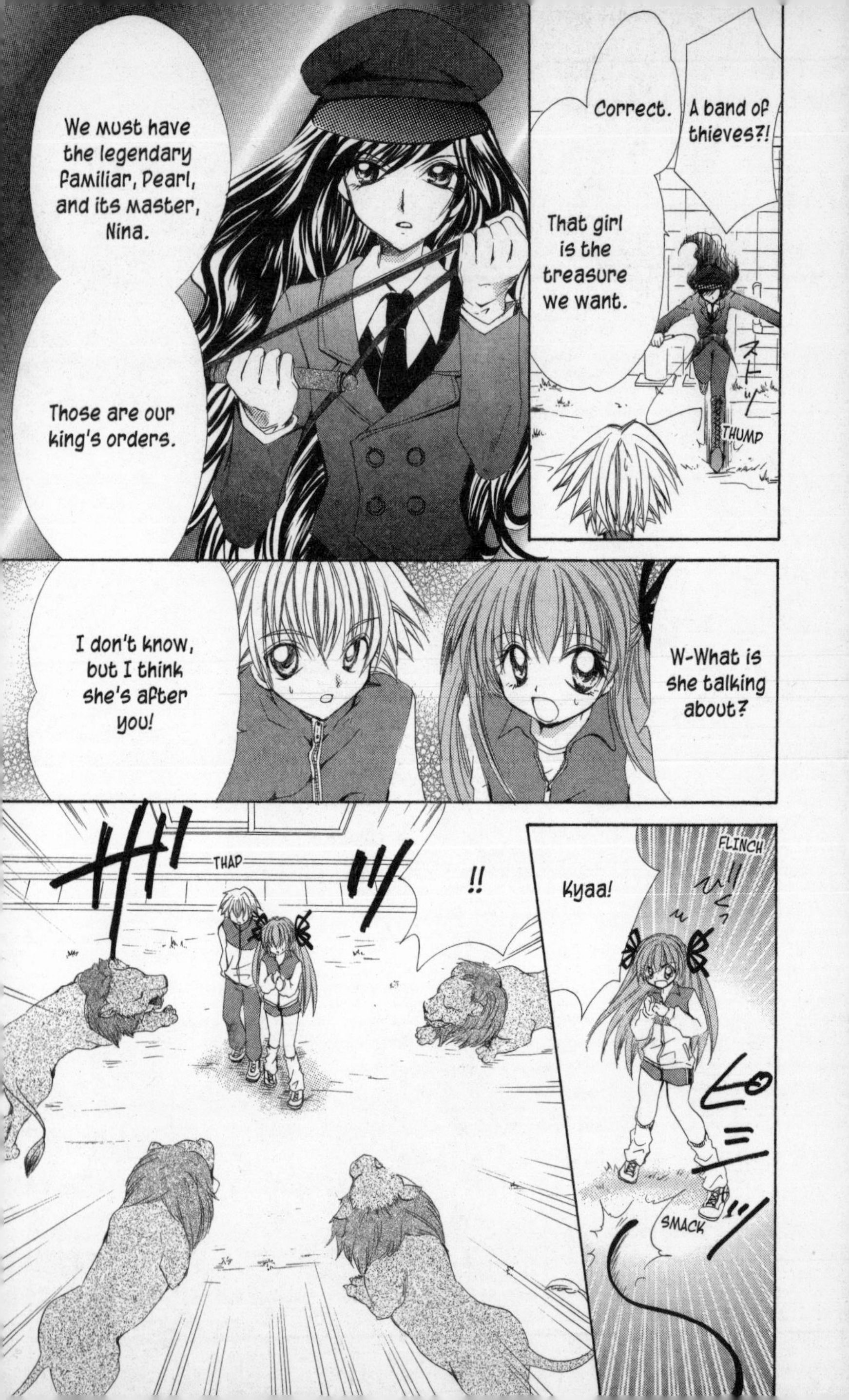
A band of thieves?!
Correct.
That girl is the treasure we want.
THUMP
We must have the legendary familiar, Pearl, and its master, Nina.
Those are our king's orders.
W-What is she talking about?
I don't know, but I think she's after you!
FLINCH
Kyaa!
SMACK
!!
THAP

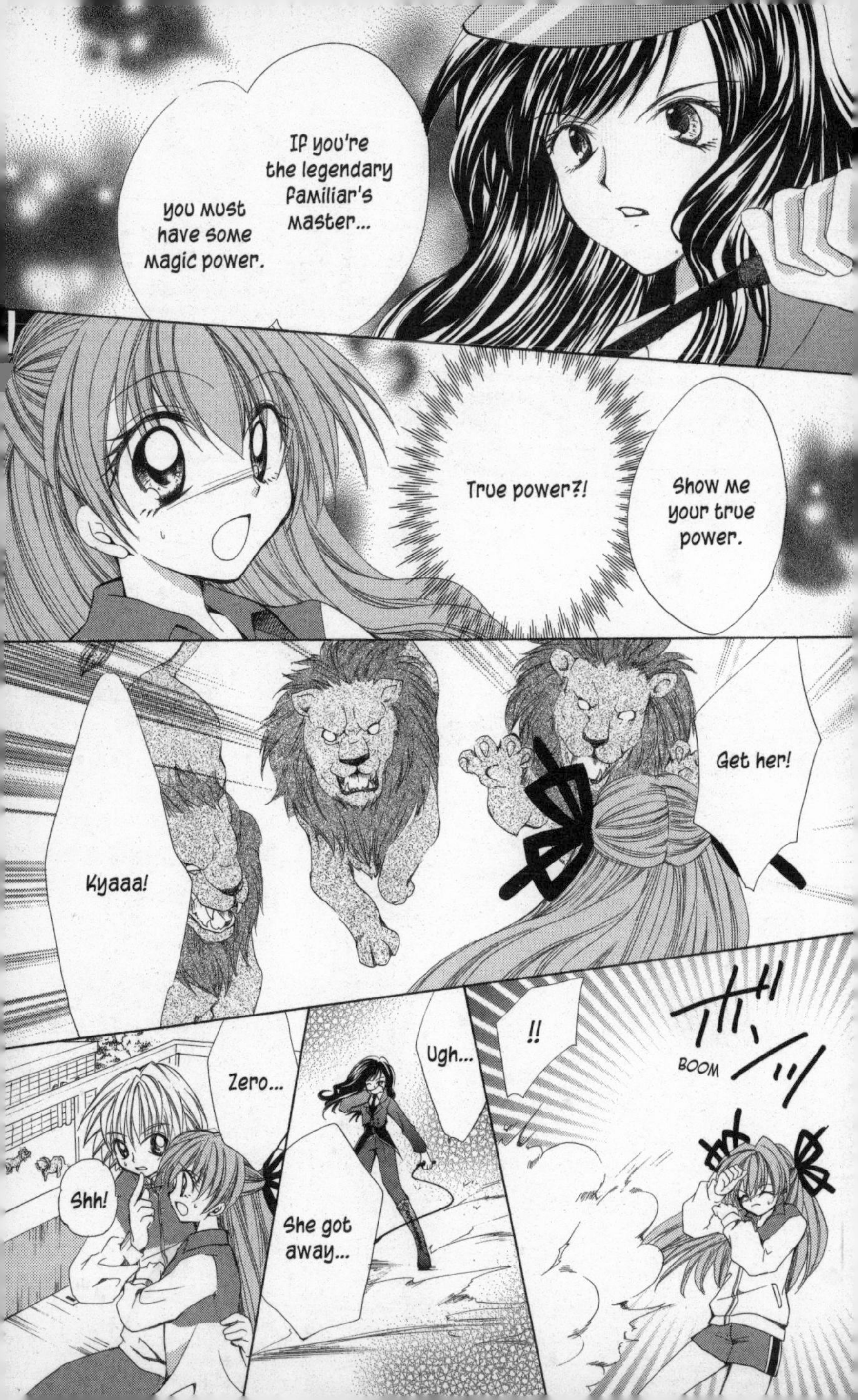
If you're the legendary familiar's master...
you must have some magic power.
Show me your true power.
True power?!
Get her!
Kyaaa!
BOOM
!!
Ugh...
She got away...
Zero...
Shh!

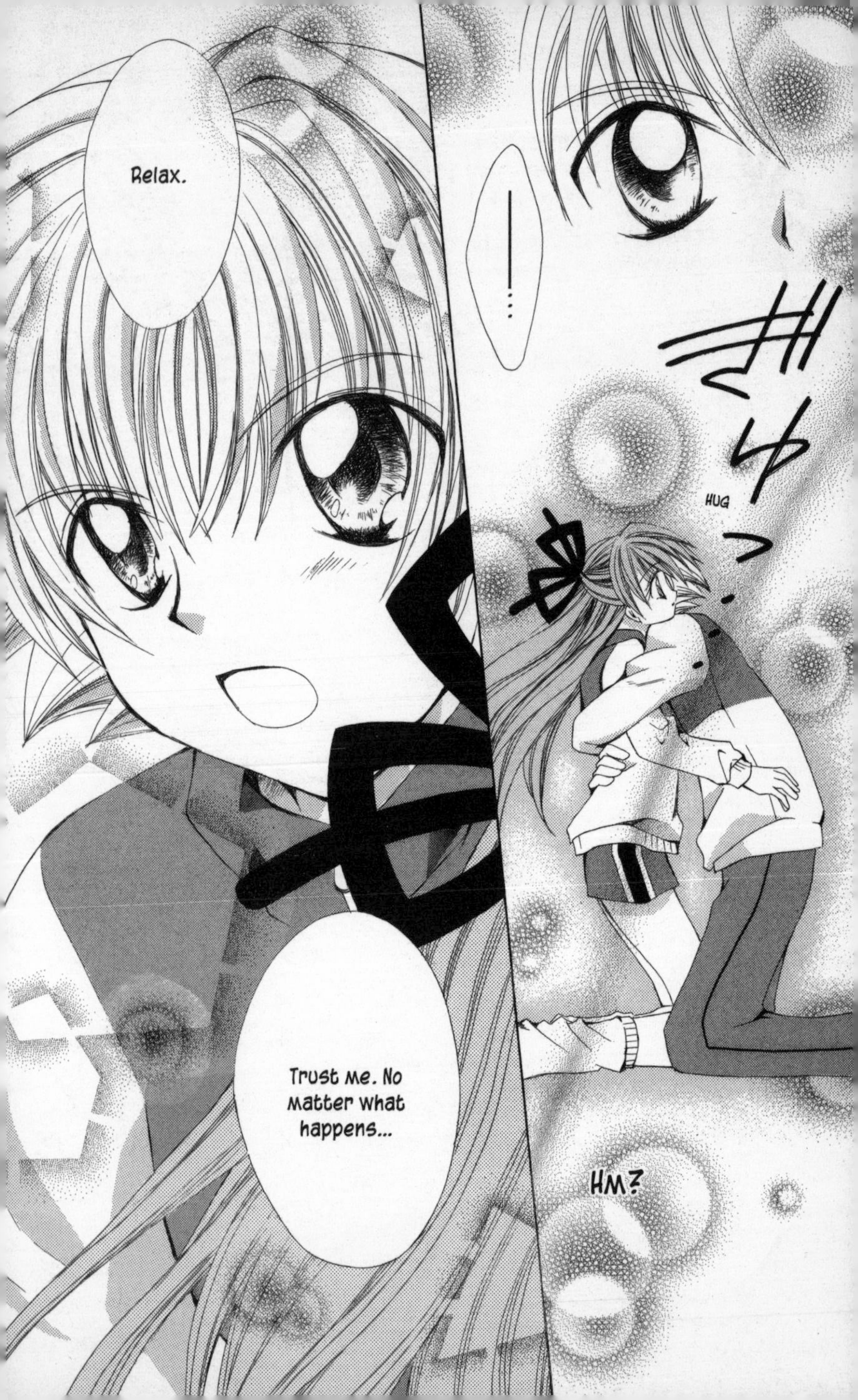
—...
ぎゅっ
HUG
HM?
Relax.
Trust me. No matter what happens...

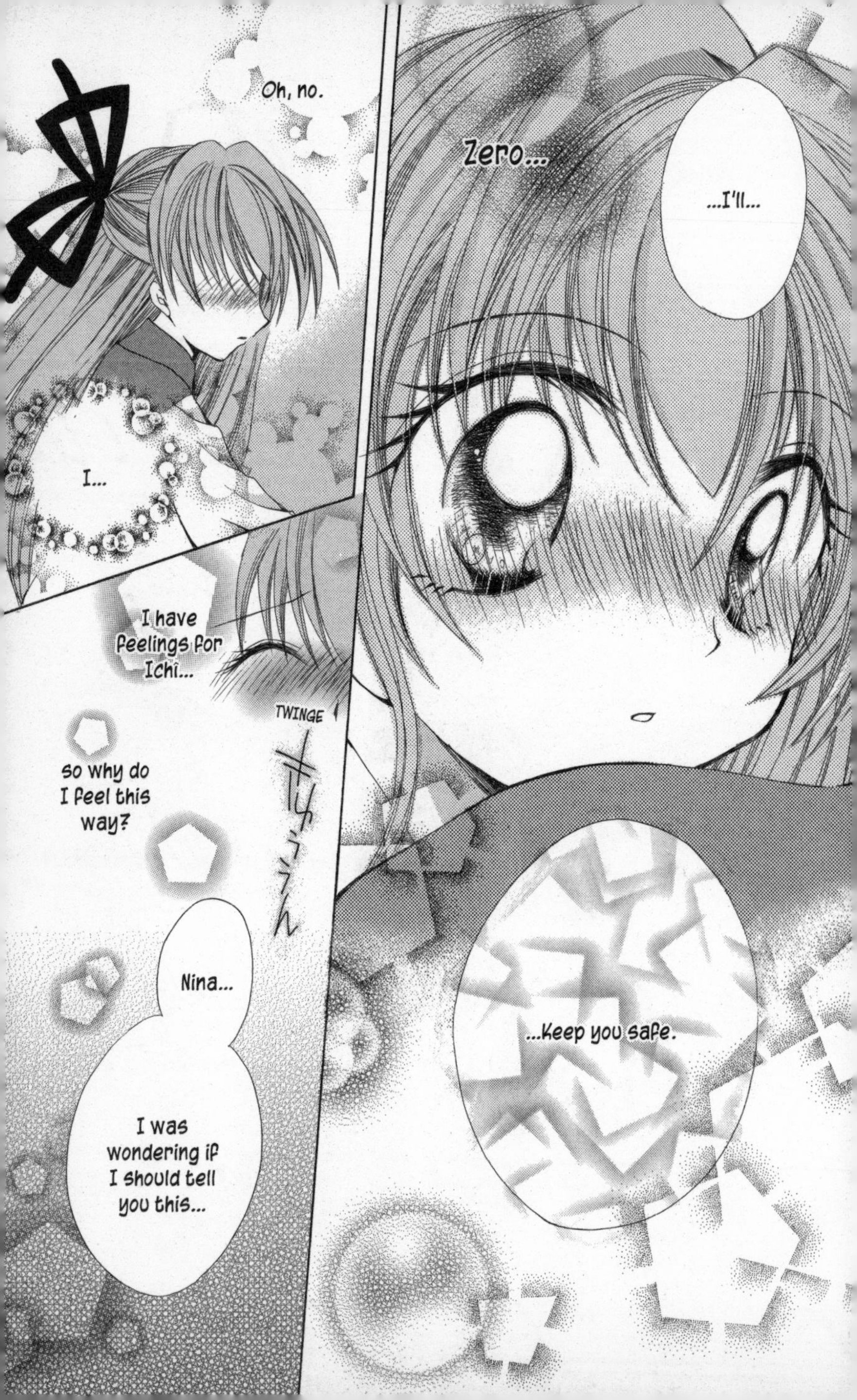

Zero...
...I'll...
...Keep you safe.
Oh, no.
I...
I have feelings for Ichi...
so why do I feel this way?
TWINGE
Nina...
I was wondering if I should tell you this...

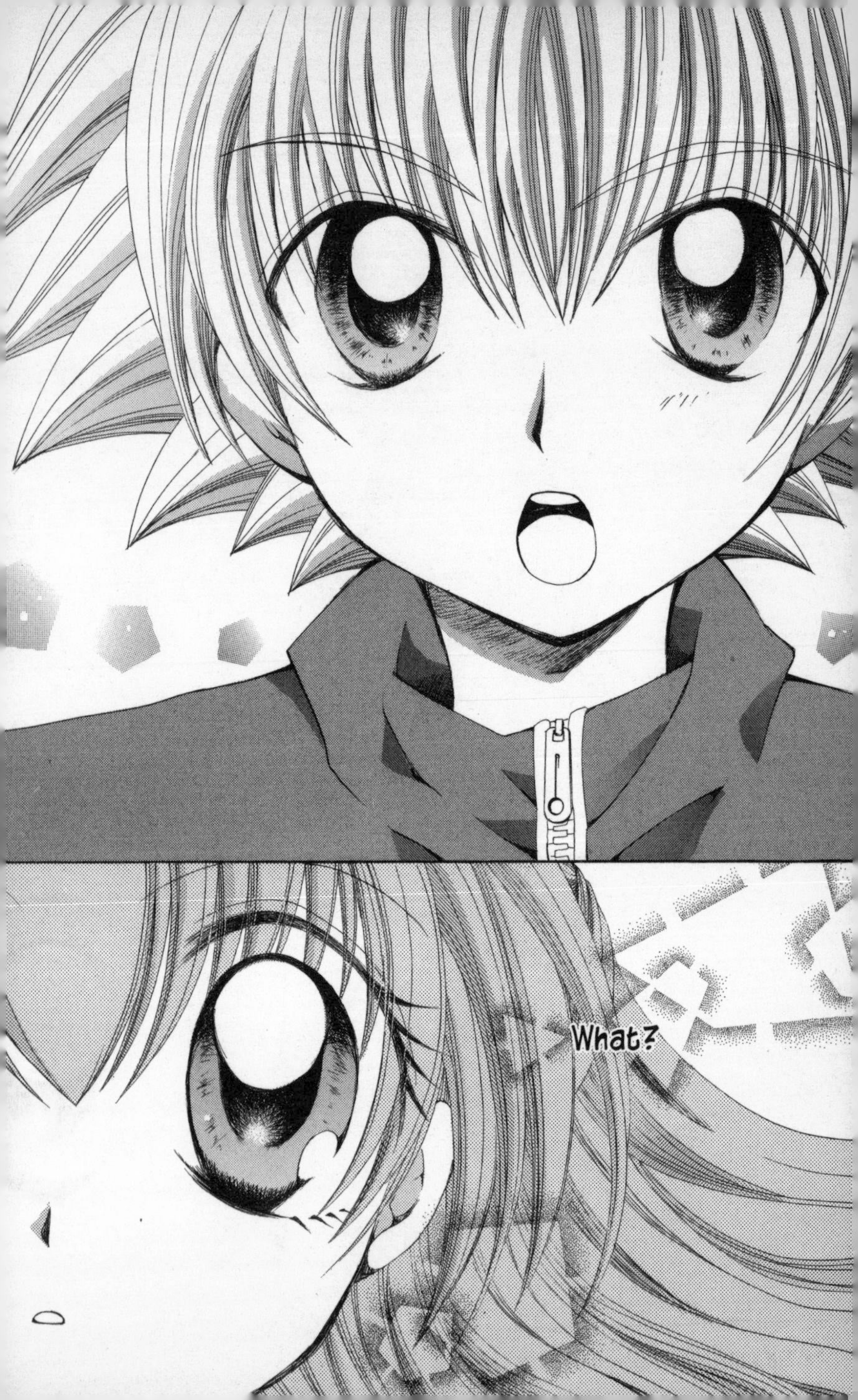
What?

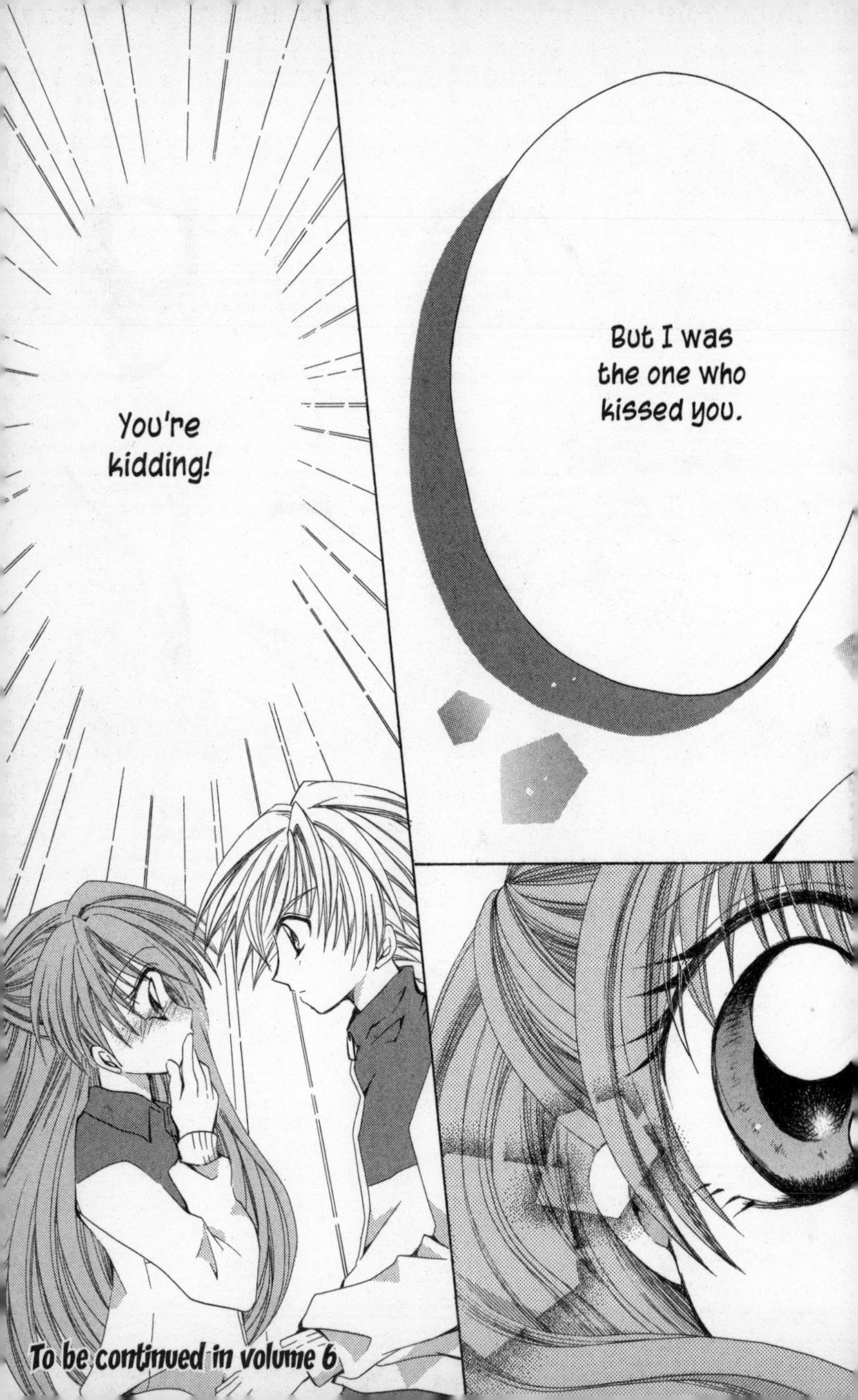
But I was the one who kissed you.
You're kidding!
To be continued in volume 6

Rokka's Dream

Mini☆Theatre: TAKE 2

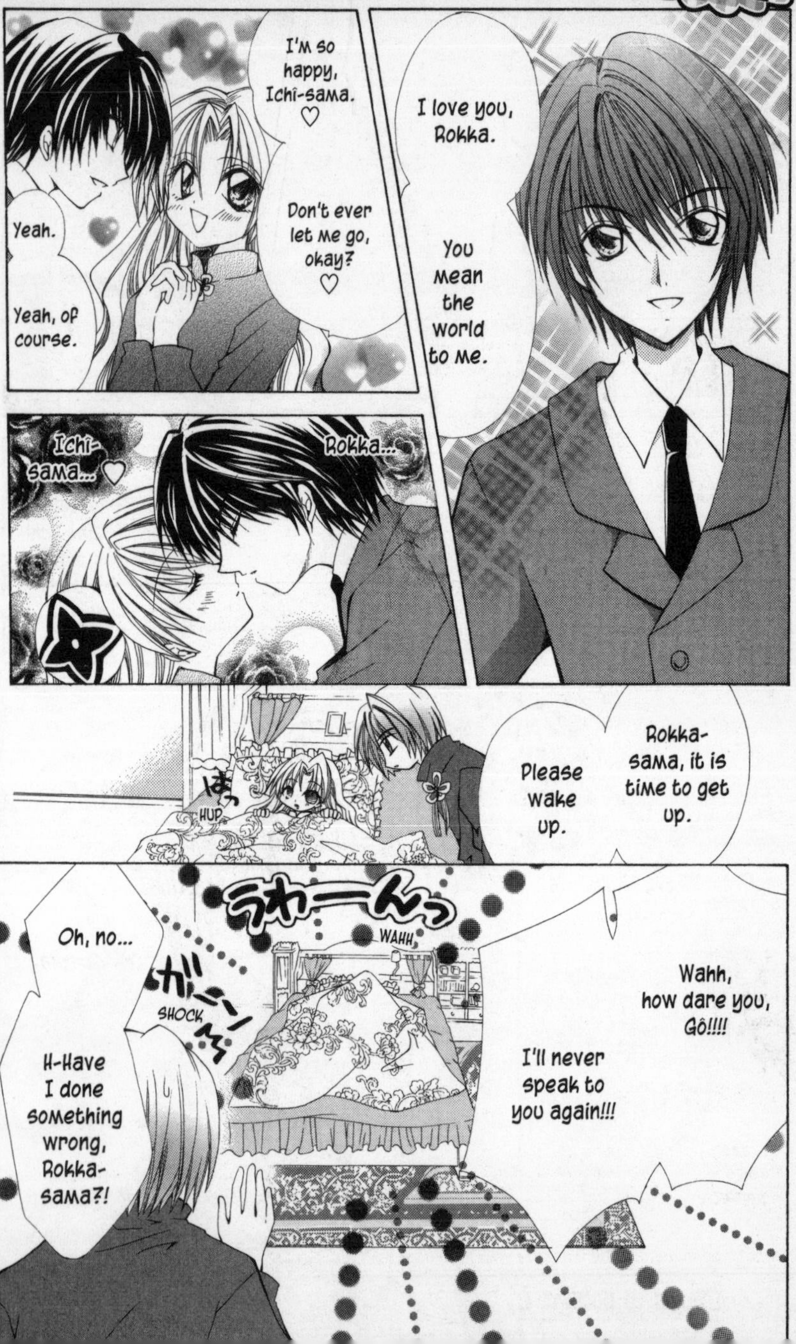
I love you, Rokka.
You mean the world to me.
I'm so happy, Ichi-sama. ♡
Don't ever let me go, okay? ♡
Yeah.
Yeah, of course.
Rokka...
Ichi-sama... ♡
Rokka-sama, it is time to get up.
Please wake up.
はっ
HUP
Wahh, how dare you, Gô!!!!
I'll never speak to you again!!!
うわーんっ
WAHH
ガーン
SHOCK
Oh, no...
H-Have I done something wrong, Rokka-sama?!

Rokka's Dream 2

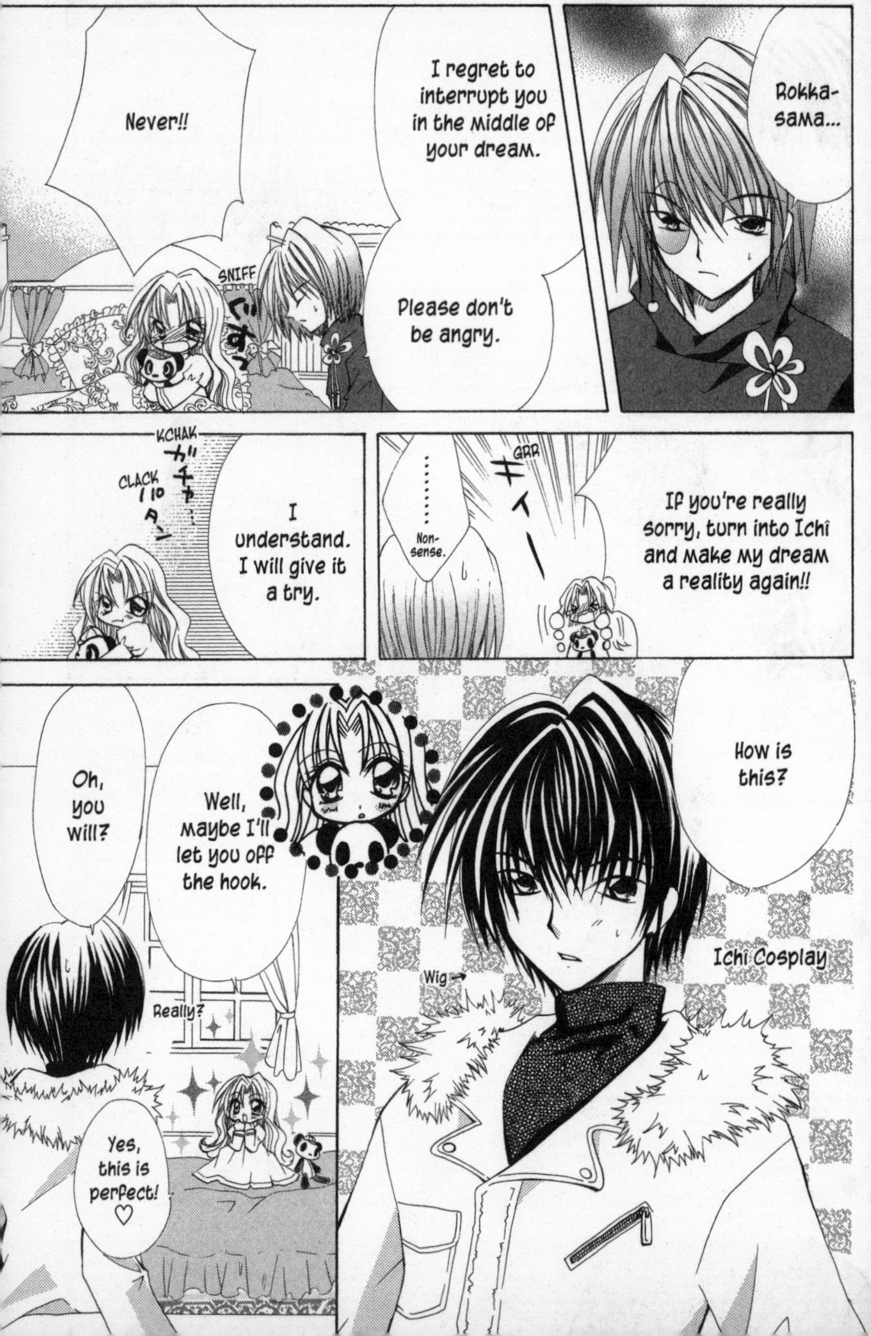
Rokka-sama...
I regret to interrupt you in the middle of your dream.
Please don't be angry.
Never!!
SNIFF
If you're really sorry, turn into Ichi and make my dream a reality again!!
GRR
......
Non-sense.
KCHAK
CLACK
I understand. I will give it a try.
How is this?
Ichi Cosplay
Wig
Well, maybe I'll let you off the hook.
Oh, you will?
Really?
Yes, this is perfect! ♡

A Woman's Pride (Heart's Way)

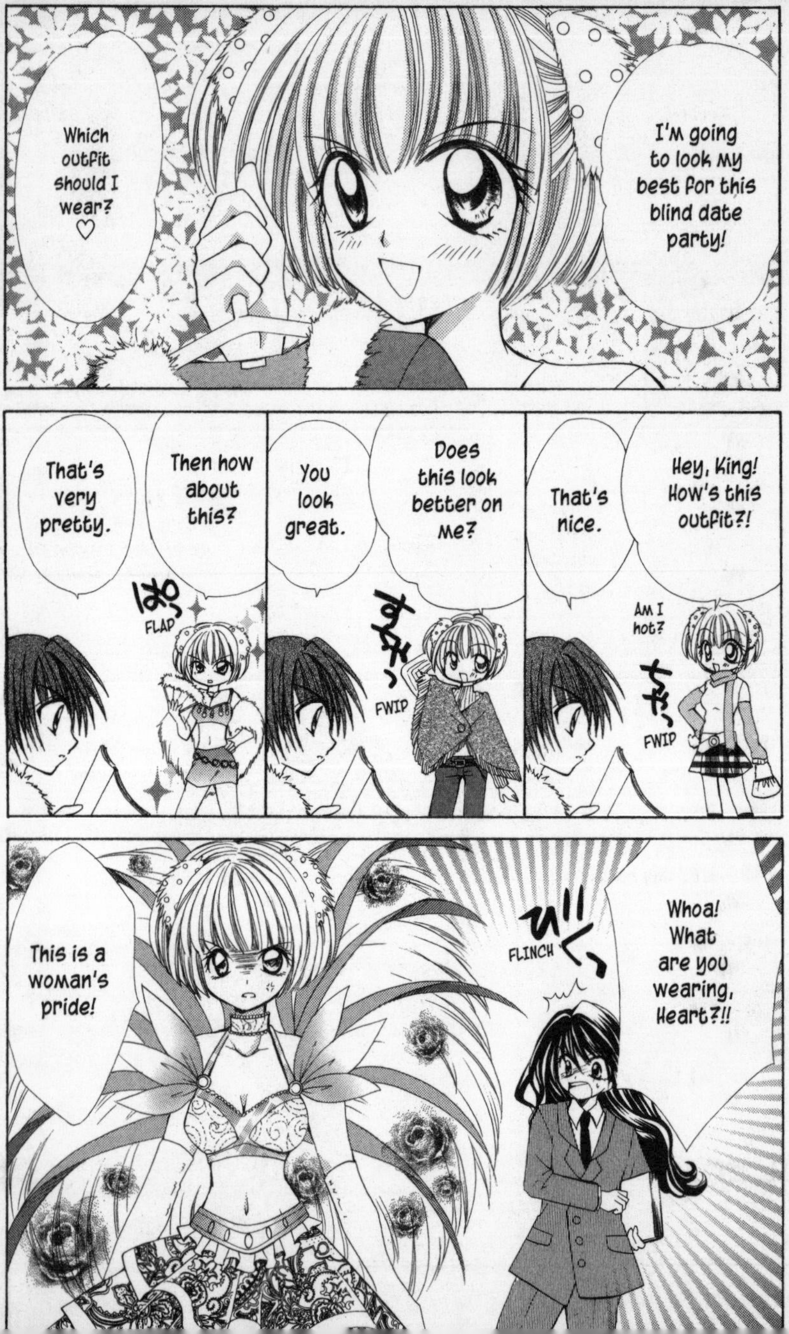
I'm going to look my best for this blind date party!
Which outfit should I wear? ♡
Hey, King! How's this outfit?!
Am I hot?
ちゃっ
FWIP
That's nice.
Does this look better on me?
FWIP
You look great.
Then how about this?
ぱっ
FLAP
That's very pretty.
Whoa! What are you wearing, Heart?!!
びくっ
FLINCH
This is a woman's pride!

Making Remedies (Spade's Way)

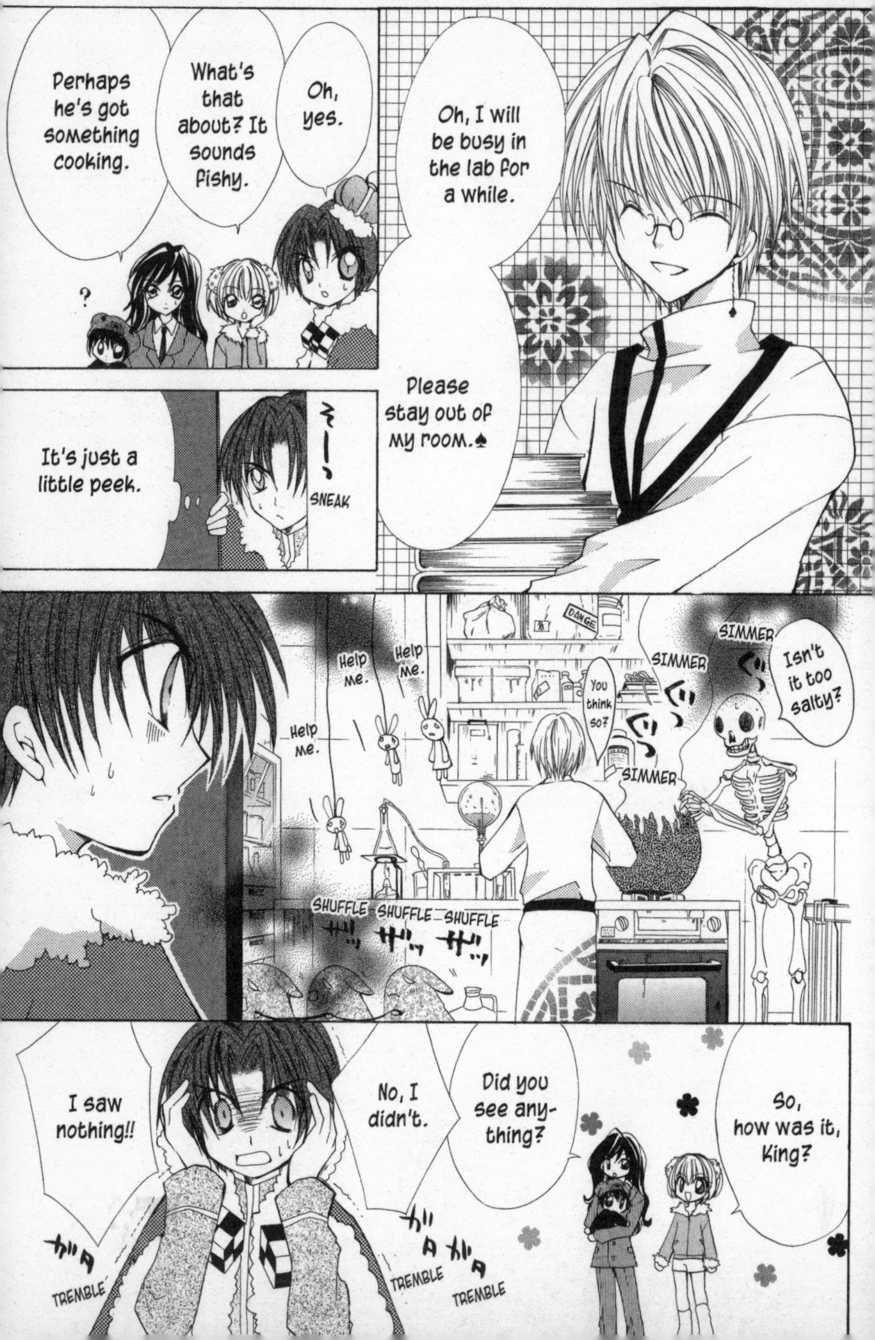

Oh, I will be busy in the lab for a while.
Please stay out of my room.♠
Oh, yes.
What's that about? It sounds fishy.
Perhaps he's got something cooking.
?
SNEAK
It's just a little peek.
SIMMER
Isn't it too salty?
SIMMER
SIMMER
You think so?
DANGE
Help me.
Help me.
Help me.
SHUFFLE
SHUFFLE
SHUFFLE
So, how was it, King?
Did you see anything?
No, I didn't.
TREMBLE
TREMBLE
I saw nothing!!
TREMBLE

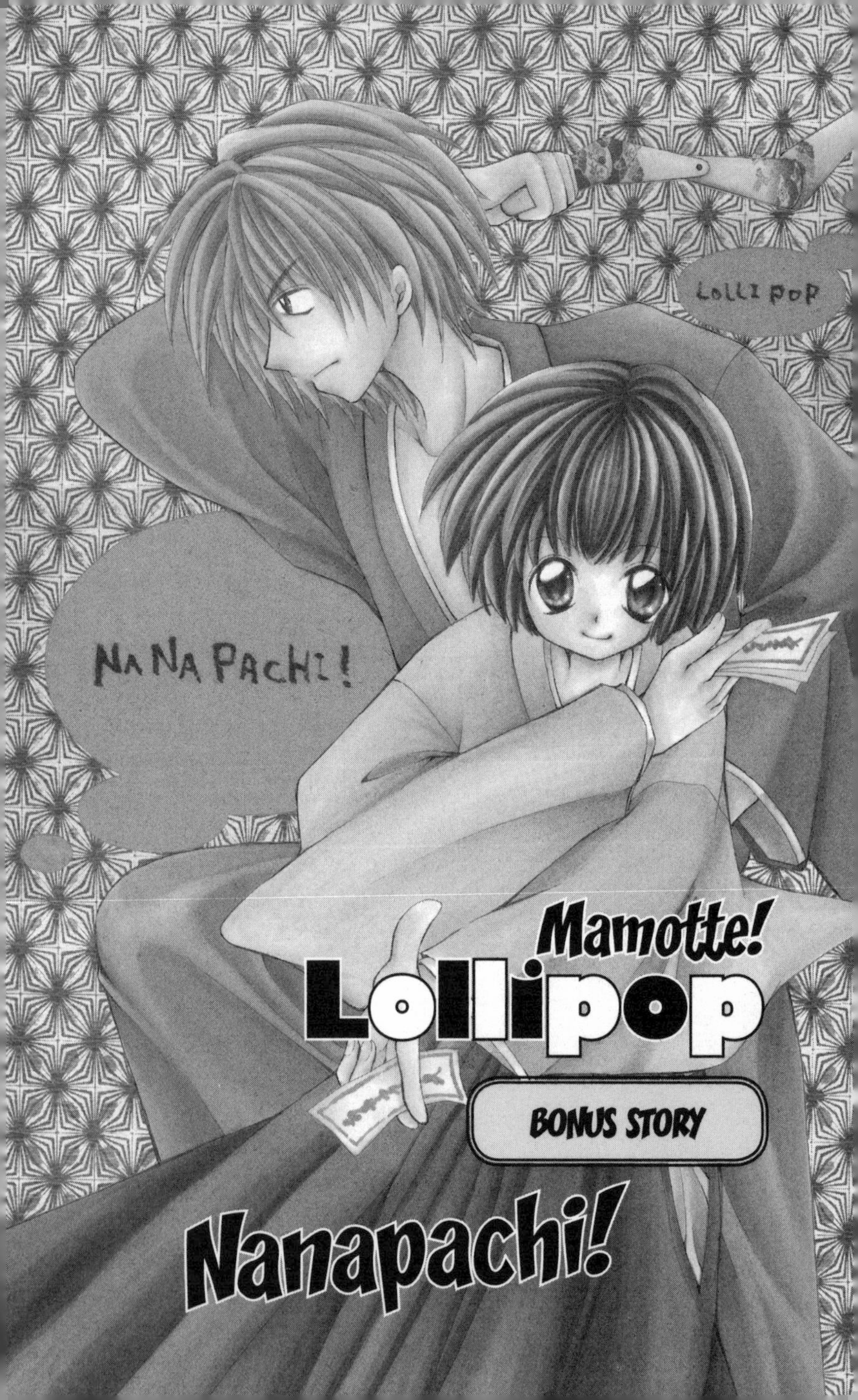

LOLLI POP
NA NA PACHI!
Mamotte!
Lollipop
BONUS STORY
Nanapachi!

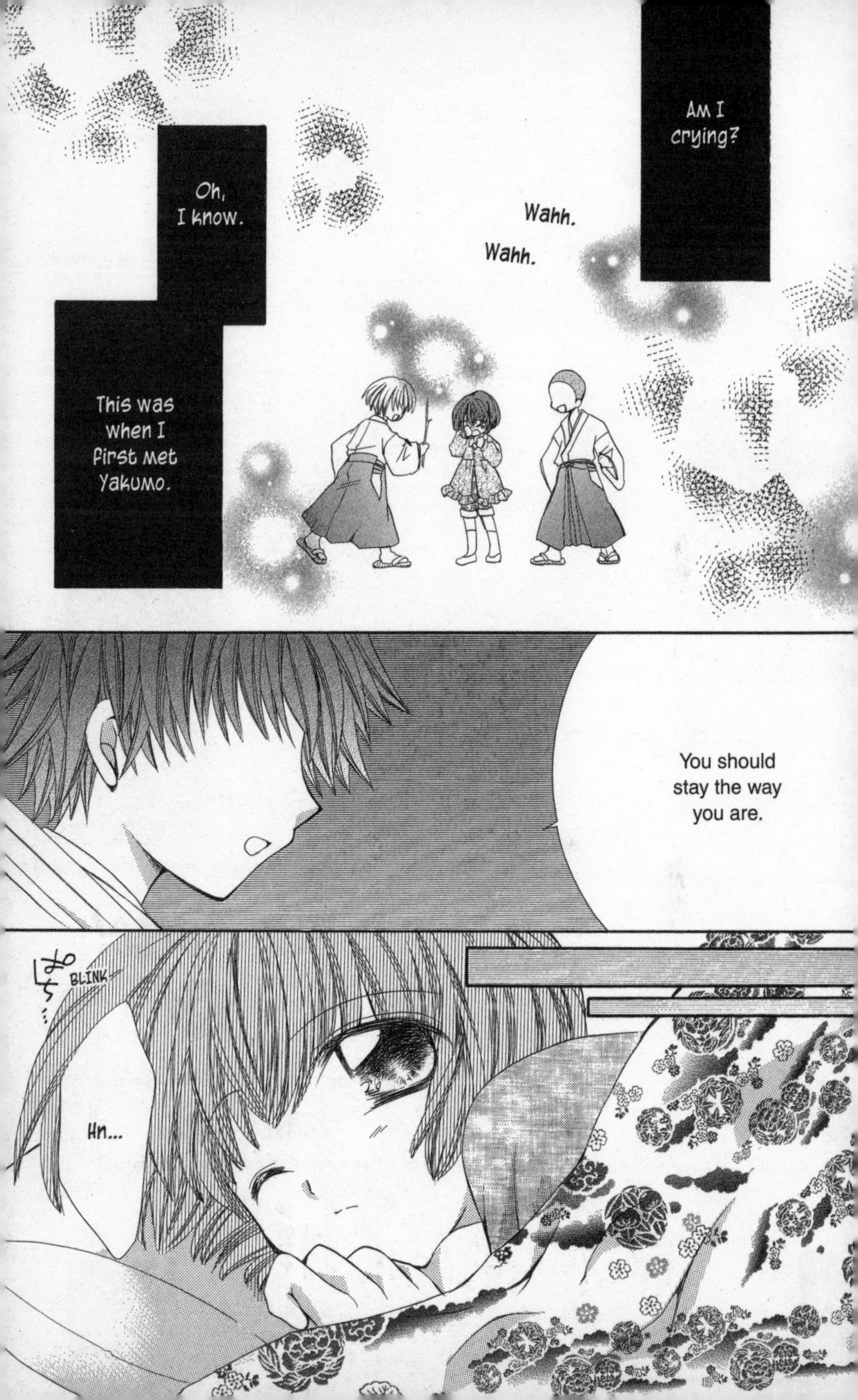
Am I crying?
Wahh.
Wahh.
Oh, I know.
This was when I first met Yakumo.
You should stay the way you are.
BLINK
Hn...

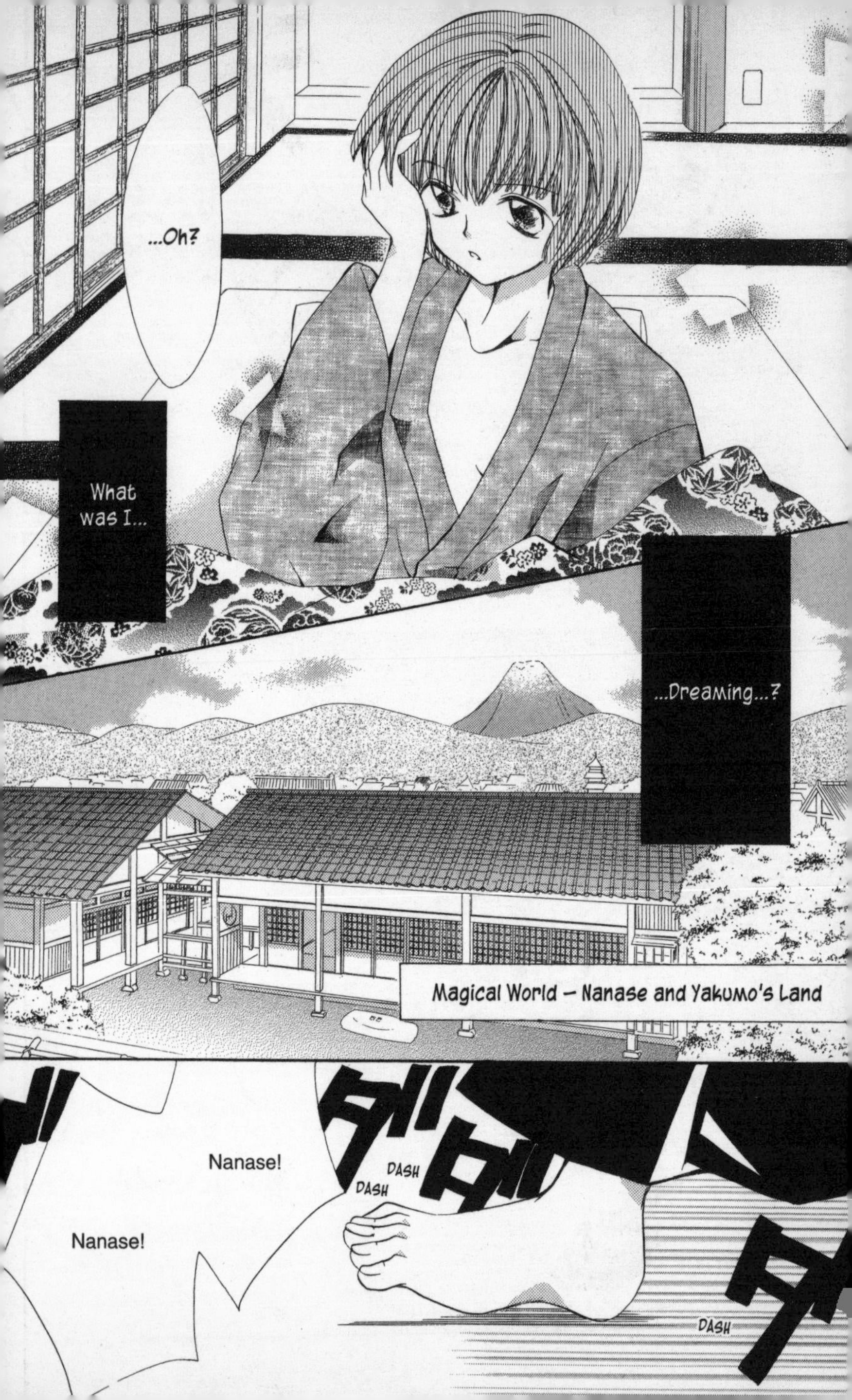
...Oh?
What was I...
...Dreaming...?
Magical World – Nanase and Yakumo's Land
DASH
DASH
DASH
Nanase!
Nanase!

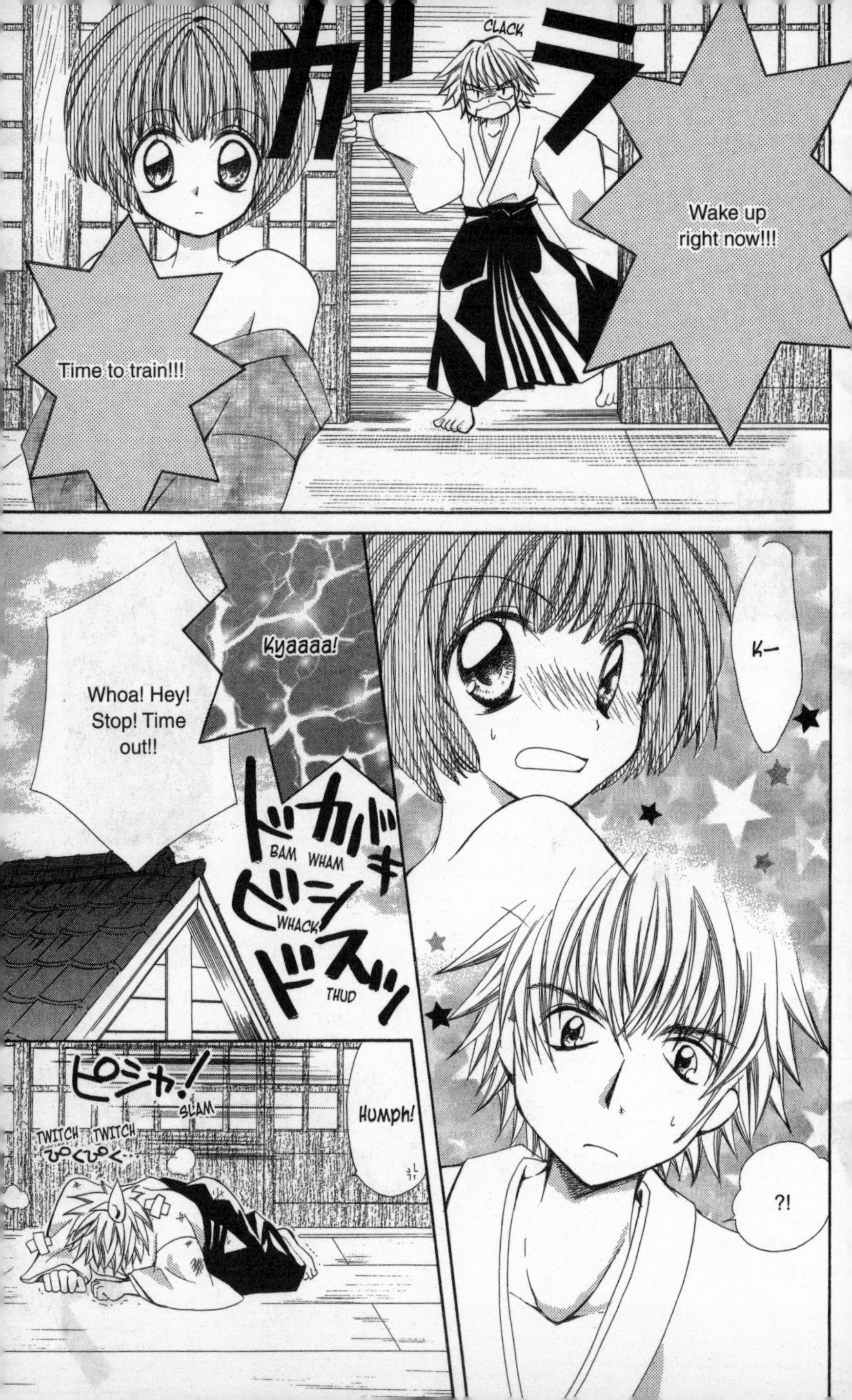

ガラ
CLACK
Wake up right now!!!
Time to train!!!
K–
?!
Kyaaaa!
Whoa! Hey! Stop! Time out!!
ドカバキ
BAM WHAM
ビシ
WHACK
ドスッ
THUD
Humph!
ピシャ!
SLAM
TWITCH TWITCH
ぴくぴく

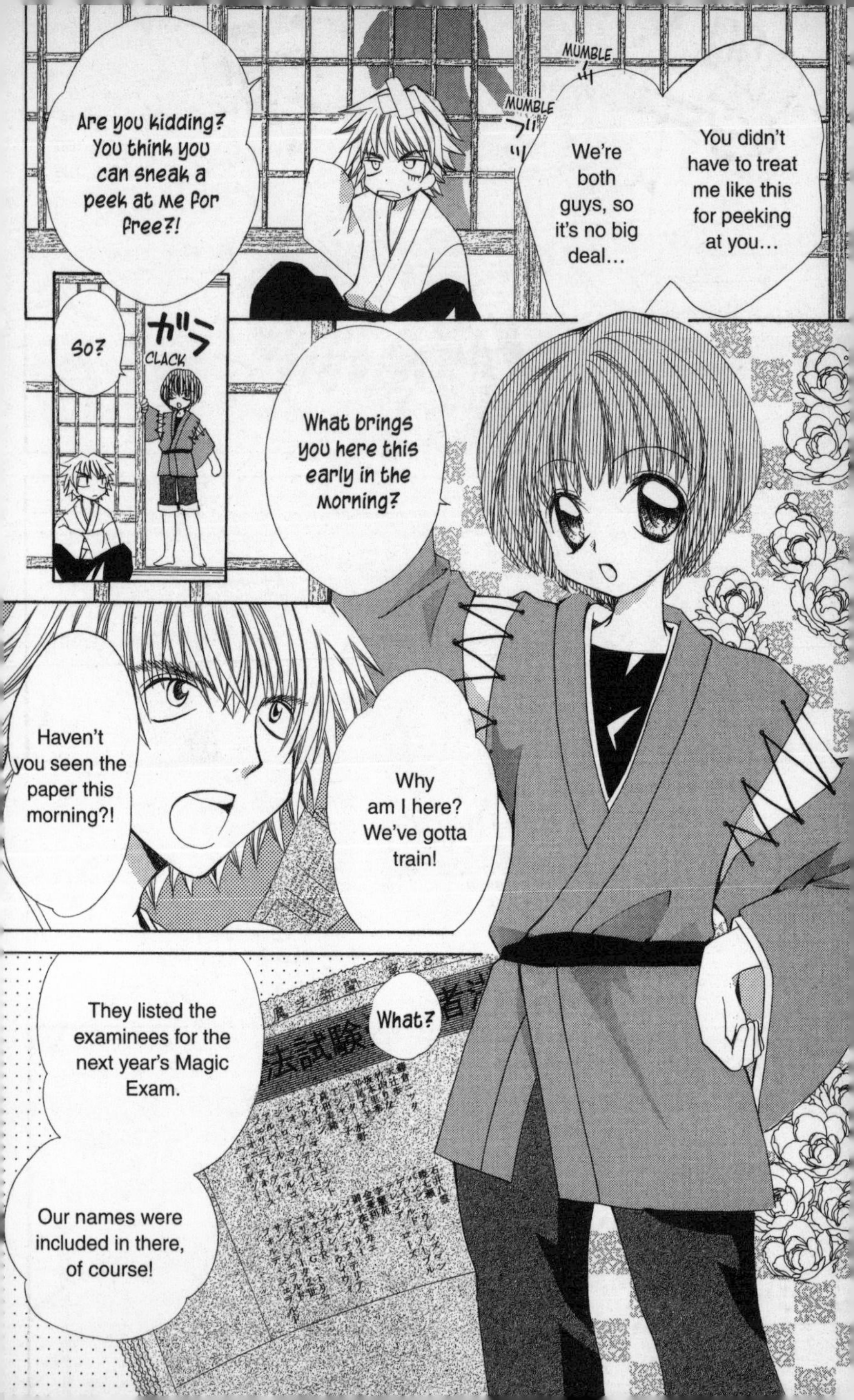
MUMBLE
MUMBLE
You didn't have to treat me like this for peeking at you…
We're both guys, so it's no big deal…
Are you kidding? You think you can sneak a peek at me for free?!
What brings you here this early in the morning?
Why am I here? We've gotta train!
What?
ガラ
CLACK
So?
Haven't you seen the paper this morning?!
They listed the examinees for the next year's Magic Exam.
Our names were included in there, of course!

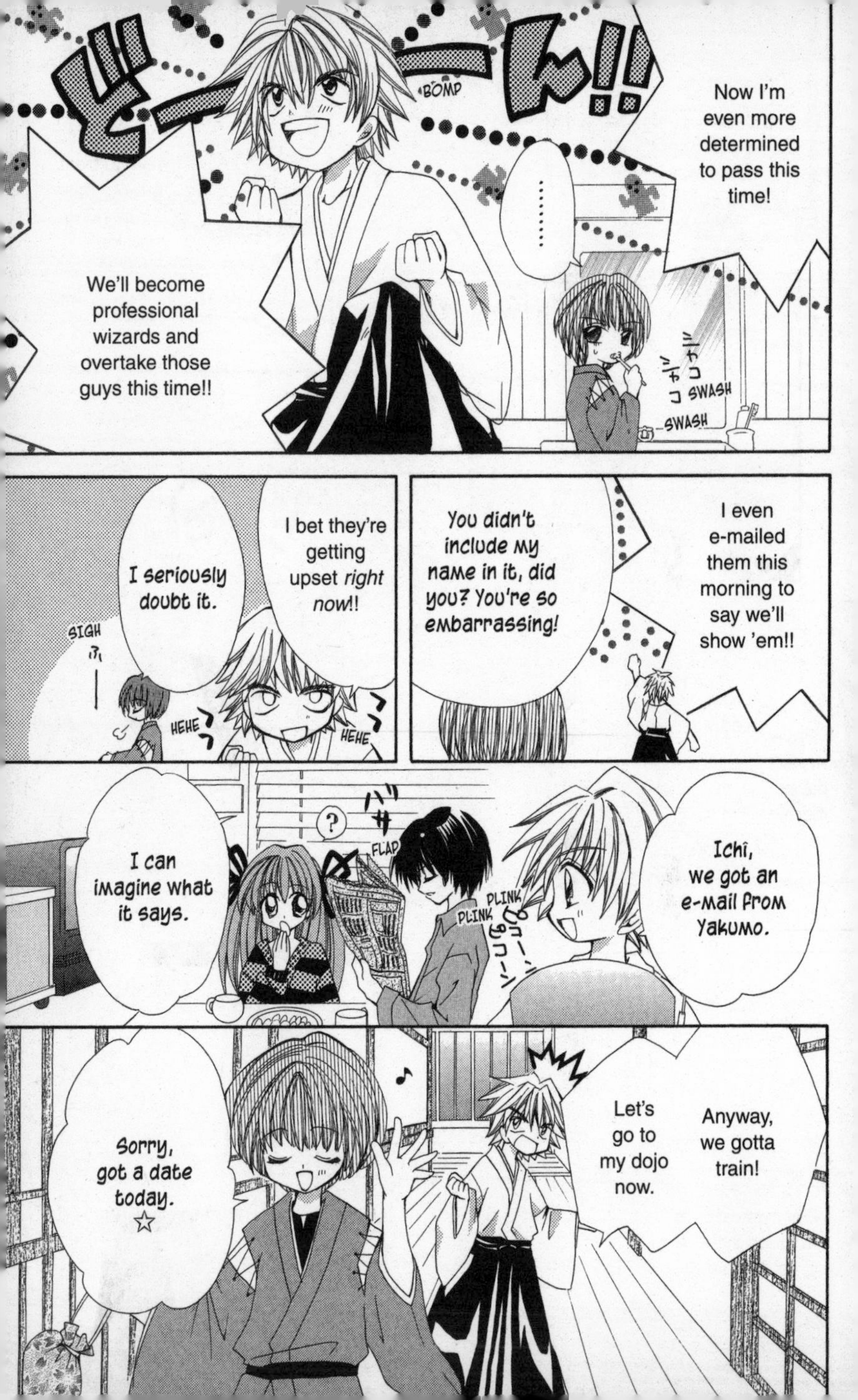
どーーん!!
BOMP
Now I'm even more determined to pass this time!
……
シャコシャコ
SWASH
SWASH
We'll become professional wizards and overtake those guys this time!!
I even e-mailed them this morning to say we'll show 'em!!
You didn't include my name in it, did you? You're so embarrassing!
I bet they're getting upset *right now*!!
HEHE
HEHE
I seriously doubt it.
SIGH
Ichi, we got an e-mail from Yakumo.
PLINK
PLINK
FLAP
?
I can imagine what it says.
Anyway, we gotta train!
Let's go to my dojo now.
Sorry, got a date today. ☆

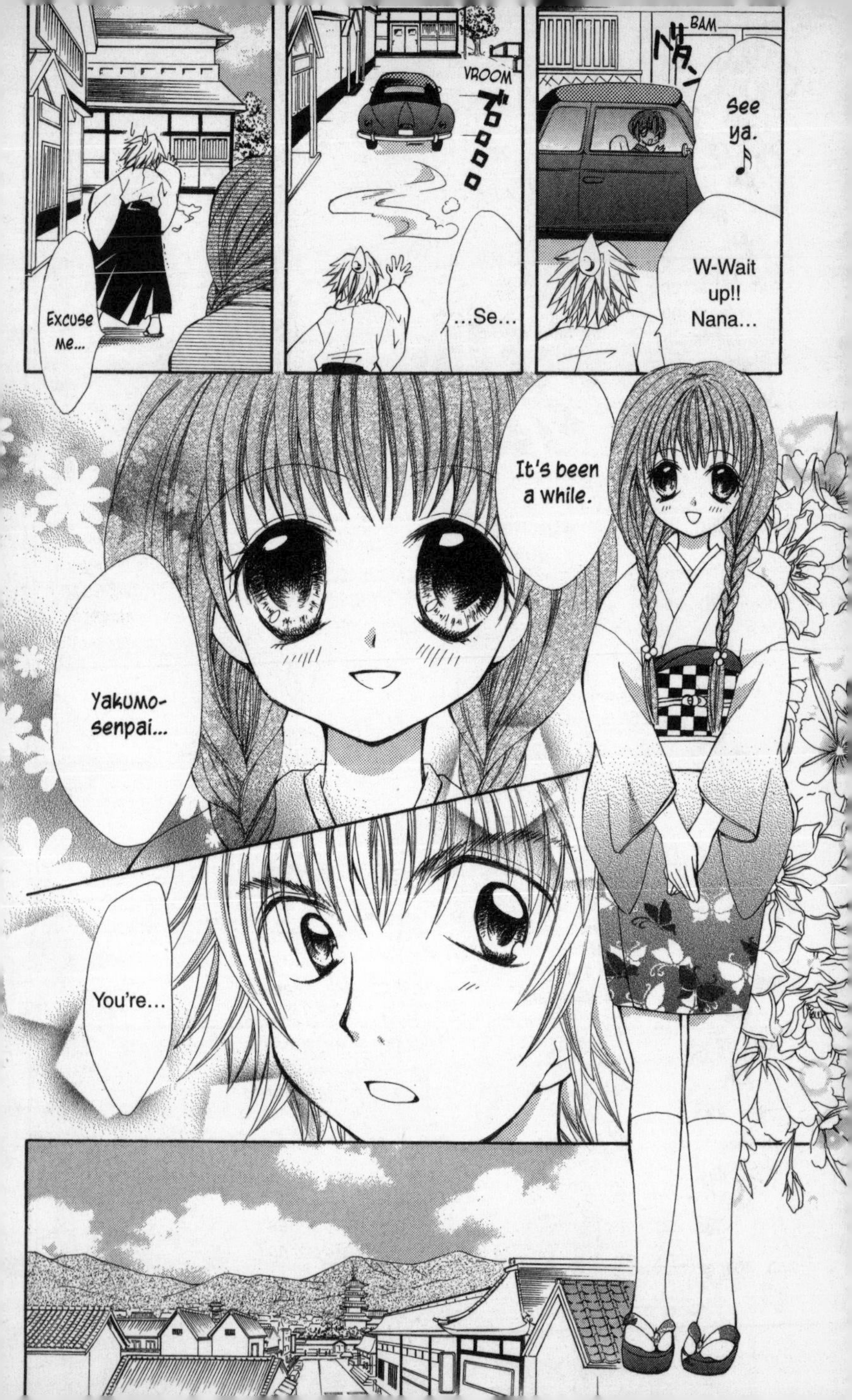
BAM
See ya. ♪
W-Wait up!! Nana...
VROOM
...Se...
Excuse me...
It's been a while.
Yakumo-senpai...
You're...

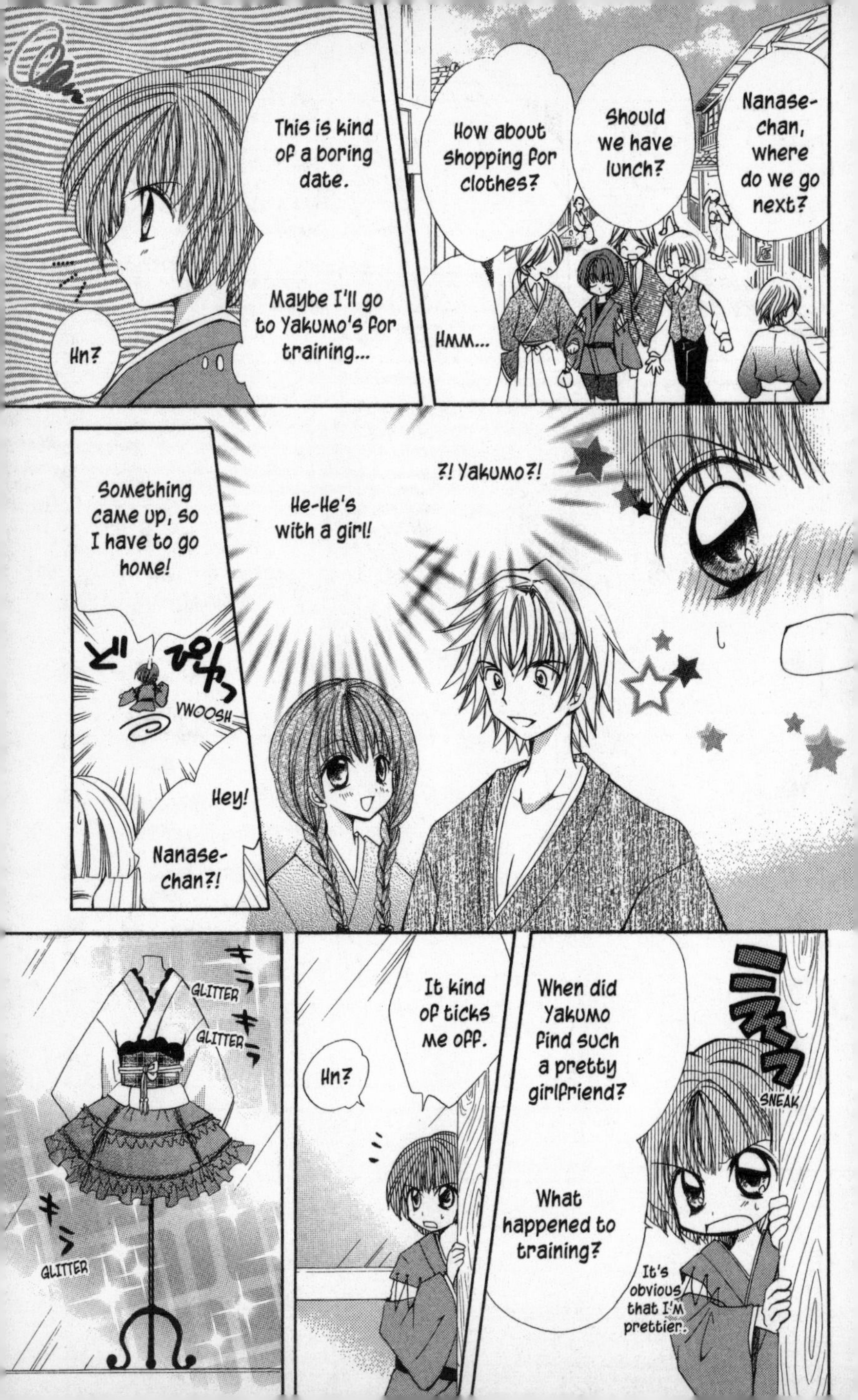

Nanase-chan, where do we go next?
Should we have lunch?
How about shopping for clothes?
Hmm...
This is kind of a boring date.
Maybe I'll go to Yakumo's for training...
....
Hn?
?! Yakumo?!
He-He's with a girl!
Something came up, so I have to go home!
VWOOSH
Hey!
Nanase-chan?!
SNEAK
When did Yakumo find such a pretty girlfriend?
What happened to training?
It's obvious that I'm prettier.
It kind of ticks me off.
Hn?
GLITTER
GLITTER
GLITTER

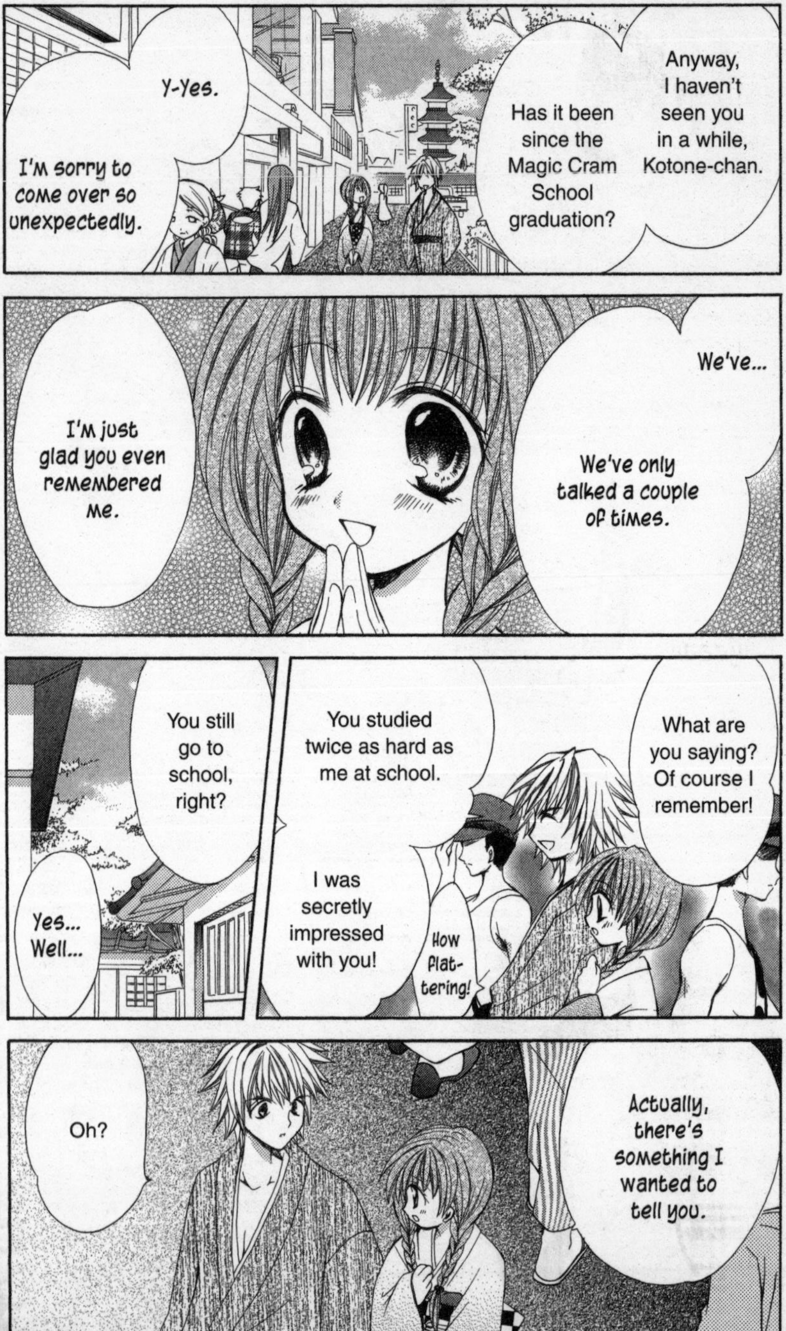
Anyway, I haven't seen you in a while, Kotone-chan.
Has it been since the Magic Cram School graduation?
Y-Yes.
I'm sorry to come over so unexpectedly.
We've...
We've only talked a couple of times.
I'm just glad you even remembered me.
What are you saying? Of course I remember!
You studied twice as hard as me at school.
I was secretly impressed with you!
How flat-tering!
You still go to school, right?
Yes... Well...
Actually, there's something I wanted to tell you.
Oh?

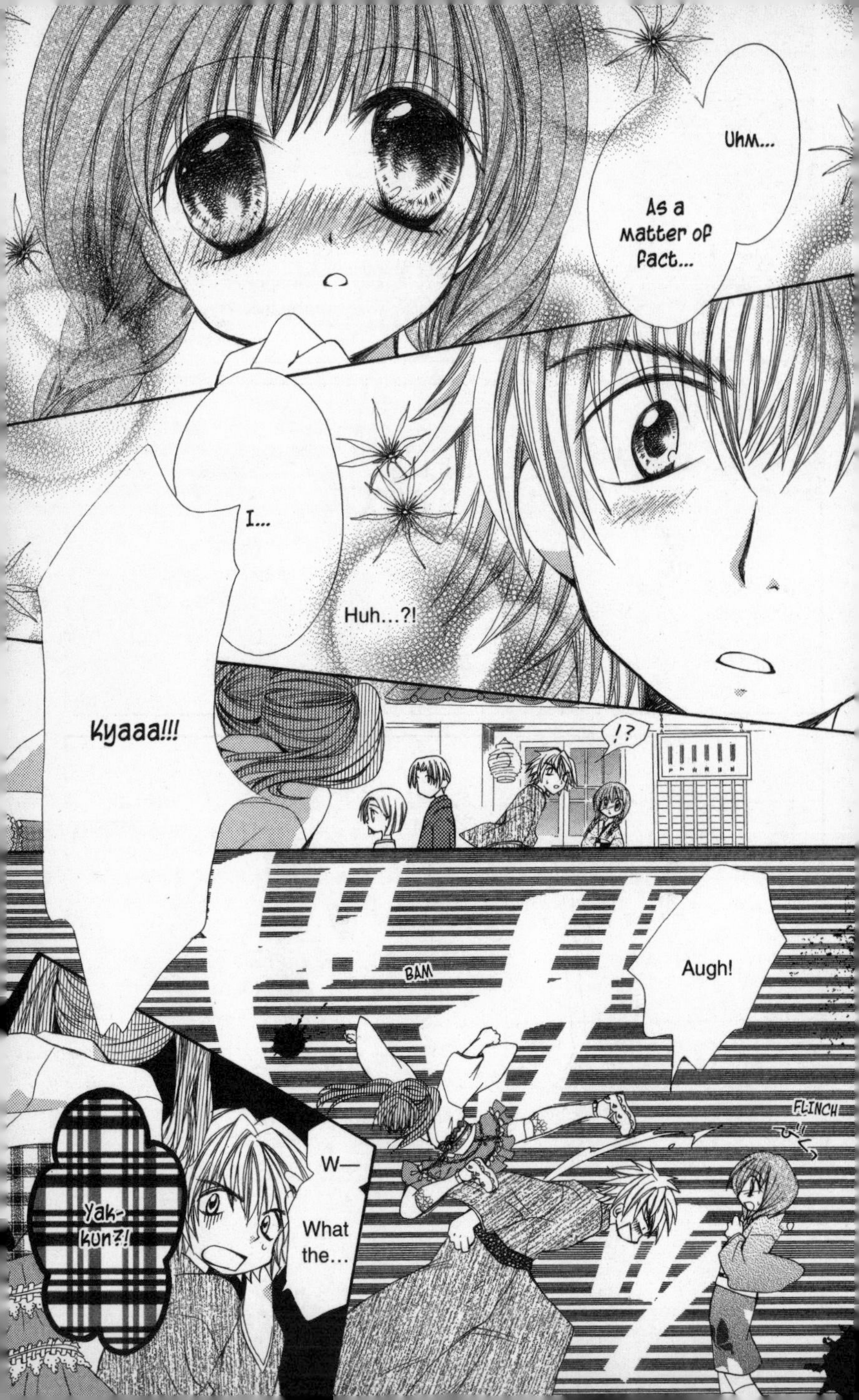
Uhm...
As a matter of fact...
I...
Huh...?!
Kyaaa!!!
!?
Augh!
BAM
FLINCH
W—
What the...
Yak-kun?!

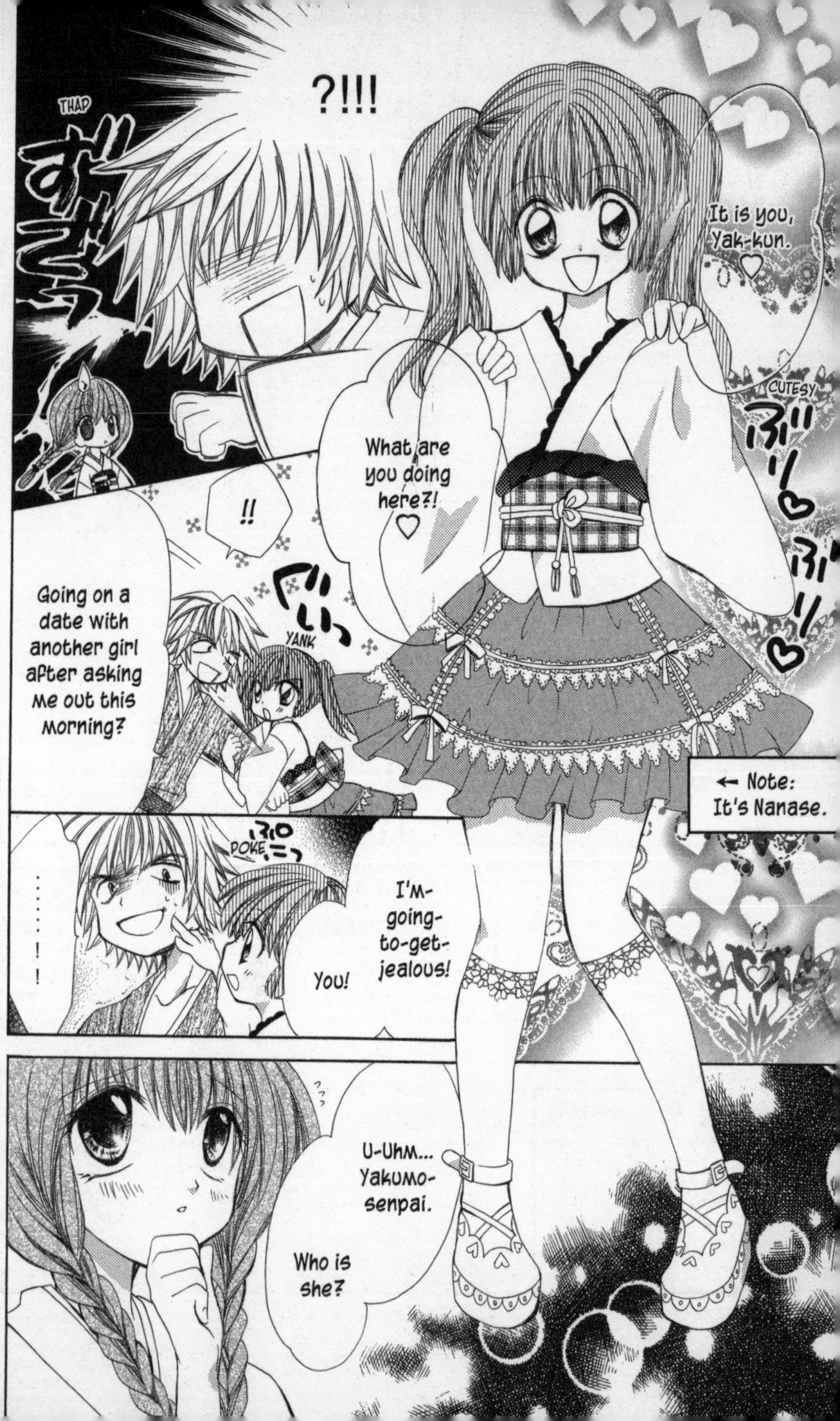
It is you, Yak-kun. ♡
CUTESY
What are you doing here?! ♡
← Note: It's Nanase.
?!!!
THAP
!!
Going on a date with another girl after asking me out this morning?
YANK
POKE
I'm-going-to-get-jealous!
You!
......!!
U-Uhm... Yakumo-senpai.
Who is she?

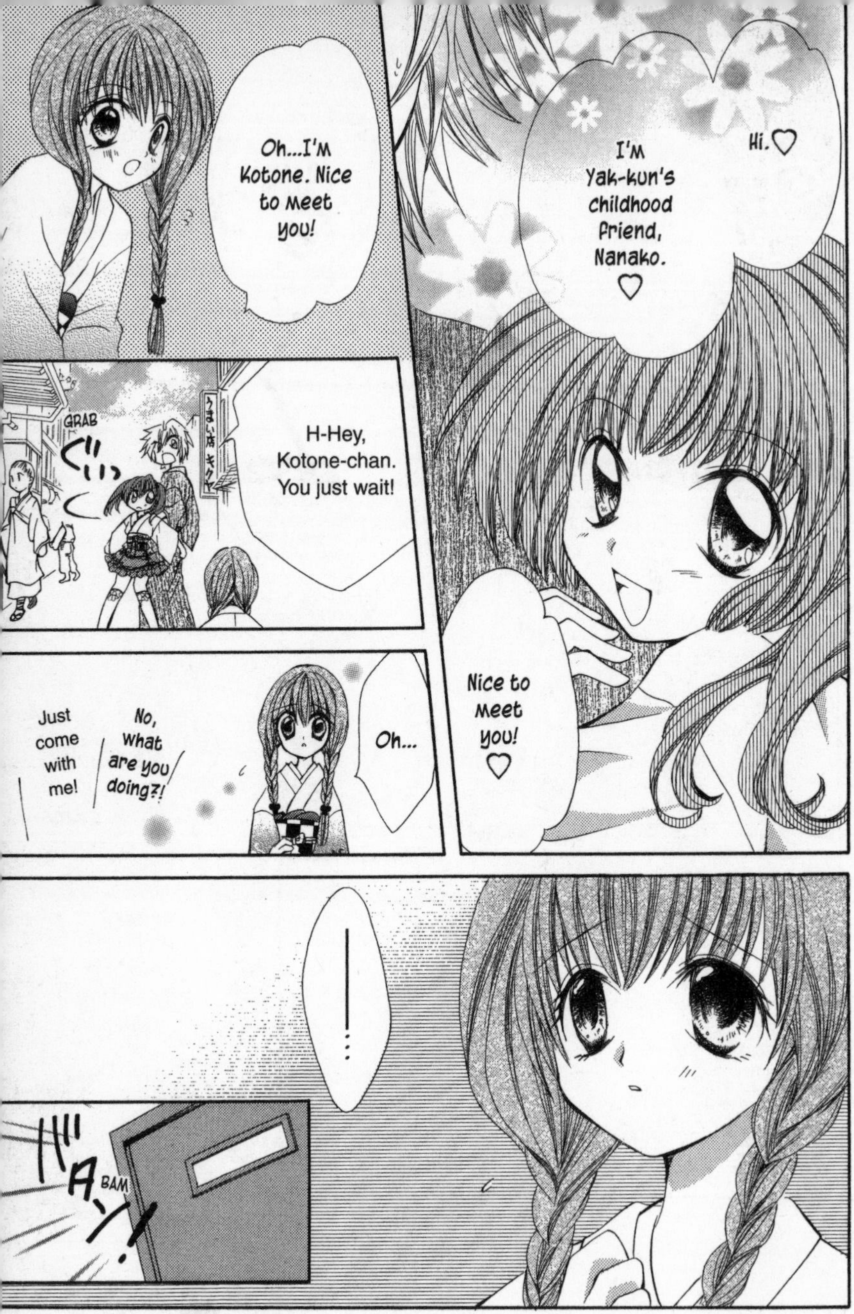
Hi. ♡
I'm Yak-kun's childhood friend, Nanako. ♡
Nice to meet you! ♡
Oh...I'm Kotone. Nice to meet you!
H-Hey, Kotone-chan. You just wait!
GRAB
Oh...
No, what are you doing?!
Just come with me!
—...
BAM

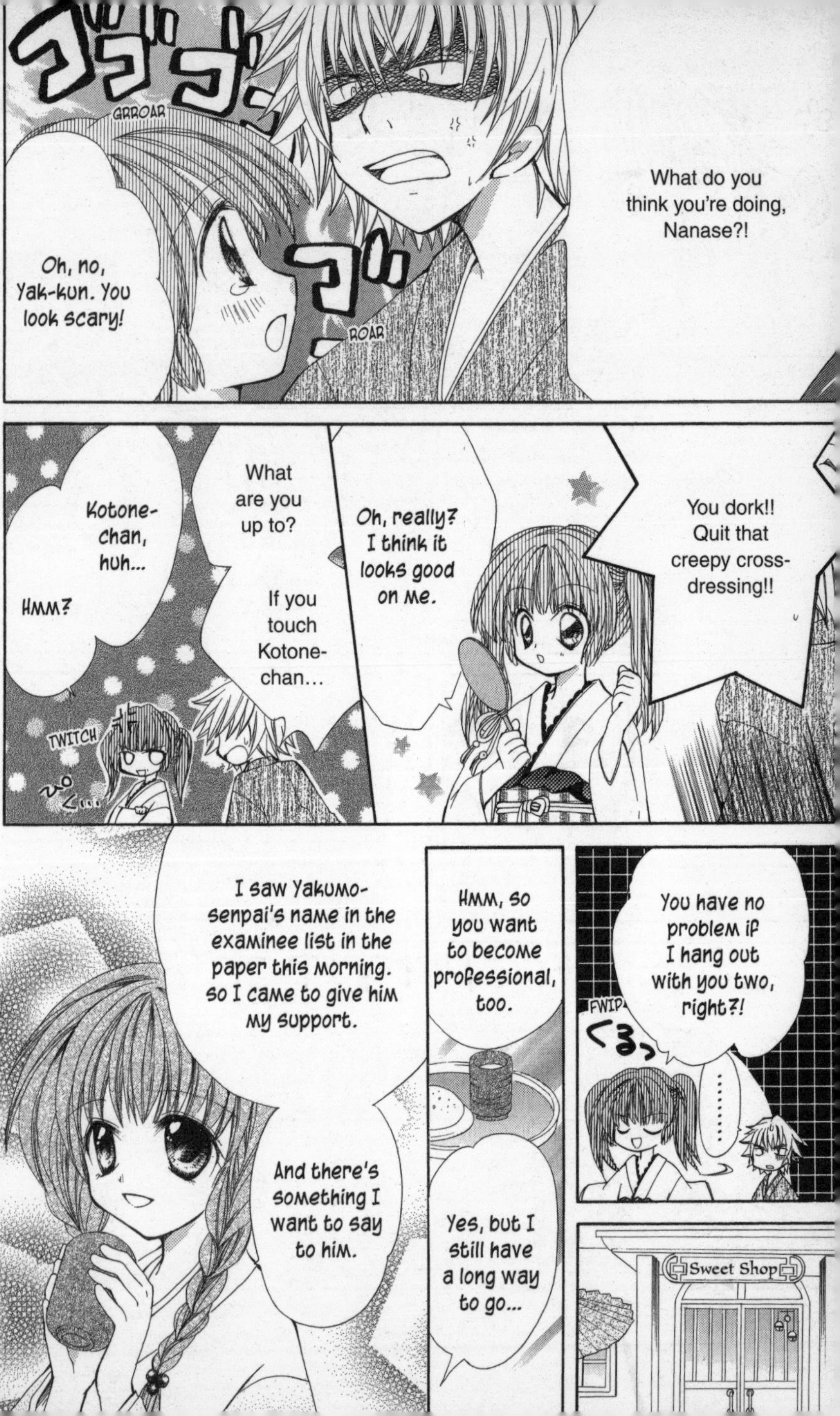
What do you think you're doing, Nanase?!
GRROAR
ROAR
Oh, no, Yak-kun. You look scary!
You dork!! Quit that creepy cross-dressing!!
Oh, really? I think it looks good on me.
What are you up to?
If you touch Kotone-chan…
Kotone-chan, huh...
HMM?
TWITCH
You have no problem if I hang out with you two, right?!
FWIP
......
Sweet Shop
Hmm, so you want to become professional, too.
Yes, but I still have a long way to go...
I saw Yakumo-senpai's name in the examinee list in the paper this morning. so I came to give him my support.
And there's something I want to say to him.

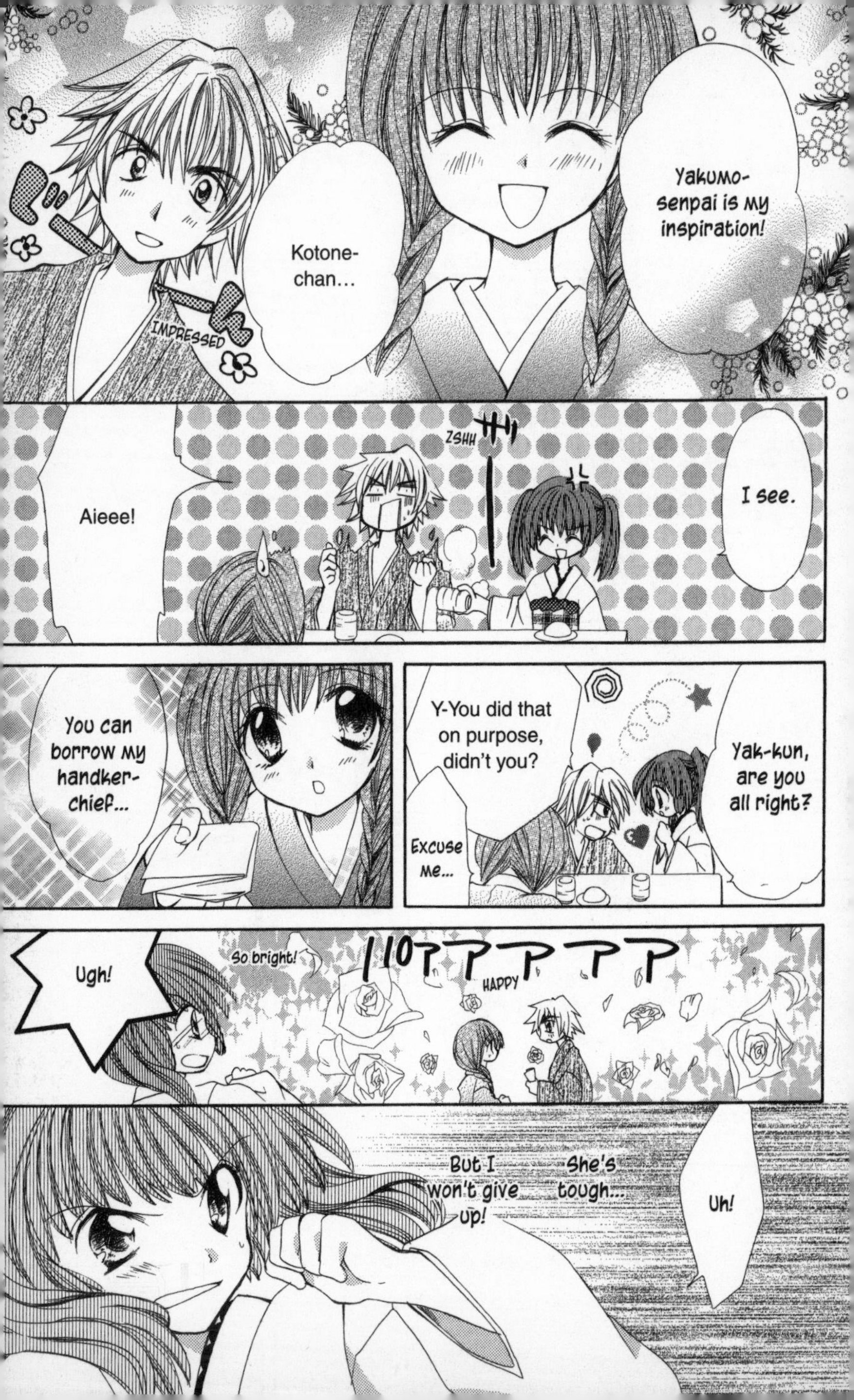
Yakumo-senpai is my inspiration!
Kotone-chan...
IMPRESSED
I see.
ZSHH
Aieee!
Yak-kun, are you all right?
Y-You did that on purpose, didn't you?
Excuse me...
You can borrow my handkerchief...
HAPPY
So bright!
Ugh!
Uh!
She's tough...
But I won't give up!

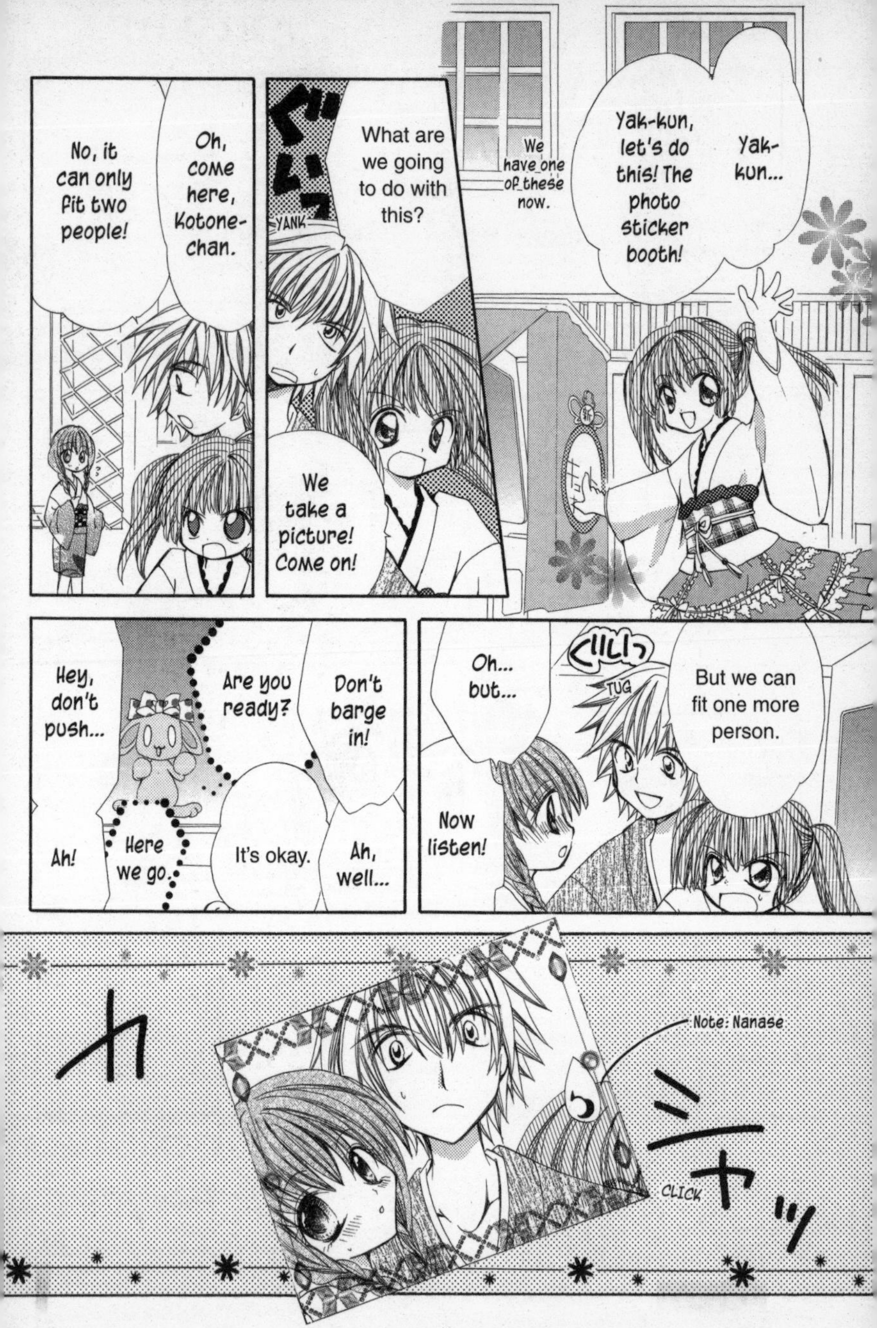
Yak-kun...
Yak-kun, let's do this! The photo sticker booth!
We have one of these now.
ぐいっ
YANK
What are we going to do with this?
We take a picture! Come on!
Oh, come here, Kotone-chan.
No, it can only fit two people!
But we can fit one more person.
くいっ
TUG
Oh... but...
Now listen!
Don't barge in!
Are you ready?
Hey, don't push...
Ah, well...
It's okay.
Here we go.
Ah!
カシャッ
CLICK
Note: Nanase

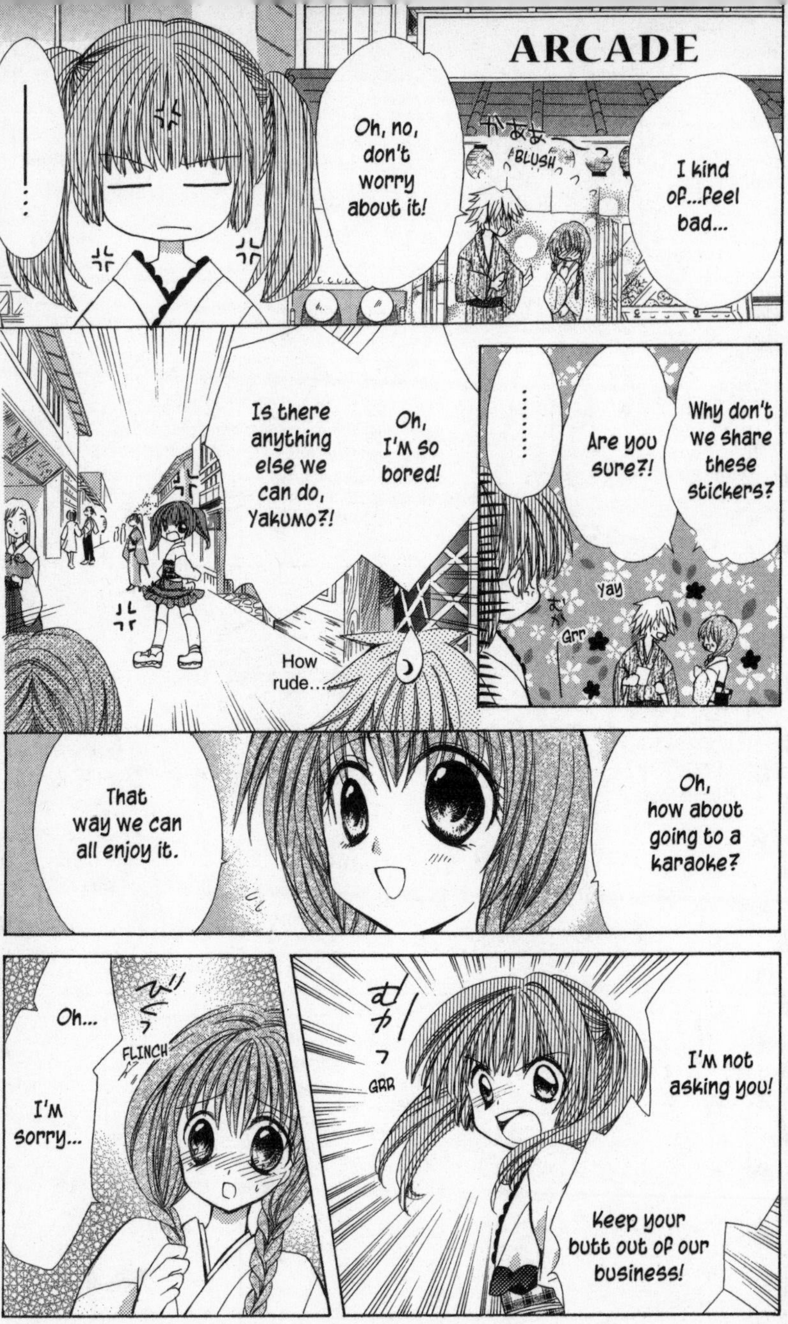
ARCADE
I kind of...feel bad...
BLUSH
Oh, no, don't worry about it!
—......
Why don't we share these stickers?
Are you sure?!
......
Yay
Grr
Oh, I'm so bored!
Is there anything else we can do, Yakumo?!
How rude...
Oh, how about going to a karaoke?
That way we can all enjoy it.
I'm not asking you!
GRR
Keep your butt out of our business!
FLINCH
Oh...
I'm sorry...

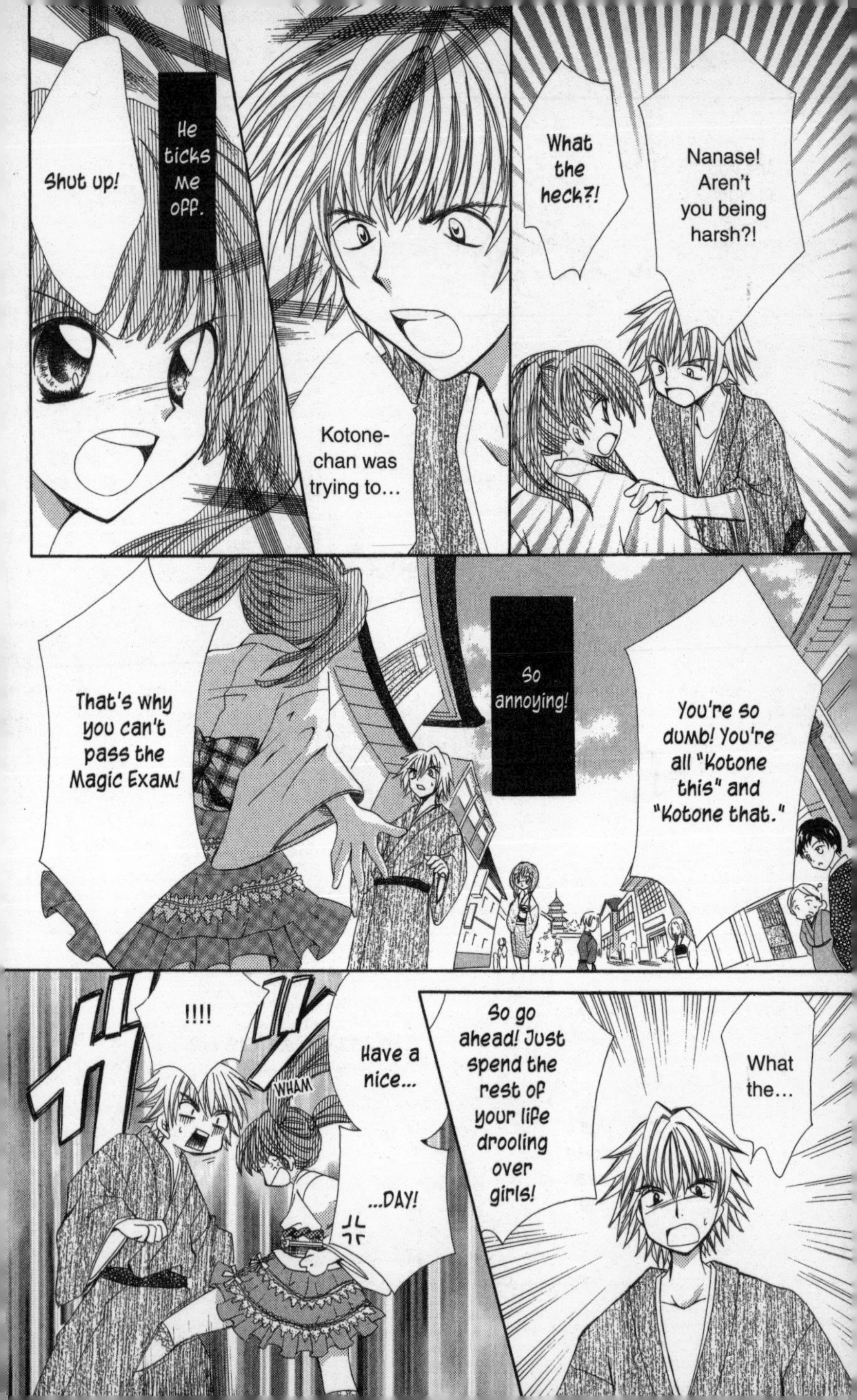

Nanase! Aren't you being harsh?!
What the heck?!
Kotone-chan was trying to…
He ticks me off.
Shut up!
You're so dumb! You're all "Kotone this" and "Kotone that."
So annoying!
That's why you can't pass the Magic Exam!
What the…
So go ahead! Just spend the rest of your life drooling over girls!
Have a nice...
!!!!
WHAM
...DAY!

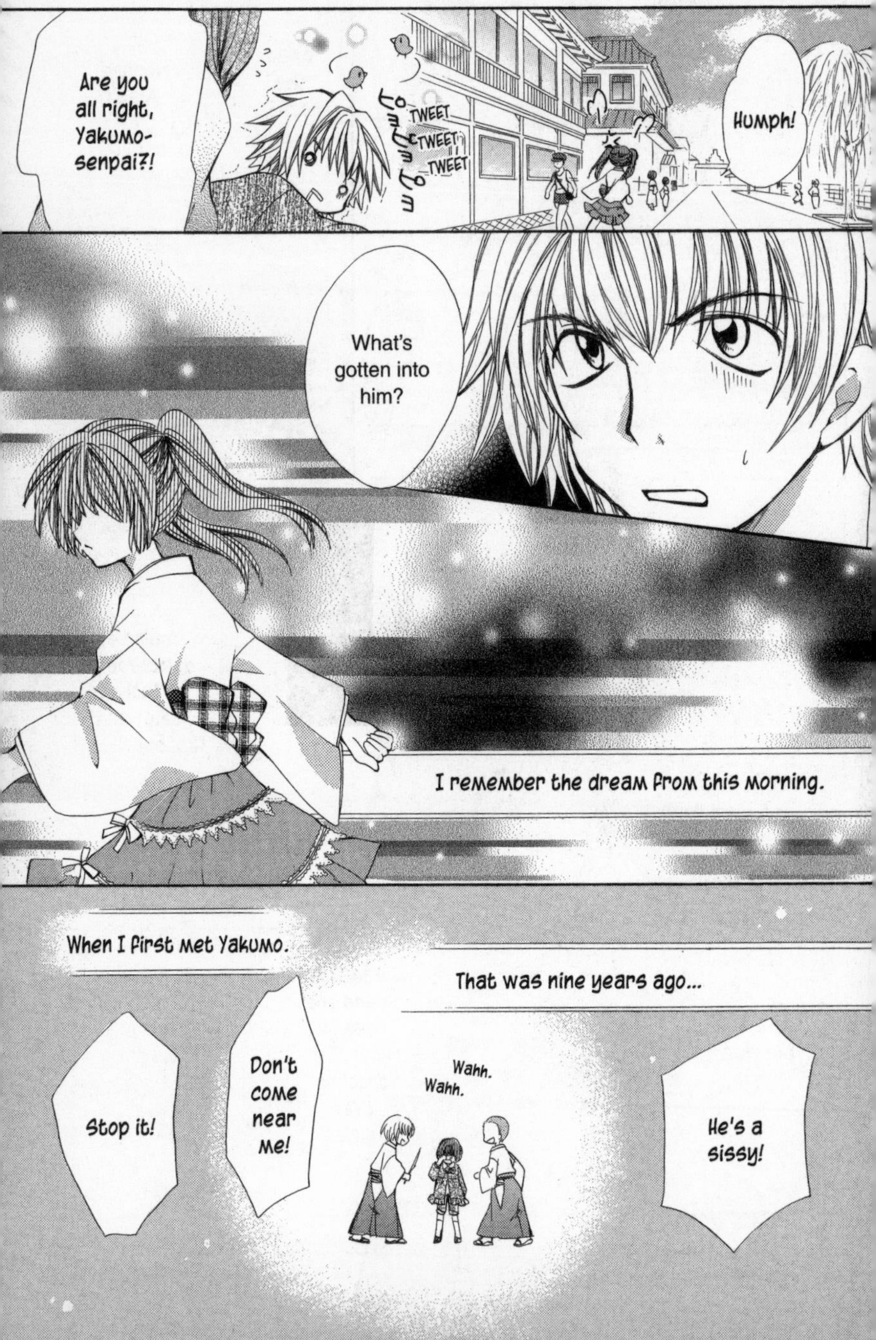
Humph!
TWEET TWEET TWEET
Are you all right, Yakumo-senpai?!
What's gotten into him?
I remember the dream from this morning.
When I first met Yakumo.
That was nine years ago...
He's a sissy!
Wahh. Wahh.
Don't come near me!
Stop it!

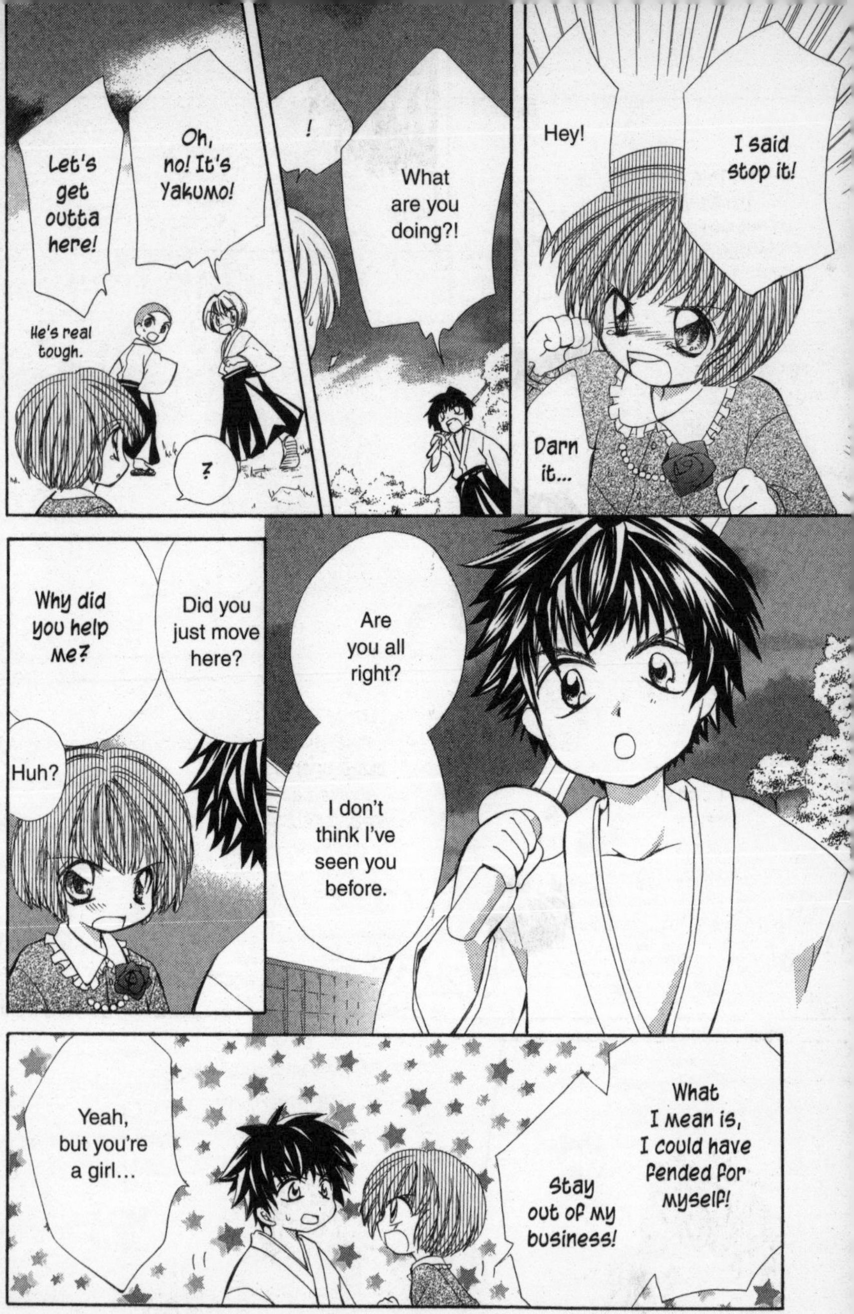
I said stop it!
Hey!
Darn it...
What are you doing?!
!
Oh, no! It's Yakumo!
Let's get outta here!
He's real tough.
?
Are you all right?
I don't think I've seen you before.
Did you just move here?
Why did you help me?
Huh?
What I mean is, I could have fended for myself!
Stay out of my business!
Yeah, but you're a girl...

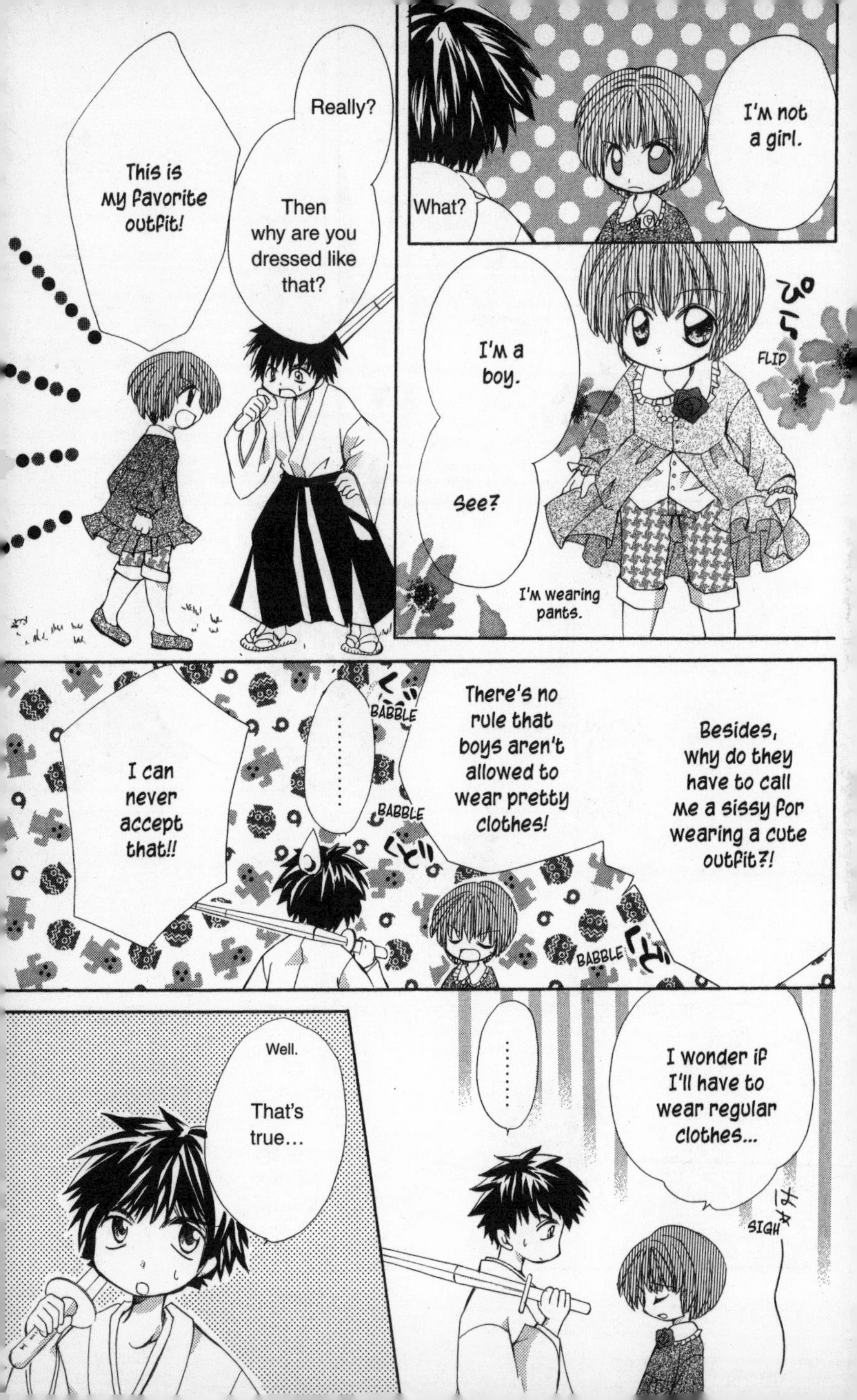
I'm not a girl.
What?
I'm a boy.
See?
FLIP
I'm wearing pants.
Really?
Then why are you dressed like that?
This is my favorite outfit!
Besides, why do they have to call me a sissy for wearing a cute outfit?!
There's no rule that boys aren't allowed to wear pretty clothes!
BABBLE
BABBLE
BABBLE
......
I can never accept that!!
I wonder if I'll have to wear regular clothes...
SIGH
......
Well.
That's true...

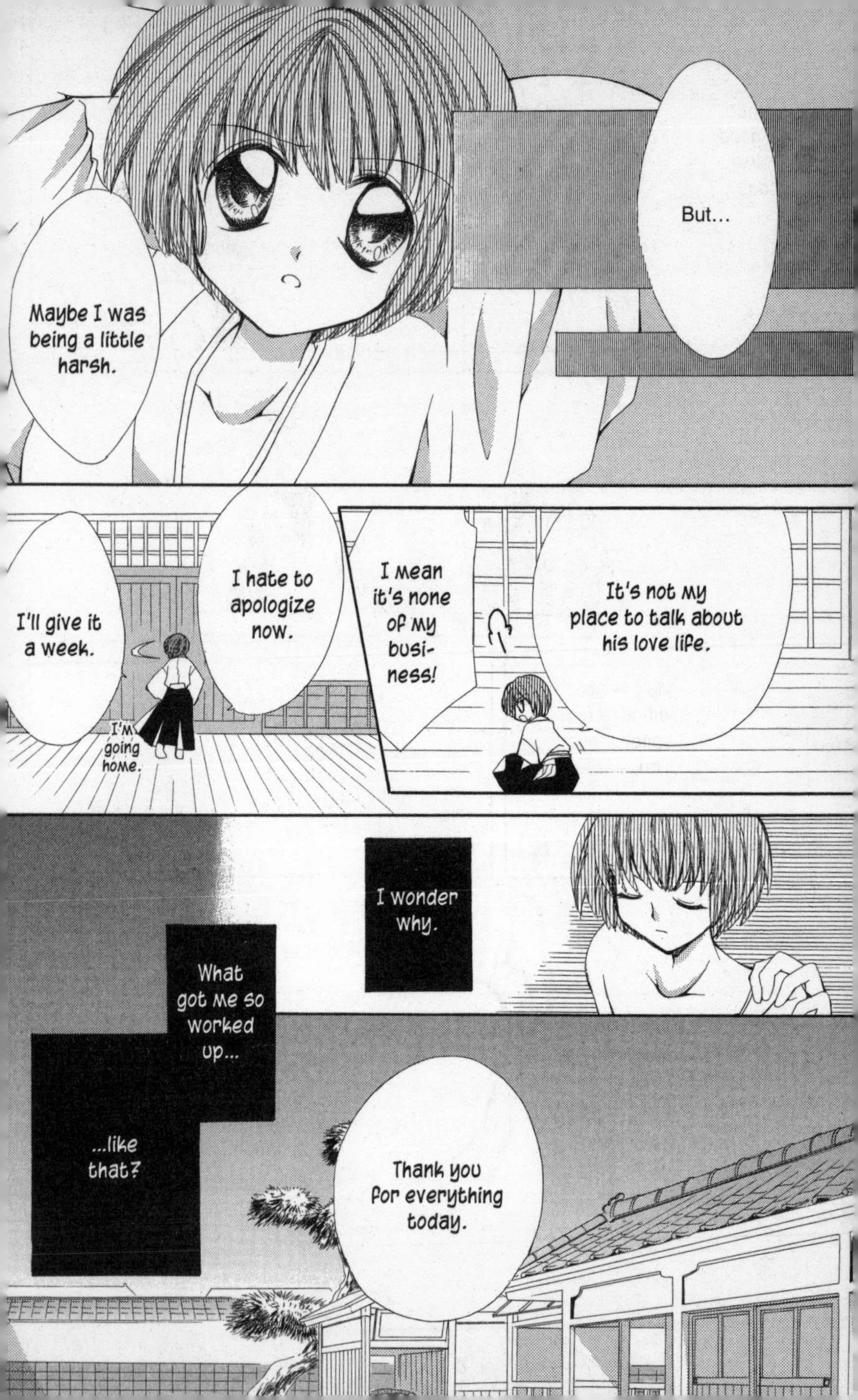

But...
Maybe I was being a little harsh.
It's not my place to talk about his love life.
I mean it's none of my business!
I hate to apologize now.
I'll give it a week.
I'm going home.
I wonder why.
What got me so worked up...
...like that?
Thank you for everything today.

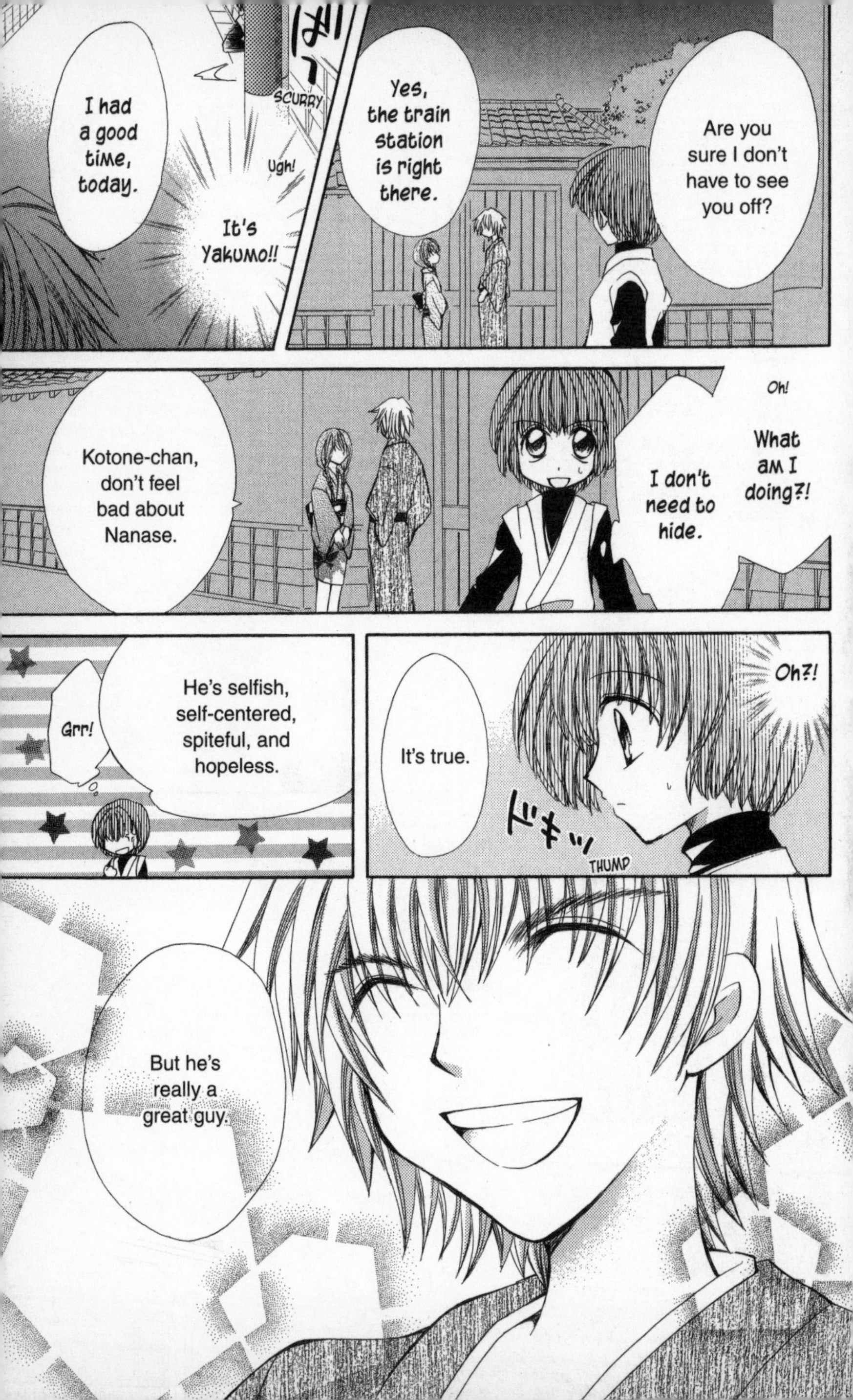
Are you sure I don't have to see you off?
Yes, the train station is right there.
ぱっ
SCURRY
Ugh!
It's Yakumo!!
I had a good time, today.
Oh!
What am I doing?!
I don't need to hide.
Kotone-chan, don't feel bad about Nanase.
Oh?!
ドキッ
THUMP
It's true.
He's selfish, self-centered, spiteful, and hopeless.
Grr!
But he's really a great guy.

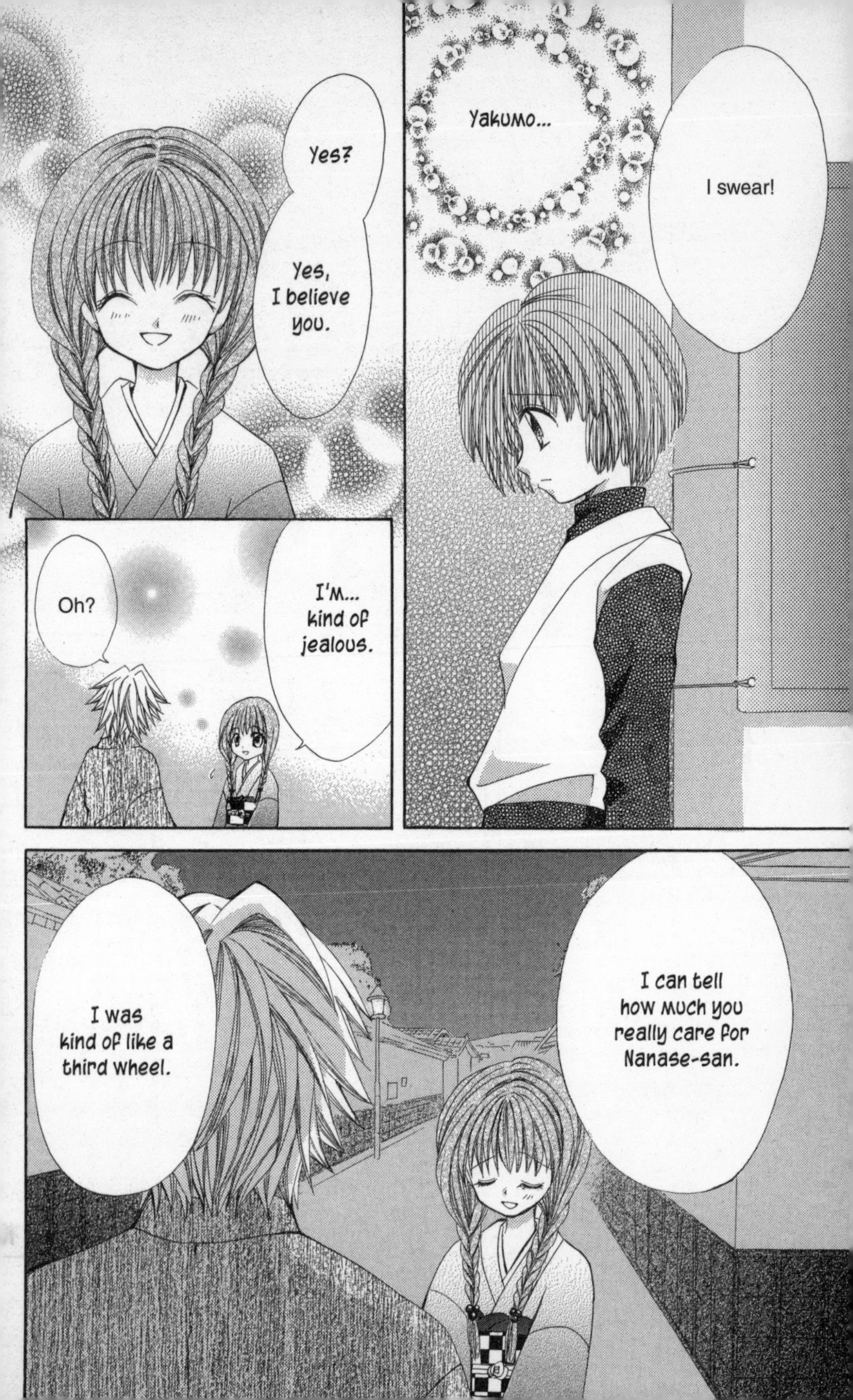
I swear!
Yakumo...
Yes?
Yes, I believe you.
I'm... kind of jealous.
Oh?
I can tell how much you really care for Nanase-san.
I was kind of like a third wheel.

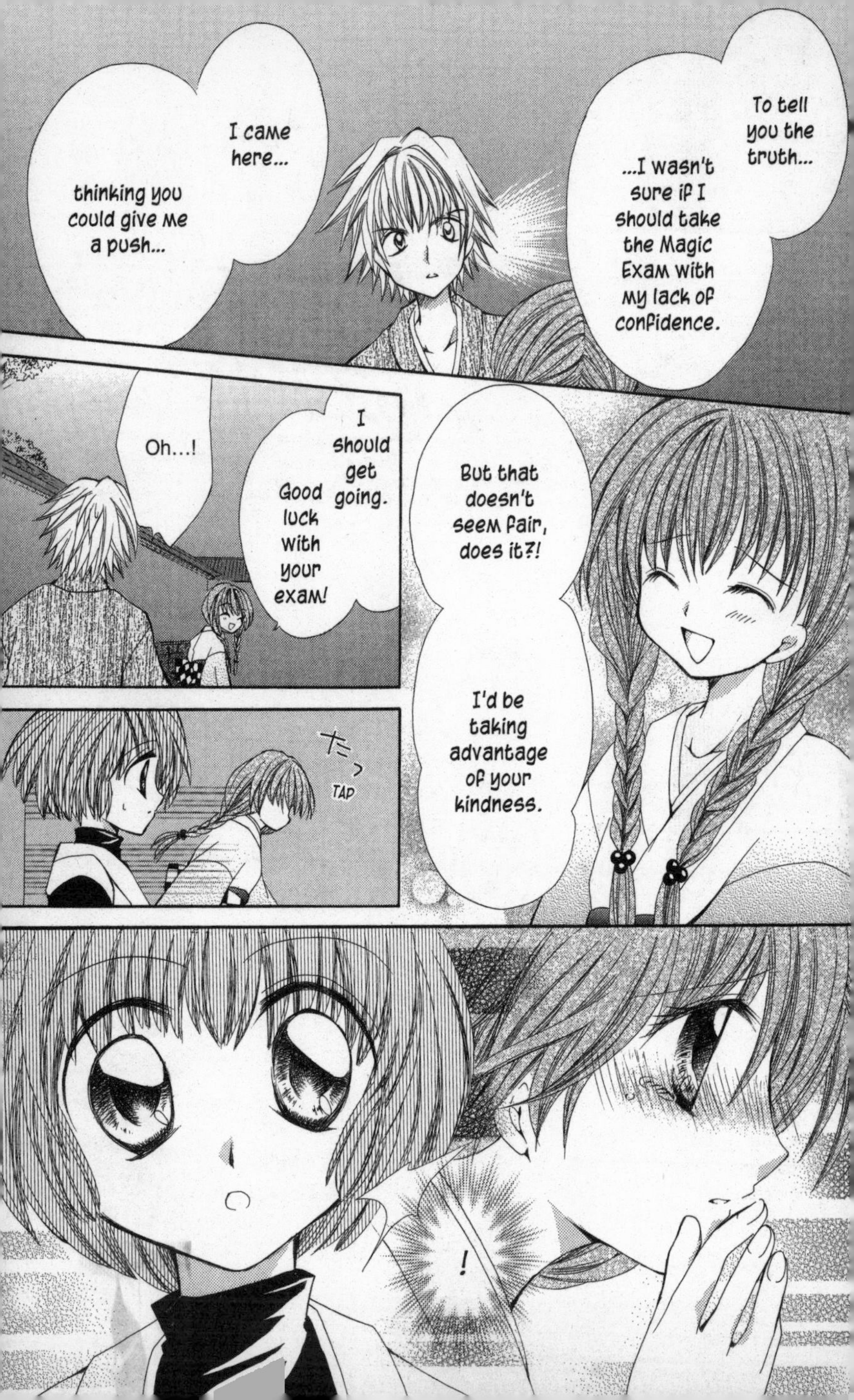
To tell you the truth...
...I wasn't sure if I should take the Magic Exam with my lack of confidence.
I came here...
thinking you could give me a push...
But that doesn't seem fair, does it?!
I'd be taking advantage of your kindness.
I should get going.
Good luck with your exam!
Oh...!
たっ
TAP
!

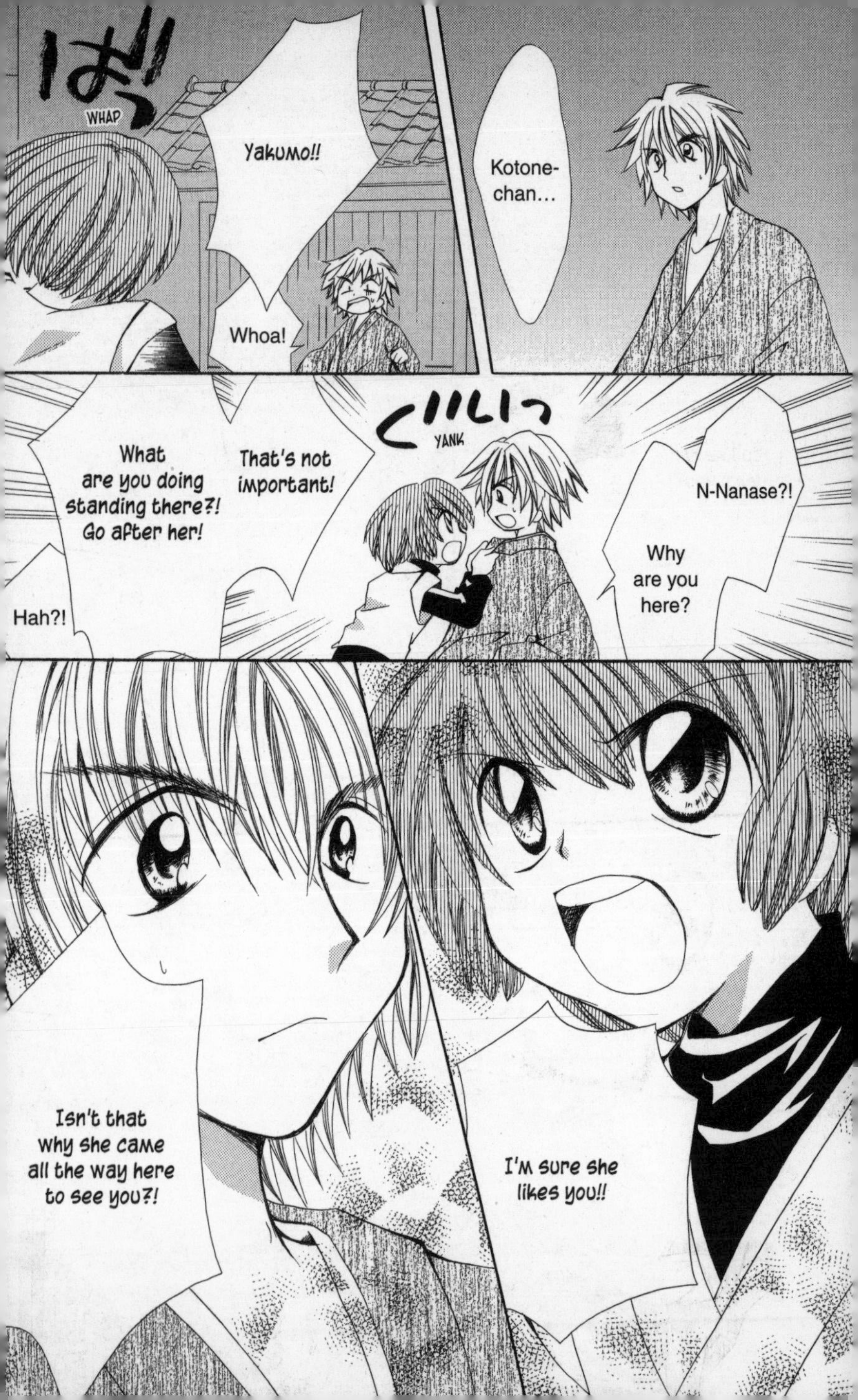

Kotone-chan…
Yakumo!!
WHAP
Whoa!
N-Nanase?!
Why are you here?
YANK
That's not important!
What are you doing standing there?! Go after her!
Hah?!
I'm sure she likes you!!
Isn't that why she came all the way here to see you?!

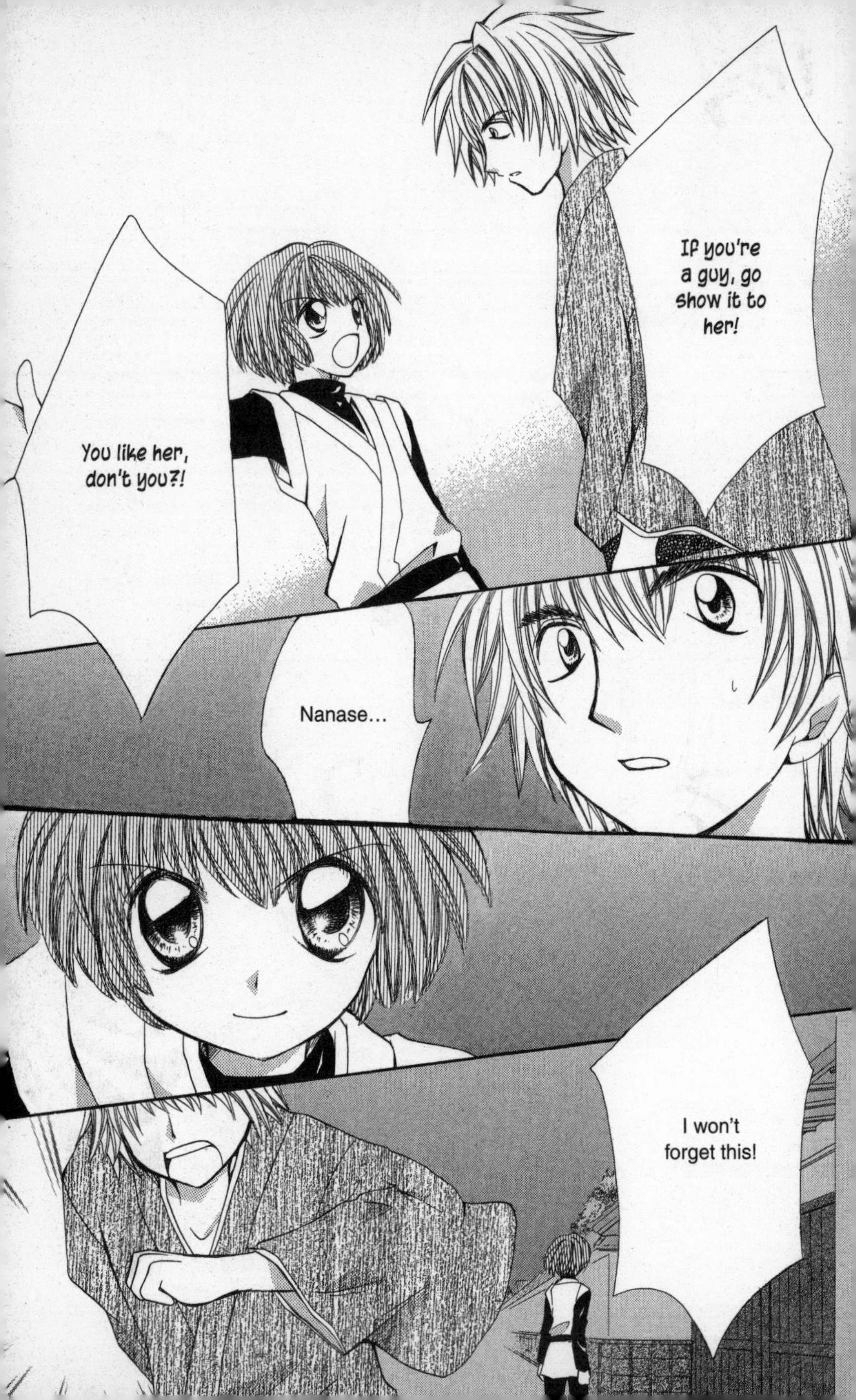
If you're a guy, go show it to her!
You like her, don't you?!
Nanase...
I won't forget this!

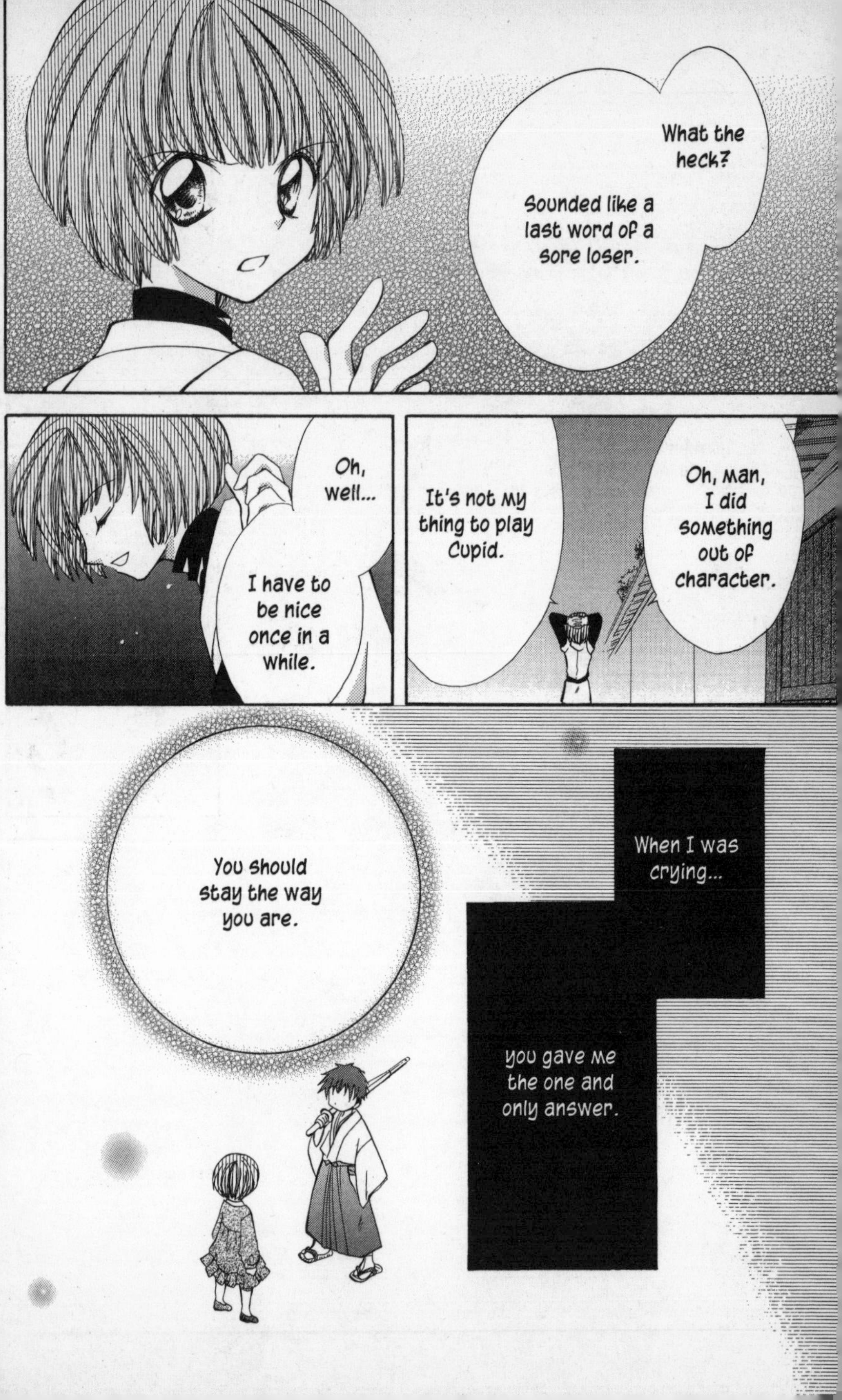
What the heck?
Sounded like a last word of a sore loser.
Oh, man, I did something out of character.
It's not my thing to play Cupid.
Oh, well...
I have to be nice once in a while.
When I was crying...
you gave me the one and only answer.
You should stay the way you are.

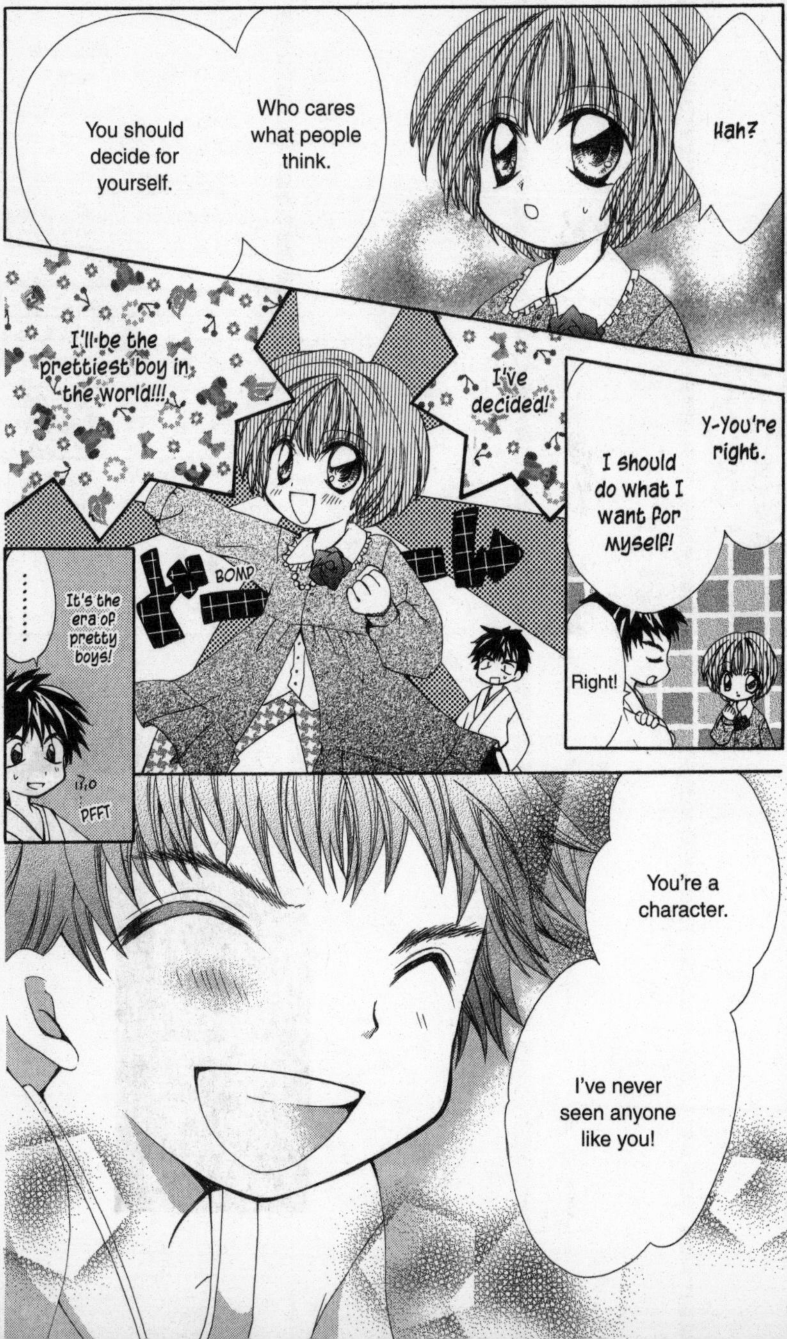
Hah?
Who cares what people think.
You should decide for yourself.
Y-You're right.
I should do what I want for myself!
Right!
I've decided!
I'll be the prettiest boy in the world!!!
BOMP
It's the era of pretty boys!
......
PFFT
You're a character.
I've never seen anyone like you!

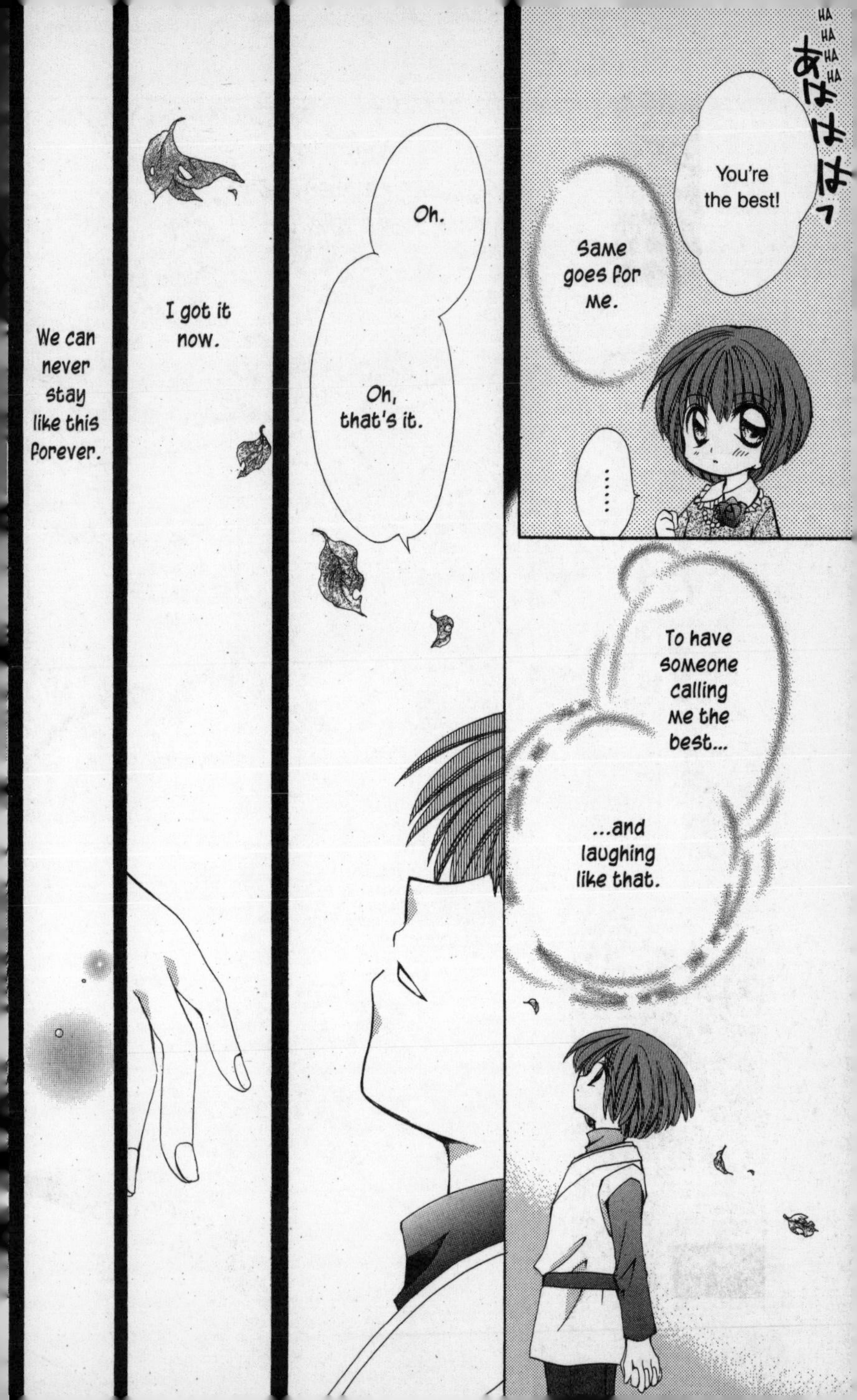
HA HA HA HA
あははは っ
You're the best!
Same goes for me.
......
To have someone calling me the best...
...and laughing like that.
Oh.
Oh, that's it.
I got it now.
We can never stay like this forever.

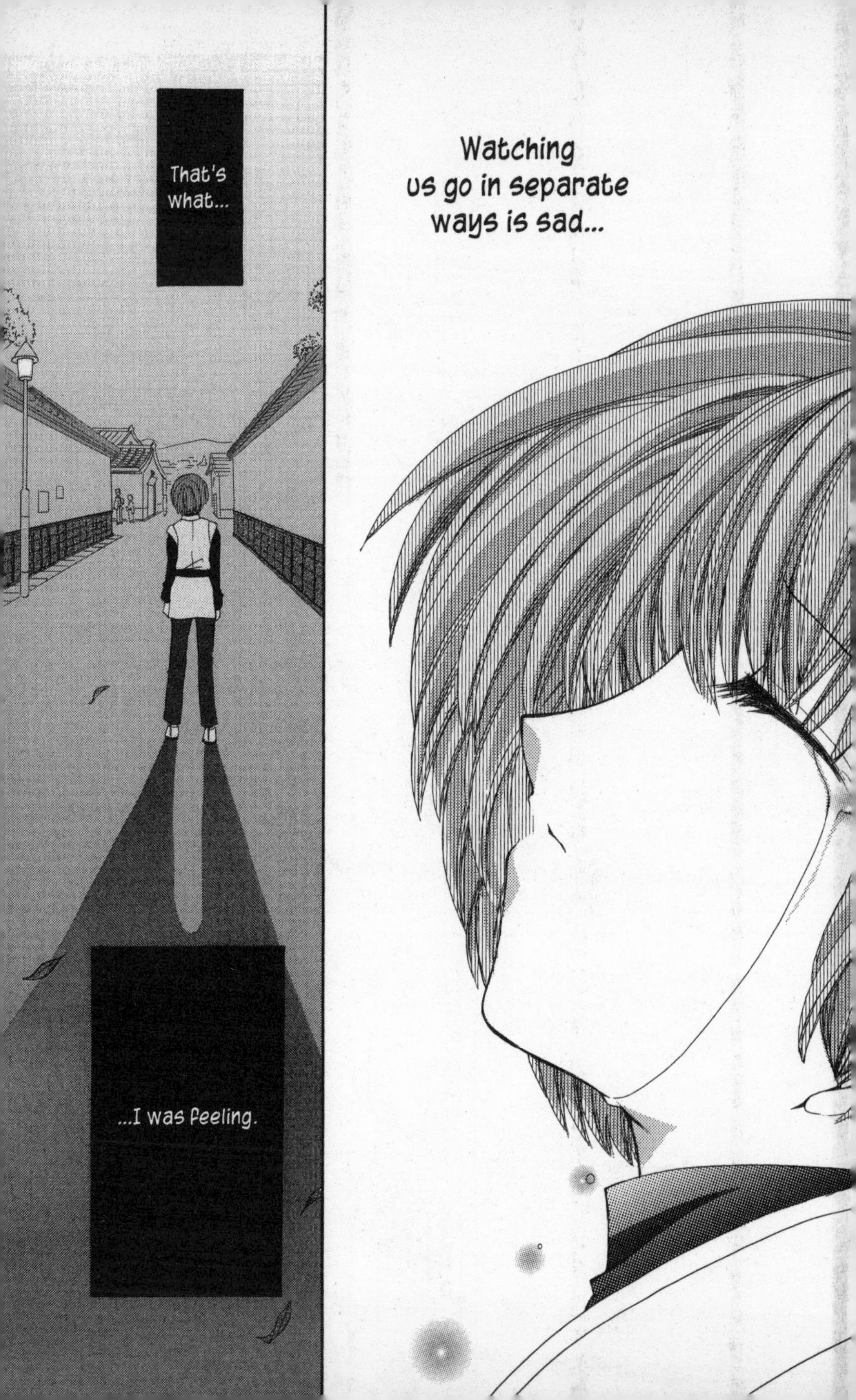
Watching us go in separate ways is sad...
That's what...
...I was feeling.

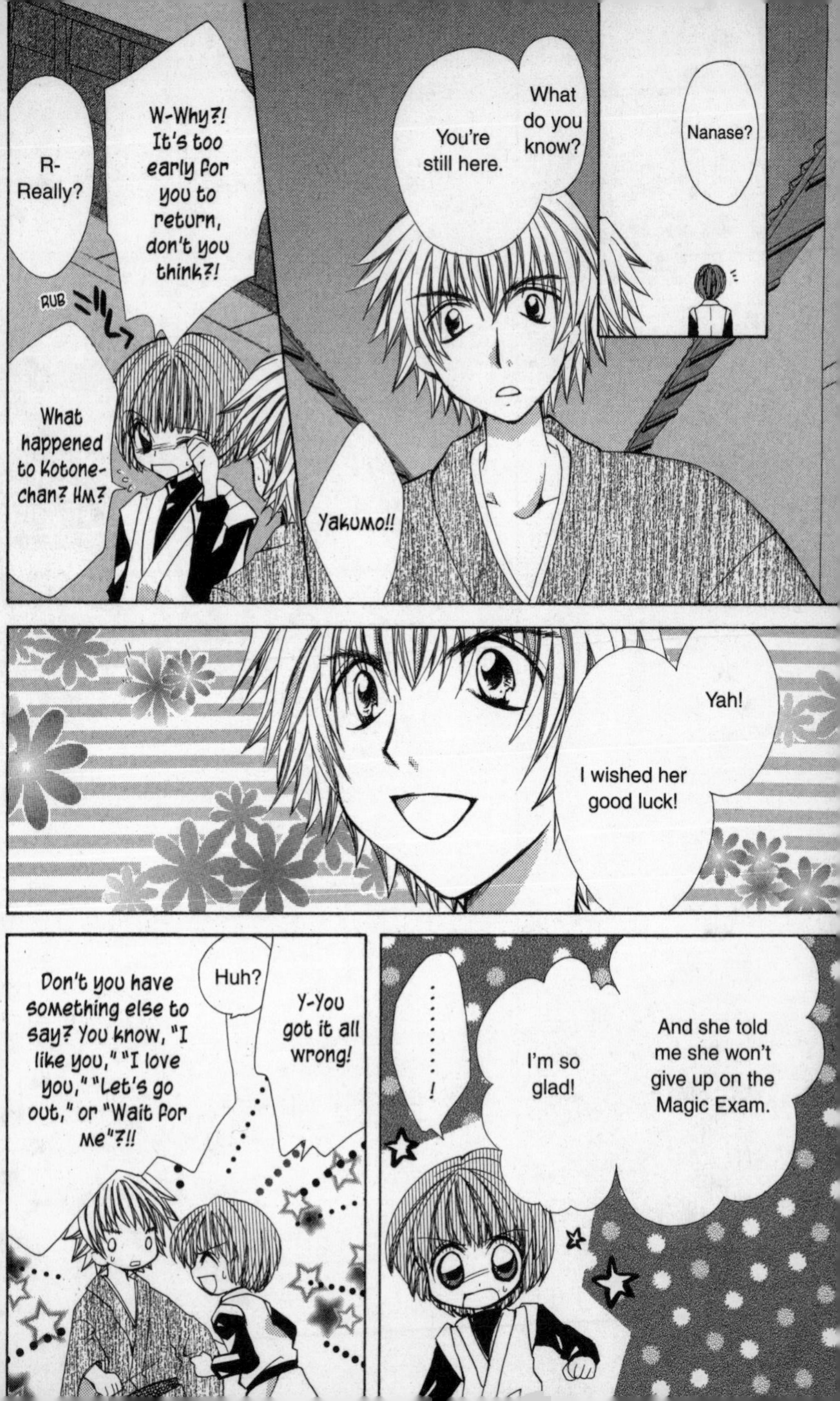
Nanase?
What do you know?
You're still here.
Yakumo!!
W-Why?! It's too early for you to return, don't you think?!
R- Really?
RUB
What happened to Kotone-chan? Hm?
Yah!
I wished her good luck!
And she told me she won't give up on the Magic Exam.
I'm so glad!
.........!
Y-You got it all wrong!
Huh?
Don't you have something else to say? You know, "I like you," "I love you," "Let's go out," or "Wait for me"?!!

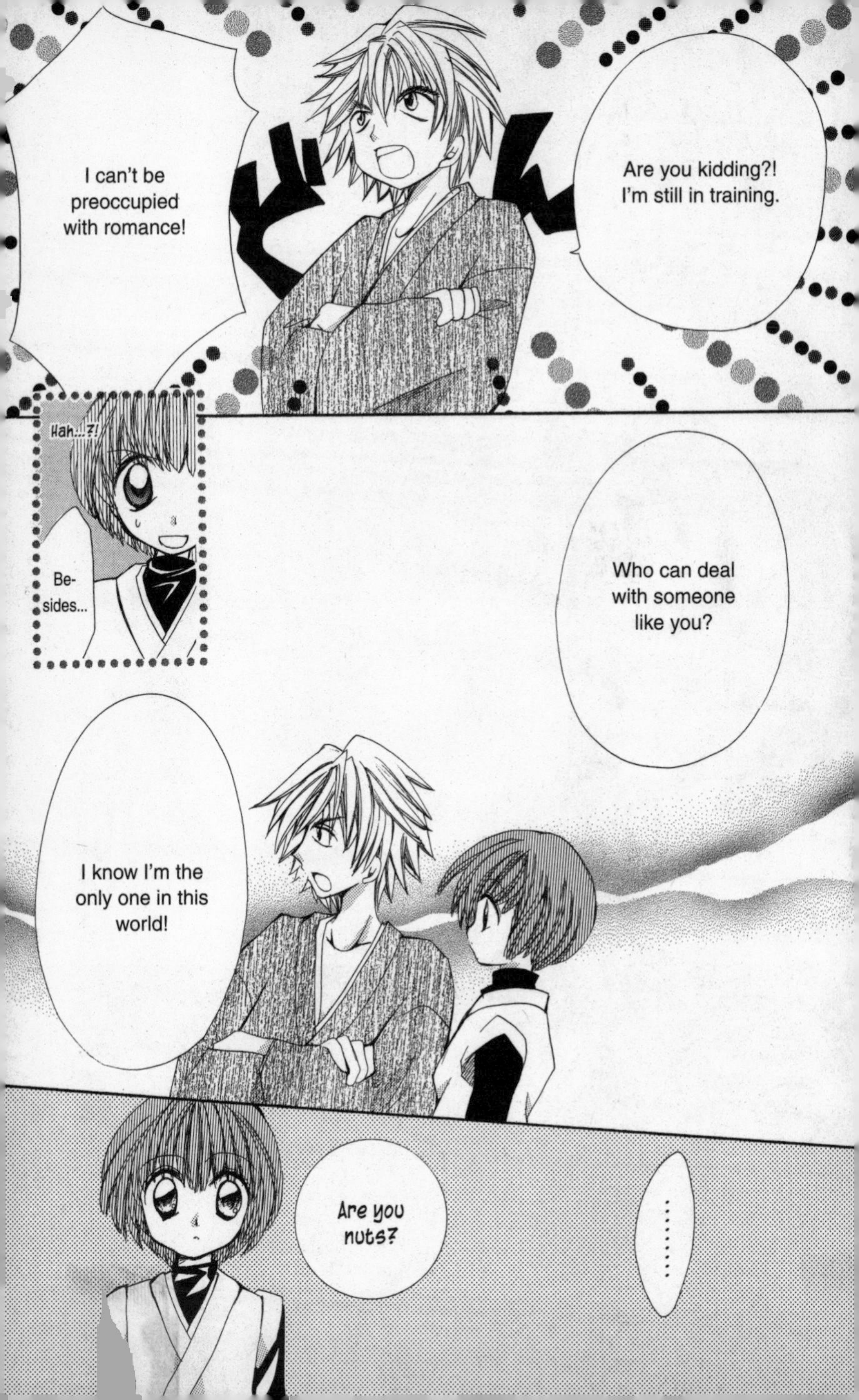
Are you kidding?! I'm still in training.
I can't be preoccupied with romance!
Who can deal with someone like you?
I know I'm the only one in this world!
Hah...?!
Be-sides...
....
Are you nuts?

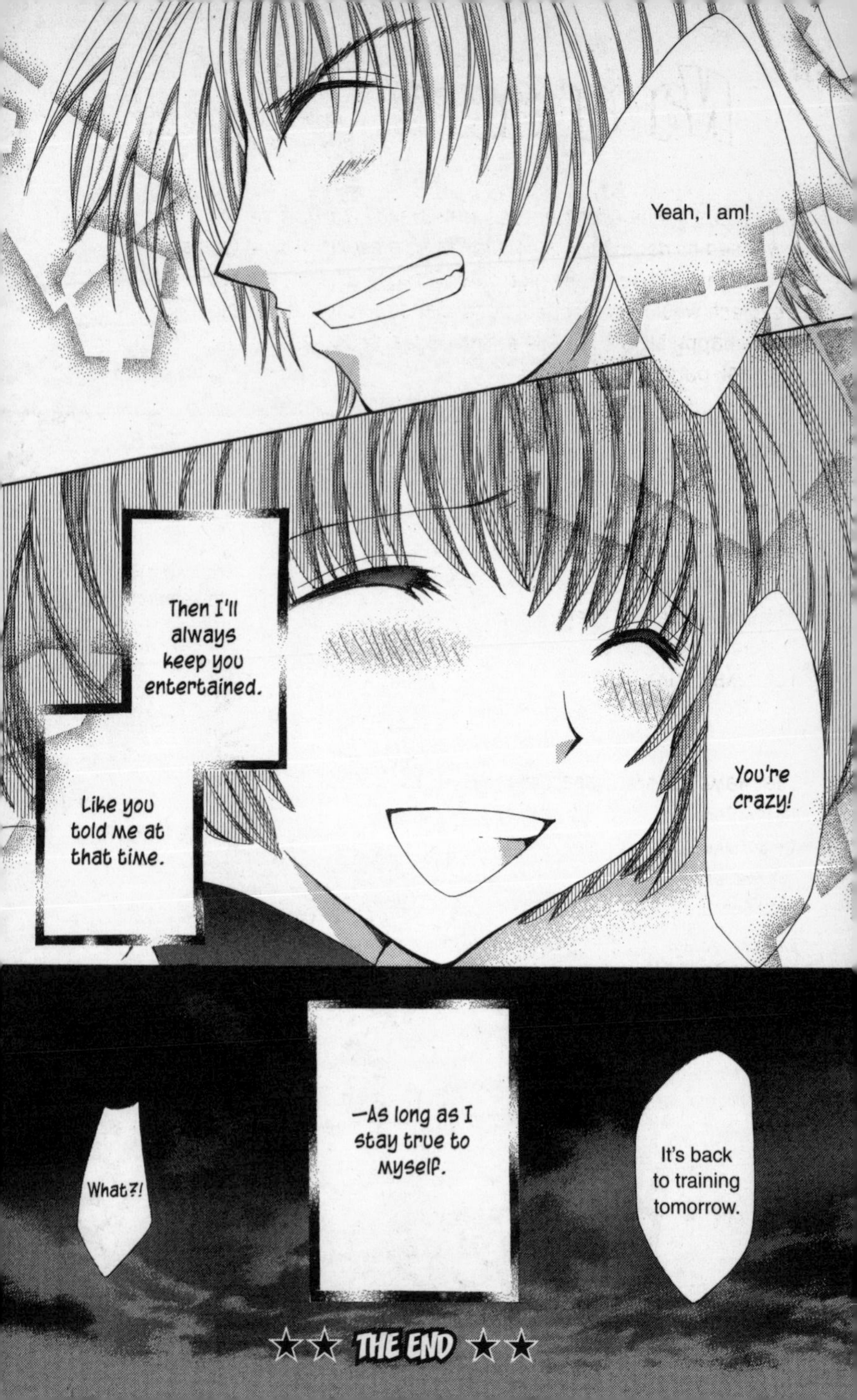
Yeah, I am!
You're crazy!
Then I'll always keep you entertained.
Like you told me at that time.
It's back to training tomorrow.
—As long as I stay true to myself.
What?!
THE END

Nanapachi!

•This is a bonus story about Nanase and Yakumo I've always wanted to do! It took a considerable amount of time (possibly six months) to put the plot on a paper. I was afraid the project would be dropped, but I managed to complete it! I was happy that I got the extra pages and even a splash page in color!!

• I really enjoy drawing these guys. I love them!! (Silly me.) You grow to love them more as time goes by.

• The characters' last names were published in the newspapers. I was amazed that some readers noticed they weren't released in the magazine.

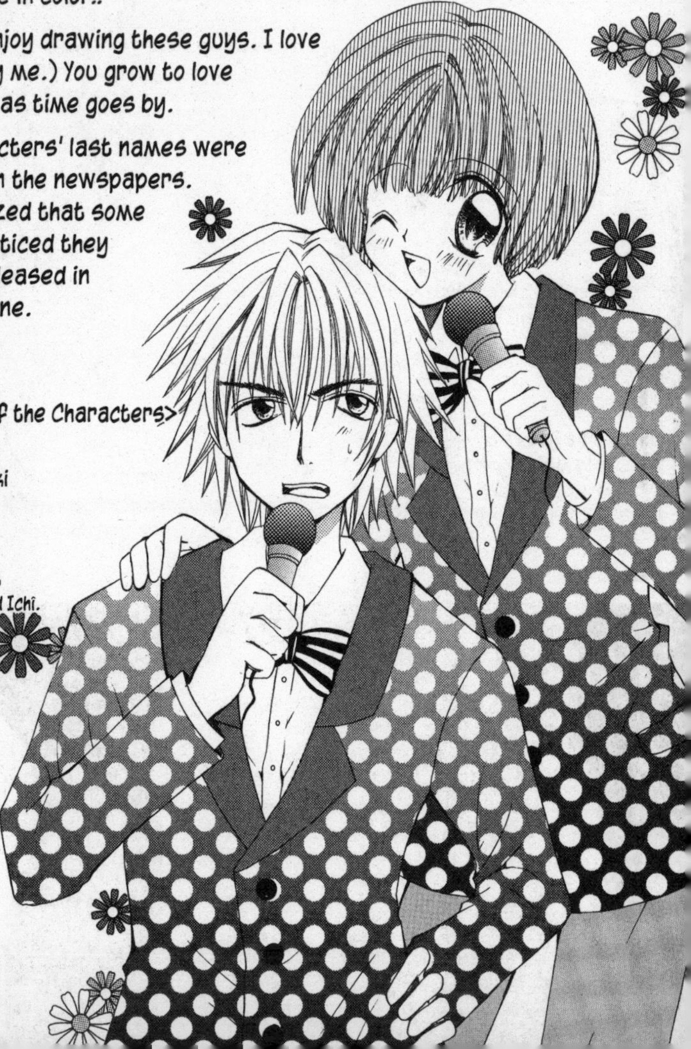

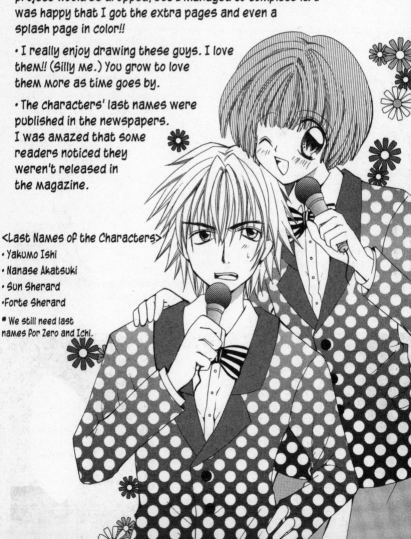

<Last Names of the Characters>

- Yakumo Ishî
- Nanase Akatsuki
- Sun Sherard
- Forte Sherard

* We still need last names for Zero and Ichî.

It's New Year's Eve! Lollipop Mini☆Theatre: TAKE 3

The Watch-Night Bell Ringing Contest?!

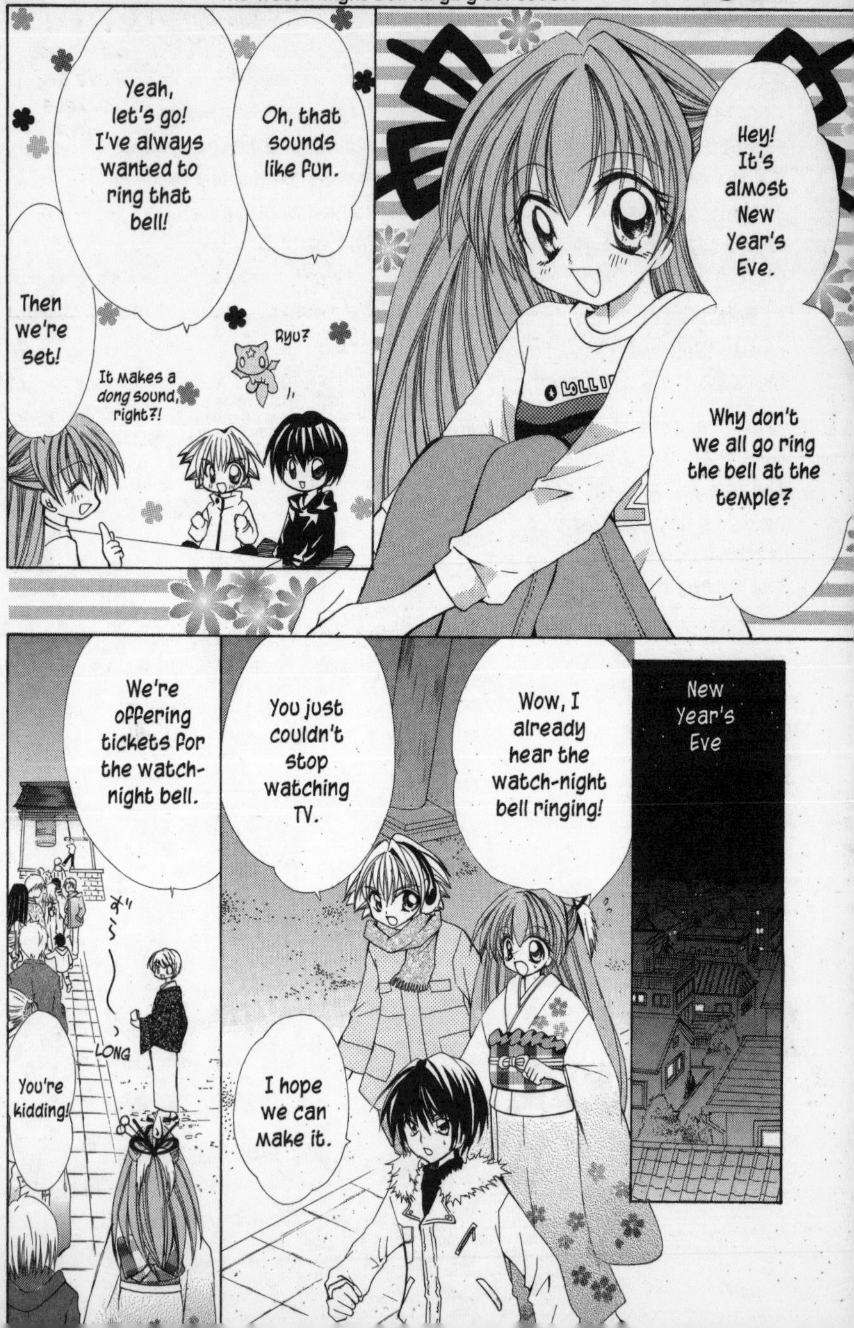

Hey! It's almost New Year's Eve.
Why don't we all go ring the bell at the temple?
Oh, that sounds like fun.
Yeah, let's go! I've always wanted to ring that bell!
Ryu?
Then we're set!
It makes a dong sound, right?!
New Year's Eve
Wow, I already hear the watch-night bell ringing!
You just couldn't stop watching TV.
I hope we can make it.
We're offering tickets for the watch-night bell.
LONG
You're kidding!

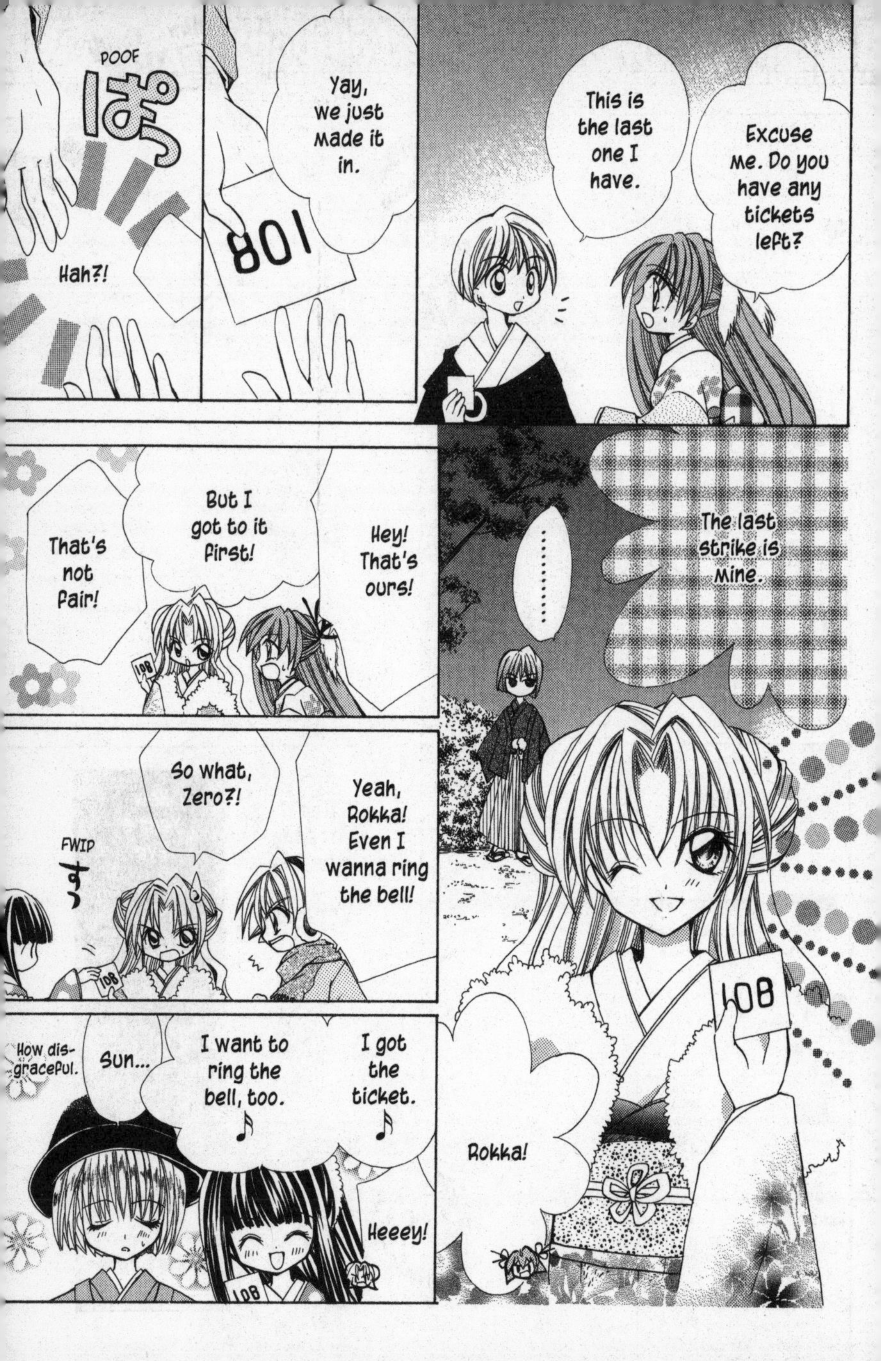
Excuse me. Do you have any tickets left?
This is the last one I have.
Yay, we just made it in.
801
POOF
ぽっ
Hah?!
The last strike is mine.
......
108
Rokka!
Hey! That's ours!
But I got to it first!
That's not fair!
108
Yeah, Rokka! Even I wanna ring the bell!
So what, Zero?!
FWIP
す
108
I got the ticket. ♪
I want to ring the bell, too. ♪
Heeey!
Sun...
How disgraceful.
108

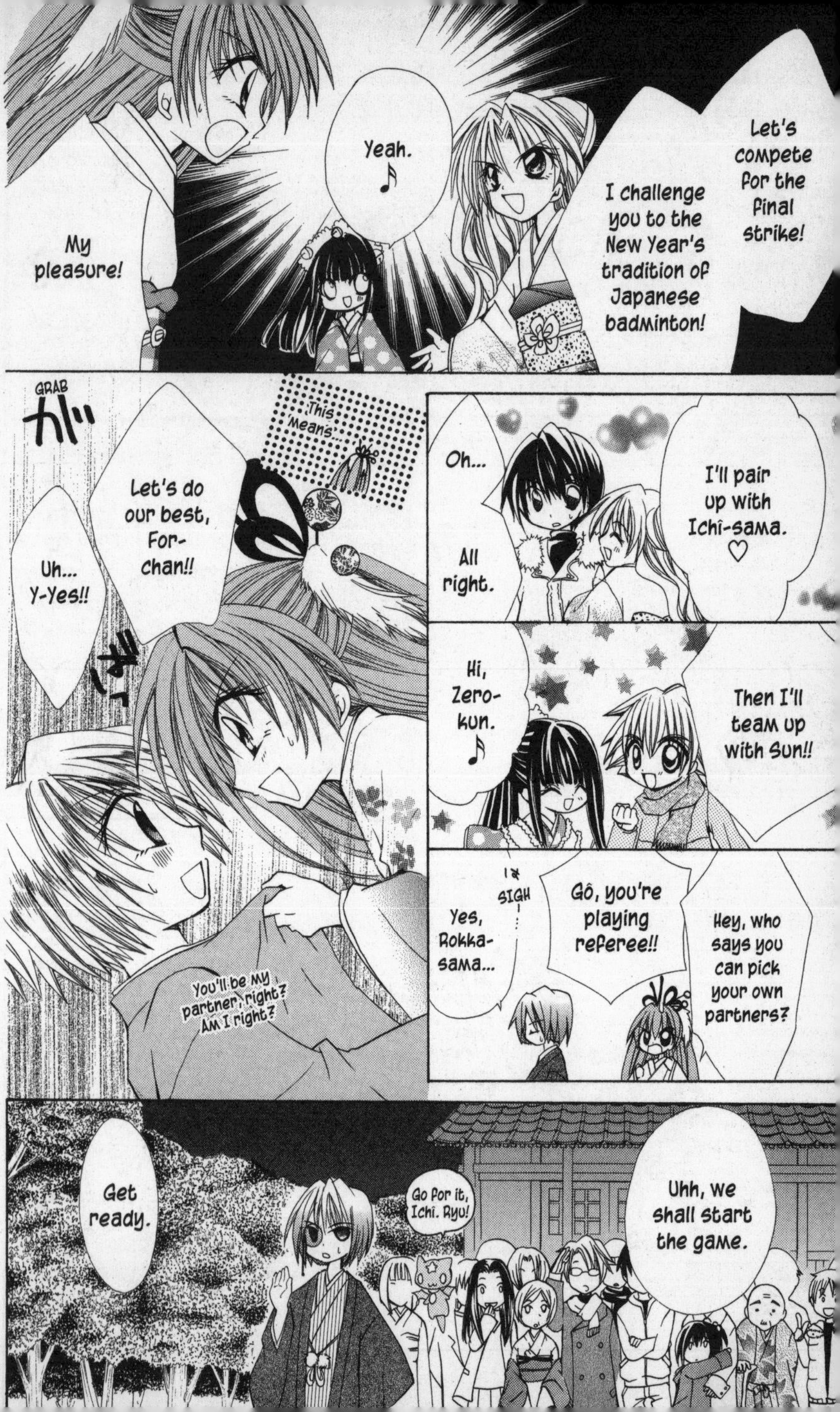
Let's compete for the final strike!
I challenge you to the New Year's tradition of Japanese badminton!
Yeah. ♪
My pleasure!
I'll pair up with Ichî-sama. ♡
Oh... All right.
Then I'll team up with Sun!!
Hi, Zero-kun. ♪
Hey, who says you can pick your own partners?
Gô, you're playing referee!!
SIGH
Yes, Rokka-sama...
This means...
Let's do our best, For-chan!!
GRAB
Uh... Y-Yes!!
You'll be my partner, right? Am I right?
Uhh, we shall start the game.
Go for it, Ichî. Ryu!
Get ready.

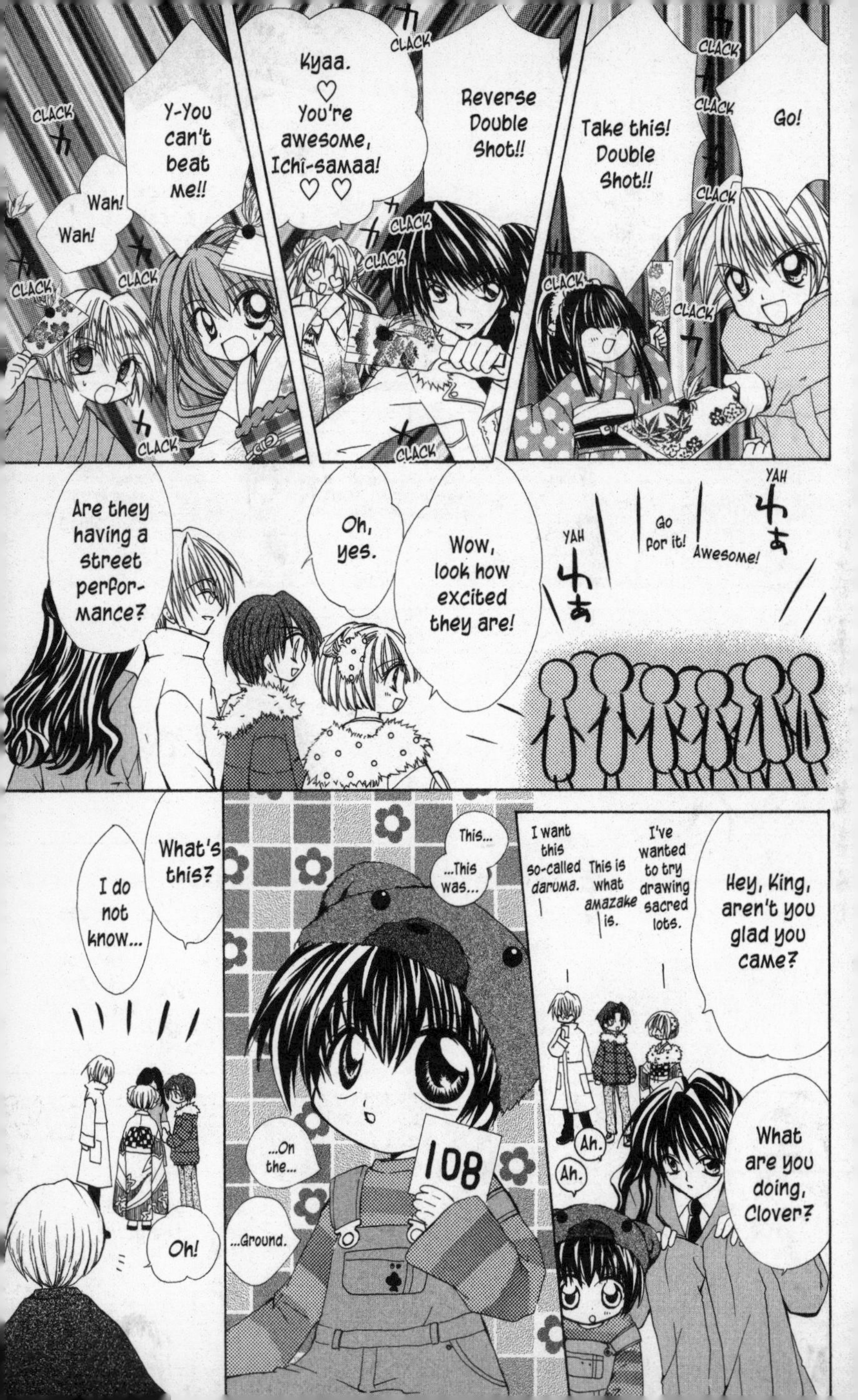
CLACK
Go!
CLACK
Take this! Double Shot!!
CLACK
CLACK
CLACK
CLACK
Reverse Double Shot!!
Kyaa. ♡ You're awesome, Ichî-samaa! ♡ ♡
CLACK
CLACK
CLACK
CLACK
Y-You can't beat me!!
Wah!
Wah!
CLACK
CLACK
CLACK
YAH
Awesome!
Go for it!
YAH
Wow, look how excited they are!
Oh, yes.
Are they having a street performance?
Hey, King, aren't you glad you came?
I've wanted to try drawing sacred lots.
This is what amazake is.
I want this so-called daruma.
Ah.
Ah.
What are you doing, Clover?
This...
...This was...
...On the...
...Ground.
108
What's this?
I do not know...
Oh!

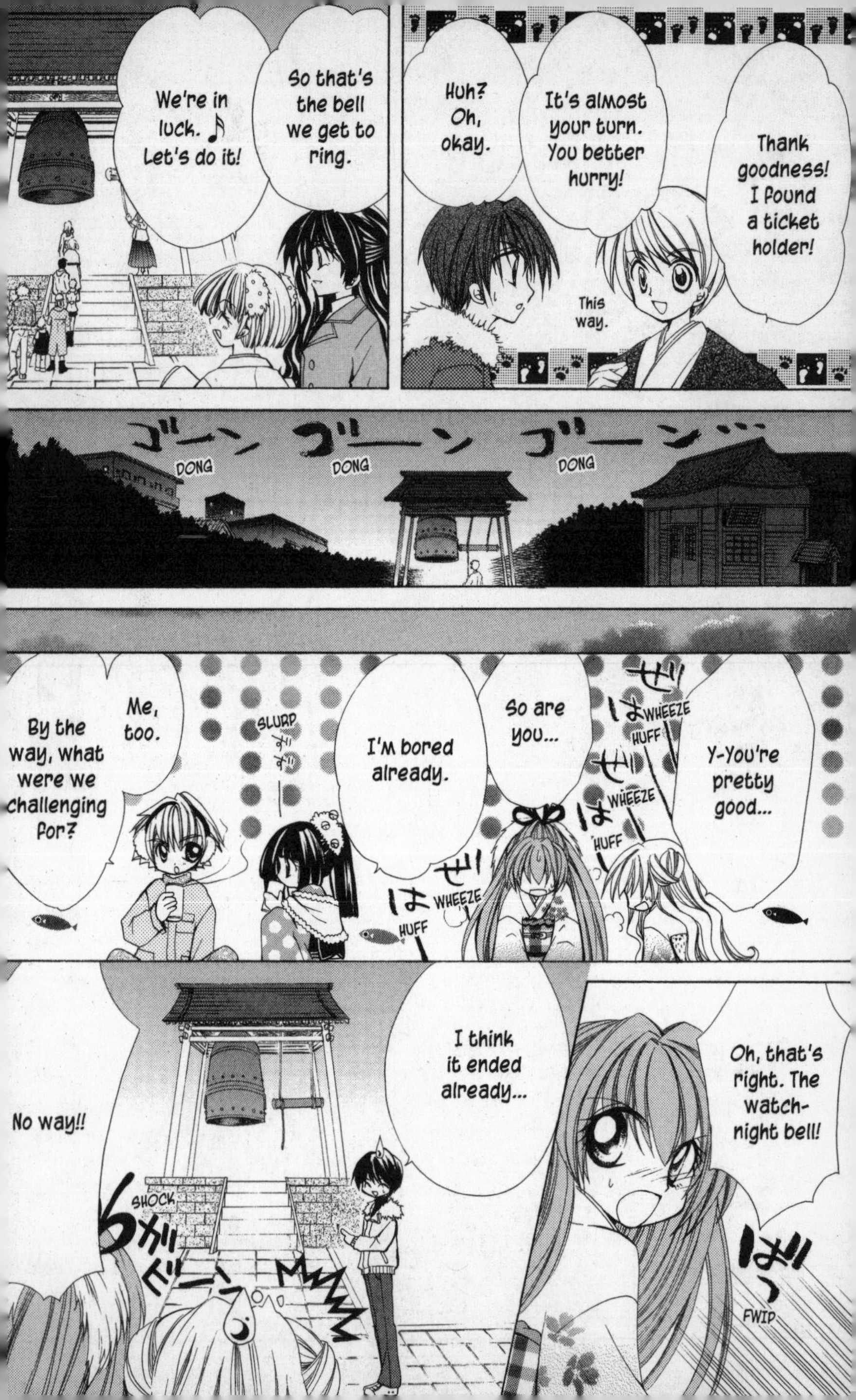
Thank goodness! I found a ticket holder!
It's almost your turn. You better hurry!
Huh? Oh, okay.
This way.
So that's the bell we get to ring.
We're in luck. ♪ Let's do it!
ゴーン
DONG
ゴーン
DONG
ゴーン
DONG
Y-You're pretty good...
WHEEZE
HUFF
WHEEZE
HUFF
So are you...
WHEEZE
HUFF
I'm bored already.
SLURP
Me, too.
By the way, what were we challenging for?
Oh, that's right. The watch-night bell!
FWIP
I think it ended already...
No way!!
SHOCK

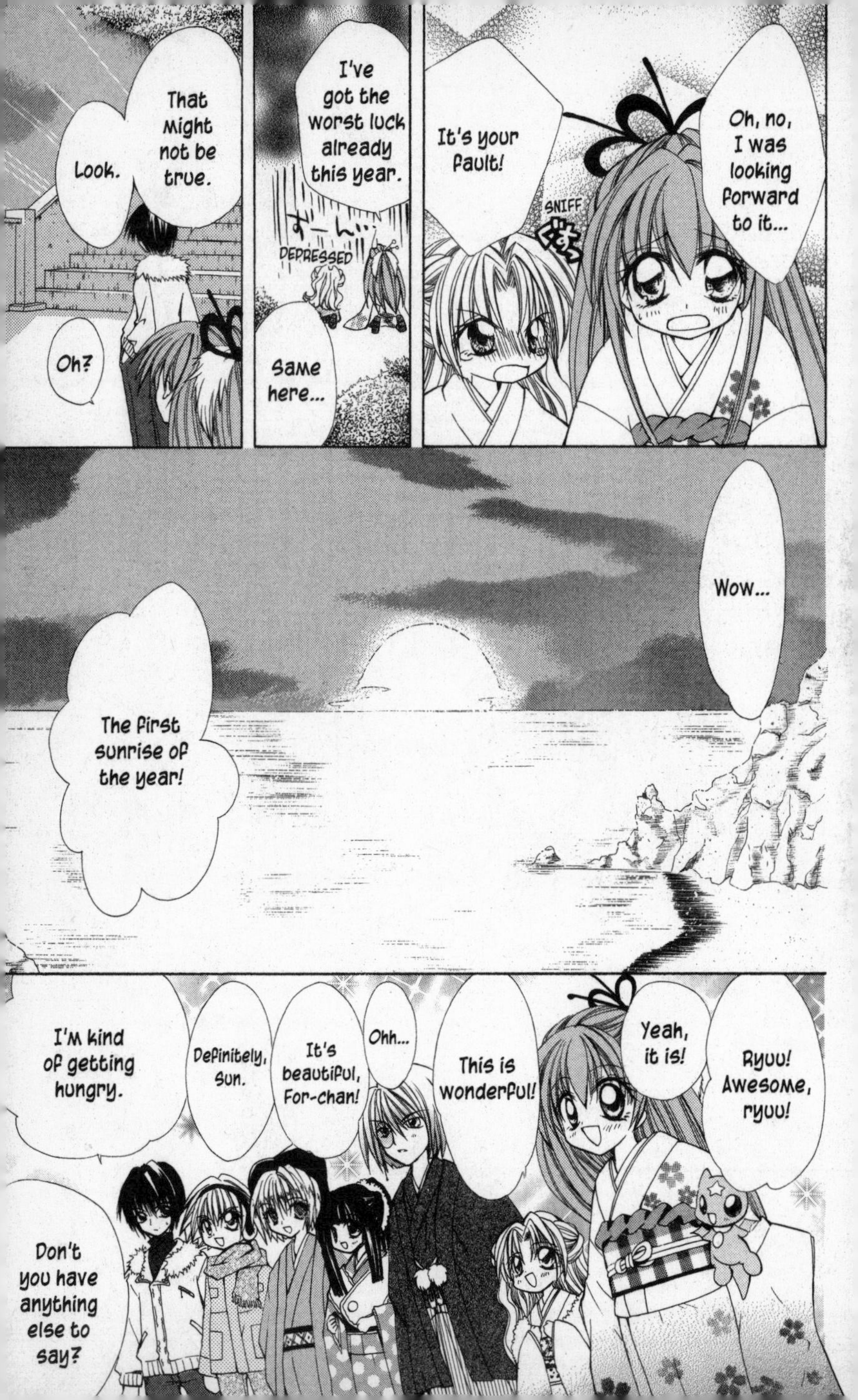

Oh, no, I was looking forward to it...
SNIFF
ぐすっ
It's your fault!
I've got the worst luck already this year.
ずーん…
DEPRESSED
Same here...
That might not be true.
Look.
Oh?
Wow...
The first sunrise of the year!
Ryuu! Awesome, ryuu!
Yeah, it is!
This is wonderful!
Ohh...
It's beautiful, For-chan!
Definitely, Sun.
I'm kind of getting hungry.
Don't you have anything else to say?

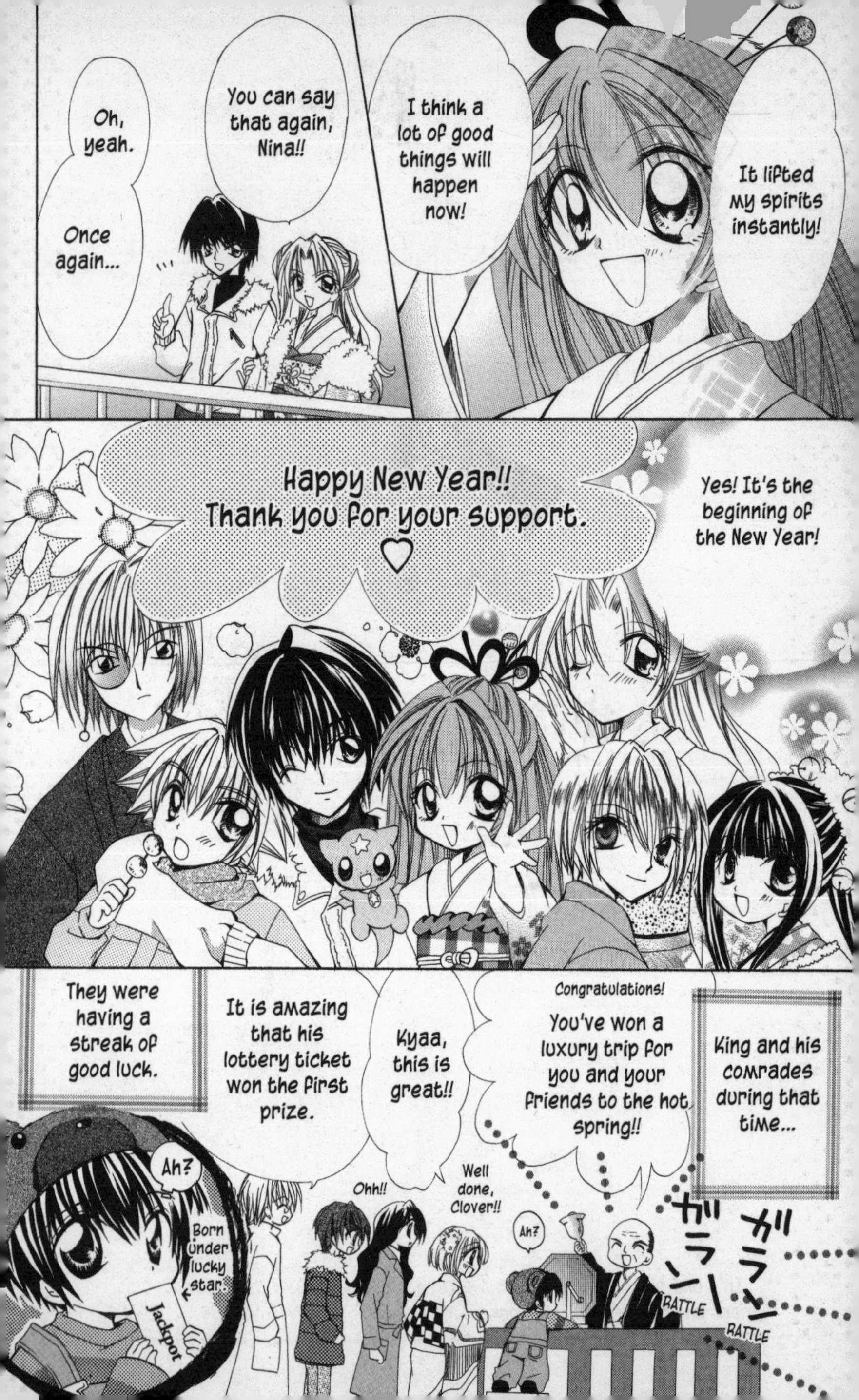
It lifted my spirits instantly!
I think a lot of good things will happen now!
You can say that again, Nina!!
Oh, yeah.
Once again...
Yes! It's the beginning of the New Year!
Happy New Year!! Thank you for your support. ♡
King and his comrades during that time...
Congratulations!
You've won a luxury trip for you and your friends to the hot spring!!
Kyaa, this is great!!
It is amazing that his lottery ticket won the first prize.
They were having a streak of good luck.
ガラン
RATTLE
ガラン
RATTLE
Ah?
Well done, Clover!!
Ohh!!
Ah?
Born under lucky star.
Jackpot

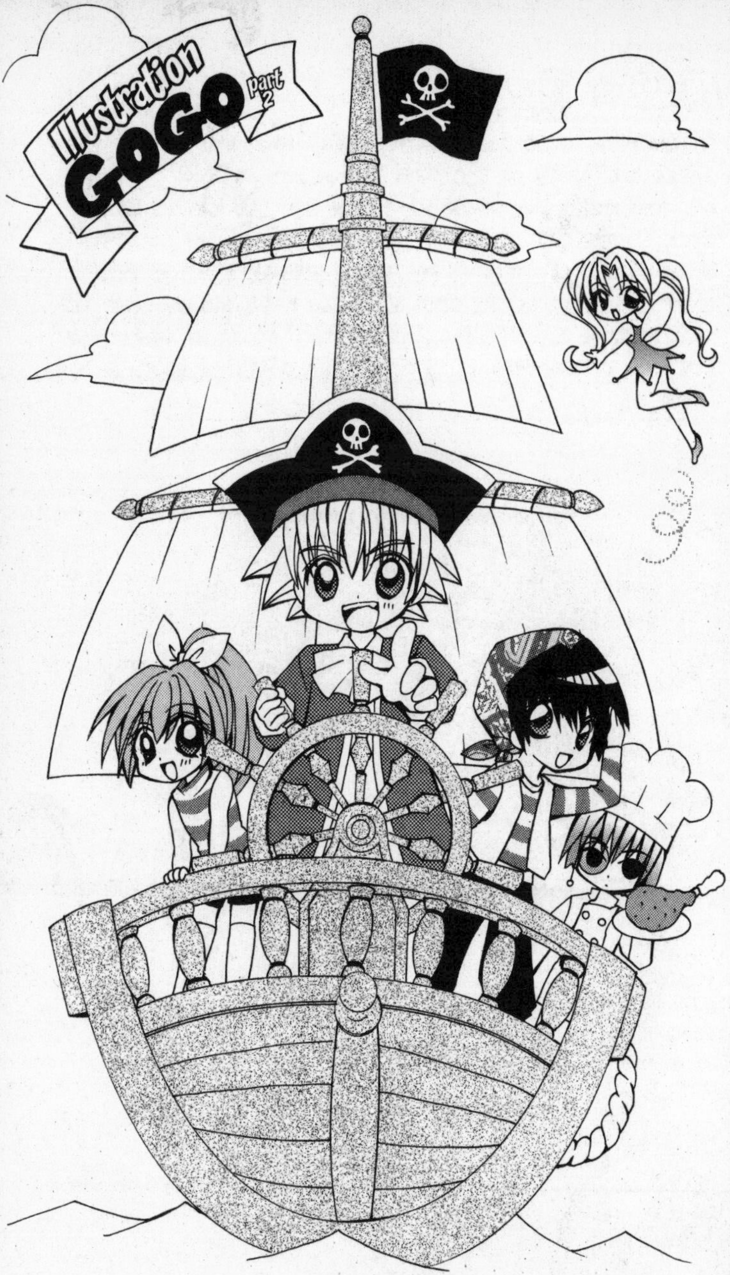
Illustration GoGo part 2

It's the pirate series! It looks very fun! Let's go on an adventure to hunt the treasure!! Zero looks perfect as a captain! We're still looking for illustration requests! Send them in with your fan letters!

Mini ★ Theatre

It was nice to do the Mini ★ Theatres again. ♡ ♡ These are mainly on the main characters, and King and his comrades. Slapstick comedy is fun, but it's tough to draw so many characters. These 16 pages are chock-full of stories! I'm glad that my editor enjoyed the watch-night bell story at the end. If I could have had my wish, I'd include more characters. It's too hard to do all *Mamotte! Lollipop* characters, but because that kind of story is fun, I love it!

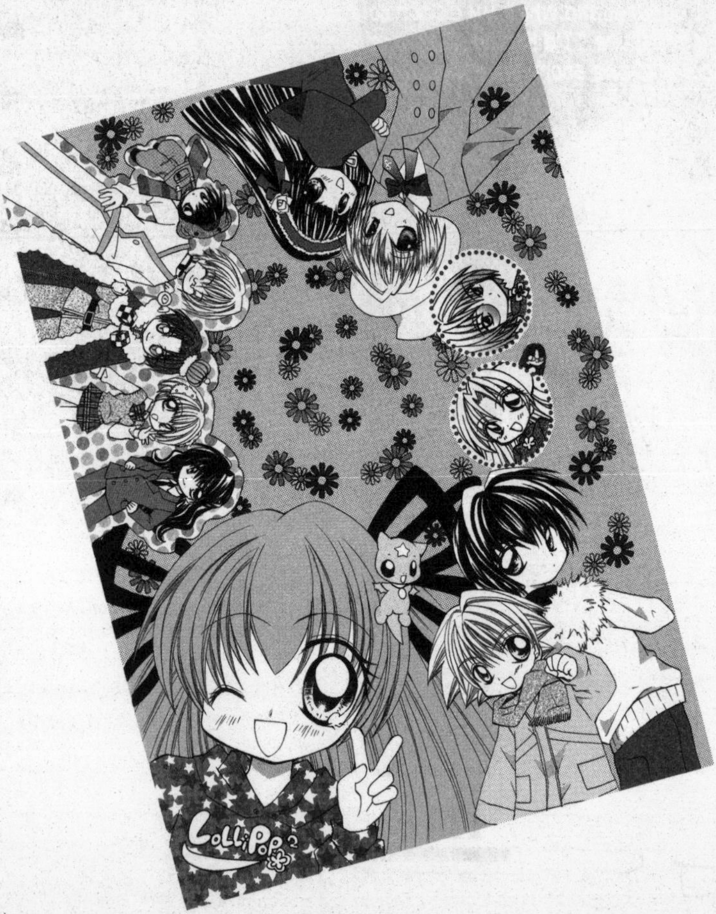
LolliPop 2

Bye-Bye ★

This is the last page. Thank you for reading all the way to the end. I can't believe we're in the fifth volume. I'm so grateful to everyone for letting me do such a long series. But it still continues!! I'm happy about that!!

The story in the magazine is reaching the best part and even I'm excited to find out what will happen. Even though you have a plot in mind, you actually end up drawing something completely different. Now I understand when my editor told me "a serialization is like a living creature." I'd like to draw the manga as I look forward to the outcome of the story with my readers. I hope you'll support Volume 6!

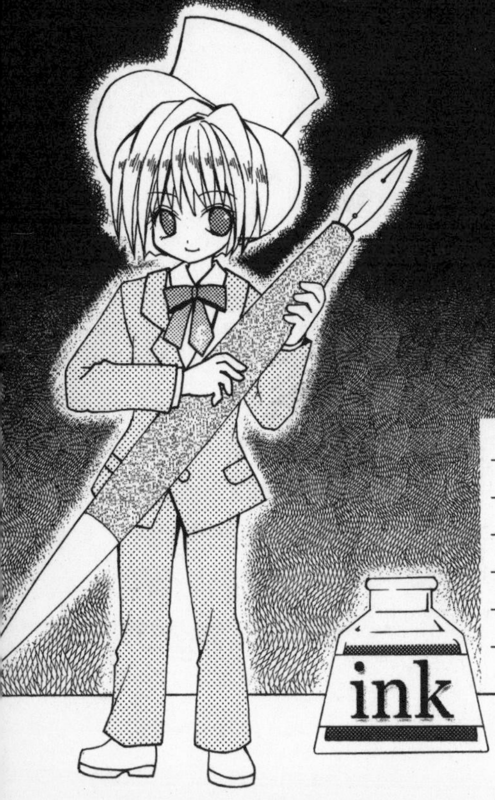
ink

2005. 1. 24

Special Thanks

Yunori Morie, Kumi Katuoka, Nahoru Mita, Tomo Miyakawa, Mai Sukou, Yanomichi, Hozumix, and special guests M. Sekiya...and you!

When's my turn?

It's Ichi for Volume 1. ♪

ABOUT THE CREATOR

Michiyo Kikuta

Born in Ibaraki Prefecture on February 10th. Aquarius. Blood type B. She entered and won second place in the 31st Nakayoshi New Faces Manga Award with the manga *Giniro Moyô* in the year 2000, which then made its debut in *Nakayoshi Haru-yasumi Land* (Nakayoshi Spring Break Land) in 2001. Her featured works are *Mamotte! Lollipop* and *Medical Magical*. She enjoys clothes shopping and loves sweets.

Translation Notes

Japanese is a tricky language for most Westerners, and translation is often more art than science. For your edification and reading pleasure, here are notes on some of the places where we could have gone in a different direction in our translation of the work, or where a Japanese cultural reference is used.

Title: *Mamotte! Lollipop*
Mamotte means to protect and Lollipop, as we later come to know, is a tool that will help save the heroine from danger.

Names
The characters in *Mamotte! Lollipop* have names based on Japanese numbers. For example, Zero for *zero* (zero); Ichî for *ichi* (one), Nina for *ni* (two), and Sun for *san* (three).

Kyaa and *Gyaa*
Kyaa is a girlish scream. Though it sometimes indicates fright or surprise, it's usually a scream of delight. *Gyaa*, on the other hand, nearly always indicates real fright, embarrassment, or pain.

Ryu
Pearl has a habit of ending all its lines of dialogue with the word *Ryu*. It is a play on the word *ryû*, which means "dragon."

B4, page 59
B4 is a standard paper size in Japan (kind of like 8-1/2" by 11" or 11" by 14" in the U.S.), which measures 257 millimeters by 364 millimeters, or 10.1" by 14.3".

Mame Maki, page 59

Though it is not a national holiday, *setsubun mame maki* or the "bean-throwing festival" is always held on the day before the first day of spring, according to the lunar calendar. People throw roasted soybeans at *oni* or "ogres" to drive out evil spirits and bad luck.

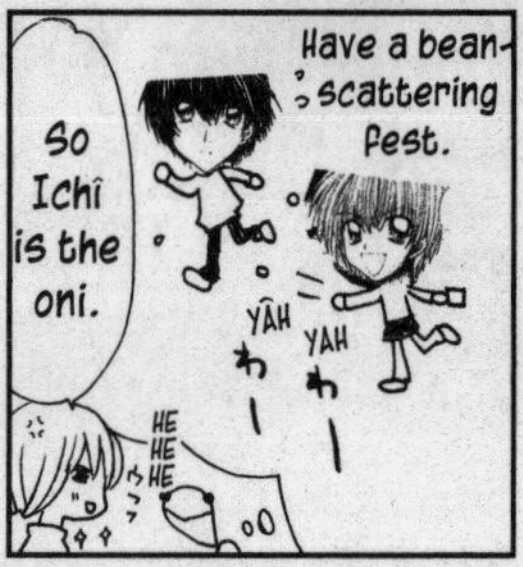
Have a bean-scattering fest.
So Ichî is the oni.
YAH
YAH
HE HE HE

Buchô, page 64

This title is used for club leaders.

Goddess, page 79

The actual word the creator uses is *megami*, which literally means "goddess." This is the affectionately joking title the creator gives to her assistants.

Singing comedian, page 79

The reference in the original Japanese was to the Guitar Samurai, a character created by the Japanese stand-up comedian Yôku Hata. While dressed in a kimono, he would sing sarcastic songs about celebrities, ending each song by slashing the air with his guitar, as if swinging a sword.

Blind date party, page 84

A "blind date party," or *gôkon*, is a popular custom with young Japanese boys and girls. At a blind date party, the two hosts, one male and one female, will each invite friends of their same gender. Although the hosts know each other, everybody else is meeting for the first time.

Kansai Dialect, page 101

Yakumo speaks in Kansai dialect, which is a dialect spoken specifically in the Kansai region of the country. This dialect is often rendered in manga as an American Southern accent, or as some other regional accent, which is not exactly accurate. Therefore, we've used a special font to denote that Yakumo's speech sounds a little different from everyone else's.

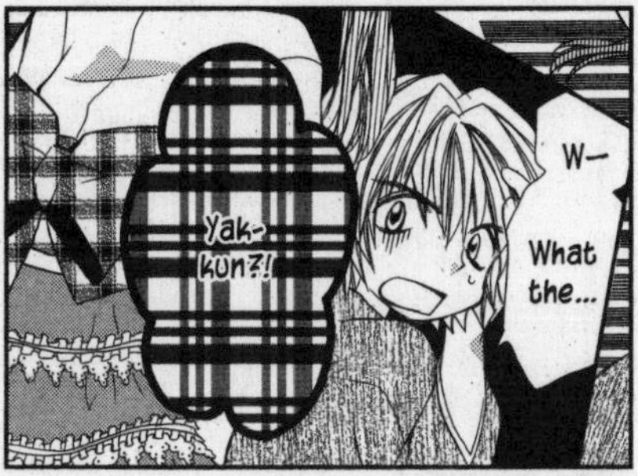
W—
What the...
Yak-kun?!

Yak-kun, page 157

This is a pet name Nanase invented for Yakumo in his attempt to make himself appear cute in his disguise as a girl.

Ring the bell at the temple, page 182

This is a special midnight custom. At midnight, the *Joya no kane* or a "watch-night bell" is struck by a group of 108 parishioners at the temples all over Japan.

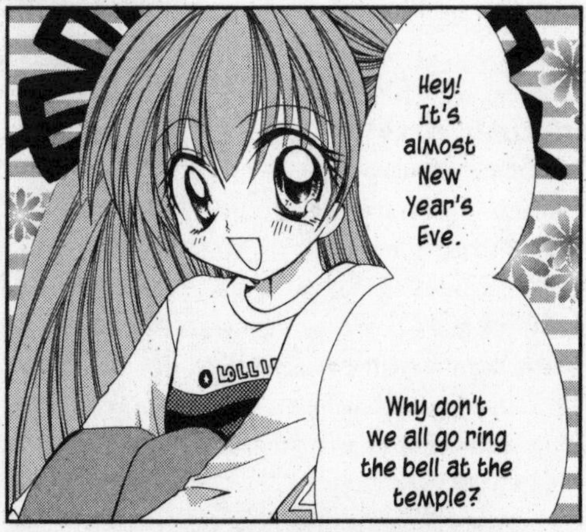
Hey! It's almost New Year's Eve.
Why don't we all go ring the bell at the temple?

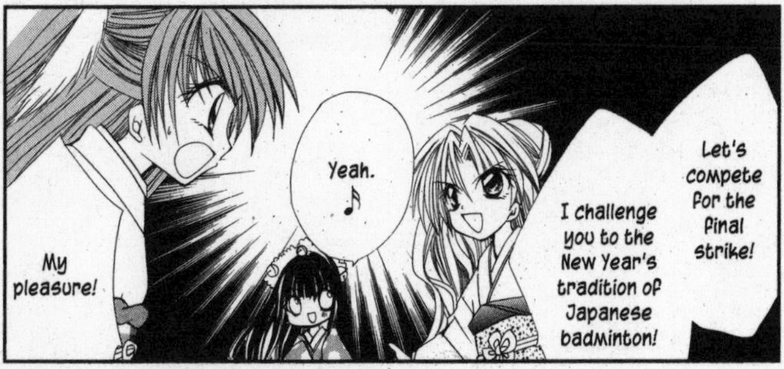
Let's compete for the final strike!
I challenge you to the New Year's tradition of Japanese badminton!
Yeah. ♪
My pleasure!

Japanese badminton, page 184

A Japanese badminton-like game known as *Hanetsuki* is tradionally played on New Year's with an ornamental wooden paddle called *hagoita* and a shuttle called a *hane*.

Drawing sacred lots, page 185

Literally meaning "sacred lottery," *omikuji* are random fortunes written on little folded papers found in shrines and temples in Japan. They are supposed to reveal an overall vision of the person's future, but also specific predictions about finances, health, romance, and so on.

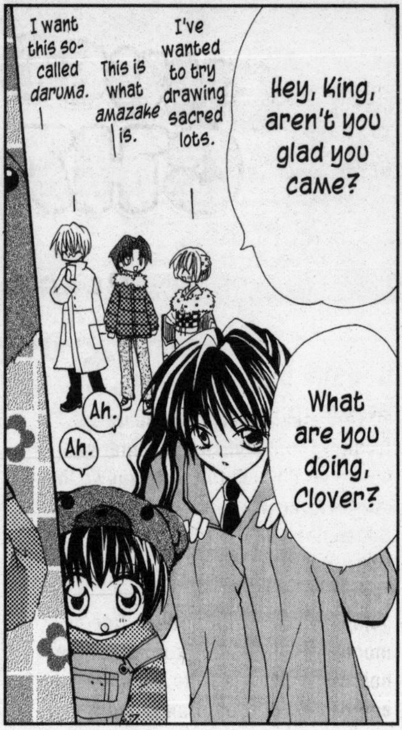

Hey, King, aren't you glad you came?
I've wanted to try drawing sacred lots.
This is what amazake is.
I want this so-called daruma.
What are you doing, Clover?
Ah.
Ah.

***Daruma*, page 185**

Daruma is a hollow and round Japanese wish doll modeled after Bodhidharma, the founder of Zen Buddhism. It has a face with a mustache and a beard, but no eyes. One fills in the right eye using black ink at the time of making a wish and completes the other when that wish comes true.

***Amazake*, page 185**

Literally meaning "sweet sake," this is a traditional sweet, non-alcoholic Japanese drink made from fermented rice. It is usually offered at the temples on New Year's.

SHUGO CHARA!

PEACH-PIT

Creators of *Dears* and *Rozen Maiden*

Everybody at Seiyo Elementary thinks that stylish and super-cool Amu has it all. But nobody knows the *real* Amu, a shy girl who wishes she had the courage to truly be herself. Changing Amu's life is going to take more than wishes and dreams—it's going to take a little magic! One morning, Amu finds a surprise in her bed: three strange little eggs. Each egg contains a Guardian Character, an angel-like being who can give her the power to be someone new. With the help of her Guardian Characters, Amu is about to discover that her true self is even more amazing than she ever dreamed.

Special extras in each volume! Read them all!

VISIT WWW.DELREYMANGA.COM TO:
• Read sample pages
• View release date calendars for upcoming volumes
• Sign up for Del Rey's free manga e-newsletter
• Find out the latest about new Del Rey Manga series

RATING   T AGES 13+

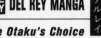

DEL REY MANGA デルレイ

The Otaku's Choice

KITCHEN PRINCESS

STORY BY MIYUKI KOBAYASHI
MANGA BY NATSUMI ANDO
CREATOR OF ZODIAC P.I.

HUNGRY HEART

KITCHEN PRINCESS
1
custard pudding
christmas cookie
onion gratin soup
MIYUKI KOBAYASHI
NATSUMI ANDO
Creator of Zodiac P.I.

Najika is a great cook and likes to make meals for the people she loves. But something is missing from her life. When she was a child, she met a boy who touched her heart—and now Najika is determined to find him. The only clue she has is a silver spoon that leads her to the prestigious Seika Academy.

Attending Seika will be a challenge. Every kid at the school has a special talent, and the girls in Najika's class think she doesn't deserve to be there. But Sora and Daichi, two popular brothers who barely speak to each other, recognize Najika's cooking for what it is—magical. Could one of the boys be Najika's mysterious prince?

Special extras in each volume! Read them all!

VISIT WWW.DELREYMANGA.COM TO:

- Read sample pages
- View release date calendars for upcoming volumes
- Sign up for Del Rey's free manga e-newsletter
- Find out the latest about new Del Rey Manga series

RATING T AGES 13+

DEL REY MANGA デルレイ

The Otaku's Choice

SHIN MIDORIKAWA

NEVER STOP BELIEVING

Since ancient days, the Gaius School of Witchcraft and Wizardry has trained the fiercest swordsmen and the most powerful wizards.

Now one boy could become the greatest of them all. If he studies hard. If he is true to his friends. If he believes.

And if he survives . . .

Special extras in each volume! Read them all!

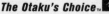

TOMARE!

止まれ

[STOP!]

You're going the wrong way!

Manga is a completely different type of reading experience.

To start at the *beginning,* go to the *end*!

That's right! Authentic manga is read the traditional Japanese way—from right to left. Exactly the *opposite* of how American books are read. It's easy to follow: Just go to the other end of the book, and read each page—and each panel—from right side to left side, starting at the top right. Now you're experiencing manga as it was meant to be!